International Banking

A Functional Approach

International Banking

A Functional Approach

Suk-Joong Kim

The University of Sydney, Australia

NEW JERSEY • LONDON • SINGAPORE • BEIJING • SHANGHAI • HONG KONG • TAIPEI • CHENNAI • TOKYO

Published by

World Scientific Publishing Co. Pte. Ltd.
5 Toh Tuck Link, Singapore 596224
USA office: 27 Warren Street, Suite 401-402, Hackensack, NJ 07601
UK office: 57 Shelton Street, Covent Garden, London WC2H 9HE

Library of Congress Cataloging-in-Publication Data
Names: Kim, Suk-Joong, author.
Title: International banking : a functional approach /
Suk-Joong Kim, The University of Sydney, Australia.
Description: New Jersey : World Scientific, [2023] | Includes bibliographical references.
Identifiers: LCCN 2023014996 | ISBN 9789811262319 (hardcover) |
ISBN 9789811262326 (ebook for institutions) | ISBN 9789811262333 (ebook for individuals)
Subjects: LCSH: Banks and banking, International.
Classification: LCC HG3881 .K46927 2023 | DDC 332.1/5--dc23/eng/20230503
LC record available at https://lccn.loc.gov/2023014996

British Library Cataloguing-in-Publication Data
A catalogue record for this book is available from the British Library.

For any available supplementary material, please visit
https://www.worldscientific.com/worldscibooks/10.1142/13024#t=suppl

Desk Editors: Aanand Jayaraman/Thaheera Althaf

Typeset by Stallion Press
Email: enquiries@stallionpress.com

Printed in Singapore

To my wife and family

Preface

During the second half of the previous century and the first two decades of the current one, there have been notable changes in the operating environments of financial intermediaries, especially banks. These changes have been influenced by various factors, such as the evolving dynamics of the international financial order since World War II, the deregulation of major financial systems that encouraged financial innovation, and the emergence of disruptive financial technologies.

The internationalisation of US banks coincided with the predominance of the US in the global financial system. However, the emergence of bank-driven economies in the European Union and later in the Eurozone, along with the rapid growth of the Japanese economy in the 1970s and the impressive rise of the Chinese economy in the early 2000s, posed a significant challenge to the dominance of US banks in the global financial system. Consequently, the ranking of global banks has reflected the changes that have occurred over the years. The dominance of US banks was eventually overtaken by Japanese banks in the 1980s and 1990s, followed by the resurgence of European banks in the 2000s and the rise of Chinese banks since the 2010s.

The offshore eurocurrency market, established in the late 1950s, and the deregulation of financial systems in advanced economies from the early 1980s, led to significant financial innovation and increased international competition. As financial systems became increasingly globalised, both in advanced and emerging market economies, there were heightened linkages among various financial systems. This provided international banks with opportunities to minimise their cost of funds and maximise their income from international operations. However, the downsides of such globalisation were made clear through various financial crises in both advanced and emerging market economies. The spillover effects of major financial crises, such as the Global Financial Crisis of 2007–2009, across the world led to debates on the actual benefits of financial globalisation, particularly regarding the role of international banks, in recent times.

The banking industry is currently experiencing a paradigm shift as a result of the emergence of fintech, a disruptive financial technology. What was once viewed as a niche product catering to underserved customers, fintech is now posing a threat to the traditional commercial and investment banking models. Smaller financial firms are utilising big data technologies to compete against established banks in terms of cost and credit risk assessments of borrowers. Additionally, blockchain technologies have several implications for the payment services offered by traditional banks. Moreover, central bank digital currency has the potential to disrupt the role played by banks in facilitating monetary policies and providing payment system functions.

This book provides a comprehensive understanding of the traditional roles played by international banks and offers an analysis of the dynamic nature of the international financial environment in which they operate. My intention in writing this book is for it to serve as a valuable resource for advanced students and researchers pursuing studies in international banking and finance. My aspiration is that this book will equip them with the requisite knowledge to understand and evaluate the diverse challenges and opportunities that international banks encounter within the constantly evolving landscape of the global financial market.

About the Author

Suk-Joong Kim is Professor of International Finance and Banking at the University of Sydney Business School. After obtaining PhD in Financial Economics from the University of Sydney, he joined the University of New South Wales, where he held various positions, including Associate Head of the School of Banking and Finance. He returned to the University of Sydney in 2010 and performed diverse roles in the school, including Head of Discipline of Finance.

Throughout his career, he has published more than 80 articles in various leading academic outlets, two single-authored research books, and three edited/coedited research book volumes. His research interests include foreign exchange markets, international capital flows and market integration, international banking, and sovereign credit ratings. Suk-Joong has also served on the editorial boards of several leading journals in his research fields, including the *Journal of International Financial Markets, Institutions & Money, International Review of Financial Analysis, International Review of Economics and Finance, and Research in International Business and Finance*, among others. Additionally, he is the organiser of the Sydney Banking and Financial Stability Conference held at the University of Sydney Business School.

Contents

List of Exhibits

Introduction

This book is divided into two parts. The first part is titled *Part 1: The Fundamentals of International Banking* and comprises six chapters that delve into the basics of international banking. Chapter 1 of this book, titled *International Banking Functions, Theories, and Types*, acquaints readers with the major functions and theories of international banking. The chapter commences by summarising the traditional role of international banks in providing international trade finance functions to international traders. It then surveys their intermediation role, which involves seeking opportunities in international financial markets through participation in the eurocurrency and foreign exchange markets, to reduce funding costs, hedge risks, and maximise investment returns. Additionally, the chapter touches on how international banks participate in sovereign lending via loan syndication. The motivations behind the internationalisation of banks are also discussed, including defensive expansion (also known as follow-the-customer expansion), taking advantage of new market opportunities and regulation differentials. The chapter also provides an overview of various organisational forms of foreign banks, ranging from correspondent banking to full banking presence, such as foreign branch and subsidiary banking operations in the target foreign markets. The chapter concludes with examples of various linkages between the motivations and organisational forms of international banking. It emphasises that banks seeking to expand to international markets should have clear goals in the target markets and adopt appropriate forms of banking presence consistent with these goals.

Chapter 2: Internationalisation of Banks from the US, Japan, and China explores the internationalisation experiences of banks from the US, Japan, and China. US banks faced regulatory restrictions in their domestic market operations, particularly with the Glass–Steagall Act, which mandated the separation of commercial and investment banking operations, and the McFadden Act, which limited the domestic expansion of banking operations beyond state borders. These regulatory measures shaped the architecture of the US banking system throughout the last century and motivated US banks to explore foreign markets with less onerous regulations. The emergence of opportunities in emerging markets, such as Western Europe in the 1950s, Latin America in the 1970s, East Asia, and Eastern Europe in the 1990s, enabled US banks to leverage their technical advantages in providing banking products. The primary driving force behind the internationalisation of Japanese banks was customer-driven expansion. As their corporate clients expanded into the US market, Japanese banks followed them to provide financial services in the US. The combination of an expanding economy, a high domestic saving rate, and an appreciating Yen led to Japanese banks becoming a dominant force in the international financial market throughout the 1980s and 1990s, until the onset of the Japanese banking crisis from 1998 to 2004. Similarly, Chinese banks expanded internationally to service their corporate customers in foreign markets, as encouraged by the Chinese government's 'Go Out Policy'. The policy aimed to support state-owned enterprises in exploring foreign markets and to ease the pressure of accumulating foreign currency reserves on the renminbi to revalue. Chinese banks also pursued foreign opportunities independently by acquiring stakes in foreign banks. Like Japanese banks in the 1990s, Chinese banks have come to dominate the world ranking of international banks in terms of balance sheet size since the late 2010s. The internationalisation of Chinese banks can be attributed to a similar combination of factors, including an expanding economy, a high domestic saving rate, and a bank-dominated financial system.

Chapter 3: International Trade Finance covers the various methods of financing international trade, a role that has been performed by international banks for many years. One prominent method is the letter of credit financing, where a payment guarantee is created by either the importer's bank or the exporter's bank to ensure the exporter's payment in international trade. This method is typically used for short-term trades in ordinary goods and is usually on a recourse basis. For longer-term trades in capital goods involving importers of higher risk, forfaiting is an alternative method available, mostly provided on a non-recourse basis by private institutions, including banks, due to the increased risk involved in providing financial protection. Factoring is another method of trade financing, where a factor purchases a large number of trade receivables, eliminating the need for the exporter to collect them individually. This chapter also discusses other international trade finance methods, including payment in advance, open account, consignment, and countertrade. Furthermore, many countries have established Export Credit Agencies that aid in facilitating international trade of significant importance to the country, which the private sector financial institutions may find difficult to engage in because of the heightened counterparty risk involved.

Chapter 4: Foreign Exchange Market presents the extent of foreign exchange market participation by international banks. With a daily trading volume of USD 7.5 trillion in April 2022, the foreign exchange market has seen remarkable growth in recent decades, with a significant portion of the trading activity focused on only a few exchange rates. The top four currencies — the euro, Japanese yen, British pound, and Chinese renminbi — priced in US Dollars, represented 51.7% of global volume in April 2022. This, combined with the market's sizeable trading volume, has resulted in the lowest transaction costs compared to other financial markets. The foreign exchange market comprises a direct dealing market and a broker market segment, with banks participating to provide services to their corporate clients and the market as a whole. Banks also trade on their own account, exploiting any information advantage they may have in the market, while also providing market-making and broking services.

Chapter 5: Eurocurrency Market delves into the eurocurrency market, exploring the participation of international banks within it. The eurocurrency market is an offshore extension of domestic interbank money markets that deals with multiple currencies. The key feature of this market is the separation of currency between the market and the instruments. For instance, multinational banks can engage in USD-denominated transactions in London, which is an example of eurodollar trading, the most significant segment of the eurocurrency market, accounting for 60% of market volume. As eurocurrency transactions take place offshore and involve currency separation, the government of the currency denomination, such as the US government for eurodollar transactions, has no legal jurisdiction over them. This feature of the eurocurrency market was attractive to international investors seeking protection from political conflicts in the country of the currency denomination during the geopolitical upheavals of the 1960s. The market's growth coincided with international banks' expansion into various foreign markets. The deregulation of the financial system in major economies from the early 1980s weakened the case for eurocurrency market in terms of financial innovation. However, it still provides asset protection for international investors from the government of the currency denomination.

Chapter 6: International Loan Syndication of this book discusses the role of international banks in loan syndication. International loans are often much larger than domestic loans and subject to additional risks, such as political, currency, regulation, and country risks. Therefore, these loans are usually syndicated, meaning that a group of lenders, including banks and institutional investors, come together to fund a borrower and spread the risk among them. Each lender in the syndicate contributes a portion of the loan and may also have a designated management or administration role that earns them fee income in addition to their share of the interest income. Large international banks have a competitive advantage in originating loans and often act as the book runner or lead arranger, while other participating banks can share some of the management responsibilities, such as credit risk analysis, loan underwriting, and loan usage monitoring, or simply provide funding and rely on other banks for management duties. By exploiting the comparative advantage of all participating banks in a syndicate, loan syndication results in an optimal distribution of responsibilities within the lending group. One of the clear benefits of loan syndication is that it allows the participating banks to share information, risk, and responsibilities, reducing the information asymmetry that exists between lenders and borrowers. In addition, the borrower enjoys an advantage in this arrangement as working with the lead arranger in a loan syndicate increases their chances of securing the desired loan amount at a lower cost overall, as opposed to borrowing from multiple lenders individually. The size of the loan syndication market has fluctuated over the years, reflecting various episodes of financial crises since the 2000s. In 2021, the market recorded a volume of USD 5.4 trillion, with advanced country borrowers accounting for 87% of the total volume. US borrowers accounted for as much as 58% of the total volume.

Part 2: International Financial Crises and Secret Money expands on the topics covered in the first part and aims to equip readers with knowledge of how international banks are affected by international banking crises, sovereign debt crises, financial secrecy, and international money laundering. *Chapter 7: International Banking Crisis* provides an overview of the origins and effects of international banking crises. These crises refer to a state in which a financial system experiences a sequence of monetary losses and the depreciation of financial and non-financial assets that endanger the stability of the banking system. Government interventions are often necessary to save failing financial institutions. Between 1971 and 2017, there were 151 banking crises, with the majority (126) occurring in developing economies (Laeven and Valencia, 2018). Nevertheless, notable crises were also observed in advanced economies, such as the Global Financial Crisis. Two main factors tend to precede a banking crisis. The first is excessive credit growth that leads to financial bubbles, which when burst can paralyse the banking system. The second is excessive risk-taking by banks following deregulation, which can cause financial instability. The price of a banking crisis can be steep, with an average fiscal cost of rescuing the banking sector reaching as high as 13% of GDP between 1971 and 2017. Developing countries bore the brunt of the cost, with rescue costs as high as 14% of GDP, in contrast to 9% in advanced economies (Laeven and Valencia, 2018).

Chapter 8: Banking Crisis in Emerging Economies delves into the causes of banking crises in emerging economies. Commercial banks, being intermediaries in financial transactions, are vulnerable to mismatches between their assets and liabilities. These mismatches result from the shorter-term, less liquid nature of their liabilities, and their being in smaller denominations, relative to their assets. In developed financial systems, tools are available to manage these risks and protect them from shocks. Due to the underdeveloped financial sectors in emerging economies, the absence of readily available risk management tools can increase their vulnerability to banking crises, which in turn can have severe consequences. The factors contributing to banking crises in emerging economies can be classified into two categories: micro and macro factors. Micro factors include poor risk management by banks due to inadequate credit risk assessment and management skills, as well as distorted incentives arising from government ownership of banks and connected lending. Weak accounting and legal frameworks also make it difficult to accurately assess the health of the banking sector in a timely manner. Macro factors include inadequate preparation for financial liberalisation, where inefficient domestic banks face competition from more efficient foreign banks, leading to instability in the banking sector, macroeconomic volatility, inflexible exchange rate systems that cannot absorb external shocks, and domestic lending booms and bubbles that eventually burst.

Chapter 9: Banking Crisis in Advanced Economies delves into the causes of banking crises in advanced economies. The banking crises that occurred in the late 1980s and early 1990s in advanced economies shared similar characteristics with those observed in emerging economies. In both cases, banks lacked risk management skills and struggled to compete with one another. This was due to the underdeveloped financial and economic systems in emerging economies and strict regulations in advanced economies that limited competition. When banks faced sudden competition due to financial and economic system liberalisation or entered a deregulated environment, they were incentivised to take excessive risks that were difficult to manage. However, recent banking crises in advanced economies, including the Global Financial Crisis (GFC), were unique to the characteristics of the advanced financial system. This was due to the development of new and complex financial products resulting from continued financial engineering. For example, Collateralised Debt Obligations (CDOs) based on mortgage loans became increasingly complex in structure and underlying asset composition, making it almost impossible to assess their credit quality accurately. Moreover, naked Credit Default Swaps written on CDOs allowed third parties to speculate on their default probability, exacerbating the aggregate risk exposure to the CDOs in the financial system. The lack of regulation on these products allowed excessive risk-taking behaviour that eventually led to the collapse of confidence and the GFC. Overall, the key factor underlying all banking crises is the ineffective management of bank risk-taking activities.

In *Chapter 10: Country risk analysis*, the focus is on country risk analysis, which sheds light on the additional risks involved in lending to sovereign governments. Compared to corporate borrowers, loans to government borrowers are riskier since it is not possible to take legal action against a defaulting sovereign. While sovereigns have the option to default on their loans with no immediate consequence, it could lead to reputational damage, resulting in being locked out of the international loan market. The relationship between a banking crisis and a sovereign debt crisis is bi-directional. A banking crisis has the potential to worsen the fiscal position of the sovereign to such an extent that doubts may arise about its capacity to service external debt obligations and allocate additional funds to support the banking sector. Conversely, as a consequence of a weakened sovereign, the decreasing value of government securities that banks hold in their asset portfolio may expose the banking sector to further vulnerability. The term 'country risk' comprises several risks, including political, transfer, sovereign, and currency risks. International banks must assess both credit and country risks of foreign borrowers. There are two ways to evaluate country risk: internal risk evaluation, in which lenders examine the borrower's country risk using statistical or checklist methods, and external risk evaluation, which depends on third-party evaluations such as sovereign credit ratings or country risk indexes generated by credit rating agencies or other third-party entities.

Chapter 11: International Debt Crisis examines the nature of international debt crisis episodes, with a focus on the causes and consequences of sovereign debt crises in both emerging and advanced economies since the 1970s. According to Laeven and Valencia's (2018) report, there were 75 sovereign debt crises between 1971 and 2017, with all but two occurring in emerging economies. The most notable case of an emerging economy sovereign debt crisis was the Latin American debt crisis in the 1980s, which began with Mexico's default announcement in August 1982 and quickly spread to other countries in the region. The response from the international community, led by US money centre banks and later the US government, included loan rescheduling, debt-for-equity swaps, and the creation of a secondary market for emerging market debt. Mexico experienced difficulties again in 1994 due to rising political risk and domestic economic troubles. The Russian debt crisis in 1998 had similar characteristics, with a combination of currency and debt crises leading to a loan moratorium for 90 days. However, the recovery was relatively quick due to rising oil prices. The Eurozone debt crisis from 2009 to 2015 was the most recent and notable sovereign debt crisis in advanced economies. While the Eurozone maintained a relatively balanced external position, some member countries, such as Greece, Portugal, and Spain, experienced continued budget and current account deficits, funded mostly by bank loans within the union. Furthermore, the expansion of bank lending fuelled real estate booms in Spain and Ireland. The Troika, consisting of the European Union, the European Central Bank, and the IMF, provided rescue funding to troubled countries, and lenders were forced to reduce debt. The combined efforts of all parties resulted in meaningful recoveries for all countries from 2015.

Chapter 12: Financial Secrecy and Secret Money examines the concept of financial secrecy, along with its supply and demand. Financial secrecy is the act of withholding bank clients' financial information from third parties, including tax authorities in their home countries. The demand for financial secrecy can arise from various reasons, including personal, business, and political motives. Countries that offer a favourable legal and policy environment for financial and legal institutions to provide financial secrecy to international clients are usually preferred. Tax havens and offshore financial centres are examples of such jurisdictions that offer low or zero tax rates in addition to financial secrecy, attracting wealthy individuals and corporations seeking to avoid taxes. Nevertheless, conventional tax havens have faced scrutiny from advanced country governments and international organisations like the OECD and IMF, resulting in the creation of lawful strategies for transferring profits from high-tax to low-tax countries. These corporate tax havens comply with international exchange programs while exploiting legal loopholes to help corporations avoid taxes. Switzerland is one of the oldest and most well-known tax havens globally, with its banking sector providing offshore private banking services to many wealthy individuals and corporations worldwide. The Swiss bank secrecy Act of 1934 justifies Swiss banks' provision of financial secrecy to their customers. Although Swiss banking secrecy has suffered some setbacks, it is likely to continue providing services to foreign clients for the foreseeable future.

Chapter 13: International Banks and Money Laundering explores the topic of international money laundering, which involves disguising the source of assets to avoid financial or legal scrutiny. Unlike tax evasion, which is commonly associated with traditional tax haven jurisdictions like Switzerland and the Cayman Islands, money laundering activities can occur anywhere. In 2009, criminal proceeds totalled around USD 2.1 trillion, equivalent to roughly 3.6% of global GDP. Out of this, drug trafficking contributed 20% of criminal proceeds and an estimated 75% of all criminal proceeds that were laundered. Money laundering typically involves three stages: placement, layering, and integration. In the placement stage, cash proceeds from criminal activities are placed in banks. In the layering stage, the illegal assets are transferred multiple times between bank accounts. In the integration stage, the assets are used for what appear to be legal purposes. International efforts to combat money laundering have taken various forms, including the OECD's Fighting Action Task Force (FATF) setting recommendations for governments and financial institutions to adopt. Governments also impose Anti-Money Laundering (AML) procedures on their financial institutions to prevent banks from being used in the money laundering cycle, especially during the placement and layering stages.

Part 1

The Fundamentals of International Banking

Chapter 1

International Banking: Functions, Theories, and Types

1.1. Introduction

International banking refers to the provision of financial (banking) services to clients in many different (legal and banking) jurisdictions. The services provided may include transactions with foreign as well as domestic residents relating to offering the following services: deposit-related products and extending loans in domestic and foreign currencies; facilitating foreign currency transactions; advising clients on foreign exchange and other financial risk hedging services; participating in international loan syndications; facilitating international trade finance for clients, etc. In today's world of highly integrated financial architecture, deregulated banking activities, market openness, fast and secure flow of information, and value transfer, the playing fields of banks are not limited to the domestic market. Instead, a whole spectrum of financial services in many different geographical markets is available even for small domestic banks as well as large multination banks. In addition, the development of communication and payment-related technologies combined with the widespread adoption of mobile Internet devices allow financial technology (or FinTech) start-ups to challenge traditional financial institutions in domestic and potentially international intermediation activities.

International banks are also referred to as multinational banks. Although the two terms *international* and *multinational* are sometimes used interchangeably, there is a subtle difference when they are applied to banking. Multinational banking refers to the activities of banks that own and operate physical banking facilities (e.g., branches and subsidiaries) across multiple country locations. For example, HSBC (https://www.hsbc.com/) has a presence (branches and subsidiaries) in 35 countries (as of July 2022), providing both domestic and international banking services. Thus, *multinational* relates more to organisational forms than the types of services provided. On the other hand, the term *International* banking specifically refers to traditional cross-border and cross-currency foreign banking and eurobanking[1] activities. It relates more to the types of banking services provided, not necessarily the location of the provision of the services or clients. From these definitions, it is clear that international banking services can be provided by both multinational and domestic banks, and these two terms can be used interchangeably throughout this chapter without loss of generality.

Exhibit 1.1 shows the total cross-border claims of the Bank for International Settlements (BIS) reporting banks for the fourth quarter of 1977 to the first quarter of 2022. Panel A shows international bank claims, which include total cross-border loans and other assets of the reporting banks. The initial spur to growth in the mid-1980s coincides with the deregulation of the financial system of major economies. The rapid growth from the early 2000s continued until its peak of USD 35 trillion in the first quarter of 2008 before starting a reversal. The Global Financial Crisis (GFC) which began in mid-2007 induced the withdrawal of international banking activities that continued until the fourth quarter of 2016, where it reached USD 27 trillion before it began to rebound, reaching USD 36 trillion by the first quarter of 2022. The recovery of international banking activities from 2016 is coming mostly from the USD-denominated claims, as seen by rising USD-denominated claims. On the other hand, Euro-denominated claims have been falling since the start of the GFC. Panel B shows currency shares of total cross-border claims. The USD accounted for as much as 78% of the total claims in the fourth quarter of 1983. Its share gradually declined until 2008, when it reached its lowest level of 40% of the total.

The German Mark/the Euro is the second most popular currency denomination in international assets. Its popularity started to grow from

---

[1]Eurobanking refers to those international banking activities involving financial services denominated in currencies foreign to the market where the transactions occur (e.g., an Australian bank providing a loan denominated in the USD to a Japanese multinational borrower in London). See Chapter 5.

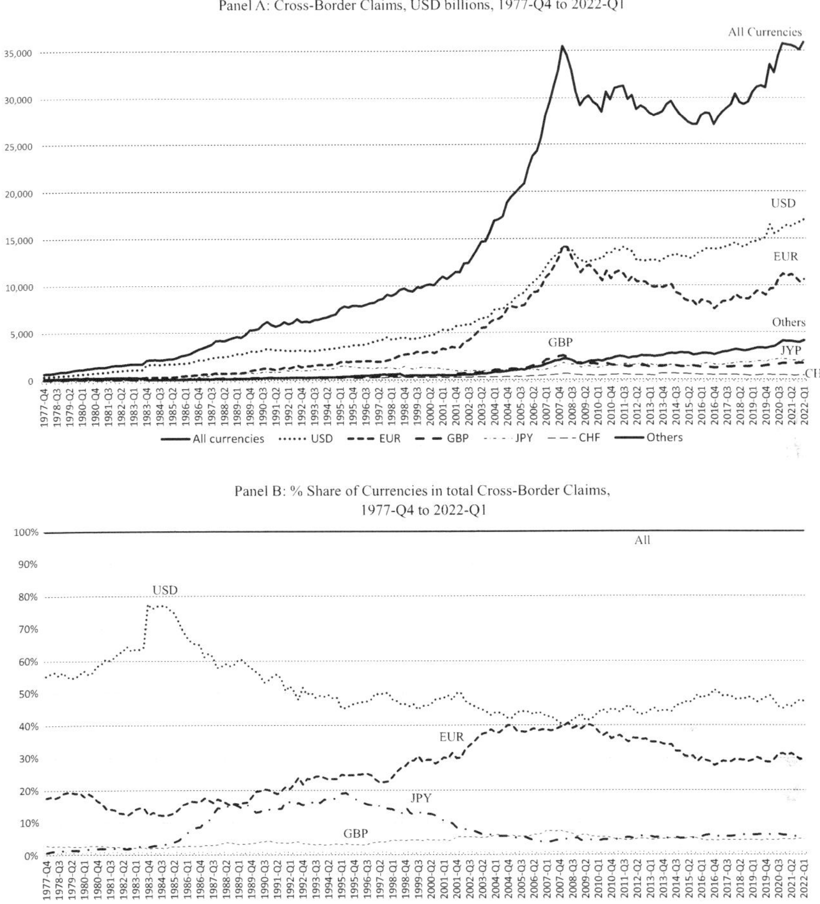

Exhibit 1.1. Cross-border claims and currency compositions of BIS reporting banks, 1977Q1–2022Q1.

Source: BIS international banking statistics, Locational banking statistics.

the mid-1980s during the financial market deregulation phase to match the USD in importance by the second quarter of 2008. The USD and the Euro accounted for 40% and 41% of cross-border bank assets, respectively, in the second quarter of 2008. However, this trend was reversed due to the weakening international positions of major European banks during the GFC of 2007–2009 and the Eurozone debt crisis of 2009–2012. By the first quarter of 2022, 47% and 30% of cross-border assets were denominated in the USD and the Euro, respectively.

The cross-border claims denominated in the Japanese Yen started to rise from the fourth quarter of 1985 and peaked in the second quarter of 1995 at 19% of the total. This coincides with the periods of the heightened international presence of Japanese banks, as seen in Panel A of Exhibit 1.2. However, the financial difficulties faced by Japanese banks since the bursting of the stock and real estate market bubbles in 1991 led to the substantial reduction of the Japanese Yen's share of the total cross-border claims to settle between 5 and 6% of the total from 2004.

Exhibit 1.2 shows the 10 largest banks in the world by total assets over the period 1996–2020. The landscape of top banks has changed significantly over the last three decades. There are a number of noteworthy developments. *First,* the average size of bank assets has increased by a factor of six, from USD 502 billion in 1996 to over USD 3 trillion in 2020. This corresponds to the significant increase in the cross-border banking activities shown in Exhibit 1.1. There also has been an even larger growth in total equity from USD 18 billion to USD 213 billion over the same period, representing a more than eleven-fold increase and reflecting the efforts of the banks and the regulators in strengthening the capital position of banks, especially after the GFC. However, the profitability of top banks, as measured by return on equity, has fluctuated across the period in line with the various episodes of financial turbulence. The profitability of banks recovered after the dip in the late 2000s.

Second, Japanese banks dominated the top 10 bank ranking from the late 1980s, and their dominance continued well into the second half of the 1990s, as evidenced by the 1996 ranking shown in Panel A, where seven Japanese banks were listed in the top 10 list. This is in large part due to the delayed response of the Japanese banks and their regulator to address the accumulating non-performing loans (NPL) created by the Japanese bubble collapse in 1991. The negative effects of not addressing the NPL are reflected in the large and negative profitability of some of the banks listed. Four of the seven banks listed reported a negative return on equity for 1996, ranging from –19.4% for Fuji bank to –6.6% for Sanwa bank. The Asian Financial Crisis of 1997 triggered the banking crisis in Japan in 1998, which highlighted the need to write off/down the accumulated NPLs. Consequently, the Japanese banks largely withdrew from the

Total Asset	Capital	Bank	Country	Total Asset USD m.	Total Equity USD m.	ROE %
		Panel A: 1996				
1	2	Bank of Tokyo-Mitsubishi	Japan	720,098	28,389	3.0
2	12	Deutsche Bank	Germany	536,319	15,581	9.9
3	9	Sanwa Bank	Japan	500,713	17,665	-6.6
4	8	Sumitomo Bank	Japan	499,604	18,594	2.0
5	7	Dai-Ichi Kangyo Bank	Japan	498,296	19,480	4.3
6	13	Fuji Bank	Japan	487,020	15,551	-19.4
7	11	Sakura Bank	Japan	477,736	15,950	-10.6
8	3	Crédit Agricole Banque Indosuez	France	477,329	22,846	7.5
9	127	Norinchukin Bank	Japan	429,234	3,092	-16.5
10	1	HSBC Holdings	UK	401,666	29,396	19.9
		Average		502,802	18,654	-0.7
		Panel B: 2004				
1	17	UBS	Switzerland	1,533,306	35,630	20.1
2	11	Mizuho Financial Grp	Japan	1,324,075	44,990	8.7
3	2	HSBC	UK	1,276,778	99,817	11.9
4	6	Groupe Credit Agricole	France	1,245,213	67,621	8.0
5	8	BNP Paribas	France	1,236,062	48,825	13.0
6	1	JP Morgan Chase	USA	1,157,248	105,653	4.2
7	18	Deutsche Bank	Germany	1,146,189	35,343	9.5
8	5	Royal Bank of Scotland Grp	UK	1,124,108	68,768	12.6
9	3	Bank of America Corporation	USA	1,112,035	99,645	14.2
10	12	Mitsubishi Tokyo Financial Grp	Japan	1,024,804	44,654	12.1
		Average		1,217,982	65,095	11.4
		Panel C: 2012				
1	19	Deutsche Bank	Germany	2,800,133	63,462	0.1
2	7	Mitsubishi UFJ Financial Group	Japan	2,664,171	117,018	0.2
3	4	HSBC Holdings	UK	2,555,579	139,590	0.2
4	11	BNP Paribas	France	2,542,880	91,858	0.1
5	3	ICBC	China	2,456,295	140,028	0.3
6	13	Credit Agricole	France	2,431,932	80,222	0.1
7	15	Barclays	UK	2,417,369	78,036	0.1
8	12	Royal Bank of Scotland (RBS)	UK	2,329,767	88,112	0.0
9	2	JP Morgan Chase & Co	USA	2,265,792	150,384	0.2
10	1	Bank of America	USA	2,136,578	159,232	0.0
		Average		2,460,049	110,794	0.1
		Panel D: 2020				
1	1	Industrial and Commercial Bank of China	China	4,307,502	380,189	11.8
2	2	China Construction Bank Corporation	China	3,638,950	316,122	12.2
3	3	Agricultural Bank of China	China	3,559,126	277,608	11.0
4	4	Bank of China	China	3,257,474	258,431	11.2
5	10	Mitsubishi UFJ Financial Group	Japan	3,096,333	143,729	3.9
6	9	HSBC Holdings	UK	2,715,152	148,359	5.9
7	5	JP Morgan Chase & Co	USA	2,687,379	214,432	17.0
8	6	Bank of America	USA	2,434,079	188,492	14.6
9	13	BNP Paribas	France	2,432,262	101,081	9.5
10	12	Credit Agricole Group	France	2,259,512	105,812	8.2
		Average		3,038,777	213,426	10.5

Exhibit 1.2. Top 10 banks in the World by total assets, 1996–2020.

Source: Euromoney (1996, 2004) and The Banker (2012 and 2020).

international banking scene, and the process of addressing the thorny NPL issue began in the early 2000s, reducing the balance sheet size for most banks. In addition, the wave of mergers and acquisition activities (both the private sector initiated and due to the government's pursuit of Too-Big-To-Fail (TBTF) policy) significantly changed the landscape of the Japanese banking sector.[2] The adjustment process of Japanese banks continued until 2005, and through M&As, structural reforms, further diversification of assets, and addressing NPLs, they started to report healthy profits from 2005. However, Japanese banks have never regained their prominence on the world stage. Mitsubishi UFJ was the only top 10 presence in the 2012 and 2020 lists shown in Exhibit 1.2.

Third, US and European multinational banks had largely replaced Japanese banks in the world rankings in the 2000s and the early 2010s. Due to their traditional cross-border banking activities and the strength of their economies, US and European banks were able to regain their position as top global banks. Due to the Eurozone debt crisis of 2009–2012, German and French banks fared worse from the mid to late 2010s.

Fourth, there have been ranking upgrades due to M&A activities between banks. For example, as noted in the second point above, a number of Japanese banks have merged to create new entities. These include Mizuho financial group (from the mergers of Dai-Ichi Kangyo Bank, Fuji Bank, and the Industrial Bank of Japan in 2002) and Mitsubishi UFJ Financial Group (from the mergers of Mitsubishi Tokyo Financial Group and UFJ group in 2005). In the US, JPMorgan Chase was an outcome of a series of mergers since 1996 involving Chase Manhattan Bank, J.P. Morgan & Co., Bank One, Bear Stearns, and Washington Mutual.

Fifth, the Chinese banks' ascendency to the world ranking is also noteworthy. The big four Chinese banks (Industrial and Commercial Bank of China, China Construction Bank, Agricultural Bank, and Bank of China) emerged in the early 2010s and started to dominate the world rankings from the mid-2010s. In 2020, the top 4 world banks were the top 4

---

[2]Hosono *et al.* (2007) provide the details of the mergers and acquisition activities in the Japanese Banking sector from 1990 to 2004. In general, they find that although the government's Too-Big-To-Fail (TBTF) policy had a significant impetus to the M&A activities, the desired goals (especially efficiency and profitability gain and reduction in NPLs) were not met. Instead, they find that the bank mergers were motivated by the desire to increase the size of their operations to take advantage of the government's TBTF policy. However, they did not find support for empire-building as a motive.

Chinese banks accounting for 48.58% of the top 10 banks' total assets. The spectacular ascendency of the Chinese banks in the world bank rankings coincides with the underlying Chinese economy's successful transformation into a global player since the early 2000s culminating in China becoming the second-largest economy in 2010.[3]

An additional observation in the top global ranking presented above is that top global banks are not necessarily global in terms of diversification of income streams. For instance, most of the Japanese banks in the 1990s relied almost exclusively on domestically generated income. Also, the top Chinese banks from the early 2000s relied heavily on domestic intermediation activities. This is an important difference from non-financial multinational corporations that are operating out of many geographical locations and draw income across these markets. Canals (1997) suggests that this difference is due to additional complexities associated with bank internationalisation compared to the internationalisation of companies in other industries.

1.2. Functions of International Banks

International banking is more about the functions that banks perform rather than the organisational aspects of banking operations. These functions are cross-border in nature and are spread across the following activities: international trade financing, activities in the interbank foreign exchange market, participation in the eurocurrency market, sovereign lending, and international investment banking activities. In this section, a brief discussion of each of the functions is provided.

1.2.1. *International trade finance*

Financing international trade has traditionally been the most important hallmark of an international bank. Due to the gap between the payment and shipment of goods, the exporter is exposed to counterparty default.

[3]Although the large Chinese banks were highly ranked in terms of various performance measures (e.g., tier 1 capital, ROA, and profitability), their income comes predominantly from traditional commercial banking activities (i.e., interest income). Conversely, large US and European banks dominated the rankings in non-interest income categories in the trading, fee, and commission income rankings in 2016.

Due to the added complications and costs arising from a distance (physical, political, legal, regulation, and cultural) between the two parties in an international transaction, the exporter is unlikely to manage the counterparty default risk effectively. Thus, international trade may not occur without an international bank providing financial and performance guarantees and gap financing. Trade financing involves the process of financing business transactions that involve the transfer of ownership of goods or providing services in return for financial remuneration. Financial institutions are usually involved in the process by providing advances to the buyer through business overdrafts, loans, and bill acceptance facilities.[4] International trade financing may be viewed as an extension of domestic trade financing with additional complications. These include geographic risk, foreign exchange risk, political risk, inflation and interest rate risk, market risk, and payment risk, just to name a few. Facilitating international trade has been one of the most important functions associated with international banking. Although domestic banks (as opposed to multinational banks) have also been providing trade payment guarantees, especially for their domestic clients, access to international financial markets and presence in multiple country locations allowed international banks to be in a better position to assess these risks and provide international trade financing more readily. In general, international trades in goods need to be financed because there is a time gap between the time of sale and receipt of payment for an exporter, and the exporter needs funding to continue the production cycle. Also, international trade involves some degree of uncertainty which may lead to a non-completion of trade. Thus, the exporter requires assurance of payment before shipment can be made.

Although domestic banks can participate in this process, international banks with access to the networks of banks located worldwide are in a better position to assess and manage the associated risks of default.

---

[4]Bill acceptance facilities allow banks to accept (or guarantee) commercial bills issued by their corporate customers (usually long-standing business customers). This enables corporations to raise funds directly from the capital market, assisted by the banks' payment guarantee. The bills are issued and traded in the domestic market and denominated in the currency of the market. The letter of credit is similar in that a bank provides a payment guarantee for its customer. However, at least two currencies are involved in this process (e.g., the AUD and the USD if an Australian importer pays the invoice of the trade in the USD).

1.2.2. *Interbank foreign exchange market*

The foreign exchange market represents a vehicle facilitating international transactions that require the transfer of value from one currency to another. For example, international trade between an Australian exporter of natural resources (e.g., coal and iron ore) and a Chinese importer is typically denominated in the USD as commodities are priced and traded in the USD, a trade vehicle currency. The Chinese exporter needs to raise the USD funds, and the Australian exporter then needs to exchange the USD funds received into the Australian Dollar. The interbank foreign exchange market is where such transactions are facilitated, and it is unique in its characteristics which distinguish it from other international financial markets. These include continuous trading on a 24-hour-per-day basis, especially between the major currencies (USD vs Euro is the most important currency pair followed by USD vs Japanese Yen); a large volume of transactions (USD 7.5 trillion per day on average in 2022, BIS, 2022); lower transaction costs measured by narrower bid and ask spreads compared to other financial instruments; and relatively unregulated operations due to cross-border nature of the transactions. International banks account for the bulk of foreign exchange trading.[5]

International banks typically perform four roles in the foreign exchange market. *First,* they provide an intermediary service to their non-financial customers. In dealing with retail customers needing foreign exchange (international travellers, investors, etc.), they act as an agent for their customers servicing their foreign exchange needs. They participate in the foreign exchange market to buy or sell foreign currencies on behalf of their customers and provide foreign exchange hedging services. They offer both spot and forward (outright and swap) contracts and over-the-counter foreign exchange derivative products to their customers. When they act on behalf of their customers, their main aim is to minimise the costs of providing these services.[6] This was the traditional service

[5]In the 2022 survey of the BIS's triennial survey of Foreign Exchange and Over-the-counter (OTC) derivatives markets, financial institutions (the sum of reporting dealers and other financial institutions) accounted for 94% of the daily turnover of USD 7.5 trillion. In the 1995's survey, the daily volume was USD 1.1 trillion, and the financial institutions' share was 84%. https://www.bis.org/statistics/rpfx22.htm.

[6]An outright forward contract requires the seller to deliver a specified amount of foreign currency at some future date. The seller of the contract assumes the resulting exchange rate

function performed by international banks. As such, this aspect of the foreign exchange business is treated as a cost centre of their operations. This portion of the foreign exchange market volume was only around 6% of the total in 2022 (see Exhibit 4.9).

Second, international banks act as brokers matching bid and ask transactions for a fee. They provide a matchmaking service whereby they match buyers' bid process to sellers' ask prices. They generate fee income by providing this service and are not acting as a counterparty to transactions. The existence of search costs makes the services provided by brokers invaluable. Brokers in major money market centres receive limit orders (specific amount and price) from other banks and work out the best bid and ask rates for a given amount for a currency pair. These best rates are known as the broker's inside spread and are released to the market upon request or via trading screens. The identities behind these best rates are usually hidden until the enquiring bank accepts the prices.

Third, international banks act as market makers and stand ready to transact on the bid and ask quotes they provide to the market. Market-making banks are expected to quote both their buying (bid) and selling (ask) prices for a specified trade size in a foreign currency. This is a common characteristic of other types of financial markets, such as interbank money markets, where market makers are expected to provide liquidity in a given currency when required. Once quotes are given, market makers must be able to honour their quotes, and they would not know beforehand which of the two rates (bid or ask) would be hit, so they must have sufficient reserves in both the foreign currencies in which they are dealing and bank reserves (i.e., money).

Fourth, international banks also trade foreign currencies on their own accounts. That is, they trade for profit, and some have grown to rely on this source of income. To the extent that the foreign exchange market is decentralised and information asymmetries exist, banks trading with superior information (e.g., advanced knowledge of macroeconomic

---

risk. A swap contract is a combination of an outright forward and a spot transaction on the opposite side in the same amount. Although this eliminates the exchange rate exposure for the customer, an interest rate exposure (due to the interest rate differential between domestic and foreign currencies) arises. In 2022, the composition of total daily volume was FX swaps: 50%, Spot: 28%, Outright forwards: 16%, currency swap: 2%, and options and other products: 4%.

announcements and monetary policy changes) can realise trading profits by trading with uninformed dealers. However, it can be argued that trading for profit in the foreign exchange market itself does not lead to economically productive activities as there are no underlying trades in goods and services. Thus, it might be questionable whether the active participation of international banks in the foreign exchange markets for profit motives is desirable from social and economic standpoints. However, the reality is that international banks' foreign exchange market activities will continue to grow thanks to the continuing growth of international financial markets and the international integration of national economies. The factors contributing to the market growth include the rapid growth of international market opportunities for both financial and non-financial corporations (e.g., emerging market opportunities, financing cross-border M&A activities), the continuous improvement of trading technologies, and the recent floating of many emerging market currencies.

1.2.3. *Participation in eurocurrency market*

International banks play a crucial role in intermediating cross-border financial flows between clients in various jurisdictions. International money markets located in financial centre locations, such as London, New York, and Hong Kong, facilitate trades of short-term credit denominated in major currencies. The eurocurrency market is the segment of the international money market where credit products traded are denominated in currencies other than the currency of the market where the transactions occur. Specifically, eurocurrency markets refer to the Over-The-Counter (OTC) interbank market for bank time deposits (short-term, up to 12 months) in the currency denomination other than the national currency of the location of the bank. For example, a domestic corporation that requires USD funds for its operation in the US can borrow the necessary USD amount from a UK bank in London. Eurobanks are international banks that engage in eurocurrency transactions and are typically foreign branches of international banks located in major money market centres. By far, the most important currency in the eurocurrency market is the USD. It is in the form of eurodollar (USD deposits and loans outside the US), accounting for approximately 62% of the eurocurrency market in 2021 (BIS Locational Banking Statistics, see Exhibit 5.2).

1.2.4. *Sovereign lending*

International banks engage in lending to sovereign borrowers. National governments often tap into the international banking market to fund infrastructure investments and other national projects, as their domestic financial markets may not be able to fund them. In general, most sovereign borrowings are in hard currencies (such as the USD and the Euro) and in large denominations. Due to the large size of the loans involved, sovereign lendings are usually syndicated with multiple international banks involved, which may also include domestic banks of the sovereign borrowers. International banks face additional risks when extending loans to sovereigns as the normal array of legal protection is not available to them when sovereign defaults occur. There have been many occurrences of international debt crises involving sovereigns. The most notable are the Latin American debt crisis in the early 1980s and the Eurozone debt crisis of 2009–2012, among others. International banks, in these cases, were forced to take alternative arrangements that invariably involved loss to the lenders. Examples include loan rescheduling, partial or full debt forgiveness, and alternative payment arrangements, such as swaps for equity, natural resources, or lower-valued debt.

1.2.5. *International investment banking*

Investment banks act as an intermediary between corporations and the capital market and offer fee-based services for arranging for their clients to access the market to raise required funds. Corporations can tap into equity markets via initial public offerings and subsequent equity raising or alternatively, issue debt instruments directly to the capital market. Investment banks act as arrangers and sometimes underwriters facilitating such capital market access for their clients. Large international banks, as shown in Exhibit 1.2, especially those from the US and Europe, provide investment banking services backed up by commercial banking presence in the location of the client. Corporations planning to issue securities (e.g., long-term bonds in the USD, either in the US or non-US markets) can entertain accessing multiple markets across many jurisdictions for large denomination debt issues. National governments wishing to privatise government-owned enterprises (e.g., electricity or other utility companies) can allocate shares to both onshore and offshore investors due to the large size of such endeavours. Such cross-border investment banking activities require international banks that can access multiple markets. Other cross-border activities of international investment banking include the following: trading, as well as underwriting, of international securities (international loans, euronotes, eurobonds, etc.); trading in international equities; and providing funds management and risk management services.

1.3. Theories of International Banking

Banks engage in international banking activities for several reasons. In this section, various determinants of bank internationalisation are examined. These include (1) defensive expansion where banks are forced to follow their customers to a foreign location, (2) accessing foreign markets to expand and diversify their balance sheets, (3) participating in the eurocurrency market, and (4) benefiting from regulation arbitrage.

1.3.1. *Defensive expansion (Follow the customer)*

Insomuch as the relationship with customers (especially corporate borrowers) is valued, banks follow them when they establish foreign operations requiring financial and local market-specific services. This is known as a defensive expansion. If the bank does not follow its customers, they are forced to seek assistance from the banks operating in the target market (domestic and multinational banks in the target market). If multinational banks are servicing these customers in the target foreign markets, they may also attempt to service them in the customers' home market as well. This will result in the bank losing customers in both home and foreign markets. In banking systems where banks traditionally played an important role in corporate governance, it is not uncommon for business corporations to have cross-shareholding arrangements with their banks (e.g., Japan and most continental European countries). Under these circumstances, companies usually deal with one bank for most of their financing. It is a natural progression for the bank to follow its customers wherever they expand to. In Japan, these banks were called a 'main bank', and in Germany, they were referred to as a 'Haus bank'.

Most multinational banks have established presence in countries that represent major export (or input) markets for their main customers, such as the Japanese banks in the US, and the US banks in Western Europe and Latin America. Australian banks' presence in foreign soils dates back to the late 19th century when they opened their offices in London due to their importance for Australian exporters.

1.3.2. *Growth potential*

In order to achieve further growth in banking activities that are not possible domestically, banks look to foreign markets for expansion. This is important because banks need to be of sufficient size (especially for capital market and currency dealing transactions) to realise scale economies. Due to a lower degree of heterogeneity of core banking products (i.e., intermediation), the marginal cost of providing international banking services in addition to servicing the domestic market is low. For instance, a credit product initially developed for the domestic market might be introduced to a foreign market (with some localisation, if needed). This is especially true if the target markets share common business, legal, and cultural characteristics with the country of the expanding banks. For example, Spanish banks found Latin American banking markets a hospitable environment. Australian banks expanded first to New Zealand and the UK due to the similarity in market conditions.

Also, if the expanding bank has a clear technical and cost superiority over local banks and the local market is in the early stage of deregulation, then expansion into that local foreign market would offer sizable profits and market share. This was the case with the US banks when they saw the opening of western European markets in the 1960s. They had both the technical expertise and the access to a cheaper cost of capital and were in a position to benefit from their expansion into the then emerging European markets.

1.3.3. *Access to money market centres*

Ready access to the interbank money market[7] has been crucial for banks' short-term money management (raising and unloading credit in various currencies). Before the advent of an efficient global payment and communication system, it was essential to have a presence in the key international money market centres such as London and New York to access the interbank market for liquidity and cost minimisation purposes.

[7] The interbank market refers to the network of (international) banks that facilitate borrowing and lending short-term money between banks.

In addition to achieving lower costs of funds through the interbank market, banks might also consider international expansion to achieve a higher return on investments. In light of the events regarding LIBOR manipulation scandals in London (the Libor Scandal of 2012, see Chapter 5), the kinds of market intelligence (and a trading edge) banks can obtain by being in the strategic markets are highlighted.

1.3.4. *International diversification benefits*

One of the core benefits of being a multinational corporation is the ability to diversify both the revenue and cost sides of its operation across multiple jurisdictions. International diversification is likely to reduce aggregate risk and enhance the profitability of multinational corporations. Similar benefits exist for banks that operate across national markets. By diversifying the sources of funds and the geographical area of fund deployment, banks may be subject to less overall portfolio risk. This is especially relevant, considering that business cycles of different regions of the world tend not to coincide perfectly. This is intuitively appealing since an opportunity for multinational banks to diversify their loan portfolios across borders would reduce their portfolio risk. In addition, expansion into emerging markets would have the potential to improve overall profitability at the same time. Recent evidence shows, however, that this strategy may not always be successful as the continued globalisation of international financial markets (even the emerging markets) increases financial contagions and thus reduces the potential for diversification benefits. MSCI (2020) reports diminished benefits of global portfolio investment diversification due to increased market correlations and geopolitical risks. However, they suggest that alternative investments may still yield global diversification benefits, such as real estate, infrastructure and ESG (Environment, Social and Governance) themed opportunities.

1.3.5. *Regulation considerations*

The existence of a considerable difference in the severity of the banking sector regulation between countries presents a tempting opportunity for the banks in heavier regulation countries to expand into less onerous regulation countries. This is because the compliance costs would be higher the more severe the regulation. One of the reasons for the internationalisation of US banks into Western Europe in the late 1960s was to escape the domestic regulation in the US that added to the costs of bank operations. For example, Regulation Q placed caps on domestic deposit rates, limiting the ability of US banks to raise funds from this source. Moreover, mandatory deposit insurance, the separation of commercial and investment banking under the Glass Steagal Act, and the limitations of state branching regulations for state-chartered banks under the McFadden Act all contributed to US banks seeking less stringent regulation jurisdictions. The emergence of the eurodollar market that was free from these cost-adding regulations provided an impetus for US banks to raise funds from this source.

As banks become internationalised, they face additional risks that must be managed effectively. Country risks (or political risks) need to be identified and managed effectively. In its extreme form, nationalisation by host governments of foreign-owned banks would lead to a significant capital loss. Alternatively, the imposition of capital control may prevent local borrowers from repaying in hard currencies, thus leading to costly processes of unwinding positions in that market. Exchange rate risk is another potentially debilitating aspect of international transactions, and currency mismatches between assets and liabilities expose banks to swings in exchange rates leading to higher uncertainty. Another consideration is the high set-up costs in internationalisation. This is especially true in commercial banking activities because of the branch networking requirement and greater efforts needed to overcome the loyalty of local customers to local banks.

In recent decades, these additional risks involved in international banking have become more prominent in international bank regulation arbitrage. Houston, Lin, and Ma (2012) report that international bank flows tend to concentrate on countries with strong investor protections, lower systemic risk, and fewer regulations. They highlight the role of the strength of the institutional environment as a prerequisite before regulation arbitrage can be effective in recent times. Karolyi and Taboada (2015) report that cross-border bank acquisitions are positively received by the stock market when the acquirers face more stringent regulations in their home countries. They regard this as evidence of international regulation arbitrage.

1.4. Types of International Banking

Different organisational forms of international banking permit different sets of international banking activities. The organisation forms range from a corresponding banking arrangement where there is little resource commitment for the banks involved to a full branch presence in the target banking market, which operates at the same level as local banks in the host country. Some forms of banking are investment-specific joint-venture banks, while others are set up to compete against the local banks in the host market.

1.4.1. *Correspondent bank*

Correspondent banking is the minimal form of international presence. A bank may have a correspondent relationship with another bank in countries where it does not have a presence. A correspondent bank relationship is established when two banks maintain a correspondent bank account with each other. Through these accounts, they service their clients in their operations in that foreign country. For example, an Australian bank might have a correspondent arrangement with a Japanese bank. The Australian bank holds a Japanese Yen cheque account with the Japanese bank, and conversely, the Japanese bank holds an Australian dollar cheque account with the Australian bank. From the Australian bank's perspective, the Japanese Yen account it holds is called a *Nostro* account (our account) and the Australian dollar cheque account it provides for the Japanese bank is called a *Vostro* account (their account).[8] These accounts are used when the clients of each bank request payments in local currencies. This arrangement is useful for servicing multinational corporate clients to conduct business worldwide through the bank's own and the correspondent bank's networks. In addition, a correspondent banking relationship involves assistance with trade financing and advising clients on local business conditions. This represents the lowest-cost solution for servicing multinational corporate clients in foreign countries without setting up operations in the host markets, but the range and quality of services provided are unlikely to be satisfactory for multinational corporate clients that require a deeper level of commitment from their banks.

1.4.2. *Representative office*

A representative office is a service facility designed to service a bank's multinational client in its foreign operation. However, it is not a direct

[8]The *Nostro* and *Vostro* accounts are held between banks and used to facilitate payment requirements arising from bilateral transactions of foreign exchange and eurocurrency transactions, in addition to transferring funds to each other on behalf of their customers.

operational presence, rather, it is a business post located in the banking district of a host country and represents the interests of the bank in the host foreign country. Its role is limited to acting as a listening post for business opportunities, monitoring correspondent relationships, and generally helping clients carry out business in a foreign country on behalf of their parent. It is suitable when a full banking presence is not called for due to insignificant market opportunities or as a probing instrument for a possible future full banking presence in the host market. In this role, representative offices collect intelligence on the conditions of the host market for their parents as well as their multinational clients operating in the host market. Typically, services provided are also very limited. They are not permitted to carry out the general intermediation business (taking deposits and lending to local borrowers) in the foreign host market as they are not a bank, but the services involved are generally more comprehensive than in a correspondence arrangement.

1.4.3. *Foreign branch*

Foreign branches of banks operate at the same level as the local banks in the host countries and are subject to the banking regulations of both the home and host countries. However, they are often subject to restrictions designed to limit their activities (such as a limit on the number of permitted branches, activities limited to business banking and retail banking not permitted, etc.). In the case of US banks, their foreign branches were not subject to home (US) reserve requirements nor were they required to pay deposit insurance on deposits taken in the foreign markets. This was the most popular method of overseas expansion by US banks. In general, due partly to branch restrictions and other potential local resistance, foreign branches usually concentrate on the wholesale business where the extensive branch network is not essential, and they perform more specialised functions more closely in line with the areas of competitive advantage of the parents. In short, foreign branches generally concentrate on the business end of the market and perform specialised functions to cater to non-retail customers in the target host market.

Foreign branches are legally a part of their parent banks which afford them the following comparative advantages compared to local competitors: *First,* they allow a much faster global payment system through the parent's access to the global network. *Second,* they can handle much larger loan volumes than their balance sheets would allow since they are backed by the balance sheets of their parents. That is, their headquarters can provide additional funds required for loans by foreign branches. *Third,* both liquidity and solvency risks can be lower than local market competitors as their parents can provide necessary liquidity on short notice if required. Foreign branches are a part of their parents' global networks, so the liquidity and solvency of their globally consolidated operations are managed instead of at the individual foreign branch operation level. *Fourth,* consistency in corporate culture is achieved. Each multinational bank strives to have distinct characteristics to appeal to its clientele, so they wish to project a particular image in the minds of their customers. For example, HSBC is known for global retail banking, Credit Swiss for private banking services, Standard Chartered for an emerging market concentration, JPMorgan for their tilt towards syndication deal-making efforts, etc. Foreign branches are a preferred form of foreign presence to instil corporate culture and specific methods of business operation. However, this can also be a source of potential problems for the banks on a consolidated basis, as a financial crisis arising from a foreign banking location can have the potential to destabilise the entire operation of the multinational bank. Also, foreign branches require substantially more effort and time to get them up to operating levels as they require building banking operations from the ground up in the host market.

Ceruttia *et al.* (2007) report that banks prefer foreign branches over subsidiaries for the host market with a higher corporate tax rate. Higher corporate taxes can be more effectively managed via profit shifting across different tax jurisdictions that foreign branch networks would allow for multinational banks. On the other hand, they find that foreign branches are not suitable in host countries with restrictive regulations on new banks and foreign bank activities. Also, host countries with higher levels of country risk make establishing and running foreign branches potentially more expensive as the branches in the host countries are more likely to require bailouts than the branches in other host countries.

1.4.4. *Subsidiary and affiliate banks*

A subsidiary bank is a locally incorporated bank with a local board of directors that is wholly or majority-owned with controlling interests by a foreign parent. On the other hand, an affiliate bank is only partially owned by a foreign parent with no controlling interest. These are appropriate when branch banking is not allowed due to a regulatory feature of the host market or more grassroots-level banking operations are required to avoid local resistance. They are subject to the banking regulations of the host country, and the foreign parent is not legally liable for the deposits of the subsidiary banks. Subsidiaries operate at the same level as local banks in the host market, and as such, they can provide a full range of banking services, and they engage in both retail and wholesale banking activities.

The advantages of subsidiaries over foreign branches are as follows: (1) banks can get a quick full banking presence in a target foreign market through mergers and acquisition activities, (2) subsidiaries with substantial local affiliations (e.g., local name and usage of local managers and employees) can face substantially less customer resistance, especially in retail banking area, (3) the parent bank is not legally liable to guarantee deposits and other liabilities of the subsidiaries (a local crisis firewall). However, cultural consistency is difficult to achieve, and as a result, it takes longer to instil the parent's specialities onto the subsidiaries, if at all.

Ceruttia *et al.* (2007) suggest that foreign subsidiaries are more suitable for the host countries with higher country risk as the bank has limited liabilities in the event of a full-blown banking crisis in the host country. Moreover, Gleason *et al.* (2006) show that the acquisition of foreign banks is more feasible than other modes of entry when the expansion aims for scale and the target markets are developing countries.

1.4.5. *Edge Act bank in the US*

Edge Act banks are subsidiaries of US (or foreign) banks created under the Edge Act 1919 and located in the US to engage in all aspects of international banking without being subjected to state laws. The US Federal Reserve is responsible for monitoring and regulating Edge Act banks. They provide intermediation services to US corporations conducting business internationally. Their initial developments were due to the Edge Act of 1919, an amendment to the United States Federal Reserve Act of 1913 that allowed federally chartered US banks to engage in foreign banking activities to compete against foreign banks servicing US multinational corporations. In addition to Edge Act banks, Edge Act investment corporations are similarly allowed under the Act but engage in investments in foreign companies rather than financial intermediation.

Foreign banks are also allowed to operate Edge Act bank and corporations. As of September 2022, there were three foreign banks operating Edge Act bank branches: Banco Itau International and Banco Santander International both in Miami, Florida; and Standard Chartered Bank International in New York, New York. There is also one foreign bank operating an Edge Act investment corporation, HSBC International Financial Corporation in Wilmington, Delaware.

1.4.6. *International banking facility for US banks*

An International Banking Facility (IBF) is a separate accounting entity within a bank operating in the US to provide intermediation service to non-US residents and companies while not being subjected to US regulations and some state and local income taxes. IBFs were developed, in December 1981, to allow US banks to compete more effectively with foreign competitors in their offshore banking activities in the eurocurrency market (Key and Terrell, 1988). Deposits taken under this facility are exempt from the Federal Reserve's reserve and mandatory deposit insurance requirements.[9] Any depository institution operating in the US can potentially operate an IBF, and these include federally or state-chartered domestic US banks, US branches and subsidiaries of non-US banks, Edge Act banks, savings and loan associations, and mutual savings banks. IBFs allow US banks to accept deposits from and make loans to foreign corporate customers within their US locations. Before the introduction of IBF, only banks operating foreign branches or subsidiaries (i.e., multinational banks) were able to service their foreign customers. After establishing an IBF, smaller US banks (e.g., state-chartered banks) could also compete for foreign customer business without leaving the US.

IBFs are allowed to undertake the following activities: take large denomination time deposits with two-day notice of withdrawal from foreign non-banking customers; take overnight funds from foreign banking

[9]The reserve requirement in the US was reduced to zero on 26 March 2020. The current deposit protection, as of 2023, provided by the Federal Deposit Insurance Corporation (FDIC), is up to USD 250,000 per deposit category. https://www.federalreserve.gov/monetarypolicy/reservereq.htm.

and official institutions; take deposits from and make loans to foreign non-banking customers on the condition that funds are only to be used for non-US operations of the IBF, and non-bank deposits and withdrawals greater than USD 100,000.

As of 31 December 2022, there were 21 large US banks that operated an IBF (11 Nationally chartered and 10 state-chartered) out of 1,997 large commercial banks as defined by the US Federal Reserve. The four largest banks were JP Morgan Chase, Bank of America, Citigroup and Wells Fargo.[10]

1.4.7. *Offshore banking unit and offshore financial centre*

International banking activities can often be conducted via Offshore Banking Units (OBUs) of multinational banks, typically located in Offshore Financial Centres (OFCs). A significant portion of international banking flows is facilitated by OFCs due to several regulatory advantages this form of banking offers. In the first quarter of 2021, 15% of all cross-border claims and 16% of cross-border liabilities of all banks reporting to the Bank for International Settlement were against OFCs.

OBUs are typically foreign branches of a bank established in a foreign location. They are established mostly to conduct eurocurrency transactions against other foreign banks that are also OBUs in that location.[11] They cater to non-resident banking businesses such as foreign exchange, eurocurrency, and over-the-counter products. They are not permitted to service local residents, and as a result, local financial regulators have no incentive to regulate or restrict the activities of the OBUs in their jurisdictions. Moreover, they allow tax-effective environments for international banking operations. They can operate as a branch or a subsidiary of a parent bank and need not be more than an office as all transactions can be carried out at the parent's headquarters.

Banks from major countries established OBUs in the early 1970s in countries closer to their business time zones (e.g., US OBUs in the

---

[10] https://www.federalreserve.gov/releases/lbr/current/.

[11] A eurocurrency transaction is defined as a short-term money market participation whereby the currency denomination of an instrument differs from the national currency of the market where the transaction occurs. For example, the eurodollar market is an inter-bank market outside the US where USD denominated short-term funds are traded. For more detailed discussions of eurocurrency markets, please refer to Chapter 5.

Caribbean countries; European OBUs in the Middle East Countries, Switzerland, and Liechtenstein; Australian OBUs in Singapore and Malaysia). They can provide more tax-effective services (and potentially financial secrecy) to their existing clients in foreign locations via their OBUs. OBUs operating as foreign branches are legally a part of their parents, whereas those established as independent entities can be legally separate from their parents. The distinction between foreign branches and wholly or majority-owned foreign subsidiaries discussed above also applies to these two different ownership types of OBUs.

In addition, OBUs can be a domestic branch of a local bank established for the purpose of conducting non-resident business. The IBF for US banks is one example. Another is the Offshore Banking Unit regime in Australia, where Australian banks can establish an independent unit to conduct offshore banking activities against non-residents, which exempts the 10% withholding interest tax for deposits and enjoys a concessional corporate tax rate of 10% (as opposed to 30% applicable to domestic corporations).

However, the OECD's forum on harmful tax practices, which was created in 1998, recognised the harmful impact of OBUs on the domestic financial system due to the concessional tax rates and the ring-fenced nature of the OBUs.[12] As a result, some countries, such as Australia, have introduced legal measures to limit or abolish their activities.[13]

Locations hosting OBUs are typically offshore financial centres whose financial systems (especially banking systems) allow external financial flows to be beyond the normal economic activities of the host countries. The list of OFCs has changed over time, and the BIS's list as of December 2020 included a total of 25 countries.[14] In addition, the IMF has

---

[12]https://www.oecd.org/tax/beps/beps-actions/action5/.

[13]The Australian federal government introduced the Treasury Laws Amendment Bill 2021 on 17 March 2021 to abolish the OBU regime. The bill aims to remove the preferential tax rate of 10% after the 2023–2024 tax year and the withholding tax exemption from 1 January 2024. In addition, the G7 countries agreed in June 2021 to set a minimum 15% global tax rate for multinational corporations. This will significantly impact the ability of corporations to avoid taxes by strategically locating their income generating activities in tax haven countries.

[14]The countries that host an offshore financial centre include Anguilla, Aruba, the Bahamas, Belize, Bermuda, British Virgin Islands, Cayman Islands, Cook Islands, Cyprus, Gibraltar, Guernsey, Isle of Man, Jersey, Liechtenstein, Macao, SAR, China, Monaco,

a similar list which is largely overlapping with that of the BIS's (see Chapter 12 for more details).

1.4.8. *Joint venture bank*

Multinational banks may choose to establish a bank in a foreign country with another bank, typically a local bank in that location. There are broadly two reasons for this approach: entry barriers and local market knowledge. Forming a joint venture with a local bank might be the only way a multinational bank can access the foreign market due to strict regulations preventing foreign bank entry. An example of regulation-induced joint ventures is multinational banks' expansion into China. Foreign corporations were required to form a joint venture with a Chinese company where the latter held a controlling interest. In 2018, the limit on foreign ownership of joint ventures was increased to 51%, and it was further relaxed on 1 April 2020 as a part of the US-China trade deals, which allows US banks to wholly own their joint ventures in China. Goldman Sachs bought out its Chinese partner to raise its ownership stake to 100% in December 2020, and JPMorgan managed to raise its stake in its joint venture with a Chinese partner to 71% in November 2020.

The second reason is to overcome the challenges posed by an inadequate understanding of the local business practices and market intelligence for a successful operation in the target market. The local knowledge gap can be successfully addressed by establishing a joint venture bank with a local partner who is an established player in that market. For example, the UBS group entered into a joint venture arrangement with Banco do Brasil in November 2019 to tap into the investment banking segment in Brazil and other countries in the region. Banco do Brasil could in turn be able to access the international network of UBS via the joint venture.

Joint venture banks must have a clear focus and the potential to benefit both parties in the joint venture. Once the barriers to entry are dismantled and the foreign bank gains enough local knowledge, the joint ventures are usually dissolved.

Montserrat, the Netherlands Antilles, Palau, Panama, Samoa, Seychelles, Turks and Caicos, and Vanuatu.

Gleason *et al.* (2006) report that for US banks, the joint venture mode of expanding into foreign markets was more profitable when the aim was complementary (e.g. expansion into non-banking areas) and the target market was more regulated or developed economies.

1.5. Linkage Between Reasons for International Banking and International Banking Forms

As detailed in the previous section, international banking activities can be conducted under various banking forms. They vary in terms of the banking activities permitted under each license and the financial commitment required. Each form is suitable for a specific scenario. Banks choose an appropriate form of foreign presence depending on the strategic reason for the expansion into a particular foreign market. Thus, there usually is a close relationship between the reasons and the organisational forms of foreign presence. Exhibit 1.3 links the reasons for the international expansion of banks and the organisation forms of their foreign operations. There can be more than one banking presence suitable for each internationalisation motivation.

1.5.1. *Customer-driven international expansion*

The follow-the-customer or defensive expansion can be in the form of correspondent banking in the first instance, which requires only a minimum presence in the target market. If a strategic business customer of a bank is expanding its business into a foreign country, as either an input market and a manufacturing hub or as an output market, the bank must establish a banking form that is suitable for effectively providing appropriate service for the customer in the foreign market. If funding and other financial services can be actioned from the headquarter location of the bank, then correspondent banking supplemented by a representative office could be sufficient. In addition to funding, the representative office can provide local market intelligence and financial advice. An advantage of this approach is lower resource commitment, which can be easily reversed if circumstances change. A downside, however, is that the range of services that can be provided is limited.

If a customer-driven expansion is project-specific and requires more substantial financial activities in the target market, then a more elevated

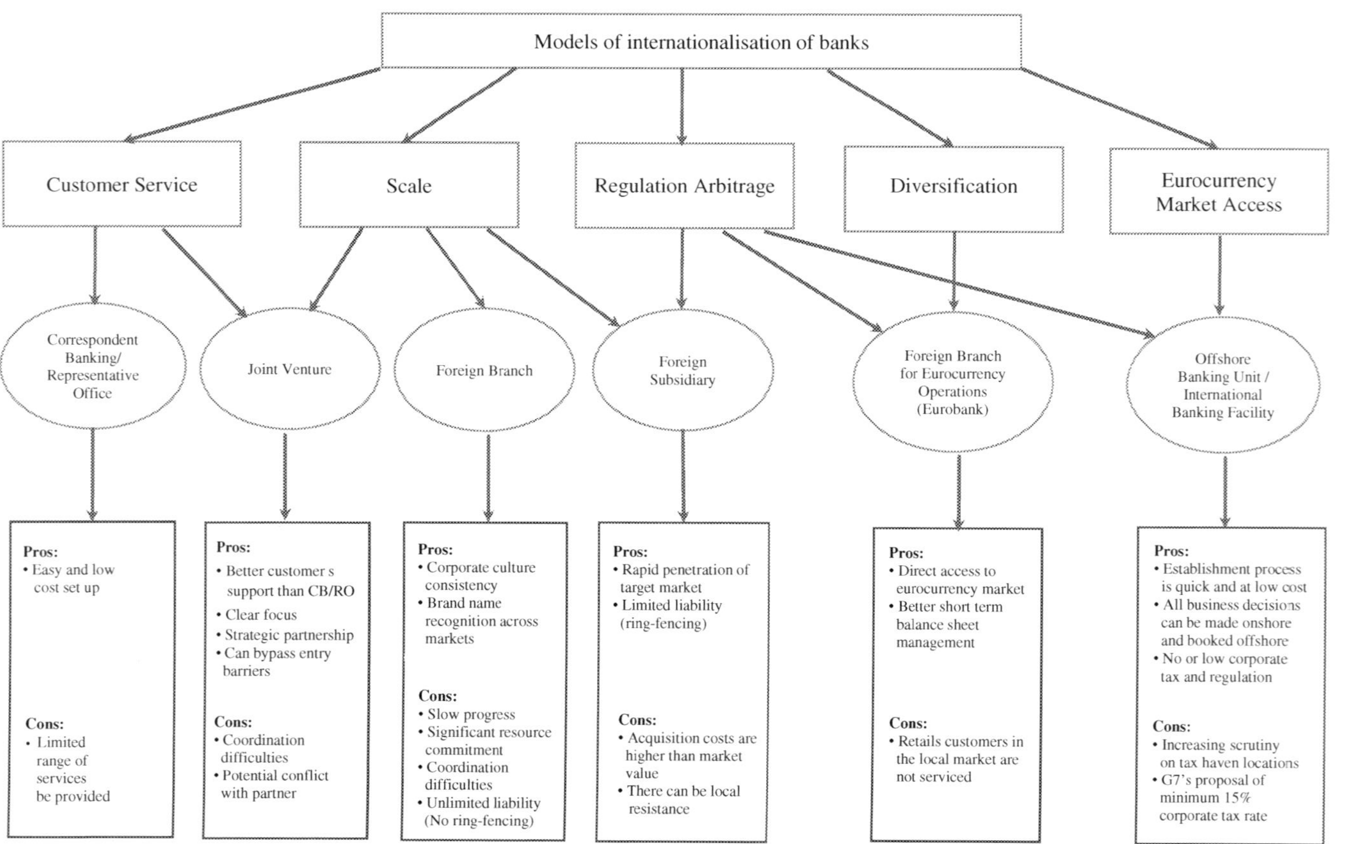

Exhibit 1.3. Linkages between the reasons for international banking and foreign banking form.

Source: Adapted from Canals (1997).

form, such as an alliance, can be considered. An alliance can be formed with a local bank in the host market to establish a joint venture bank that will provide the necessary services to the customer in the target market. It is possible that the customer's commitment can be proved to be a longer-term venture and that the target banking market could become an attractive location for expansion. One of the downsides of a joint venture bank is the potential conflicts with the local partner bank if the interests of the two banks in the partnership diverge. There may also be coordination difficulties with the partner bank, especially if a significant difference exists in bank sophistication between the partners.

Following the first contact with the target market, if a longer-term presence is called for, the bank may consider beyond the rudimentary forms of banking and establish a more permanent structure, such as a foreign branch or a subsidiary banking. These forms of banking presence would allow the bank to service its customer and local customers. However, the substantial cost and time required for such prominent expansion into the foreign market must be justified by the longer-term strategy of the bank.

1.5.2. *Scale economies*

If the aim of international expansion is to achieve scale economies, establishing full-service foreign branches is one option. International expansion is the only realistic option for banks located in relatively small economies to grow their business. For Australian banks, expanding into the nearby New Zealand market was one such option to achieve scale economies. Once successfully established, activities from the foreign branches can supplement domestic operations allowing the bank to achieve scale economies in their commercial (and investment) banking activities and a reduction in overall operating costs. In addition, this approach allows consistency of corporate culture across foreign branches, which is essential if the bank wishes to exploit its franchise value and brand name. However, a downside of this approach includes potential local resistance, especially in the retail banking space, significant resource and time requirements, and potential coordination difficulties. Furthermore, there is a potential for financial difficulties emanating from a struggling foreign branch to drag down the whole banking organisation. As the foreign branches are legally a part of the parent bank, their liabilities must be guaranteed by the parent bank if needed. For example, in 1995, Barings bank collapsed due to mounting losses suffered by its Singapore branch. A rogue trader managed to rack up GBP 825 million in losses from unhedged speculative futures trading on the Nikkei 225 index, which were beyond the capacity of the London parent bank to absorb.

Foreign subsidiaries and joint venture banking can also be considered for scale economies-driven expansion. Products and processes developed in the headquarters can be transferred to the foreign subsidiaries and joint venture banks, saving product development costs when deploying them in the foreign host market. However, these forms of full-service banking do not offer the additional benefits foreign branches do, such as instilling corporate culture, consistency in operational procedures, and integration with the bank's global network.

1.5.3. *Regulation arbitrage*

Regulation arbitrage is another motivation for the international expansion of a bank. Banks in a more onerous domestic regulation environment typically face a relatively limited scope of activities and a higher cost of conducting financial intermediation due to regulatory compliance. Moving some of their activities to jurisdictions (or facilities such as IBF) that allow more tax-effective operations would lower their overall cost of business. Moreover, this will allow the banks to compete more effectively against their international competitors headquartered in low regulation jurisdictions. Offshore Banking Units can be appropriate for this purpose. OBUs can be as simple as a postal address in an offshore financial centre if all that is required is to take advantage of the host jurisdiction's low tax and regulation status. All the investment and funding decisions are made and executed from the head office at home, but these activities are booked to the OBU for tax purposes. The offshore financial centres that host these facilities do not impose regulations on these offshore activities and offer very low or even zero effective corporate tax rates.

Foreign branches can also be useful if the longer-term international expansion strategy includes a full-banking presence in the target foreign markets. For example, US banks' expansion into foreign markets from the 1960s was partially motivated by the desire to avoid binding and costly domestic regulations.

1.5.4. *Diversification of asset and liability operations*

Diversification of asset and liability operations is also important for bank internationalisation. To reduce the credit risk of its loan portfolios, a commercial bank may consider acquiring foreign assets, including loan portfolios, in the desired target market, preferably funded by local sources in the host market. Acquiring an existing foreign bank as a wholly owned (or at least with a controlling interest in the case of a joint venture) foreign subsidiary is an appropriate option. An advantage of this approach is the potentially rapid pace of market penetration and the exposure to the target market for both asset and liability operations. This will work to diversify the overall risk of the consolidated banking operations. However, the costs involved in M&A activities can be substantial as the takeover prices can be much higher than the market price of the target bank. In addition, there can be local resistance to the takeover transaction, especially if the target bank has a loyal customer base.

If a bank wishes to diversify its short-term assets and liabilities (e.g., its money market positions), then adequate access to the international money market is essential. Due to the traditional over-the-counter nature of how money markets are organised, the bank needs a permanent and physical presence in the location where such money market activities take place, such as London, Hong Kong, and Singapore. Participants in the market must be visible and easily contactable (traditionally by phone before the advent of advanced communication networks) to be on top of current market trends. A purpose-built foreign branch (or an OBU) is established to handle the eurocurrency business. Such a foreign branch will be distinct from foreign subsidiaries or other foreign branches of the bank in the same location in that the former does not aim to service the local retail customers.

1.5.5. *Eurocurrency market access*

Eurocurrency market access is important to international banks as it offers competitive prices on both sides of liquidity management transactions, not to mention various hedging tools for interest rate and currency risks. Due to the over-the-counter nature of the eurocurrency market and the traditional voice-based communication, physical presence in the location of the eurocurrency market was compulsory for effective market participation. Multinational banks established purpose-built foreign branches in offshore market centres to act as eurobanks to engage in eurocurrency transactions. Also, OBUs were established for tax minimisation purposes. However, there have been recent OECD initiatives that limit the usefulness of OBUs as they aim to achieve a global minimum corporate tax rate of 15%. This will reduce the attractiveness of the tax benefits of establishing OBUs.

References

Bank for International Settlements (BIS, 2022), Triennial central bank survey of foreign exchange and Over-the-Counter (OTC) derivatives markets in 2022. https://www.bis.org/statistics/rpfx22.htm.

Bank for International Settlement, Locational banking statistics, https://www.bis.org/statistics/bankstats.htm?m=2069.

Canals, J. (1997). *Universal Banking*. New York: Oxford University Press, Chapter 9: Internationalisation of Banking, pp. 242–275.

Ceruttia, E., Dell'Ariccia, G. and Pería, M. (2007). How banks go abroad: Branches or subsidiaries? *Journal of Banking & Finance*, 31(6), 1669–1692. Euromoney, Various issues, https://www.euromoney.com.

Gleason, K. C., Mathur, I. and Wiggins III, R. A. (2006). The use of acquisitions and joint ventures by US Banks expanding abroad. *The Journal of Financial Research*, 29(4), 503–522.

Hosono, K., Sakai, K. and Tsuru, K. (2007). Consolidation of banks in Japan: Causes and consequences (September 2007). NBER Working Paper No. w13399, SSRN: https://ssrn.com/abstract=1014346.

Houston, J. F., Lin, C. and Ma, Y. (2012). Regulatory arbitrage and international bank flows. *Journal of Finance*, 67, 1845–1895.

Karolyi, G. A. and Taboada, A. G. (2015). Regulatory arbitrage and cross-border bank acquisitions. *Journal of Finance*, 70, 2395–2450.

Key, S. J. and Terrell, H. S. (1988), International banking facilities, International Finance Discussion Papers, No. 333, September 1988, Board of Governers of the Federal Reserve System. https://www.federalreserve.gov/econres/ifdp/international-banking-facilities.htm.

MSCI (2020). Global investing: The benefits and challenges of diversification. MSCI Research Insight.

The Banker, Various issues. http://thebanker.com.

Chapter 2

Internationalisation of Banks from the US, Japan, and China

2.1. Internationalisation of US Banks

The environment for US bank internationalisation has changed over time as the US financial system underwent numerous transformations in the second half of the last century. The internationalisation of US banks started in the 1960s when they expanded into emerging Western European countries, mainly to follow their multinational customers and explore emerging opportunities in the region. During the regulated era of the pre-1980s, one of the most important reasons for internationalisation was to avoid restrictive domestic US regulations that were not conducive to achieving economies of scale in domestic operations, especially for state-chartered banks. The process of deregulation of the US financial system started in the early 1980s leading to the repeal of the two most restrictive regulations, the McFadden Act and the Glass–Steagall Act, in 1994 and 1999, respectively. This was soon followed by similar levels of financial sector deregulation in other major financial systems of other countries from the early to mid-1980s. The ensuing deregulated environment led to waves of consolidations via domestic and cross-border M&A activities and the transition from relationship banking to transactional banking in commercial banking and other financial engineering activities. The US subprime crisis and the subsequent Global Financial Crisis of 2007–2009 exposed the inadequacies of the US financial system to deal with the unchecked and opaque risk-taking activities of the US investment banks. This led to an unprecedented level of intrabanking industry consolidation and some degree of re-regulation of the US financial system via Dodd–Frank Act 2010. Due to the global outreach of US banks and major international banks' exposure to the US financial system, the US has led many international market trends. These include the deregulation waves of the 1980s in advanced countries, financial innovations, and destructive and contagious financial crises.

The internationalisation of US banks was due to several factors, which can be grouped into push and pull factors. The push factors that encouraged US banks to expand to other countries include the restrictive regulations that hampered the domestic growth of their operations. Moreover, the relative competitiveness of their operations in the chosen mode of operation compared to their potential international competitors helped the US banks quickly seize market share once established in a foreign market. The pull factors were, first, the emergence of emerging market opportunities that the US banks could exploit. The 1960s' Western European markets offered initial expansion opportunities, which were followed by Latin American markets in the 1970s and the general opening up of market opportunities in East Asian and East European emerging market countries from the late 1980s and early 1990s. Second, US banks followed their domestic customers as they explored various international markets as both output and input markets.

2.1.1. *US financial regulation*

The banking industry has traditionally been one of the most regulated industries in a given country due to the central role banks perform in the economy, such as facilitating the payment system and creating credits. The US banking system, in particular, stands out as one of the banking systems shaped by various regulatory measures as direct responses to various economic and financial crises and political developments since the early 20th century. The US banking system in the past and currently, to some extent, showed many unique characteristics compared to other banking systems around the world. It was composed of a large number of mostly small total (assets less than USD 500 million) retail banks that were geographically, and in other aspects, restricted as opposed to a small number of large banks in other major countries such as those in Western Europe (DeYoung, 2019). Due to the parallel developments in non-banking segments of the financial system, such as the corporate debt market, banks had to compete against other banks and other sources of finance for their corporate customers. This combination resulted in the US banking system, where a large number of *de novo* banks existed, and an equally large number of banks went out of business without causing systemic economic distress.

Two types of regulations shaped the modern history of the US banking industry: the McFadden Act (1927–1994) and the Glass–Stegall Act (1933–1999). The former forced US banks to operate essentially within the state in which there were chartered, and the latter prohibited commercial banks from providing other financial services such as investment banking, insurance, and asset management services. These two types of regulations hampered the growth potential of the US banks within their domestic market.

The McFadden Act (1927–1994) essentially prohibited US banks from establishing nationwide branch bank networks. This Act permitted federally chartered national banks to branch out within the states they were located to the same extent as the state-charted banks in the same state. Previously, they were only permitted to operate out of one building (i.e., no branch banking was allowed). However, states that prohibited branch banking altogether (i.e., unit banking) severely limited the growth potential of all banks in those states. The most important restriction of this Act was the prohibition of interstate banking, whereby national banks were forbidden from operating across multiple states or owned by banks chartered in another state. This resulted in US banks remaining relatively small in size and essentially becoming regional banks susceptible to regional economic risk, which cannot easily be diversified away. In addition, economies of scale could not be achieved especially for those banks that operated in smaller states. However, many institutions effectively avoided this restriction by forming a group bank (later known as a bank holding company), where a holding company owned a group of banks across multiple states. Each member bank was operating within its state and fully complied with the regulation. By setting up as a group bank, the holding company was getting around the prohibition of interstate banking regulation while operating the banks it owned as if they were interstate branches. However, this arrangement still did not offer the full benefits of economies of scale and diversification benefits interstate branch banking would provide. The definition of a bank holding company was formally defined in the bank holding company act of 1956.[1] The McFadden Act resulted in a large number of small and inefficient banks that were kept afloat by the anti-competitive regulation. Typically, US banks were smaller in size and larger in numbers compared to their European and Japanese counterparts due mostly to this restriction. The number of commercial banks peaked at 14,261 in 1984 before declining to 4,236 by 2021 (see Exhibit 2.1).[2]

By the mid-1980s, states were allowed to determine whether to permit bank holding companies from other states to establish and operate banks in their states. Thirty-five states eventually agreed to the relaxation of the interstate banking restriction via out-of-state bank holding companies.

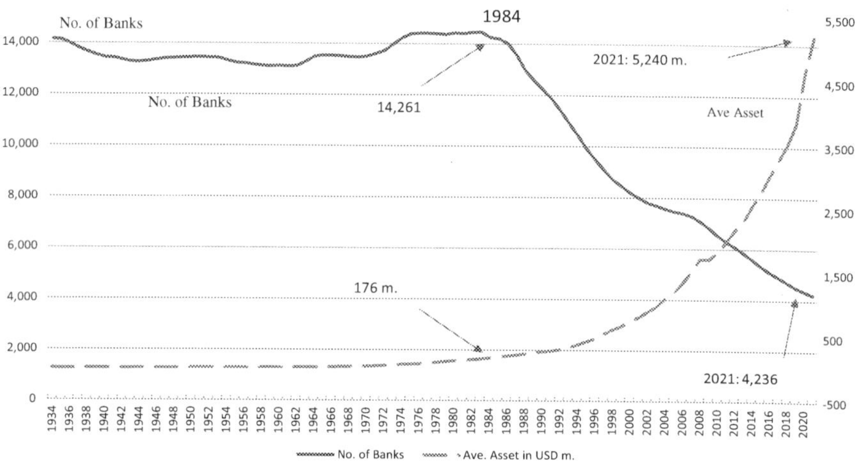

Exhibit 2.1. Total number of US commercial banks and average asset in USD m., 1934–2021.

Source: FDIC, https://www.fdic.gov/.

[1] According to the bank holding company act of 1956, a bank holding company is a company that owns at least a 25% stake in at least two banks. https://www.federalreservehistory.org/essays/bank_holding_company_act_of_1956.

[2] For comparison, there were around 200 banks in Japan and approximately 350 in the UK in 2019. In terms of the number of banks per one million people, there were 14 banks in the US, 1.6 banks in Japan and 5.2 banks in the UK.

This resulted in a flurry of bank merger and acquisition activities across state borders. As shown in Exhibit 2.1, the number of commercial banks started to fall in 1984, and at the same time, the average total bank asset grew from USD 176 million in 1984 to USD 5,240 million by 2021. In 1994, the Riegle-Neal Interstate Banking and Branching Efficiency Act effectively repealed the McFadden Act and allowed the establishment of nationwide banks that could acquire banks in other states after 29 September 1995. This Act allowed interstate and nationwide commercial banking for the first time in US banking history. The result was an immediate rise in nationwide banking operations from 1995 when the Act came into effect. In 1994, the number of US banks with interstate branches was 10 commercial banks with 30 interstate branches. These numbers rose to 456 US commercial banks with 8,876 interstate branches in 1997 (Koch and MacDonald, 2010, p. 774).

The other important regulatory restriction was the Glass–Stegall Act (1933–1999) which effectively created a sharp distinction between various functions of financial services in the US financial system. Banks involved in both commercial and investment banking activities were given a year to decide whether they would operate in one or the other. Under the Glass–Stegall Act, investment banks could underwrite corporate securities and hold stocks, but they could not perform the intermediation functions of commercial banks. Conversely, commercial banks were prohibited from holding stocks or engaging in brokerage activities. This regulation was rooted in the belief that the conflict of interest inherent in servicing clients in more than one financial market segment would lead to excessive risk-taking in stock market investment activities. For example, banks that heavily invested in the stock market were more likely to lend to those companies that the banks invested in. Also, banks were incentivised to make loans to investors who they advised as brokers. The inherent conflict of interest was believed to be one of the most significant contributing factors to the stock market crash of 1929. Commercial and investment banks were forced to concentrate on their traditional activities of financial intermediation (making loans to fund business activities rather than investing in the stock market) and capital market services, respectively. The separation of the two functions shaped the industrial structure of the US financial system into what was later known as the specialist financial system. Specialised institutions were created in each segment of the financial service industry to service customers in that segment only. Commercial banks, investment banks, asset managers, and insurance companies operated in their own protected segments.[3] The US financial system developed into a bank holding company structure whereby a holding company can potentially own and operate financial institutions in various segments, such as investment banking and commercial banking, as long as their subsidiaries are independent of each other.

Although the specialised system had the benefit of simplifying the regulation framework, a crucial downside was the inability of institutions to take advantage of the scope economies resulting from combining two or more related activities under one roof. Many other advanced economies adopted similar financial architectures that largely separated commercial and investment banking functions, and some of these countries were the UK, Canada, Australia, and Japan, to name a few. US commercial banks were, however, allowed to engage in non-commercial banking activities indirectly. *First,* under Section 20 of the Act, they could fully own investment banking subsidiaries as long as their profits did not exceed 5% of the consolidated business revenue. This limit was raised to 10% in 1989 and then to 25% in 1997. *Second,* the Edge Act (Federal Reserve Act of 1913, amended in 1919) allowed the establishment of Edge Act corporations that were set up in the US as subsidiaries of US or foreign commercial banks. These subsidiary banks were allowed to engage in non-commercial banking operations as long as they served non-US customers exclusively.

On the other hand, the separation of commercial and investment banking functions was not generally present in the (ex-UK) Western European banking markets. Especially in former West Germany, some form of universal banking was allowed where banks conducted commercial and investment banking activities within one institution. It has been argued that a universal banking system can achieve a higher level of stability due to the diversification benefits across different activities (Büschgen, 1979). This arrangement was rooted in the development of the German economy in the early 20th century. Industrial companies, and the German economy in general, relied on banks for the provision of long-term credit in place of capital markets. The long-term funding of industrial companies was often in the form of equity ownership, which naturally led to interlocking board memberships between banks and their industrial clients. As a result, banks took on a governance responsibility for their clients. This is in stark

---

[3]The Bank Holding Company Act of 1956 officially closed the loophole that allowed bank holding companies to provide insurance underwriting and erected a firewall between commercial banking and insurance activities.

contrast to the US financial system, where the capital market performs that role for publicly listed companies. There is an argument about which form of corporate governance results in more stable corporate and financial sectors. However, the answer depends on the organisational structure of the financial system in each country, so it is unlikely that this argument can be resolved easily. US banks were able to provide investment banking as well as commercial banking services in the Western European markets since the early days of their expansion into these markets, whereas they were only allowed to combine both types of activities within a single operational unit only from 1999 in their domestic market. The Gramm-Leach-Bliley Act 1999 repelled the part of the Glass–Stegall Act that resulted in the functional and organisational separation of commercial and investment banking activities, allowing investment banks and insurance companies to own commercial banks, and commercial banks to conduct investment banking activities (underwrite insurance policies and securities). The part of the Glass–Stegall Act that created Federal Deposit Insurance Corporation (FDIC) was retained.

The impact of the two regulations shaped the post-war financial architecture of the US banking system. Instead of a universal banking system, the US developed into a specialised system with a focus on the bank holding company structure for expansion. This resulted in the US banking system being composed of a large number of small banks until the mid-1980s (see Exhibit 2.1). The limited potential for domestic growth and diversification across different product groups encouraged US banks to expand to those foreign markets where such limitations did not exist.

2.1.2. *Emerging market opportunities, defensive expansion, and competitive advantage*

The regulation restriction on interstate expansion and diversification activities motivated US banks to seek opportunities beyond their domestic market. In addition, international banking markets in various regions of the world started to relax restrictions on foreign bank entry, allowing US banks to explore opportunities in these markets. These include continental European countries in the late 1960s and early 70s, Latin-American countries from the mid-1970s, and East Asian countries since the early 1990s. In addition, the creation of the eurocurrency market in London motivated US banks to participate in the foreign exchange and money market operations there.

The eurodollar market in London became a major international interbank money market for USD-denominated deposits in the 1960s. This development attracted a number of large US banks, such as Citibank, Chase Manhattan, and the Bank of America, to set up a foreign branch operation in London to take advantage of the wholesale nature of the foreign currency and eurodollar transactions unburdened by regulation. US banks also explored the opportunities opened up in the host markets from following their corporate clients to those countries. Many US conglomerates entered the emerging Western European countries seeking output markets for their products. These include IBM, Ford, and General Motors, to name a few. Once located in foreign markets, they required financial services from banks familiar with their business to help penetrate the markets successfully. This defensive expansion into foreign markets allowed US banks to service their US corporate clients in the host markets by providing financial services their clients require to prevent them from seeking those services from local or foreign banks operating in the host markets.

In Western Europe, US banks initially concentrated on currency and capital market operations serving their US corporations operating in these markets before venturing into local market intermediation and investment banking activities. In the investment banking space, they engaged in capital market operations (e.g., security underwriting and trading) and provided financial consulting services to both US and local corporations. Their skills in capital market operations honed through competition with other banks in the US capital markets proved useful in gaining market share against European banks, which were relatively uncompetitive. They also dipped their toes in the water by venturing into the financial intermediation business of commercial banking against the local population. They introduced products and services more common in the US but not universally adopted in the European market at the time, such as the general use of credit cards for consumers, the provision of money market instruments as an investment vehicle, and the securitisation of bank assets. However, their commercial banking endeavours initially proved less successful for two main reasons: *First,* significant natural entry barriers existed, such as the requirement for extensive branch networks. *Second,* their foray into the retail banking scene was met with considerable local resistance due largely to the relationship-oriented nature of retail banking. Eventually, US banks, particularly Citibank, proved to be competitive in terms of both product and price fronts compared to their local competitors and other foreign banks operating in the market.

The competitive advantage US banks enjoyed against their local counterparts in Western Europe was partially due to the development of financial system architecture in the US, which was in stark contrast to that of many Western European countries. The US financial system has evolved around the separation of commercial and investment banking activities, as discussed in the previous section. The result was the parallel development of the market for bank loans and the market for private and public (at various levels) debt instruments of various maturities and risk characteristics. Large corporations had access to capital markets and bank loans, which forced banks to be competitive in terms of both price and products, not only against other banks but also against capital market players. In comparison, the continental Western European financial systems, especially former West Germany, centred around universal banks that provided commercial and investment banking services to corporate clients. European banks were expected to provide long-term funding to corporations from all funding sources for their clients. As a result, capital market development stalled, and this, in turn, reinforced the universal banks' hold on the financing needs of their corporate customers.

The innovations brought to the Western European markets by the US banks, such as interest payable cheque accounts, overdraft facilities with consumer accounts, and generalised use of credit and debit cards, had eventually proved fruitful in both business and retail banking areas (Canals, 1997). The US banks' presence in Western Europe also had positive externalities in elevating the level of efficiency and competitiveness of host market bank competitors. In general, superior products and competitiveness (a more comprehensive range of banking products generally at lower costs, due mainly to the larger size of their global operations compared to local competitors, better recognised global brand names, better access to interbank markets for short-term credit, etc.) in the target market allowed US banks to carve out a market share, especially in their capital market-related business.

2.2. Internationalisation of Japanese Banks

The Japanese banking system has been central to the success of Japanese economic development during the second half of the last century. Commercial banks provided not only short- and long-term funding to corporations but also were responsible for the corporate governance of borrowing companies to a large extent. However, the bank-dominated financial system and the prevalence of the Main bank system (Uchida and Udell, 2019) inhibited the development of capital markets where corporations could raise long-term funds by issuing debt instruments directly to the public. This aspect of the Japanese banking system was similar to the bank governance financial system architecture of West Germany and other continental European countries until the mid- to late-1980s. Unlike the European systems, however, there had been a legal separation of commercial and investment banking activities, similar to the Glass–Steagall era of the US financial system. Therefore, the Japanese banking system combined the characteristics of both the Western European and the US financial systems. However, the scope economies of the former and the competitiveness via financial innovations of the latter were largely absent in the Japanese banking system. The internationalisation of Japanese banks was mainly due to defensive expansion and the need to have a presence in the London interbank market (Canals, 1997). The landscape of Japanese domestic and international banking operations has undergone significant changes during and after the banking crisis in Japan (1998–2004). The following sections provide further discussions.

2.2.1. *Japanese banking system*

The Japanese banking system has traditionally been partitioned into various operational segments and regions, similar to the US and other advanced countries (Uchida and Udell, 2019). There are two major types of commercial banks: city and regional banks. City banks, known as *Toshi Ginko*, operate nationally with branches across the country and are headquartered in Tokyo (Osaka for Sumitomo Mitsui). They provide domestic and international banking services to their corporate customers. Five city banks as of 2022 were all large financial groups with multiple banking and securities company subsidiaries. These are Mitsubishi UFJ financial group, Sumitomo Mitsui financial group, Mizuho financial group, and Resona Holdings (which contains Resona bank and Saitama Resona bank). The first three are the three largest banks in Japan, in that order. The fourth-largest is Japan Post Bank. However, it does not operate in the same space as city banks and caters primarily to retail customers across the country via its countrywide postal office network. In some rural and remote areas, Japan Post Bank is the only provider of financial services. They have a comparative advantage as they maintain an extensive network of post offices in the country. City banks as a group are mostly funded by domestic deposits, which accounted for 68% of their liabilities, and the three largest asset classes were loans and bills discounted (38%), cash and receivable from other banks (30%), and securities (government and corporate bonds and equities (20%) as of March 2022.[4] City banks accounted for 55% of the total assets in the banking sector in 2022. More than half of their income came from interest income (53%), followed by fees and commissions (24%). This suggests that although the city banks are large financial conglomerates that can engage in both commercial and investment banking activities, they are still commercial banks at heart.

Regional and second regional banks, known as *Chiho ginko*, are incorporated regionally and service customers located in the prefectures where they are located. As of March 2022, there were a total of 62 regional banks. Similar to the state-chartered US banks in the past, the regional banks in Japan operate within their region and provide a narrower range of services than city banks. There is an inbuilt limitation on expansion, so they tend to be much smaller in size and scope. They accounted for 30% of the banking sector's assets in March 2022. They are more concentrated in domestic intermediation than city banks. Deposits accounted for 79% of their funding, and loans and bills discounted accounted for 56% of their assets. Not surprisingly, a much higher proportion of their revenues was derived from interest income (69%).

Other types of deposit-taking institutions include trust banks and foreign banks. They play only a minor role in the Japanese financial system. Trust banks provide money trusts to retail customers and invest in corporate bonds and equities. They also make long-term corporate loans. Foreign banks, known as *Gaikoku Ginko*, are also present as foreign branches. They are regulated at the same level as local banks and concentrate on international banking activities for business and retail customers. Another group of banks that provided long-term corporate funding was long-term credit banks that raised long-term funds by issuing bonds. However, they no longer exist as a distinct type of bank in Japan due to several failures and mergers during the Japanese banking crisis (1998–2004).

Banks have traditionally played a vital role in the Japanese economy. They were the primary source of funding not only for small- to medium-sized firms but also for large corporations. Banks, as a group, provided the

[4] Japanese Bankers Association (JBA, 2023). Financial statements of all banks, https://www.zenginkyo.or.jp/en/stats/year2-01/2021-terminal/.

vast majority of credits to the private sector in Japan. During the 1980s and 1990s, banks provided, on average, 158% of GDP in credit to the private sector, representing as much as 90% of the private sector credit provided by banks (see Exhibit 2.2). Thus, there is an overwhelming dominance of banks as a funding source in the private sector. In contrast, the corresponding averages for the US are only 51% of GDP and 44% of total credits for the same period, respectively (World Development Indicator, Worldbank).

Another significant role played by banks in Japan is the corporate governance function. As one of the most important stakeholders, they influence how the borrowing firm is run, especially when the borrower is in financial difficulties. The bank-dominated financial system is typically seen in emerging market countries where information collection and processing are costly and investors are unsophisticated and generally incapable of assessing risks adequately. The general financial market underdevelopment, especially in corporate debt markets, results in financial intermediaries being tasked to perform this role on behalf of

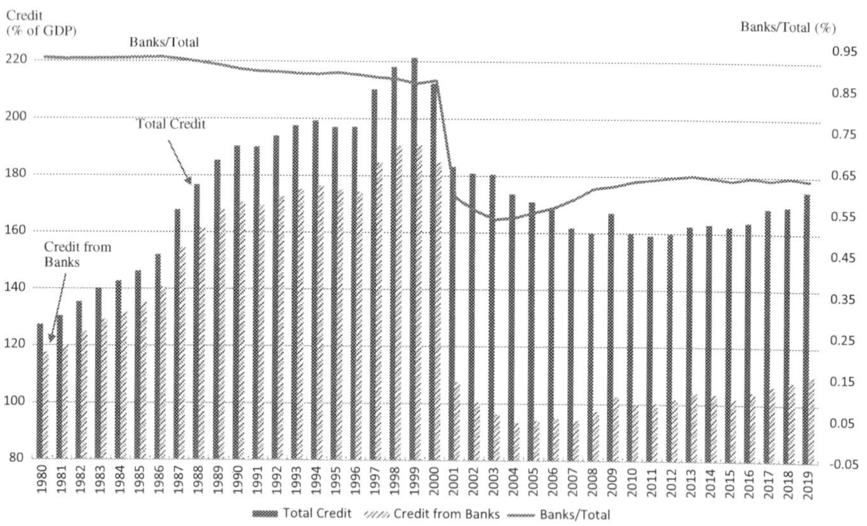

Exhibit 2.2. Total bank credit to the private sector in Japan (% of GDP).

Source: Worldbank, World Development Indicators. https://datatopics.worldbank.org/world-development-indicators/.

individual investors and depositors. However, a similar focus on bank-dominated systems existed in developed countries such as Japan and Germany. Similar to emerging market systems, non-bank capital markets were less developed in these countries resulting in limited access to a non-bank source of funds for even the largest corporations. The Japanese system took the banks' governance system to another level by cementing the relationship with a cross-shareholding arrangement between the bank and the borrowing firms. Among the board of directors, there typically would be one director who represents the lending bank's interests and performs a liaison role between the borrowing firm and the lending bank. This cross-shareholding relationship and the banks' involvement in the borrower firm is a typical feature of the focus on relationship banking, especially when the bank and the borrowers belong to the same business group (*keiretsu*). On the other hand, in the market-focused financial systems of their competitors, such as the US and the UK, the stock market disciplining mechanism took precedence in corporate governance.

Interestingly, the Japanese banking system also adopted an aspect of the US-style financial system architecture. Similar to the US's Glass–Steagall Act, a strict regulation separated commercial and investment banking operations as required by Article 65 of the Securities and Exchange Law, 1948. Commercial banks, especially large city banks, were, however, able to own securities companies (known as *Shōken Gaisha*) that deal in stockbroking and other securities trading business. The deregulation of the financial system that started in advanced economies in the early to mid-1980s also encouraged the Japanese banking system to be deregulated in the direction of a universal banking system. City, regional, and long-term credit banks were allowed to perform some investment banking functions, namely underwriting public bonds and investment advisory functions. One of the direct consequences of this part of the banking sector deregulation in Japan was the proliferation of collateralised stock market investments by corporate customers of banks. The resulting bubbles in the Japanese financial system (stock and real estate markets) from the mid- to late-1980s and their collapse in 1990 precipitated the Japanese Banking crisis in 1998. Various measures implemented to combat the recessionary impact of the twin bubble collapse throughout the 1990s proved ineffective. It was not until 2005 that meaningful recoveries were observed in the banking sector after more than a decade of economic and financial inertia.

2.2.2. *Japanese bank Internationalisation*

The emergence of Japanese banks on the world stage in the 1990s was spectacular. By 1996, seven out of the top ten banks in the world in terms of asset size (see Exhibit 1.2) were Japanese banks. The combination of the dominance of banks in the Japanese financial system and the rapid ascendence of the Japanese economy in the 1980s resulted in most large Japanese banks eclipsing their international competitors by total assets. The internationalisation of Japanese banks coincided with the internationalisation of their multinational corporation clients and a general increase in outward foreign direct investments (FDIs) from Japan in the 1980s. A combination of both external factors (a very successful export economy, low cost of domestic funding for banks, and rising value of the Yen) and internal factors (booming real estate and stock markets) in the 1980s contributed to the success of the Japanese banks on the world stage. There were three main contributors to Japanese bank internationalisation: to follow their customers (defensive expansion), to establish a presence in money market centres, and to exploit relative funding advantage on the global stage.

First, Japanese banks aimed to keep their corporate business in the foreign markets where their corporate customers operate. Qian and Delios (2008), in their empirical study of Japanese bank internationalisation for the period 1980–1998, find that banks with less intangible assets, such as management, product, and marking skills, tend to be more motivated to follow their customers to foreign markets. In addition, in most cases, the relationship between banks and their business customers goes beyond the simple borrower-lender fiduciary relationship common in the Western banking system. Rather than banks being outside creditors, they are actively involved in the corporate governance of their corporate customers, and they often belong to the same business group (known as *keiretsu*). This is similar to the old Hausbank arrangement in West Germany, leading them to hold equity stakes in each other's business.[5] Thus, the Japanese banks' initial reason for establishing operations in the US and Western Europe was to service their corporate customers who were establishing foreign operations in these target markets. In the 1970s and 1980s,

[5] This cross-shareholding arrangement was typical not only of the Japanese banking system but, to a lesser extent, of other bank-dominated financial systems in many countries.

Japanese multinationals expanded their operations in Western European countries. Canals (1997) shows that by 1989, there were a total of 501 Japanese multinational companies operating in Europe, and the UK, France, and Germany together hosted more than 63% of the total. The most prominent type of company was electronic manufacturing.

From the early to mid-1980s, Japanese car manufacturers started to open manufacturing plants in the US, either as a joint venture with a US partner or as wholly owned subsidiaries, to circumvent an increasing protectionist sentiment. These include Honda in 1982 (Ohio), Nissan in 1983 (Tennessee), Toyota in 1984 (California), Mitsubishi in 1988 (Illinois), and Subaru/Isuzu in 1989 (Indiana). The Japanese banks that served these car manufacturers were expected to follow them to the US market to provide financial and corporate governance assistance. Initially, most Japanese banks were not keen to explore other opportunities in these foreign banking markets. So, the predominant form of Japanese foreign presence in the US was agency banking, which permitted them to lend to their affiliated clients in the local currency of that foreign market financed by the transfer of funds from their headquarters in Japan or by eurocurrency funding in London. At a later stage of internationalisation, Japanese banks engaged with local customers to a limited extent, mostly in corporate banking activities and conducted investment and securities trading activities, mostly in the US. However, their impact on these activities was rather limited, unlike the significant and positive externality of the US banking presence in the European markets.

Second, the Japanese banks established their presence in London to have ready access to USD-denominated short-term credit at a relatively lower cost from the interbank market to service their Japanese multinational clients in foreign locations. Moreover, by eurocurrency trading in London's interbank markets, banks had direct access to various balance sheet adjustment instruments, such as over-the-counter derivatives in eurocurrency and foreign exchange, which can be used for both hedging and speculative purposes. These hedging tools were being developed at the time in the eurocurrency market but were generally unavailable in domestic money markets due to stringent regulatory measures. The skills in trading in these instruments could only be acquired by being visible in the market and building trading relationships with other participating banks.

Third, in contrast to US banks, Japanese banks faced neither limitations in their domestic market expansion (such as the McFadden Act in the

US)[6] nor did they possess superior financial technology that could have been exploited to compete with local banks in the host foreign markets. However, their competitive advantage in the 1980s had been lower funding costs than their foreign competitors due to a virtuous combination of low domestic interest rates, a significant domestic saving pool, accumulation of current account surplus, and the strength of the Yen. Exhibit 2.3 shows three-month deposit rates of Japan and its major competitors, the US, the UK, and Germany, from 1980 to 2019. The deposit rate in Japan was substantially lower than the corresponding rates for the other countries for the whole period, although the German rate was lower for a brief period in the early 1980s. During the Global Financial Crisis period of 2007–2009, the other countries all caught up with the lower Japanese interest rates before the US rate started to rise in 2015 due to a tightening monetary cycle in the US.

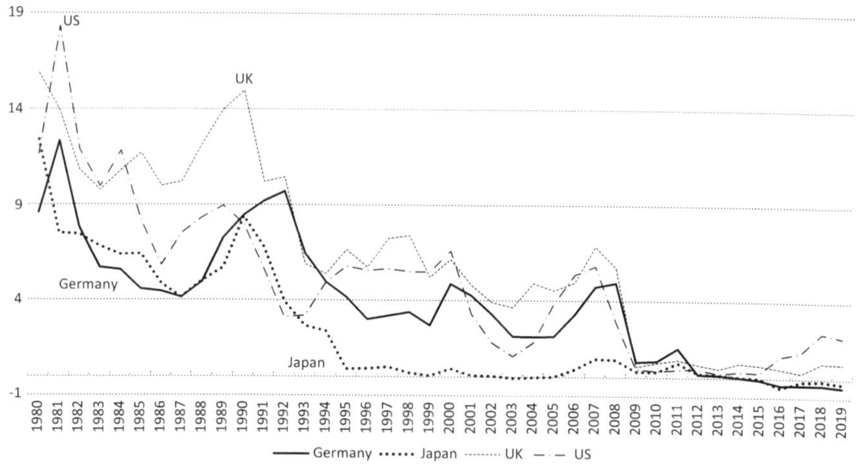

Exhibit 2.3. Three-month deposit rate in US, UK, Germany, and Japan, 1980–2019 (% pa).
Source: Refinitiv Eikon Datastream.

[6]City banks were free to expand nationally, however, regional banks were limited in their expansion capacity due to the small size and operation focus — relationship banking servicing local customers. However, there were no formal legal restrictions preventing them from growing into other segments.

Exhibit 2.4 shows national saving rates to GDP for the same group of countries. The Japanese saving rate had been above 30% of GDP throughout the 1980s and 1990s, significantly above the other three competitor countries. However, from 2006, Germany recorded more domestic savings to GDP than all the others, including Japan. Combining Exhibits 2.3 and 2.4, the abundance of domestic savings and lower deposit rates provided Japanese banks with competitiveness in competing with their international competitors in terms of undercutting them in lending interest rates. The price competitiveness of Japanese banks was, however, not matched by product competitiveness which they were lacking.

In 1981, the Japanese current account balance turned to a surplus of USD 4.7 billion. Ever since then, the current account has been in surplus, and it has been rising to its peak of USD 221 billion in 2010. The continued and growing current account surplus (especially against the US) led to the Plaza agreement in 1985, which rapidly raised the Yen's value against the USD (see Exhibit 2.5). The Yen rose in value by 73% between 1984 and 1987. However, despite the rapid and substantial appreciation of the Yen, the Japanese current account surpluses continued to accumulate,

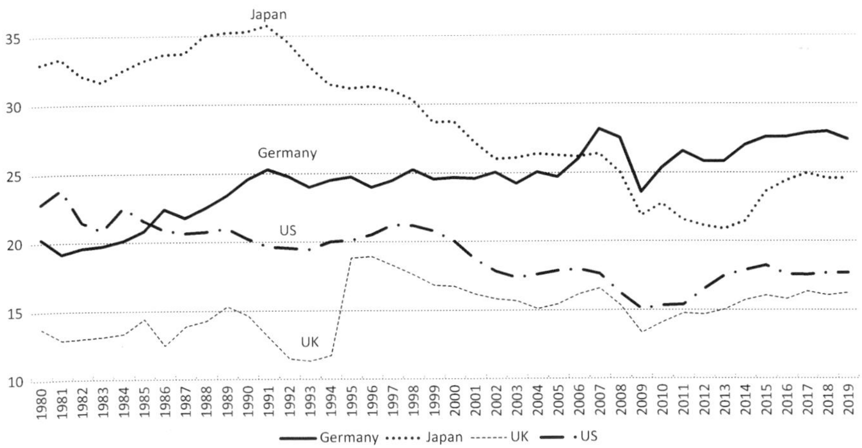

Exhibit 2.4. Gross domestic savings — US, UK, Germany, and Japan, 1980–2019 (% of GDP)

Source: Worldbank, World Development Indicators. https://datatopics.worldbank.org/world-development-indicators/.

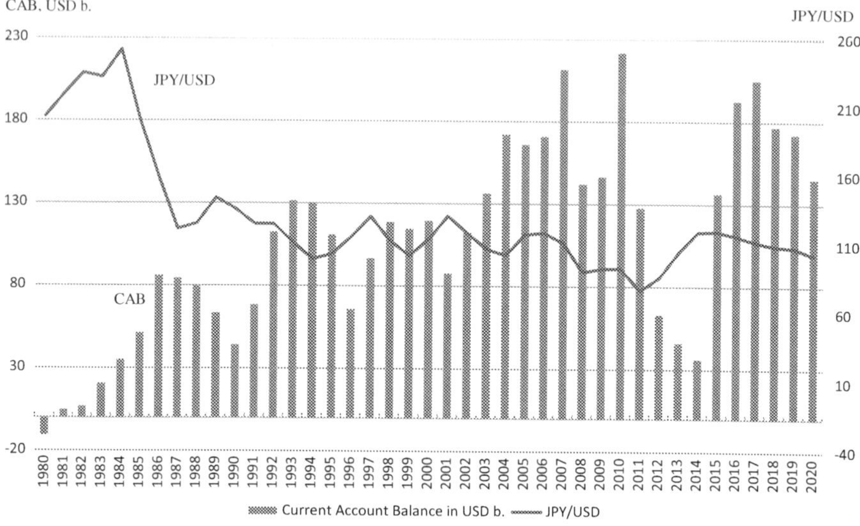

Exhibit 2.5. Current account balance and the Yen/USD exchange rate, 1980–2020.

Source: FRED database, Federal Reserve Bank of St. Louis, https://fred.stlouisfed.org/. OECD, https://data.oecd.org/trade/current-account-balance.htm.

apart from the initial negative impact on the current account balance between 1986 and 1990. The Japanese banks played a significant role in recycling the foreign currency funds from the surplus in the international financial system. In short, the Japanese banks had access to the cheap and plentiful supply of domestic funds, together with the rapidly appreciating Yen, which enabled them to undercut USD loans in the international market. Moreover, the increasing supply of foreign currency funds to recycle from Japan's continuing current account surpluses added to the significant cost advantage. These factors propelled the Japanese banks to flex their financial muscle in the 1980s and 1990s on the international stage, leading to their dominance of the international ranking by total assets (Exhibit 1.2).

2.2.3. *Japanese banking crisis (1997–2004) and the post-crisis challenges*

The collapse of the asset price bubbles in 1990 and the subsequent banking crisis in 1998 fundamentally changed the Japanese financial system, particularly the banking system. It led to several bank collapses, which was unthinkable in a bank-focused financial system with implicit protection offered by affiliated corporations and the government. This resulted in a substantial reduction in the Japanese banks' dominance of international financial intermediation activities. Also, a wave of consolidations led to the creation of mega financial groups that could potentially operate as universal banks and compete with multinational banks from the US and Western Europe on the world stage.

It is a common belief that one of the main causes of the asset inflation in Japan in the second half of the 1980s was the excessive loan growth and speculative investments following accommodative monetary policies aimed at softening the blow from the appreciating Yen since the Plaza Accord in 1985. The Yen appreciated from 236 Yen/USD in September 1985, the start of the Accord, to 154.73 by September 1986, a 42% appreciation in a year, before reaching 124.79 in May 1988, a 64% appreciation. The official interest rate was cut from 5% in January 1986 to 2.5% by February 1987. The corresponding rates in the US were 7.75% and 6%, respectively. Also, the Black Friday stock market crash in the US in 1987 was a factor in the low-interest rate environment to continue in Japan.

As in many other asset inflation episodes in recent times, the cheap and readily available bank credits from 1986 in Japan, above what was required for normal economic activities, led to excessive demand for investments in the speculative sectors of the economy. The resulting excess demand in real estate and stock markets led to excessive upward price movements (or bubbles) in these markets, reaching heights that had never been reached in history. Moreover, the Nakasone government initiated a significant expansionary fiscal policy as well in 1987, approving the equivalent of USD 43 billion stimulation package, which included a reduction of the corporate tax rate from 42% to 30% and the top marginal tax rate from 70% to 40%. The expansionary macroeconomic policies resulted in the Nikkei 225 reaching 38,915 points in December 1989. Moreover, the real estate market bubble led to the now famous comparison of the real estate prices between Japan and the US at the peak of the bubble period, that the value of the empirical palace in Tokyo was higher than the aggregate land price of the state of California in the US.

Despite successive and rapid policy interest rate increases (from 2.5% in April 1989 to 6% in August 1990) to reign in the speculative expectations in the economy, it took the start of the Gulf War in August 1990 to stop the bull sentiments. The Nikkei 225 dropped to 20,983 in September 1990, a 46% fall from one month prior, and continued its prolonged decline until late 2012. The banking sector felt one of the most important consequences of the stock market's collapse. Banks were particularly affected due to their exposure to corporate and individual borrowers who engaged in speculative investments in the stock and real estate markets (known as *zai-tech*), and the resulting investments were used as collaterals. Also, banks were significant equity holders of their strategic partners who belonged to the same business group, *Keiretsu*. As the market value of the collaterals and the value of their own stock market investments declined rapidly, a significant portion of the banks' assets became compromised. However, the resulting accumulation of Non-Performing Loans (NPLs) had gone largely unreported through various methods, such as lowering the requirement of NPL definition and evergreening of bad loans. Banks sought no significant remedies, and none were provided by the government as there was no apparent justification judging by the NPL measure of banks' health. This interfered with the normal intermediation activities in the banking sector because the accumulation of bad loans prevented banks from making further loans funded by deposits, as this would have led to the Bank for International Settlement (BIS)'s capital adequacy requirement not being met.

Exhibit 2.6 shows the twin bubbles in Japan's stock and real estate sectors that developed in the aftermath of the Plaza Accord and the subsequent credit growth from low interest rates. The rapid price rise in the two markets can be seen in the 1980s, and Nikkei peaked in the first

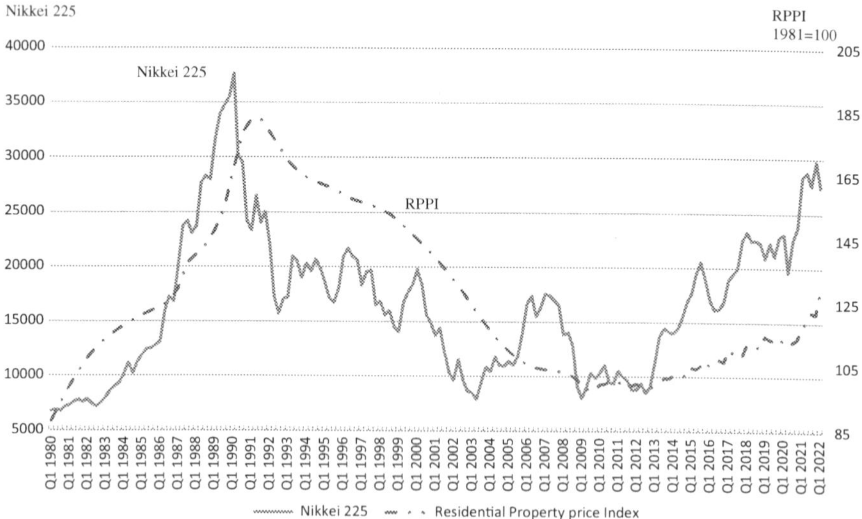

Exhibit 2.6. Nikkei 225 and retail real estate price index in Japan, Q1 1980–Q1 2022.
Source: FRED database, Federal Reserve Bank of St. Louis, https://fred.stlouisfed.org/.

quarter of 1990 before collapsing in August of that year. The real estate price index peaked in Q2 1991 and then started its rapid descent. As the majority of bank assets were tied to either stock or real estate market investments by their borrowers, the busting of the bubbles in these markets should have alerted the banks to address the accumulating NPL problems as their borrowers started to default. The responses by the government were geared towards stimulating the stock and the real estate markets in the hopes that a reversal in the fortunes would come from the aggressive expansionary policies that followed. However, the reversals did not happen until 2012, when the aggressive injection of cash into the economy combined with the Bank of Japan (BOJ)'s stock market support program started. The real estate market's recovery was much slower, although a minor reversal is noticeable from 2012 as well. The zero interest rate and the quantitative easing (that the US adopted during the resolution phase of the GFC) policies that started in the early 1990s continue to 2023, despite other OECD economies starting a tightening cycle from early 2022. The banking sector was able to postpone the inevitable throughout the 1990s by changing the definitions of NPLs and evergreening failed assets. However, the onset of the Japanese banking crisis that started in 1998 following the Asian financial crisis in 1997, however, provided urgency to address the NPL issues and eventually forced the Japanese banks to begin to reduce the bad loans collateralised by stocks and real estate investments that had lost most of their values. In 1997, the banking system in Japan began to show instability and resulted in the bankruptcies of large city banks, which was unthinkable just a few years before, as all banks were considered to be too big to fail in Japan due to the role they played in the economy. Bank of Hokkaido, one of the largest city banks, collapsed in 1997. Yamaichi securities, then Japan's second-oldest security company, the Japanese version of an investment bank specialising in stockbroking and investment management, went bankrupt in 1998 and subsequently fell into the hands of a US investment bank, Goldman Sachs. Long-Term Credit Bank and Nippon Credit Bank also failed in 1998.

Japanese banks' slow progress in adapting to the market competition-oriented model of the international financial system was identified as the root cause of many banking problems contributing to the crisis. Since the early 1980s, major economic systems started the process of deregulation, which led to intensified global competition in international financial services. Combined with the liberalisation of many emerging financial systems, the world financial architecture was increasingly shaping up as a market competition-oriented system where product, service, and competition-driven business took centre stage. Unfortunately, similar changes were not forthcoming in most Japanese banks, whose focus had been mostly on a relationship-driven banking model, and their lacklustre performances led to the *Japan Premium*,[7] which existed until the early 2000s. Together with the binding BIS's capital adequacy ratio (CAR) requirement,[8] this encouraged Japanese banks to reduce their (domestic and) international lending activities and to unravel their foreign operations to reduce their asset base to improve the CAR. Japanese banks' international positions started to fall rapidly after the outbreak of the Asian Financial Crisis in 1997. Exhibit 2.7 shows the international claims

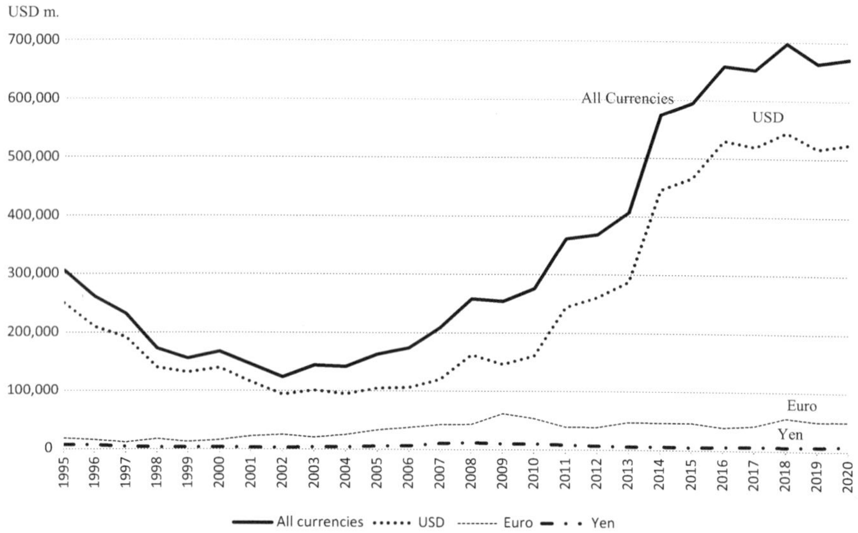

Exhibit 2.7. International claims of Japanese banks 1995–2020, USD m.

Source: BIS International Banking Statistics — Locational. https://www.bis.org/statistics/bankstats.htm.

[7]This refers to the risk premium that Japanese banks were required to pay when they borrowed from the eurocurrency market in the late 1990s to early 2000s. It was usually calculated as the difference between the LIBOR applicable for major Japanese banks and the LIBOR fix.

[8]BIS's Basel Accord I required commercial banks to keep at least 8% of risk-weighted assets in the form of tier 1 and tier 2 capital. The Basel Accord I was published in 1988 and became binding in 1992 for G10 country banks.

of Japanese banks in major currencies since 1995. Aggregate international claims against foreign borrowers in all currencies fell from USD 241 billion in 1996 to USD 172 billion in 1998 (a 41% fall) before reaching USD 123 billion in 2002 (a 74% fall) as Japanese banks repatriated funds invested in foreign markets. Domestic lending activities also fell off the cliff in 2001. As shown in Exhibit 2.2 above, the domestic private credit provided by banks fell from 184% of GDP in 2000 to 107% in 2001 and to only 93% by 2003. The banks' share of the aggregate private credit was 87%, 59%, and 53%, respectively, for 2000, 2001, and 2003.

The collapse of the twin bubbles in Japan in 1990 had set the scene for the eventual banking crisis of 1998 and, despite various measures of banking reform (Big Bang reform of 1998, series of bank rescue packages, establishment of Financial Supervisory Agency (FSA), a series of stimulation package designed to revive banks' corporate customers, and the stock market), the most important hurdle in the banking sector illness, NPLs, had not been addressed until 2001. Various measures introduced between 1998 and 2000 that were designed to stimulate the ailing banking sector failed to effectively address the core issue of NPL accumulation. When the stock market bubble collapsed in 1990, so did the market value of the collaterals for the borrowers who invested in the stock market and subsequently were in default. The Japanese government concentrated on stimulating the economy and, thus, the stock market in their efforts to reduce the NPLs of the banking sector. However, they did not attempt to address the issue directly until 2001. It was only from 2001 (after reaching its peak of nearly Yen 30 trillion or NPL ratio of 8.4% for major banks) that major banks started to write off their existing NPLs. This resulted in a drastic reduction of NPLs from 2001 to less than 1.8% by 2005 for major banks and contributed to the stabilisation of the Japanese banking sector. Although the outbreak of the GFC 2007–2009 contributed to higher NPLs between 2008 and 2013, they averaged around 2.4% before falling to 1.19% by 2017.

Exhibit 2.8 shows the NPL ratio and return on assets (after tax) of the Japanese banking sector since 1998. The NPL rose from 5.3 in 2000 to 8.4 in 2001 as the government encouraged the banks to address the NPLs, and as they started to write off their bad loans, the NPL ratio deteriorated immediately, and this is also reflected in the falling ROA to –7.5% by 2003. The improvement in both measures are visible by 2004.

In response to significant challenges imposed by the banking crisis, one of the responses of the Japanese banking sector was M&A activities

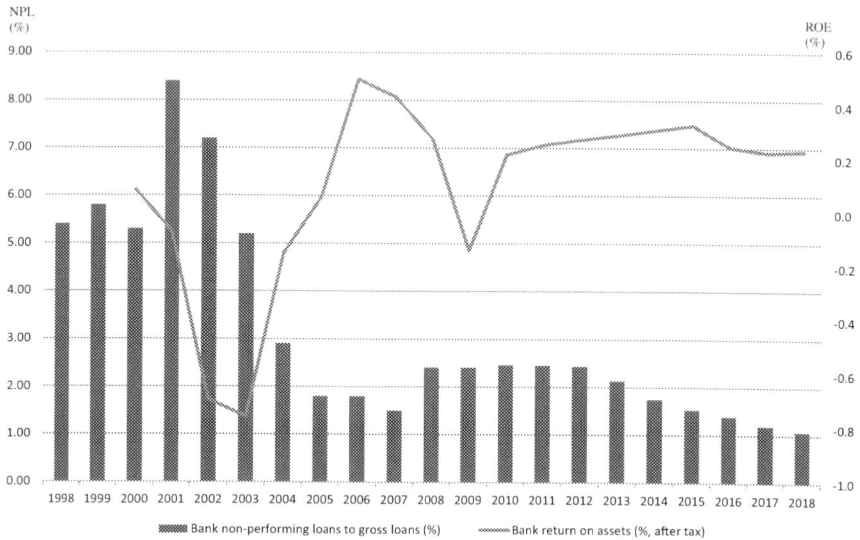

Exhibit 2.8. NPL ratio and ROA (after tax) of Japanese banks, 1998–2018.

Source: Worldbank, World Development Indicators. https://datatopics.worldbank.org/world-development-indicators/.

in the late 1990 and early 2000s (Hosono *et al.*, 2007). The number of city banks fell from 11 in 1995 to only 5 in 2015. The five city banks resulted from a series of M&A activities between 1996 and 2005, as shown in Exhibit 2.9. In addition to the M&As within Japan, city banks have been active in acquiring financial assets, especially in Europe, since 2011, thanks to the strong Yen against the Euro between 2008 and 2012,[9] government sponsorship (a war chest of USD 43 billion government credit line extended to the Japan Bank for International Cooperation (JBIC) and the top three Japanese banks), and seemingly undervalued European assets during the Eurozone debt crisis period. For example, Sumitomo Mitsui acquired a list of European assets, including RBS aviation capital in Dublin, Ireland. It can be seen in Exhibit 2.7 that the international claims of Japanese banks started to recover in 2003 after they began to reduce NPLs in 2001. Except for a small dip in 2008 during the height of the GFC period, international claims continued to

[9]The Yen appreciated from around 167 to 95 Yen per EUR from July 2008 to July 2012.

City Banks (Creation year, Total Assets in Mar 2021)	Merged from	Merged from	Merged from
Mitsubishi UFJ (Oct 2005, USD 2,357 b)	Mitsubishi Tokyo Financial Group (Apr 2001)	Bank of Tokyo Mitsubishi (1996)	Bank of Tokyo Mitsubishi Bank
		Mitsubishi Trust and Banking Nippon Trust Banking Tokyo Trust Bank	
	UFJ (United Financial of Japan) Group (Apr 2001)	Sanwa Bark Tokai Bank Tokyo Trust and Banking	
Sumitomo Mitsui Financial Group (Apr 2001, USD 1,957 b)	Sakura Bank Sumimoto Bank		
Mizuho Financial Group (2003, USD 1,803 b)	Mizuo Holdings (Sep 2000)	Dai-Ichi Kangyo Bank Fuji Bank Industrial Bank of Japan	
Resona Bank (Oct 2002, USD 364 b)	Renamed from Daiwa holding (Oct 2002)	Daiwa bank holding, Dec 2001 Parent group of Daiwa, Kinki Osaka Bank and Nara Bank Asahi Bank	
Saitama Resona Bank (Mar 2003, USD 173 b)	Formed from Asahi bank branches — 100 branches in Saitama and 3 branches in Tokyo		

Exhibit 2.9. Mergers and Acquisitions resulting in five city banks.

Source: Official websites of the five city banks and the Japanese Bankers Association.

rise and gathered pace from 2013, when quantitative easing policies were instituted.

Despite potentially significant benefits from the M&A activities, such as cost reduction through a reduction in service duplication, realising economies of scale, and better strategic focus, Harada and Ito (2008) suggest that the most important motivation behind these mergers was to take advantage of the government's too big to fail (TBTF) policy. As a result, the M&As were not carefully designed, and the intended operational efficiency improvements have not been eventuated. Interest income from wholesale lending activities still dominates other income sources, suggesting that even after the M&As, the core of banking activities has not changed significantly. Indeed, despite improving their capital positions, the top five Japanese banking groups still lag behind their international competitors from North America and Western Europe in terms of asset-side operation diversification as measured by non-interest income ratios and profitability.[10]

2.3. Internationalisation of Chinese Banks

2.3.1. *Chinese economic growth*

China's ascendance on the world economic stage started in earnest in the early 2000s when China was awarded the 2008 Beijing Olympic games on 13 July 2001, followed by joining the World Trade Organization on 11 December 2001. Since the early 2000s, China has produced a breathtaking pace of economic and financial development year after year. The real GDP growth rate for the 1990s and the 2000s averaged 9.5% and 9.8% per annum, respectively. The most recent decade of the 2010s shows a smaller but still impressive average growth rate of 7.3% (World Development Indicators). China surpassed Japan in 2010 to become the second largest economy in the world, and the gap between the largest economy, the US, and China has been narrowing (see Exhibit 2.10).

China has adopted a very successful strategy of attracting foreign direct investments (FDIs) from major economies and multinational corporations from the early 1990s to set up a manufacturing hub, exporting to

[10]The average non-interest to interest income for the top four Japanese financial groups was 0.7 compared to the average of 1.9 for the top 25 world banks (www.thebanker.com) in 2016. The ROA averages were 0.35 and 0.68, respectively.

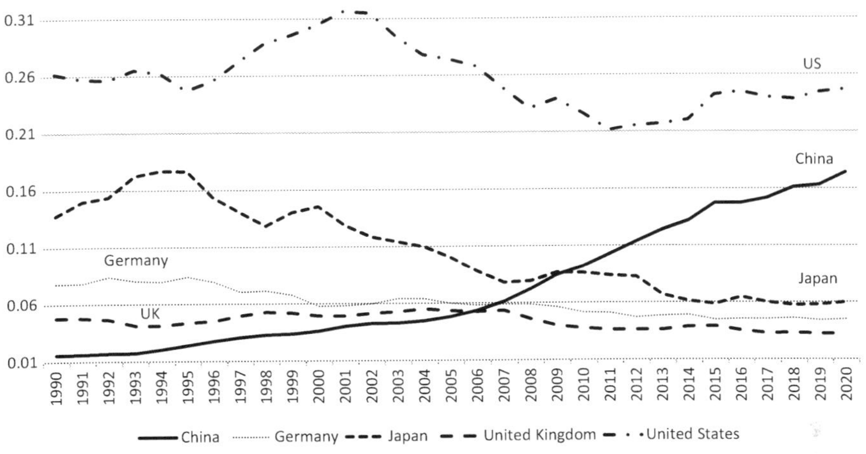

Exhibit 2.10. Top five countries by GDP (% of world total), 1985–2020.

Source: Worldbank, World Development Indicators. https://datatopics.worldbank.org/world-development-indicators/.

major markets in North America and the EU. The export-driven secondary industry focus of the Chinese economic development strategy followed the usual development path of many countries that have gone before it, such as Japan and Korea in the same region. Incoming FDIs from the US and European countries directed at establishing a manufacturing presence in China, targeting their home markets, have led to impressive growth in China's exports. China overtook Japan in 2005, Germany in 2010, and the US in 2013 to become the largest exporting country in the world, accounting for 12% of the world total in 2020 (the US was second with 9.5% of the world total, see Exhibit 2.11). This shows that the global economy is now more exposed to China in terms of global supply chain risks should there be disruptions in the production capacity of Chinese suppliers. During the COVID-19-induced lockdown of Shanghai in the first half of 2022, which is the most important trading port for international trade in China, most of the global supply chain came to a halt, demonstrating the vulnerability of the global economy to political and economic risks emanating from one part of the global supply chain.

Gradually, the growing Chinese economy attracted FDIs directed at the domestic economy as an output market. For instance, multinational car

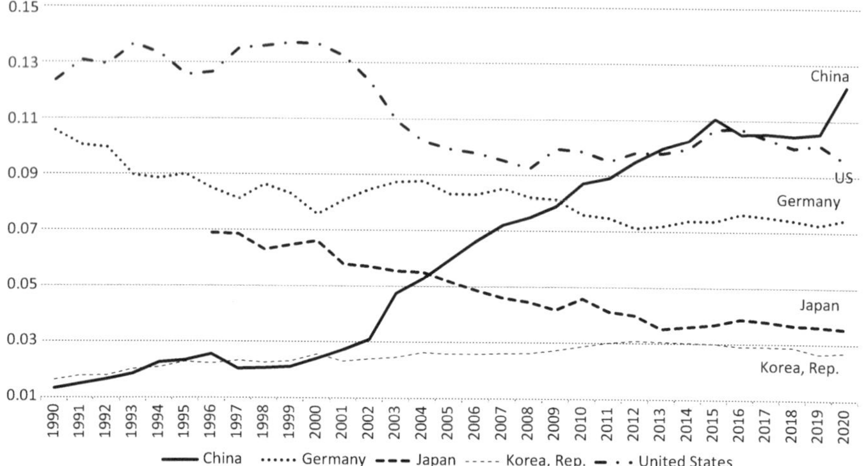

Exhibit 2.11. Top five exporting countries (% of world total), 1985–2020.

Source: Worldbank, World Development Indicators. https://datatopics.worldbank.org/world-development-indicators/.

manufacturers established manufacturing plants in China. Volkswagen was the first entrant, soon followed by American and Japanese companies and other German brands to cater for the domestic Chinese market. The growing contribution of Chinese domestic economic activities towards its GDP started to outstrip the impressive export performances, as shown as a falling share of exports in GDP from 2007 (see Exhibit 2.12). The percentage of exports as a contributor to GDP peaked at 36% in 2006 and gradually declined to 18.5% in 2019. This is a similar level observed in economies such as the US and Japan, which rely more on the domestic economy than exports, unlike export-driven economies, such as Germany and the UK. This suggests that as the world is becoming more exposed to China, its economy is becoming less exposed to the world's economy.

In addition, despite the appearance of staggering economic success since the early 2000s, the Chinese economy is still in its early stages of internationalisation. For example, McKinsey Global Institute (2019) reports that although there were 110 Chinese firms in global Fortune 500 companies, most of their revenues (80%) were drawn domestically. China imports six times more Intellectual Property (IP) than it exports, and

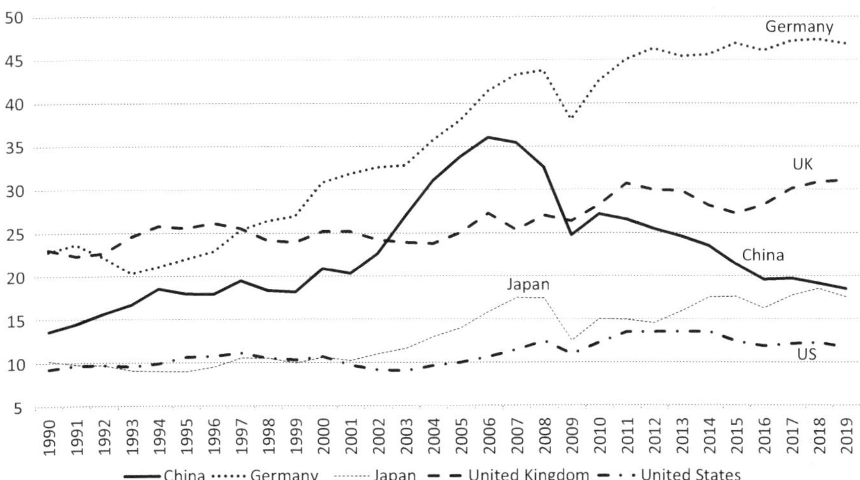

Exhibit 2.12. Export as a contributor to GDP (% of GDP), 1985–2019.

Source: Worldbank, World Development Indicators. https://datatopics.worldbank.org/world-development-indicators/.

less than 6% of its financial system is foreign-owned despite it being the third-largest in the world. Also, there was only one Chinese company that was listed in *Forbes*' list of the most valuable brands in 2020 (Huawei at 93).[11] One would expect that as the Chinese economy continues to become sophisticated and Chinese companies globalise, these metrics would approach those of its major competitors, such as the US and European counterparts. However, the outlook is not very clear on the future of the Chinese economy mainly for two reasons. *First,* the trade conflict that started in 2018 with a round of tit-for-tat tariff increases by the Chinese and the US governments look likely to continue for some time as it has escalated into geopolitical conflicts. *Second,* the rise of domestic electronic and car industries in China is in the process of displacing multinational companies that operate manufacturing presence in China for the domestic Chinese markets. The rising labour costs compared to other competing countries in the regions, such as Vietnam and India, and increasing competition from Chinese competitors reduced the

[11] https://www.forbes.com/the-worlds-most-valuable-brands/#54859dab119c.

attractiveness of China as a manufacturing hub and an output market. The subsequent withdrawal or scaling down of operations of a number of multinational companies would limit the speed of the globalisation of the Chinese economy.[12]

2.3.2. *Chinese banking system*

Similar to other emerging market countries, the banking system is the most important funding channel that intermediates between domestic savers and borrowers (businesses and individuals). The combination of a high national saving rate (average saving rate to GDP of 43% from 1990 to 2020), continued growth of the economy at a faster rate, and the underdevelopment of the non-bank financial sector led to the significant growth of bank assets from the early 2000s.

In terms of total bank assets, the Chinese banking system has been the largest in the world since it surpassed that of Japan in 2013. Its aggregate asset was USD 21 trillion in 2017, which was twice the size of the second-largest banking system in the US, with USD 12 trillion, and three times the size of Japan (see Exhibit 2.13). This resulted in the four largest banks in China being listed as the top four banks in the world in 2020 (see Exhibit 1.2). These are the Industrial and Commercial Bank of China (ICBC), China Construction Bank (CCB), Agricultural Bank of China (ABOC), and Bank of China (BOC). In addition, they are also recognised as global brands by BrandDirectory.[13] The top four Chinese banks' brand rankings were 7, 12, 17 and 27 for ICBC, CCB, ABC and BOC in 2023 respectively.

Chinese banks provided significantly more domestic credit than the other major countries with which China competes. China provided 182% of its GDP as credit to the private sector in 2020, compared to 146% in the UK, 109% in Japan, 86% in Germany, and 54% in the US (see Exhibit 2.14). Moreover, China is the only country among its competitors that rapidly expanded its banking sector in the 2010s. This is not

[12]The notable multinationals that have announced, already withdrawn from or scaled down their Chinese operations by 2022, include Hyundai motors, Samsung electronics, Toshiba, Apple, Dell Computers, and Nike, among others.

[13]https://brandirectory.com/rankings/global/table.

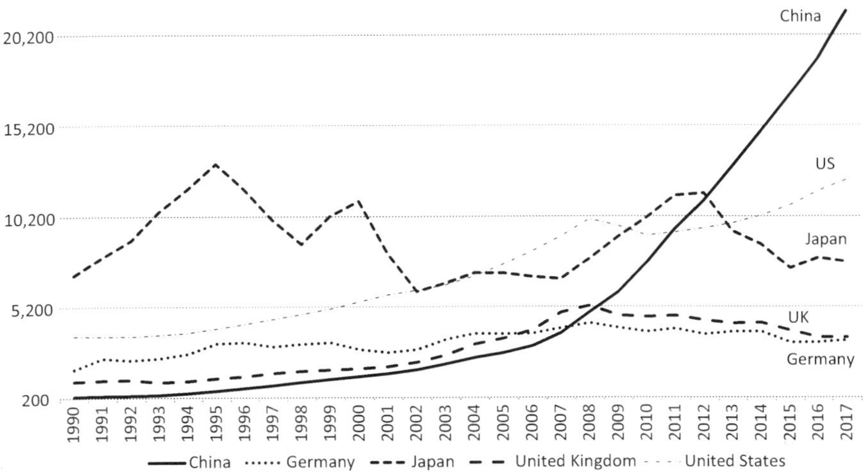

Exhibit 2.13. Assets of deposit money banks (USD b.), 1985–2020.

Source: Worldbank, World Development Indicators. https://datatopics.worldbank.org/world-development-indicators/.

surprising given the dominance of the domestic banking sector in corporate funding due to the lack of alternatives to bank loans.

Exhibit 2.15 reports various characteristics of the banking system in China and other major countries. Chinese banks are relatively under-capitalised compared to the others, with only 14.7% of regulatory capital to risk-weighted assets, and the NPL ratio is marginally higher but still at a very healthy level of 1.8% in 2021.[14] Chinese banks provide the vast majority of loans to domestic borrowers (98.7%). The US also shows an exceedingly high domestic loan concentration at 96.7%, unlike the German and UK banks. On the other hand, foreign banks in China provided only a small fraction of domestic loans accounting for only 7.4% of GDP, similar to Japan (11.8%). Not surprisingly, highly integrated banking markets such as Germany and the UK allowed higher foreign bank penetration (51.4% and 99% of GDP, respectively). Chinese banks are generally more profitable (higher ROA and ROE) with higher interest

[14]However, Klapper *et al.* (2019) cast some doubt on the accuracy of the reported NPL figures as the loose regulatory definitions of bad loans and the practice of evergreening would lead to underestimating the bad loans in the system.

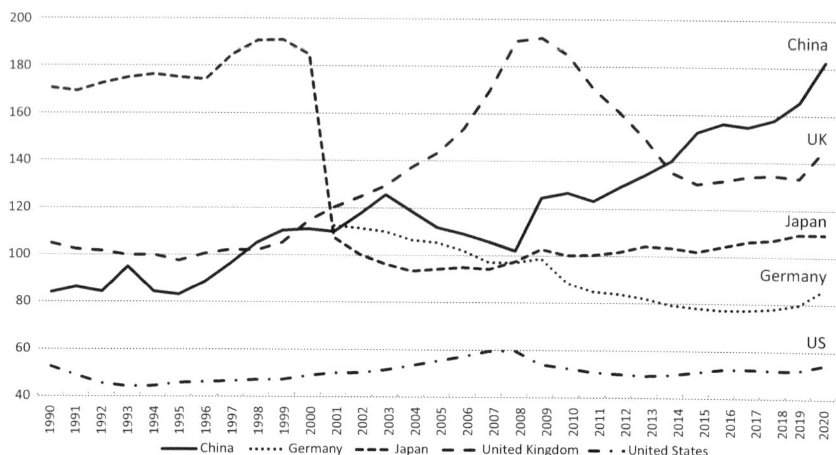

Exhibit 2.14. Domestic credit provided by the banking sector (% of GDP), 1985–2020.

Source: Worldbank, World Development Indicators. https://datatopics.worldbank.org/world-development-indicators/.

margins and lower overheads in their operations. However, their operation is not as diversified as the other banking markets in generating non-interest income activities, such as fee income-based products (the lower non-interest rate to total income ratio). Finally, Chinese banks are less accessible via their branches, operating only 8.8 locations per 100,000 people, which is significantly less compared to the others.

Another critical aspect of the Chinese financial system in recent decades is the rise of the shadow banking system. Shadow banking refers to credit intermediation that occurs outside the formal banking system within a country by non-bank financial institutions that are outside the reach of bank regulators. Banks also participate in shadow banking activities through off-balance-sheet activities. The size of shadow banking activities in China, as measured by shadow savings instruments, increased from RMB 0.6 trillion to 26.9 trillion (the equivalent of USD 84 billion to 3.8 trillion) from 2002 to 2017 (Klapper *et al.*, 2019). The main reasons identified for the popularity of shadow banking in China were restrictive regulations of the banking sector and the underdevelopment of capital markets that could provide alternative investment outlets. *First,* the restriction that

	China	Germany	Japan	United Kingdom	United States
	2021Q2	2021Q1	2020Q3	2020Q4	2021Q1
Regulatory Capital to Risk-Weighted Assets	14.7	19.2	16.9	21.6	16.3
Regulatory Tier 1 Capital to Risk-Weighted Assets	12.0	17.2	14.8	18.5	14.5
Non-performing Loans Net of Provisions to Capital	-9.3	6.8	8.4	6.8	5.2
Non-performing Loans to Total Gross Loans	1.8	1.1	1.1	1.2	1.1
Sectoral Distribution of Loans to Total Loans					
Residents	98.7	79.7	91.2	47.5	96.7
Deposit-takers	1.8	13.8	4.7	6.4	6.1
Central bank	0.0	15.8	0.0	0.0	
Other financial corporations	4.5	2.6	10.2	13.8	8.5
General government	0.0	3.9	8.6	0.2	1.4
Nonfinancial corporations	51.5	15.4	38.0	7.2	36.4
Other domestic sectors	40.8	28.4	29.8	19.9	44.2
Nonresidents	1.3	20.3	8.8	52.5	3.3
Loans from nonresident banks to GDP (%)	7.4	51.4	11.8	99.0	18.7
Return on Assets	0.8	0.3	0.2	0.6	0.3
Return on Equity	9.5	4.1	4.5	10.1	3.0
Bank overhead costs to total assets (%)	0.9	1.8	0.8	2.4	2.5
Interest Margin to Gross Income	79.0	69.5	60.1	40.6	64.3
Bank noninterest income to total income (%)	26.6	48.1	43.1	38.7	33.2
Bank branches per 100,000 adults	8.8	12.9	34.0	25.1	31.2

Exhibit 2.15. Bank soundness indicators.

Source: IMF Financial Soundness Indicators.

capped deposit interest rates at arbitrarily low levels designed to lower borrowing costs for state-owned enterprises increased demand for higher-yielding instruments. Non-banks and also banks later on created and marketed wealth management products (similar to money market instruments in other countries) that provide higher yields but do not enjoy regulatory protection as these are not deposits (Klapper *et al.*, 2019). *Second,* the 75% regulation cap on loan-to-deposit ratio, enacted in 1995 and removed in 2015, pushed the big four banks to seek a non-deposit source of funds to satisfy ever-increasing loan demands. They were the tools of credit expansion from the equivalent of USD 586 billion fiscal stimulus-driven credit expansion during the global financial crisis of 2008.

Although shadow banking caters for the segments of the market that the formal banking system cannot easily service, the growth of unregulated shadow banking activities started to pose threats to system safety. In response to this, the Chinese government started a program to reduce the size of shadow banking and has successfully reduced it from 60% of GDP to 40% (Sutton and Taylor, 2020). Although the corporate bond market has been gradually increasing in size (0.007% of GDP in 2000 to 4.16% by 2017), there have not been meaningful developments in alternative financial investment vehicles for savers. Also, for banks, the reduction in the volume of shadow banking activities, especially their off-balance-sheet wealth management product business, made it more challenging to manage their activities on both sides of the balance sheet. Therefore, it appears that the Chinese government's drive to reduce shadow banking activities has been effective. However, the development of other capital market alternatives for both investors and banks alike is still lacking. Given that the shadow banking sector is likely to play an important role in the foreseeable future as the Chinese economy and the capital market develop, an appropriate set of regulations is needed to control the inherent risk it poses to the financial system. Sun (2019) suggests that specific macroprudential tools, such as reserves for asset activities and risk-taking activities, be applied separately to banks' shadow banking activities and traditional shadow banking operations.

2.3.3. *Chinese bank internationalisation*

2.3.3.1. *Motivations for internationalisation*

There are broadly three factors responsible for the Chinese banks' internationalisation from the early 2000s. These are defensive expansion, the Chinese government's international expansion drive, and pursuing new markets/strategic assets. The first two motivations are closely tied to each other, and the third results from the first two. He *et al.* (2019) report that out of the Chinese banks they surveyed, 100% of the respondents picked the defensive motive, and over 70% also picked the other two motivations. They also listed profit and diversification motives and competition with other Chinese banks.

First, following the customer or defensive expansion is also a key motivation for the Chinese banks' internationalisation as it was for the US and Japanese banks who preceded them to dominate the international banking scene in earlier decades. Relationship banking plays a crucial role in bank internationalisation in this respect. Similar to other emerging market countries, general financial system underdevelopment necessitated the concentration of bank-dominated financial intermediation. Chinese companies rely heavily on commercial banks for their financial needs, and when they were encouraged to explore overseas markets, the need for Chinese banks to internationalise their operations intensified. Chinese banks value long-term relationships with their clients over short-term transactional benefits (Selmier, 2019). Relationship banking requires cultivating a long-term relationship with customers to gather soft as well as hard information about their business operations, risks, and potentials. Confidential information about borrowers obtained through such a relationship plays a crucial role in lending decisions, and the resulting relationship is likely to bind the bank strategically to the borrowers for a longer term. Moreover, relationship banking has the benefit of being able to assess their clients' credit risk better through a history of association with them. The reduced information uncertainty thus aids in improved bank asset management.

Second, the Chinese government encouraged state-owned enterprises (SOEs), both industrial companies and financial institutions, to expand internationally to explore opportunities in foreign markets. The inward FDIs from the early 1990s in China contributed to the meteoric rise of the Chinese economy, as documented above. This 'Go Out Policy' was initiated in 1999 in an attempt to reduce pressure on the RMB to revalue, given the accumulating foreign currency reserves from the accumulation of trade surplus. The major aims of the policy were to expand outward FDIs and achieve the international presence of Chinese companies. Consequently, Chinese companies started to venture into foreign markets to invest in foreign assets.

There have been waves of overseas mergers and acquisitions by Chinese companies acquiring foreign assets. For example, Chinese companies purchased USD 55 billion's worth of assets in the US in 2016 until the trade conflicts with the US in 2018 all but stopped this trend.[15] The most notable US assets that Chinese investors purchased are IBM's personal computer business in a USD 2.3 billion deal and Motorola mobile hardware division for USD 2.9 billion, both by Lenovo in January 2014 in the IT industry; Smithfield Foods by Shuanghuang International in the retail food industry in a deal worth USD 4.7 billion in May 2013; and AMC entertainment by Dalian Wanda Group in a USD 2.6 billion deal in 2012 (but subsequently sold off most of its stakes at a great loss by 2021) in the entertainment industry, to name a few examples. This trend of

---

[15] South China Morning Post (2019). https://www.scmp.com/business/china-business/article/2181096/chinese-acquisitions-us-companies-fell-drastic-95-cent-2018.

purchasing US assets by Chinese companies conjures memories of a similar buying spree of iconic US assets by Japanese companies in the 1980s that sparked political tensions. However, this trend was recently curbed, as evidenced by a drastic drop in investment in the US to USD 3 billion in 2018 due to the recent trade conflict. As most of these external asset acquisitions are by state-owned or controlled corporations and the large banks who have them as clients are also state-owned, it naturally follows that their banks are also expected to follow them into the foreign markets. Thus, the most important motivation for Chinese banks for internationalisation is 'Follow the customer'.

Also, as they are state-owned banks, they are required to follow government policies to aid their Chinese corporate customers abroad and expand their operations accordingly (He *et al.,* 2019). For example, the world's largest bank, the Industrial and Commerce Bank of China (ICBC), boasts its presence in 48 countries as of October 2021. The growth of the Chinese banks has been remarkable in their rapid and considerable domination of the global banking league table. As shown in Exhibit 1.2, the ranking of the world's top banks is dominated by many of the Chinese commercial banks, especially the big four: ICBC, China Construction Bank (CCB), Bank of China (BOC), and Agricultural Bank of China (ABC). However, despite the global outreach of these large banks, their dominance is due mostly to their commercial banking activities in the domestic market (see Exhibit 2.15) and against their Chinese corporate customers in the overseas markets, and their foreign operations account for only a small proportion of their overall business (less than 10% in 2012, Standard and Poors, 2012). The dominance of the big four Chinese banks does not extend to investment banking activities such as fee and commission income and trading income segments. The low level of product and customer diversification of Chinese banks appears to be related to the current lack of expertise in activities other than servicing their existing customers.

The Chinese government initiated three ambitious complementary global initiatives in 2013 that provide opportunities for Chinese banks to internationalise. These are the Asian Infrastructure Investment Bank (AIIB), the Belt and Road Initiative (BRI), and the internationalisation of the Chinese currency, RMB. The AIIB was proposed in 2013 and started to operate in December 2015 with the aim of competing with the Asian Development Bank and the World Bank in facilitating infrastructure investments in Asia. As of March 2023, there are 106 member countries from around the world. China contributed 29% of the total subscriptions giving them 27% of voting rights. The more important role of the AIIB is arguably to facilitate the BRI that was also proposed in 2013. Its aim is to invest in a large number of countries in strategic locations to form sea and land routes known as 'Silk Road Economic Belt'. The infrastructure initiative focused on Asia and Africa, and some examples of investments include ports, railroads, airports, power stations, and dams. Another initiative that complements the Chinese government's global ambition is the internationalisation of its currency, the RMB. The aim is to compete with the USD to become an international trade vehicle and reserve currency. This requires a strong domestic economy, an open and well-developed capital market, and official support from the government. China has made significant progress on all three fronts. The importance of the RMB as an international currency has been growing as a result. As the proportion of international trade transactions denominated in the RMB rises, the demand for the currency from the rest of the world will rise, and the case for the RMB becoming one of the international reserve currencies will strengthen. SWIFT reports that the RMB is the most popular currency in the Asia Pacific for payments in their trade with China in 2021.[16] In August 2015, the RMB overtook the Japanese Yen to become the fourth largest global payment currency accounting for 2.79% of the global total, after the USD (44.82%), the Euro (27.20%), and the GBP (8.45%) (Swift, 2015). The increasing role of the RMB is also reflected in its rising global share of foreign exchange market trading. It accounted for 6.6% in 2022 and ranked 4th in the foreign exchange turnover ranking, a significant increase from 0.8% (ranked 10th) in 2010 (BIS, 2022 and Exhibit 4.4). On 1 October 2016, the IMF added the RMB to its Special Drawing Rights (SDR) basket. The other currencies in the basket are the USD, the Euro, the Pound Sterling, and the Japanese Yen. Since the RMB is not yet a freely converting currency, the role of the state-owned Chinese banks in facilitating RMB-denominated transactions becomes important. It is also reported that the RMB accounted for 2.45% (or USD 287.46 billion) of the global foreign exchange reserves held by other countries in the first quarter of 2021.[17] Despite successive rounds of relaxing restrictions on

[16]https://www.swift.com/news-events/webinars/rmb-ranked-first-asia-pacific-payments-greater china.

[17]Yuan's share of global reserves hits new high at 2.45%: IMF — Global Times, https://www.globaltimes.cn/page/202107/1227563.shtml.

inward capital investments, the RMB is not yet fully convertible as of 2021. This is one of the challenges for the currency to become a truly viable alternative to the USD as an international reserve currency. IMF (2022) classifies the RMB as having 'Crawl-like arrangement' with a long list of binding controls on capital account flows.

Third, Chinese banks have explored foreign opportunities along with defensive expansion by purchasing stakes in foreign banks. However, these investment activities were limited to a small number of cases, and investment amounts were relatively small compared to other major banks' M&A activities. For instance, ICBC purchased a 20% stake in South Africa's Standard banking group in 2008 for USD 5.6 billion, an 80% stake in Bank of East Asia in Hong Kong for USD 140 million in 2012, and the global market business of Standard banks in London in 2004 (Selmier, 2019). Instead of international expansions via the M&A route, Chinese banks have largely taken a slow road to internationalisation. That is, they seem to prefer to grow organically, which is a slow process of establishing foreign branches and greenfield subsidiaries, rather than acquiring a going concern in the target market, which would provide a rapid penetration and possibly less resistance from the existing customer base (Selmier, 2019). The main reason for the organically grown path is the cultural consistency greenfield expansions offer and the degree of control the expanding Chinese banks, and ultimately the Chinese government, can have on most, if not all, of the operational aspects of the foreign operation. If one expands via M&As, it would be very difficult, if not impossible, to instil corporate culture from back home to the acquired entity with foreign directors and management. Also, it would be very difficult for the Chinese government to control the activities of the foreign subsidiaries if they were not purpose-built from the ground up. Thus, the desire to maintain relationship banking with the expanding banks' corporate clients from China, who are also subjected to the Chinese government directives, is paramount in designing an organisation form of foreign expansion for Chinese banks. Indeed, He *et al.* (2019) report that greenfield expansion dominates M&A for the top four Chinese banks. During 2001 and 2013, out of 54 foreign expansions by ICBC, greenfield expansions accounted for 43 cases, and there were only 11 cases of M&A. CCB had 22 greenfield expansions and only three M&As. For the BOC and the ABC, all of their expansions were greenfields (71 and 10, respectively).

2.3.3.2. *Challenges for Chinese banks and their international presence*

Although Chinese banks have made significant inroads into the global banking system by the sheer size of their balance sheets, they are facing challenges to their continued international expansions. Most importantly, the government initiatives that put Chinese corporations outward and hence Chinese banks have met with resistance from many corners. Many host countries of Chinese corporations' M&A activities are increasingly wary of potential negative implications for their markets. For example, under the Trump presidency, the US started to block Chinese companies from purchasing tech sector assets in the US in 2018 and blocked a Chinese company from purchasing a Korean semiconductor company. The trade conflict that started in 2018, with China and the US imposing tariffs on each other, continued under the Biden administration that came to power in 2021. In addition, the BRI is being met with increasing global resistance after some of the countries fell into financial difficulties due to the non-economical nature of some of the infrastructure projects. For example, Sri Lanka's Hambantota port project ended up in the hands of the Chinese government after the Sri Lankan government was unable to repay the financing of the project provided by Chinese banks. This example is a cautionary tale for other countries. On the other side of the spectrum, the Australian federal government cancelled two projects that the state of Victoria signed with the national development and reform commission of China in October 2018 after introducing the federal foreign investment veto law in October 2019. This global resistance to the BRI and the general expansion of Chinese corporations limit the degree to which Chinese banks can service their Chinese corporate clients in foreign markets.

As Chinese corporations tapped into Wall Street for funding for their expansions, they made a noticeable impact as their IPOs were wildly successful. For example, when it was launched in 2014 and raised USD 21.8 billion, Alibaba's IPO became the biggest of its kind in US financial history. However, as trade conflict continues and some of the US-listed Chinese companies have been reporting misleading accounting information,[18] the

[18] In the well-known case of Luckin Coffee, it was revealed that the company had inflated its 2019 reported sales by as much as USD 310 million. The revelation came after an

Chinese government's restrictions on foreign-listed Chinese corporations have come to light. That is, the Chinese government would not allow foreign regulators or exchanges to audit Chinese companies even if they are cross-listed in foreign equity markets. This further restricted the role of Chinese banks in servicing their clients in foreign markets.

As Chinese banks operate in multiple jurisdictions, they experience challenges in complying with local regulations. This was mainly due to their lack of complete understanding of the regulatory compliance in the host country. Also, when operating in multiple locations, adherence to host country regulations and client needs may not have been in line with the aim of the Chinese government. In either case, failure to comply with local laws and regulations resulted in hefty fines for some of the large Chinese banks. For example, the ABC received a USD 215 million penalty from the New York banking regulator in 2016 for a violation of anti-money laundering laws. The BOC agreed to a settlement of USD 2.3 million against Office of Foreign Assets Control (OFAC) in August 2021 for violating its Sudan Sanctions Regulation. A more than USD 42 million fine to ICBC was issued for improper handling of ADRs in 2019. There are also other cases outside the US, for example, USD 6 million to CCB in South Africa and EUR 3.7 million to the ICBC in Luxembourg. If these violations of host country regulations were due to a lack of complete understanding of the relevant regulations, one would expect that there would be improvements in compliance as they gain experience in the host market operation. However, if they were due to inconsistencies between the Chinese government's policies and host countries' regulatory requirements, such as foreign market-listed Chinese companies not being permitted to provide financial details of their operations in China to foreign regulators, then this problem is unlikely to be resolved easily.

Another challenge for Chinese banks is coming from domestic regulation. In the late 2010s, Chinese regulators cracked down on shadow banking activities in an effort to defuse the systemic risk they imposed. Commercial banks were able to bypass various regulations limiting their intermediating business by engaging in shadow banking activities mostly via wealth management products as a funding source to finance risky lending activities. Six banks received RMB 150 million (equivalent to USD 22 million) fines in 2018 for breaching regulations on shadow

investigative report by a short seller Muddy Waters. Luckin Coffee was subsequently delisted from NASDAQ in June 2020.

banking. The People's Bank of China (the Chinese central bank) imposed an equivalent of USD 1.77 million in fines on four banks in August 2021 for improper handling of customer credit information. Also, non-bank financial companies were also subjected to regulation crackdowns. In November 2020, the Chinese regulator stopped ANT financial's IPO, an affiliate of Alibaba, in the last hour due to the perception of its negative impact on financial system safety. Alibaba's stock, listed on the New York Stock Exchange, dropped by 8% in response to the news. To make matters worse for the Chinese banks, the looming real estate crisis that became apparent in 2021 due to the difficulties faced by many real estate developers has the potential to raise the non-performing loans of many Chinese banks to uncomfortable levels as the real estate investments were mostly financed by bank credit. If real estate bubbles burst, this would have a severe implication for the health of Chinese banks, which may force them to defend their domestic operations by reducing their overseas-held assets. Hence, there is a potential for a much reduced international presence of Chinese banks as a result, similar to Japanese banks' withdrawal from international markets during the post-bubble period in Japan.

In summary, Chinese banks are still in an early stage of internationalisation, and their international activities account for only a small fraction of their income. Only the Bank of China showed respectable foreign profits, accounting for 29.86% of its consolidated operations in 2017 (Zhang *et al.*, 2020). That is, the impressive global ranking of Chinese banks is largely due to the sheer size of their domestic assets. Moreover, foreign banks' share of the Chinese banking market is shrinking. Foreign banks accounted for 1.4% of China's banking assets in 2015, a non-trivial reduction from 2.4% in 2007. Also, only 7.4% of loans in China were extended by foreign lenders in 2021. Combining these observations, it is evident that the Chinese banking system is not fully open to the rest of the world, and Chinese banks' international activities are paltry compared to their domestic assets. Moreover, Chinese banks face internal and external challenges that could further limit their international activities.

References

Bank of Japan, Financial System Report, Various issues. http://www.boj.or.jp/en/research/brp/fsr/index.htm/.

Büschgen, H. E. (1979). The universal banking system in the Federal Republic of Germany. *Journal of Comparative Corporate Law and Securities Regulation*, 2, 1–27.

Canals, J. (1997). *Universal Banking*. Oxford University Press, New York, Chapter 9: Internationalisation of Banking, pp. 242–275.

DeYoung, R. (2019). Banking in the United States, in Oxford Handbook of Banking, 3rd ed., edited by Berger, A. Molyneux, P. and Wilson, J., Oxford University Press.

Harada, K. and Ito, T. (2008). Did mergers help Japanese mega-banks avoid failure? Analysis of the distance to default of banks, NBER Working Paper No. 14518, December 2008.

He, W., Boateng, A. and Ring, P. (2019). Motives, choice of entry mode, and challenges of bank internationalisation: Evidence from China. *Thunderbird International Business Review*, 61, 897–909. https://doi.org/10.1002/tie.22062.

Hosono, K., Sakai, K. and Tsuru, K. (2007). Consolidation of banks in Japan: Causes and consequences (September 2007). NBER Working Paper No. w13399, SSRN: https://ssrn.com/abstract=1014346.

International Monetary Fund (2022). Annual report on exchange arrangements and exchange restrictions 2021, July 2022.

Klapper, L., Soledad, M. Peria, M. and Zia, B. (2019). Banking in China, in Oxford Handbook of Banking, 3rd ed., edited by Berger, A. Molyneux, P. and Wilson, J., Oxford University Press.

McKinsey Global Institute (2019). China and the world, Inside the dynamics of a changing relationship, Report, 1 July 2019. https://www.mckinsey.com/featured-insights/china/china-and-the-world-inside-the-dynamics-of-a-changing-relationship.

Qian, L. and Delios, A. (2008). Internalization and experience: Japanese banks' international expansion, 1980–1998. *Journal of International Business Studies*, 39, 231–248.

Selmier, W. T. (2019). Why Chinese bank internationalisation is gradual — A historical institutional perspective. *Transnational Corporations Review*, 10(4), 318–332.

Sun, G. (2019). China's shadow banking: Bank's shadow and traditional shadow banking, BIS Working Paper, No. 822.

Sutton, M. and Taylor, G. (2020). Shadow financing in China, Reserve Bank of Australia Bulletin, December.

Uchida, H. and Udell, G. (2019). Banking in Japan, in Oxford Handbook of Banking, 3rd ed., edited by Berger, A. Molyneux, P. and Wilson, J., Oxford University Press.

Zhang, C., Zhang, T. and Tan, T. (2020). Internationalisation of Chinese banks: How to strengthen and enhance overseas operations and management. *Advances in Economics, Business and Management Research*, 126, 144–156.

Chapter 3

International Trade Finance

3.1. Introduction

One of the earliest and traditionally most important roles performed by commercial banks is facilitating international trade. Trade finance involves the process of financing business transactions that require a transfer of ownership of goods or providing services in return for financial remuneration. Since there is a time gap between the shipment of goods by the exporter and when the importer receives it, the exporter faces the risk of counterparty default. On the other hand, if the exporter fails to deliver the product, the importer faces the loss of resources already committed, such as the cost of the import if prepaid, marketing campaigns for the product, and the cost of establishing a distribution network for the product. There can also be unforeseen risks that are unrelated to the default risk of either party, such as natural disasters during transportation, political uncertainties leading to port blockages, trade conflicts, and an enactment of capital controls that prevents hard currency payments. For these reasons, both parties in a trade seek financial protection before they perform their obligations to avoid counterparty risk. That is, the exporter prefers to be paid before shipping the product, and the importer prefers to receive it in good order before paying for it. If neither party is willing or able to assume the counterparty risk in whole or in part, trade between the two parties will not occur. Financial institutions, most commonly commercial banks, are then tasked to remove the counterpart risk to allow both parties to engage in the trade.

Banks are usually involved in the process by providing advances to the buyer through business overdrafts, loans, and bill acceptance facilities.[1] International trade financing can be viewed as an extension of domestic trade financing, however, there are additional complications. These include geographic, foreign exchange, political, inflation, interest rate, market, and hard currency payment risks. Facilitating international trade has been one of the most important functions associated with international banking. Although domestic banks (as opposed to multinational banks) have also been providing trade payment guarantees, access to global financial markets and a presence in multiple country locations allowed international banks to be in a superior position to assess and manage risk much more effectively. In general, international trades in goods need to be financed because there is a time gap between the time of sale and receipt of payment by the exporter, and the exporter needs funding to continue the production cycle. Also, international trade involves a degree of uncertainty that may lead to the non-completion of a trade. Thus, the exporter needs payment assurance before shipment can be made.

There are broadly three forms of trade financing involving banks providing financial guarantees in some form. These are the letter of credit/banker's acceptance financing, forfaiting, and factoring. Other types of trade financing usually involve banks providing payment-related services without providing financial or non-financial guarantees for either party in the transaction. These include prepayment, consignment, open account, account receivable financing, and countertrade. Both groups of trade financing are discussed in the following sections.

3.2. International Trade Finance by Letter of Credit

Letter of credit (LC) financing is the most common method of financing international trade. It is oriented toward short-term international trade

[1] Bill acceptance facilities allow banks to accept (or guarantee) commercial bills issued by clients (usually long-standing business customers). This will enable them to raise necessary capital directly from the capital market, helped by the banks' payment guarantee. This is essentially a domestic instrument, so the currency of the denomination is the same as the local currency of the parties involved. The letter of credit is similar in that a bank provides a payment guarantee for its customer. However, at least two currencies are involved in this process (e.g., the AUD and the USD if an Australian importer has to pay in the USD).

duration of 30–180 days. Either the exporter's or the importer's bank provides the necessary financial guarantee (payment guarantee) on behalf of the importer. The other bank's role is usually limited to payment and document processing without financial commitments. This frees exporters from having to rely solely on their importers' credit standing and integrity, thus allowing less well-known firms to engage in international trade. The most common arrangement is for the importer's bank to provide this financial guarantee and the exporter's bank to assist in the paperwork. The former is called an opening bank, and the latter an advising bank in this arrangement. The letter of credit created in this process is called an import letter of credit. If the importer is located in a country with a high level of economic and financial uncertainties and its bank is relatively unknown, then the exporter might be able to convince its own bank to provide the financial guarantee required. In this case, the roles would be reversed between the two banks, and the resulting letter of credit would be an export letter of credit. Many countries with export-driven economies operate government banks or agencies specifically set up to provide assistance to their exporters, and the export letter of credit is included in the list of support. This is discussed in a later section of this chapter. On rare occasions, both banks can provide financial guarantees, either taking a portion of the guarantee, each adding up to 100%, or providing a backup guarantee to the other bank.

3.2.1. *Example of letter of credit creation process*

This section discusses the process of financing an international trade via an import letter of credit in more detail. Four main parties are involved in this process: the importer and the exporter, located in separate countries, and their two respective banks. In addition, an additional financier can enter this arrangement as a money market investor. There are four key documents being created in the process; these are a letter of credit (LC) issued by the importer's bank upon the request from the importer, a bill of exchange which is either a sight or a time draft issued by the exporter requesting payment, a banker's acceptance, and a bill of lading (or airway bill if good are sent by air).

We take an example of trade between an Australian wine producer and a Korean wine importer to illustrate the process of an import letter of credit-financed international trade. In order to effect the trade, the exporter must ensure that full payment to the exporter is guaranteed by a bank with good standing. The importer, K-WineImports, applies for a documentary import letter of credit from its local bank, Woori bank, as shown in Exhibit 3.1. In particular, it states that the payment is via negotiating a time draft, which is shown in Exhibit 3.2 (Panel A). The draft, also known as a bill of exchange, is issued by the exporter to request payment from the importer under the conditions set in the LC. The payment is in favour of the exporter's bank, and it will be effected in 30 days' time after the initial sighting by the importer's bank in the case of a time draft. Alternatively, payment falls due immediately after sighting it by the importer's bank in the case of a sight draft. Once it is accepted for payment by the importer's bank, it becomes a banker's draft, which can be freely traded in the money market if desired. The banker's acceptance is shown in Exhibit 3.2 (Panel B).

In this example, there are a total of 16 steps involved, as illustrated in Exhibit 3.3. Steps 1 through 4 occur before the shipment of the wine, which is step 5. Steps 6 through 11 occur immediately after shipment. An external financier, a money market investor, may also participate in this process and steps 12 and 13 depict such a transaction. At the maturity of the time draft, payment processing is shown in steps 14–16. We detail the steps involved in this trade below.

3.2.1.1. *Before shipment: Steps 1–4*

Assume a Korean importer, K-WineImports, of world wines wishes to add Australian wines to its catalogue. Its search results revealed a small Australian wine producer, Fine Aussie Wines, located in Hunter Valley, NSW, Australia, would be a good fit. In **Step 1**, K-WineImports contacts Fine Aussie Wines and makes an agreement to purchase 1,000 mixed cases of Australian wines worth AUD100,000. They agree on the terms of the sale and sign a contract specifying the conditions. The terms of sale include the price, variety, and quantity of wine, the terms of payments (30 days in this case), the currency denomination of the trade, the banking arrangements, etc.

In **Step 2**, the importer approaches its bank, Woori Bank, for an import letter of credit and submits an application, including the contract details. The importer's bank, in this instance, is referred to as an opening bank (OB) since it is the one creating or 'opening' an LC account with associated financial obligations. OB approves the LC application after

Agreement for Documentary Letter of Credit
L/C Number 123456

Woori Bank
Hoehyeon-dong, Jung-gu,
Seoul, Korea

Advising Bank:

Commonwealth Bank of Australia,
Darling Park Tower 1, 201 Sussex
Street, Sydney, New South Wales,
Australia

Applicant:

K-WineImports,
123 MyungDongGil,
Seoul, Korea

Beneficiary:

Fine Aussie Wine
Pty. Ltd, 123
Wine Avenue,
Hunter Valley,
NSW, 2310,
Australia

Amount:
AUD 100,000

Expiry date: December 31 2023 in the country of beneficiary
Latest shipment date: November 30 2023

We hereby issue this irrevocable documentary letter of credit in favour of the beneficiary noted above which is available by negotiation of draft at 90 days sight drawn on Woori Bank bearing the cause 'drawn under documentary credit no. L/C1234 of Woori Bank' and accompanied by following documents:

1 Signed commercial invoice in triplicate.
2 Packing list issued by beneficiary
3 Australian customs invoice
4 Marine insurance policy
5 Full set of original clean shipped 'On BOARD' ocean bills of lading issued by shipping company plus two non-negotiable copies made out to order of Woori Bank. Marked 'FREIGHT PREPAID' and notify the applicant.
6 Evidencing shipment of 1,000 cases of wine produced by Fine Wine Pty Ltd, comprising of
    200 cases each of Cabernet Sauvignon
    200 cases of Merlot
    200 cases of Shiraz
    200 cases of Riesling
    200 cases of Sauvignon Blac

Exhibit 3.1. Import letter of credit.

Panel A: Time draft

BILL OF EXCHANGE

DRAWN TO CONDITION OF LETTER OF CREDIT #123456
DATED DECEMBER 31 2023 OF WOORI BANK ON ACCOUNT OF
K-WINEIMPORTS,123 MYUNGDONGGIL, SEOUL, KOREA

DATE: 30 NOVEMBER 2023

30 Days After Sight Of This Bill

Pay to the Order of **Commonwealth Bank of Australia** AUD 100,000

Fine Aussie Wine Pty. Ltd
123 Wine Avenue
Hunter Valley, NSW, 2310
Australia

Panel B: Banker's acceptance

BILL OF EXCHANGE

DRAWN TO CONDITION OF LETTER OF CREDIT #123456
DATED DECEMBER 31 2023 OF WOORI BANK ON ACCOUNT OF
K-WINEIMPORTS,123 MYUNGDONGGIL, SEOUL, KOREA

ACCEPTED

DATE: 30 NOVEMBER 2023

30 Days After Sight Of This Bill

WOORI BANK
HOEHYEON-
DONG, JUNG-
GU,
SEOUL, KOREA

Pay to the Order of **Commonwealth Bank of Australia** AUD 100,000

AUTHORIZED
SIGNATURE

Fine Aussie Wine Pty. Ltd
123 Wine Avenue
Hunter Valley, NSW, 2310
Australia

Exhibit 3.2. Time draft and banker's acceptance in international trade.

Source: Adapted from Madura (2018).

checking the application and the credit standing of the importer. Exhibit 3.1 details the LC opened by OB, Woori bank, in favour of the exporter's bank, Commonwealth bank. The LC sets out the terms of shipment and documents that must be presented to OB for payment. In **Step 3**, OB sends the LC via airmail, telexes, or SWIFT,[2] or other electronic means, to the exporter's bank. The exporter's bank is an advising bank (AB) as it only provides an advisory and payment processing

[2]Society for Worldwide Interbank Financial Telecommunications.

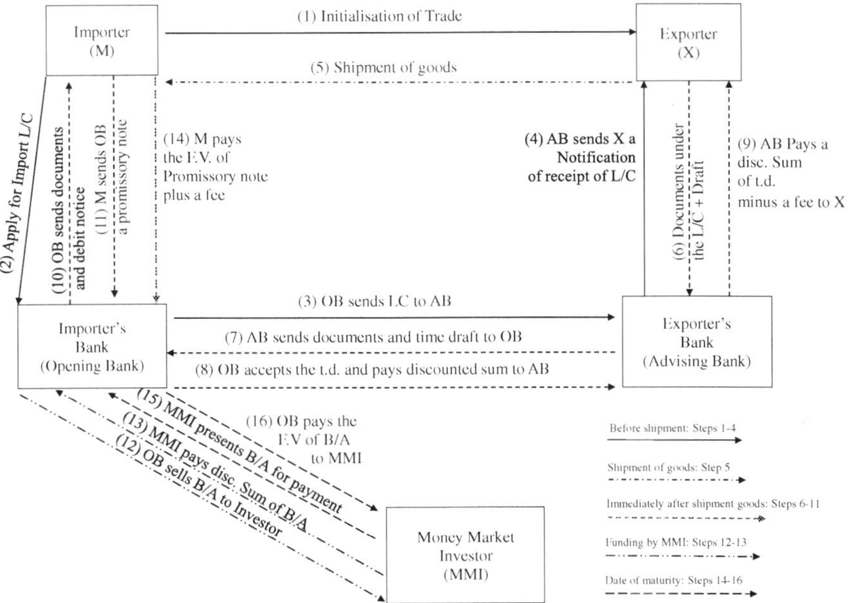

Exhibit 3.3. An import letter of credit financed international trade.

Source: Adapted from Eun *et al.* (2021) and Madura (2018).

service. AB then sends a notification of the receipt of the LC to the exporter in **Step 4**.

3.2.1.2. *Shipment of goods: Step 5*

After receiving a notification of an approved LC indicating a payment guarantee for the sale, the exporter organises shipment of the 1,000 cases of wine as agreed (**Step 5**). The documents prepared in this step include shipping-related documents, such as a bill of lading, insurance documents, and a bill of exchange (or draft). *A bill of lading* is a receipt issued by a shipping company for goods shipped on board a named vessel. It includes the terms and conditions under which the shipping company carries the goods and also acts as a document title (ownership) to the goods. It must be presented to the shipping company when the shipment is collected at the destination port. If the shipment is by air, an airway bill replaces a bill of lading. *A bill of exchange* comprises three parties to the contract: a drawer who draws the bill (exporter), a drawee who is a party to whom the bill is addressed (importer or its bank who is responsible for making the payment), and a payee (exporter or its bank). This can be either a sight draft which requires an immediate payment upon sight of the document by the drawee (similar to a bank cheque which is essentially a sight draft) or a time draft which is a payment order to pay the trade amount by a specified future date.

3.2.1.3. *Immediately after shipment: Steps 6–11*

In **Step 6**, immediately after shipping the wine to the importer, the exporter sends all the required documents under the LC to its bank and a bill of exchange to AB. Exhibit 3.2 (Panel A) shows the bill of exchange created in the process. It clearly states the amount to be paid to the exporter's bank and the due date of payment. AB then sends the documents and the bill of exchange (a time draft in this case) to OB for further processing (**Step** 7). In **Step 8**, OB examines the completeness and validity of the documents forwarded by AB and accepts the bill of exchange if everything is in order. OB officially accepts the bill by putting its stamp on the bill for a paper-based bill of exchange or updating its electronic record for an online bill. OB then provides a commitment to pay the amount in full at maturity to AB.[3] Once it is accepted, the bill of exchange becomes a banker's acceptance (BA) that can be traded in the secondary market. Exhibit 3.2 (Panel B) shows the BA created from this process. At the same time as accepting the bill, OB discounts the BA and credits the discounted value to AB.[4] AB in turn pays the exporter the proceeds minus a fee (**Step 9**). By this point, the process is completed for the exporter, and it can use the discounted funds received to finance the next production cycle. In **Step 10**, OB sends all the shipping documents along with a debit note to the importer to be used for the collection of goods upon arrival. The importer then sends a promissory note (with AB as the payee) with a face value equal to the invoice amount and the same maturity as that of the BA in **Step 11**. When the wines arrive, the importer inspects the conditions of the shipment for damages and compliance with the original sales

[3] In the case of a sight draft, OB needs to pay the full amount stipulated to AB at this point.

[4] Discounting of BA can also be carried out by AB. In this case, AB can either hold the BA until maturity or sell it on the capital market for immediate payment.

agreement and, if satisfied, collects them from the shipping company by presenting the bill of lading it received from AB in Step 10.

3.2.1.4. *Money market investor: Steps 12 and 13*

Once OB discounts the BA and pays AB, it may choose to sell the BA in the secondary market for a discounted sum of the face value (**Steps 12 and 13**).[5] This creates the necessary cash inflow for OB to fund the cash outflow in Step 8.

3.2.1.5. *Date of maturity of the BA: Steps 14–16*

At the maturity date of the BA, the importer honours the promissory note and pays the face value of the note plus a fee to OB (**Step 14**). OB, in turn, pays the face value of the BA to the holder of the BA upon presentation (**Steps 15 and 16**).

Exhibit 3.4 summarise the level of participation of each party in the LC process in this example. The importer and the exporter successfully achieve the aim of the trade. The importer receives the goods in good order as specified in the LC and pays the face value of the agreed amount at the maturity of the LC period. The exporter receives a discounted sum of the invoice amount from its bank shortly after successfully shipping the goods. The two banks service their clients and earn fee income. The importer's bank takes on the responsibility of opening the LC, and it earns a fee equal to the difference between the price of the BA received from the importer and the discounted amount of the LC paid to the exporter's banks. The exporter's bank receives a fee from the exporter for handling the paperwork and payment services. Finally, the money market investor earns an interest income equal to the difference between the face value of the BA and the discounted sum of the face value it paid to the importer's bank. In this arrangement, the importer's bank is the one that provides a payment guarantee in this trade, so its fee income should be the highest among the three financial market participants.

---

[5]Alternatively, OB may choose to hold the BA until maturity. This is because a BA represents an excellent tool for liquidity management due to low default risk (thanks to the bank's guarantee), relatively higher returns than other short-term instruments (such as treasure bills, overnight cash, etc.) and high liquidity.

Money/ Goods Flow	Importer	Exporter	Opening Bank	Advising Bank	Money Market Investor
In	Goods (12)	Discounted sum of Invoice amount (9)	Discounted value of BA from Money Market Investor (13) Face value of B/A (PN) plus a fee from importer (14)	Discounted value of BA from OB (8)	Face value of BA to money market investor (16)
Out	Face value of Invoice plus fee (13)	Goods (5)	Discounted value of B/A to AB (8) Face value of B/A to money market investor (16)	Payment of the discounted sum minus a fee to the exporter (9)	Discounted value of BA from Money Market Investor (13)
Net Income			Fee(13)	Fee (9)	Difference between (16) and (13)

Exhibit 3.4. Direction of flows of goods and money.

3.2.2. *Different types of letters of credit*

Exhibit 3.3 is an example of an unconfirmed, irrevocable LC where the payment guarantee is provided only by OB. If the LC is confirmed, an additional guarantee is provided by AB, and this affords an additional layer of protection for the exporter by having two banks guarantee payments. There are, however, many different variations to the process described above, depending on the extent of the responsibilities of each of the four participants. Most importantly, different types of letters of credit are associated with each variation.

The LC discussed in the previous example is guaranteed only by OB and is *unconfirmed* by AB. If AB confirms it, it will provide an additional layer of protection for the exporter, as AB is now committed to making the payment if OB fails to do so. Although another bank located in the importer's country may act as a second bank, it is more common for the exporter to ask its own bank to act in this role if the exporter is still concerned about the creditworthiness of the importer's banks. A separate Letter of credit can be drawn by AB (or another bank) based on the terms of the first LC. Alternatively, the LC opened by OB can be amended to include this additional commitment by AB or another bank. A *confirmed* LC adds little practical benefits but incurs additional costs to the exporter if OB has a solid reputation with sound management practices and is located in a politically stable country. However, if OB is not well known and is subjected to significant country risk, this additional protection may be worthwhile even at the extra cost.

A *revocable* LC is where OB can unilaterally amend the conditions of or cancel the LC at any time before the payment is made without consent from the exporter, the beneficiary. This is intended to provide a means of arranging payment rather than guaranteeing it. Clearly, this is not ideal for the exporter as there can be no firm guarantee of payment. As such, this form of LC is not frequently used in practice. An *irrevocable* LC is one that cannot be changed or cancelled in any way without the consent of all parties involved. This is to ensure that, once agreed upon, all the trade terms are final and cannot be unilaterally modified in any way.

Most LCs are for financing a short-term one-off international trade valid for a single transaction. However, there are instances where a sequence of transactions with the same terms and conditions between the same two trade partners can occur. A single LC written for one transaction can be used again for subsequent ones, provided that the terms of the transactions and the risk characteristics of the importer do not change across the transactions. In the LC example discussed in the previous section, if K-Wineimports is satisfied with the initial trade and wishes to import the same amount and variety of wines every two months over the next 12 months, then as long as Fine Aussie Wines agrees, one revolving LC can be drawn instead of six separate non-revolving ones. In general, thus, a *revolving* LC is suitable when the same terms and conditions (regarding the price and quantity of goods, payment conditions, carrier, banks involved, etc.) apply over a number of separate transactions between the importer and the exporter (e.g., revolving contracts to supply specified units of certain goods every period). However, depending on the number of revolving periods allowed, the total amount of credit involved could be very large, and as such, revolving letters of credit are usually revocable. A *cumulative revolving credit* allows the unused portion of the limit amount in each period to be used in a later period, whereas a non-cumulative credit does not.

A transferable (and irrevocable) LC is one where the whole or some of the LC amount to an exporter can be transferred to another party (a secondary beneficiary), who is typically a supplier to the exporter. This is useful when a major supplier to the exporter needs a guarantee of financial performance by the exporter. In our example, if Fine Aussie Wines, the exporter, needs to pay its suppliers (caskets, wine bottles, and other equipment suppliers), it can ask the LC to include a provision for a portion of the amount to be transferable to a third party. If the suppliers are required to be paid before a discounted sum of the LC is paid to Fine Aussie Wines, then it can ask for an appropriate provision to be added to the LC at the time of issuance. There can be an additional fee payable to OB for this extra service.

In terms of exporter protection, the followings give varying degrees of protection in descending order:

1. an irrevocable LC issued by a reputable domestic (i.e., located in the exporter's country) bank,
2. an irrevocable LC issued by a foreign (i.e., located in the importer's country) bank and confirmed by a reputable domestic bank,
3. an irrevocable and unconfirmed LC issued by a foreign (i.e., located in the importer's country) bank,
4. a revocable LC.

3.3. Forfaiting

Forfaiting is a process of financing an international trade when LC financing is not available. There can be broadly three such cases: *First,* LCs are for financing short-term international trades of less than 180 days, in general, and cater for a wide variety of trade transactions. Banks do not typically issue LCs for a term longer than 12 months, so they are not suitable for longer-term transactions. *Second,* LC financing is generally unavailable in international trades when the credit standings of the importer and its bank are considered too low, and the exporter's bank is unwilling to provide a financial guarantee. Third, there may be a significant country risk in the importer's country, such as potential foreign exchange controls and other systemic risks. As a result, the financial guarantee provided in LCs opened by the importer's bank would not be satisfactory to the exporter or its bank. However, the exporter may still be keen to engage with the importer as the importer's country presents significant opportunities despite the high level of risk. In these cases, without a bank providing support via an LC, the exporter in a longer-term or a risker international trade must bear the default risk until the maturity of the trade or find an alternative method of transferring the risk and secure an early payment. Forfaiting is one such alternative available to exporters in that situation. It is suitable for international trades in specific goods, mostly capital goods and equipment worth USD 100,000 in value and higher that require longer terms (typically 1–5 years) for settlements. The importer of capital goods often requires a long enough time to generate an income stream to pay off the import.

Forfaiting allows such an alternative whereby the exporter can secure an early payment from a third party that also assumes the counterparty risk (Beard and Thomas, 2006). The name of this form of trade financing is derived from a French word, *forfait*. The exporter forfeits all future payments related to the trade receivables to the forfaiteur for a discounted sum on a non-recourse basis. That is, once the forfaiteur pays the discounted sum to the exporter, there is no recourse to the exporter even if both the importer and importer's bank fail to pay the full value of the receivables at maturity. The counterparty default risk is completely transferred to the forfaiteur. However, the exporter is still responsible for successfully completing the shipment with proper documentation and for the quality and quality of the goods sent. Forfaiting benefits the exporter since it receives the upfront payment of the discounted sum of the face value minus a fee and so is free from various risks associated with the payment transaction (currency risk, political risk, etc.). The forfaiteur (forfaiting firm) assumes all the risks, and so it needs to be compensated by applying a heavier rate of discount to the face value of the receivables than the current market discount rates for BAs with the same terms to maturity. The risk premium applied to the discount rate depends on the perceived default risk of the importer, the political and economic environment of the importer's country, and other risk dimensions.

Forfaiting has its origin in the difficulty faced by traders in the east-west trades in the 1960s, where western exporters found it difficult to locate banks or government agencies to finance exports to countries behind the iron curtain in eastern Europe. The risks were considered too high for western banks to participate, and the credit standing of the banks in the importer's countries was considered too low. Thus, demand existed for a financial institution to provide service to the parties involved in this trade. Credit Suisse (via its subsidiary A. G. Zurich) was one of the first banks to facilitate a forfaiting-based sale of US grain to eastern European importers. The US exporters received immediate payment, and the eastern European importers received a term credit. This process is suitable for trades involving little-known importers located in a country with higher inherent risks. This form of trade financing has helped economic development in many developing regions of the world from the 1960s. However,

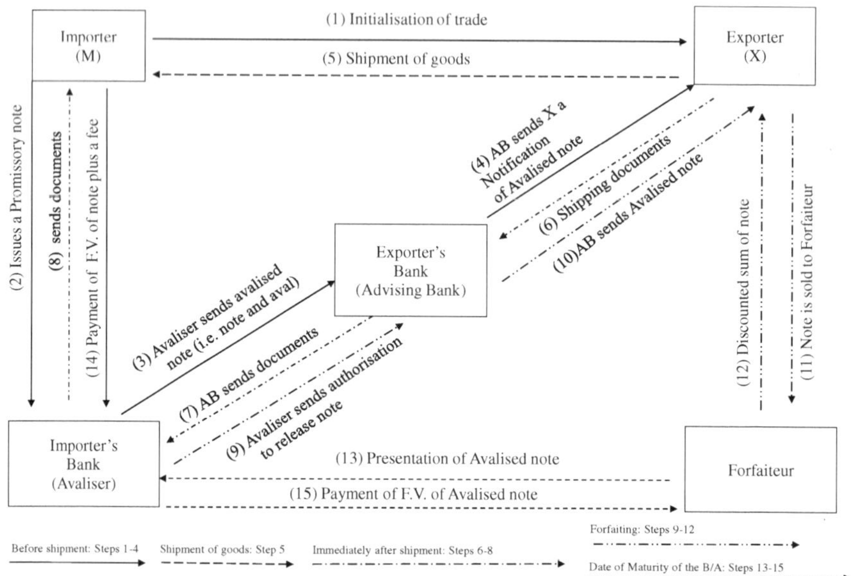

Exhibit 3.5. A forfaiting process.

Source: Adapted from Bishop (2004).

forfaiting remains substantially European in nature, with the rest of the developed world accounting for only a fraction of the global volume.

Steps involved in the forfaiting process illustrated in Exhibit 3.5 are explained in the following section.

3.3.1. *Before shipment: Steps 1–4*

In **Step 1**, the importer and exporter agree on the terms of the sale and sign a contract specifying the conditions. The terms of sale to be agreed upon include the price and quantity of the sale, terms of payments, currency denomination of the trade, and banking arrangements. In **Step 2**, the importer approaches its bank for a payment guarantee on a promissory note it is issuing in the amount of the face value of the trade. The importer's bank provides an aval, which is a document stating the bank's payment guarantee on the Promissory note. The promissory note together with the aval is referred to as an avalised note, and the importer's bank is now called an avaliser. The avaliser passes the avalised note to the exporter's bank (AB) in **Step 3,** which in turn sends a notification of its receipt to the exporter (**Step 4**).

3.3.2. *Shipment of goods: Step 5*

In **Step 5**, the exporter prepares the shipment of goods and the necessary trade documents, a bill of lading, and insurance documents.

3.3.3. *Immediately after shipment: Steps 6–8*

The exporter sends all the required documents to AB (**Step 6**). AB then forwards the documents to the avaliser (**Step** 7). The importer then receives the documents (**Step 8**) and uses them to collect the goods.

3.3.4. *Forfaiting: Steps 9–12*

In **Step 9**, the avaliser sends an authorisation to the exporter's bank to release the avalised note to the exporter. The exporter receives the note (**Step 10**) and then sells it to the Forfaiteur (**Step 11**) for a discounted sum.

3.3.5. *Date of maturity: Steps 13–15*

At the date of maturity, the Forfaitur presents the avalised note to the avaliser for payment (**Step 13**). The avaliser then pays the Forfaiteur the face value of the note (**Step 15**), drawing from the account of the importer (**Step 14**).

Although the forfaiting process is similar to the BA process, there are important differences. *First,* the trade receivables are sold to a forfaiting firm (a forfaiteur, usually a bank) on a non-recourse basis. Should OB and the importer fail to honour the financial commitment, the loss is borne by the forfaiteur. The Forfaiteur forfeits the right to force the exporter to pursue the defaulting importer. On the other hand, LC trades are on a recourse basis. So, if the importer or its bank fails to pay the required amount of the trade, the money market investor in the LC example in the previous section has recourse against the exporter. In forfaiting, once the exporter sells the avalised note to the forfaiteur, the exporter is free from any financial obligations to the forfaiteur even if the importer or its bank fails to pay the forfaiteur at maturity. *Second,* although some governments accept BAs as collateral for discounted loans, which gives the holders additional flexibility in liquidity management, only private institutions participate in the forfaiting process due to its higher risk nature.

3.4. Factoring

Factoring has been used for financing domestic transactions for quite a long time, especially in developing countries in Asia and Latin America, although it has not been commonly used by US exporters. However, factoring has also been used in financing international trade in recent years. Factoring firms (mostly a bank or bank-owned subsidiary and is called a *factor*) provide up to 80–85% of an invoice amount to the exporter, usually on a non-recourse basis at the time of export, with the remainder minus a fee paid when the importer pays in full. Factors simply take over the responsibility of collecting trade receivables from the exporter. They collect the receivables directly from the importer in its local country in accordance with local business practices so as to minimise conflict. Factoring can be with or without a recourse agreement. Factoring is suitable for exporters who sell to a large number of importers. In essence, factoring is similar to forfaiting. However, one important difference is that factoring caters for a large number of relatively small trade receivables, whereas forfeiting is usually for an individual (and mostly large denominated sums) receivable.

Exhibit 3.6 shows a typical factoring process. As soon as a trade agreement is made between the exporter and the importer (**Step 1**), the exporter enters an agreement with a factor to buy the receivable resulting from this trade (**Step 2**). The exporter may also consult the factor before finalising the trade, in which case the first two steps are reversed. The factor then sends a notification of the factoring agreement to the importer (**Step 3**). The exporter ships the goods along with the associated shipping documents (**Step 4**). This differs from the LC and the forfaiting processes we discussed in the previous sections, where the shipping documents are first sent to OB. Once the shipment is completed and the importer receives the goods in good order, the factor pays 80% (it varies between 80–85%) of the trade invoice to the exporter on a non-recourse basis (**Step 5**). At this point, the responsibility of collecting payment lies solely with the factor, and the exporter is free to move on to the next production cycle without recourse. At maturity of the trade term, the importer pays the full value of the invoice to the factor (**Step 6**). If there is a default by the importer,

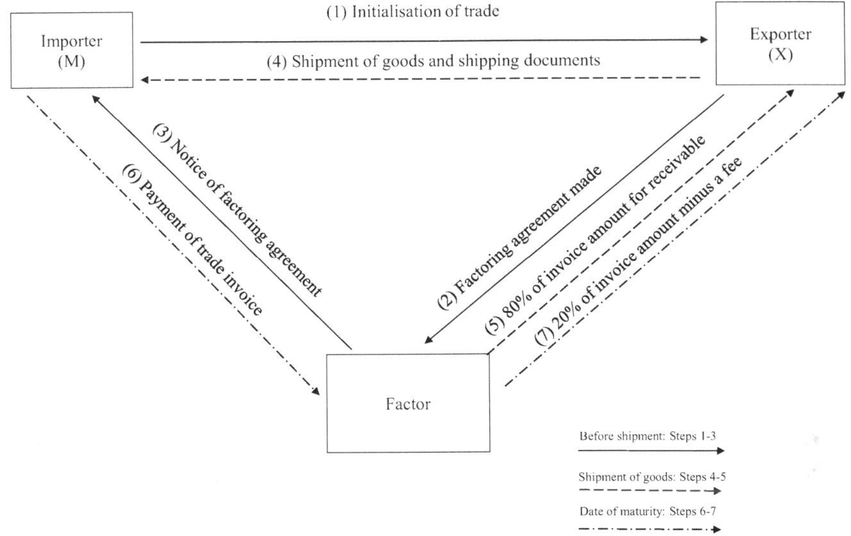

Exhibit 3.6. A factoring process.

then Step 6 will not occur at maturity, and so the following step (Step 7) will also not occur. The factor is expected to negotiate with the defaulting importer for a resolution. If there is no default in Step 6, the factor then pays the remaining 20% of the trade invoice minus a fee to the exporter (**Step** 7).

Exhibit 3.7 summarises the characteristics of LC, forfaiting, and factoring-based international trades. Banks are involved in all three forms of international trade finance, and each form is suitable for specific circumstances. LC financing is suitable for short-term international trade in general goods where the importer is able to obtain a payment guarantee from a bank with good international credit standing. Forfaiting is suitable for medium to long-term trades when the exporter requires immediate payment on a non-recourse basis due to the higher risk of the trade. Factoring is appropriate for exporters with multiple short-term trade receivables that need to be used to finance the next round of the production cycle. LC and forfaiting generate a short-term instrument that can easily be traded in the secondary market. Whereas LC is universally used across many international trades, forfaiting is more popular in Europe and factoring is mostly used in the developing countries of Asia and Latin America.

	Characteristics	Letter of credit	Forfaiting	Factoring
1	**Purpose**	Importer's bank providing financial guarantee to exporter via banker's acceptance	Exporter selling a right to a trade receivable (via a promissory note issued by importer and guaranteed by its bank) to a forfaiteur for immediate payment	Exporter selling trade receivables to a factor for an immediate payment
2	**Recourse/Non-Recourse to exporter**	Recourse	Non-recourse	Both Recourse and Non-recourse
3	**Trade duration/receivable maturity**	Short durations, 30–180 days	Medium to long term, 3–5 years	Short durations, less than 90 days
4	**Type of products traded**	Ordinary goods	Capital goods or equipment	Ordinary goods
5	**Trade amount**	Wide variety of invoice amounts	Minimum USD500,000 in most cases	Small denominations, and multiple accounts
6	**Proportion of face value covered**	100%	100%	80–90%
7	**Who pays the fees**	Exporter and Importer	Importer	Exporter
8	**Negotiable Instrument**	Banker's acceptance is negotiable	Avalised note is negotiable	Not applicable
9	**Tradeable in the secondary market**	Yes	Yes	Not applicable
10	**Exporters using this service**	Across the world	Initially East-West trades in European countries	Developing Asian and Latin American countries

Exhibit 3.7. Comparisons among letter of credit, forfaiting and factoring.

3.5. Other Forms of Trade Finance

3.5.1. *Payment in advance (Cash in advance)*

In situations where an importer's capability to make payments in time and/or the importer's bank lacks credibility in providing a payment guarantee, the exporter may insist on advance payment before shipment is made. This situation may arise when the importer has a less than acceptable reputation in past dealings or when some possibility of the importer's government imposing payment restrictions (foreign exchange controls, for example) exists.

3.5.2. *Open account*

When the importer and the exporter have been doing business with each other for a long time without any payment-related problems (non-payment, delay in payment, etc.), they can simplify the payment process by trading on an open account basis. The importer can ask the exporter to add the value of the current shipment of goods to the account that the former holds with the latter, and the account will be paid at regular intervals. This is suitable when there is no perceived risk of default on the part of the importer and the longer-term trade commitments between the two parties necessitate such a cost-saving measure.

3.5.3. *Consignment*

In cases where the exporter wishes to retain ownership of the goods until they are sold, it may send the goods on a consignment basis. This implies that the payment is not made until the goods are sold in the market, and the importer has the revenue from the sale to pay the exporter. In the meantime, the ownership of the goods remains with the exporter. This arrangement suits a situation when the exporter has a positive view of the market potential and the integrity and commitment of the importer, but the importer is unable to secure a letter of credit.

3.5.4. *Countertrade*

Popular forms of counter trades include barter trade; counter purchase, where exporters are required to spend a specified portion of the trade value in purchasing goods or services in the importer's country; buyback agreements that require exporters to buy goods produced from the products they sold to the importers; and switch trade which is used when exporters who are paid in kind sell it to a switch trader who in turn conducts further countertrade until hard currency position is achieved. One advantage of countertrade is for exporters to have access to developing countries that are otherwise unable to obtain trade financing or have access to hard currencies. A well-known example of a countertrade is between Pepsi-Cola and the Soviet Union in the 1970s. The former exported the soft drink to the latter in return for an exclusive 10-year distribution and marketing rights for Stolichnaya Vodka in the US, which led to the creation of a premium vodka market in the US.

3.6. Export Credit Agencies

Exports are a method of expanding the size of an economy beyond what its domestic market would allow. By tapping into demands from foreigners, a country can develop key industries that require scale economies and higher entry requirements, even if the domestic market is of insufficient size. Importing the technologies and materials needed to support a country's export sector is thus crucial in the economic development of many current and past developing countries that focus on international trade. Banks and other financiers of international trade provide financial protection for both exporters and importers in their own countries. As discussed in the previous sections, there are various methods of providing support for international trade. Normally, banks and other financial institutions are involved on their own to provide this service for their clients via an LC, forfeiting, and factoring services. In other cases, private institutions may not be able to get involved due to higher inherent risks in international transactions because of the types of goods being traded and the counterparty involved. Government agencies may then step in to facilitate international transactions that private sector banks may regard as beyond their risk tolerance. Many advanced and developing countries run export-import banks or export credit agencies (ECA) to provide direct or indirect financing for domestic companies engaged in international transactions in their countries. Exhibit 3.8 lists some of the export finance agencies across the world that are set up to provide financial and non-financial support to their country's international traders.

ECAs can be privately owned banks, government agencies, or some combination of both. They can take the form of a bank and specialise in financing international trades in the forms discussed in the previous sections in this chapter, along with performing normal financial

Country	ECA	Website
Algeria	Compagnie Algérienne Assurance et de Garantie des Exportations, (CAGEX)	https://www.cagex.dz/
Australia	Export Finance Australia (EFA)	https://www.exportfinance.gov.au/
Austria	Oesterreichische Kontrollbank AG (OeKB)	https://www.oekb.at/
Bangladesh	Export Import Bank of Bangladesh Limited	https://www.eximbankbd.com/
Belgium	Office national du Ducroire/Nationale Delcrederedienst (ONDD)	https://www.credendo.com/
Brazil	Brazilian Guarantees Agency (ABGF)	https://www.abgf.gov.br/
	Brazilian Development Bank (BNDES)	http://bndes.gov.br/
Canada	Export Development Canada (EDC)	https://www.edc.ca/
Mainland China	Export Import Bank of China (Exim)	http://english.eximbank.gov.cn/
	China Export & Credit Insurance Corporation (Sinosure)	https://www.sinosure.com.cn/
	China Development Bank (CDB)	http://www.cdb.com.cn/
	People's Insurance Company of China (PICC)	http://picc.com/
Hong Kong	Hong Kong Export Credit Insurance Corporation	http://www.hkecic.com/
Colombia	Banco de Comercio Exterior de Colombia (Bancóldex)	
Czech Republic	Export Guarantee and Insurance Corporation (EGAP)	https://www.egap.cz/
	Czech Export Bank	https://www.ceb.cz/en/
Denmark	Eksport Kredit Fonden (EKF)	https://www.ekf.dk/en
Egypt	Export Credit Guarantee Company of Egypt, (ECGE)	https://www.ege-eg.com/
Estonia	Kredex Krediidikindlustus (EST)	https://kredex.ee/
Finland	Finnvera and its subsidiary Finnish Export Credit Ltd (FEC)	https://www.finnvera.fi/
France	Compagnie Française d'Assurance pour le Commerce Extérieur (COFACE)	https://www.coface.com/
	Direction des Relations Economiques Extérieures (Ministère de l'Economie) (DREE)	https://data.bnf.fr/fr/
Germany	Euler Hermes Kreditversicherungs AG	https://www.eulerhermes.com/
	AuslandsGeschäftsAbsicherung der Bundesrepublik Deutschland	https://www.agaportal.de/
Greece	Export Credit Insurance Organisation (ECIO)	https://oaep.gr/
Hungary	Hungarian Export Credit Insurance Ltd (MEHIB), Hungarian Export Import Bank	https://exim.hu/en/
India	Export Import Bank of India, ECGC Limited	https://www.ecgcltd.in/
Iran	Export Guarantee Fund of Iran (EGFI)	https://egfi.ir/
Israel	Israel Foreign Trade Risks Insurance Corporation, (ASHRA)	
Italy	SACE S.p.A. Servizi Assicurativi del Commercio Estero	https://www.sace.it/
Japan	Japan Bank for International Cooperation (JBIC)	https://www.jbic.go.jp/
	Nippon Export and Investment Insurance (NEXI)	https://www.nexi.go.jp/
Jordan	Jordan Loan Guarantee Cooperation (JLGC)	https://www.jlgc.com/
Luxembourg	Office du Ducroire (ODD)	https://odl.lu/
Mexico	Banco Nacional de Comercio Exterior (Bancomext)	https://www.bancomext.com/en/
Morocco	Société Marocaine d'Assurance à l'Exportation	https://www.smaex.com/
Netherlands	Atradius	https://group.atradius.com/
New Zealand	Export Credit Office (ECO)	https://exportcredit.treasury.govt.nz/
Nigeria	Nigerian Export Import Bank	https://neximbank.com.ng/
Norway	The Norwegian Guarantee Institute for Export Credits (GIEK), Export Credit Norway	https://www.eksfin.no/
Pakistan	The EXIM Bank of Pakistan	http://eximbank.gov.pk/
Poland	**Korporacja Ubezpieczeń Kredytów Eksportowych (KUKE)**	https://kuke.com.pl/en
Portugal	**Companhia de Seguro de Créditos**	https://www.cosec.pt/
Russia	Export Insurance Agency of Russia	https://www.exiar.ru/
Saudi Arabia	Saudi Export Program, (SEP)	http://www.sfd.gov.sa/
South Africa	Export Import Credit Insurance Agency (EICIA)	https://www.ecic.co.za/
South Korea	Korea Trade Insurance Corporation (KSURE)	https://www.ksure.or.kr/en/
	The Export Import Bank of Korea (KEXIM)	http://www.koreaexim.go.kr/
Slovakia	Export Import Bank of the Slovak Republic (Eximbank SR)	
Sri Lanka	Sri Lanka Export Credit Insurance Corporation (SLECIC)	https://www.slecic.lk/
Spain	Compañía Española de Seguros de Crédito a la Exportación CESCE (Ministerio de Economía)	https://www.cesce.es/
Sweden	Exportkreditnämnden (EKN)	https://www.ekn.se/
Switzerland	Swiss Export Risk Insurance (SERV)	https://www.serv-ch.com/en/
Taiwan	Export–Import Bank of the Republic of China	https://www.eximbank.com.tw/
Turkey	Export Credit Bank of Turkey (Türk Eximbank)	https://www.eximbank.gov.tr/en
Ukraine	Export Credit Agency (ECA)	
United Arab Emirates	Etihad Credit Insurance (ECI)	https://eci.gov.ae/
United Kingdom	United Kingdom Export Finance (UKEF)	https://www.gov.uk/
United States	Export Import Bank of the United States (ExIm Bank), CoBank	https://www.exim.gov/

Exhibit 3.8. Export Credit Agencies in countries around the world.

Source: Listed countries' ECA websites.

intermediation functions. Alternatively, they can be set up as non-bank government or privately held agencies that provide direct (loans to exporters and importers) and indirect funding (loans to the banks of exporters and importers that will make loans to their customers). In addition to financing and payment guarantees, they also provide insurance services to help international trade. Their role has become more important, especially after the two recent global crises (the Global financial crisis of 2008 and the European debt crisis of 2009) as banks became more risk-averse.

References

Beard, A. and Thomas, R. (2006). *Trade Finance Handbook.* Thomson.

Bishop, E. (2004). *Finance of International Trade*. Elsevier.

Eun, C., Resnick, B. and Chuluun, T. (2021). *International Financial Management*, 9th ed., McGrawHill, New York.

Madura, J. (2018). *International Financial Management*, 13th ed., Thompson. Chapter 19 Financing International Trade.

Chapter 4

Foreign Exchange Market

4.1. Introduction

Commercial banks have traditionally provided foreign exchange services for various types of customers. They service their retail and corporate customers in their foreign exchange requirements by buying or selling foreign currencies on behalf of their customers. They offer both spot and forward[1] (outright and swap) contracts and over-the-counter foreign exchange derivative products. When they act on behalf of their customers, their main aim is to minimise the costs of providing the service, and their role is not to take risks in the market. This is the traditional service function performed by international banks. As such, foreign exchange trading was treated as a cost centre of their operations. In addition to customer service-driven participation, commercial banks also trade foreign currencies on their own accounts. That is, they trade for profit, and some have grown to rely on this source of income. The foreign exchange trade volume for the profit motive has taken a significant portion of the market, consistently accounting for the bulk of the market activities. Trading in foreign exchange by itself does not lead to economically productive activities, so it is questionable whether the active participation of

[1] An outright forward contract requires the seller to deliver a specified amount of foreign currency at some future date. The seller of the contract assumes the resulting exchange rate risk. A foreign exchange swap contract is a combination of an outright forward and a spot transaction on the opposite side in the same amount. This eliminates the exchange rate risk for the company initiating the swap.

international banks in the foreign exchange market for profit motives is desirable. However, the foreign exchange market activities of international banks will continue to grow as they seek further profit opportunities. The contributing factors are the rapid growth of international market opportunities for both financial and non-financial corporations (e.g., emerging market penetrations and financing cross-border M&A activities in foreign currencies), the continuous improvement in trading technologies, and the floating of many emerging market currencies.

4.2. Characteristics of the Foreign Exchange Market

The key characteristics of the foreign exchange market distinguish it from other international financial markets. These are (1) continuous trading on a 24-hr/day basis, (2) large volume, (3) lower transaction costs, and (4) relatively unregulated operations. The following sections discuss these characteristics:

4.2.1. *Continuous trading*

The three main currencies, the USD, the Euro, and the Yen, are being traded in all major locations in addition to their local trading time zones, allowing a 24-hour trading day. There are three main trading locations corresponding to different time zones within a calendar day: the Asia-Pacific, European, and North American trading zones, following the Sun each day. Exhibit 4.1 shows the timeline of foreign exchange market opening hours across a trading day, from right to left. As a calendar day t begins, the major Asia-Pacific markets open in sequence, first the Sydney market, followed by the Tokyo, Hong Kong, and Singapore markets. Towards the tail end of the Asia-Pacific trading hours, the European markets start to open, first the major continental markets in Paris and Frankfurt, followed by the London market. There is an overlap of at least two hours where the Asia-Pacific and the European markets are trading simultaneously. The North American market opens as the Asia-Pacific market trading concludes for the day, and the European markets trade into the afternoon hours. There are at least three hours of overlap between the European and the North American trading hours. As the calendar day t comes to a close and the North American markets close for the day, the Asia-Pacific markets, headed by the Sydney market, start for the calendar day $t + 1$.

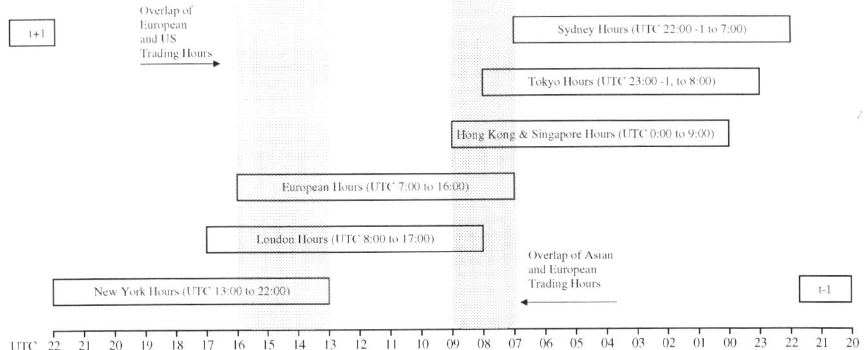

Exhibit 4.1. Timeline of foreign exchange market operating hours.

Source: Author's calculations based on 8 am to 5 pm trading hours in each market.

The foreign exchange market trades national currencies (more precisely, bank deposits in various currencies), and the USD acts as an anchor currency that is used to price each national currency as an asset. All currencies are quoted against the USD, and cross-exchange rates between two non-USD currencies are calculated from the two relevant bilateral rates. The most important currency assets in the foreign exchange market were the Euro (EUR), the Japanese Yen (JPY), the British Pound (GBP) and the Australian Dollar (AUD) between 2007 and 2019, and the Chinese Yuan (RMB) replaced the AUD in the fourth spot in 2022 (see Exhibit 4.4). Exhibit 4.2 shows the 24-hour trading patterns of the top four major currencies (the AUD as the 4th spot) traded on the Electronic Broking System (EBS) platform on 30 January 2015.

It is noticeable that for each exchange rate, there are three peaks of market activities. The first is around early Asian/late morning Sydney trading hours. During these hours, the local market trading (JPY transactions in Tokyo and AUD transactions in Sydney) of the Japanese Yen and the Australian Dollar dominates other currencies. The second peak is around late Asia-Pacific/early London trading hours. The third and the most active trading hours are London afternoon/New York morning hours, when the two largest markets (London and New York) are both operating, where the trading volumes are at their highest within a 24-hour period. In general, the trading volume for each currency is at its peak during the business hours of the local market. The Euro and GBP are most actively traded during the European and New York market trading overlap. The

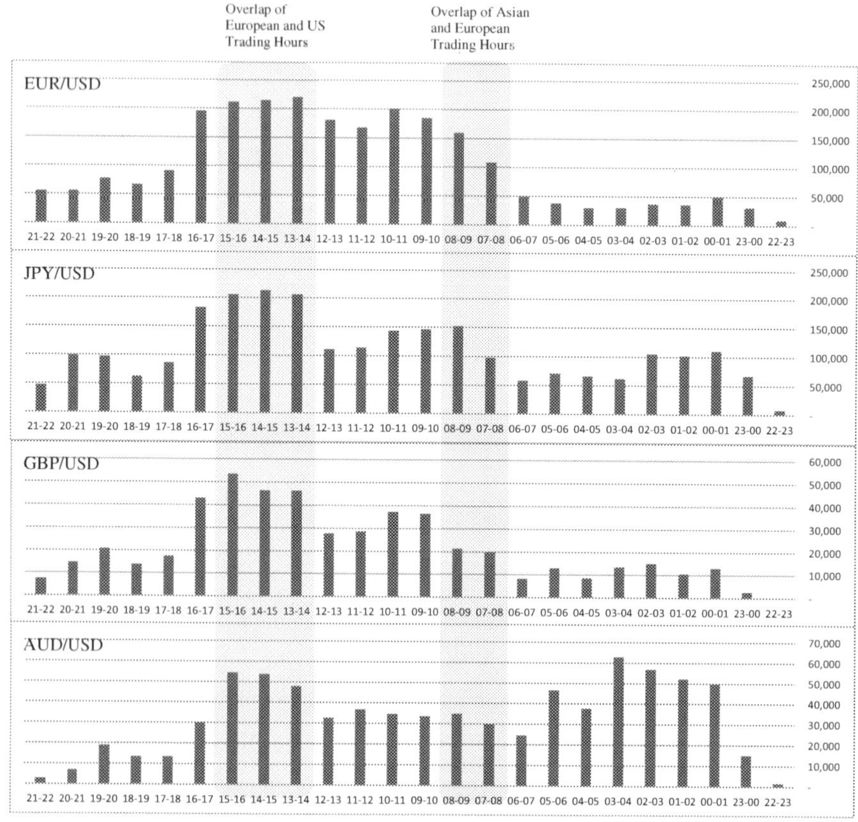

Exhibit 4.2. Intraday quote and trading volume of major exchange rates.

Source: Author's calculation based on the daily quote and trading volume on 30 January 2015 on the EBS platform.

AUD shows the highest trading volume during the Asia-Pacific hours. The JPY, however, has its highest trading volume in the European and New York trading hours while the Tokyo market is closed for the day, suggesting strong demand for the currency outside its local market trading.

Due to the 24-hour trading of the main currencies, foreign exchange traders are not limited by their regional markets' business hours. Rather, they are expected to be on top of important market developments on a 24-hour basis, although the volume of trading of each currency is heaviest during the operating hours of its national market, except for the JPY. This

24-hour nature of foreign exchange market operation provides several advantages over other financial markets, such as equity and other centrally organised markets. *First*, international banks with foreign exchange trading posts in key time zones (Tokyo, Hong Kong, Zurich, London, and New York) can manage their portfolio holdings of major currencies across the 24-hour horizon. *Second*, the price discovery process is continuous and reflects information as it arrives. In most other markets where they close for trading overnight, it is possible to have large jumps in prices at the market open to account for the accumulation of tradable information during market closure. *Third*, there are neither trading limits nor trading halts like those common in many equity and futures markets, making continuous rebalancing of currency portfolios possible. In short, continuous trading across many time zones allows easy market entry and exit to take advantage of information asymmetries that may develop in the market.

4.2.2. *Large volume*

The Bank for International Settlement (BIS) has conducted tri-annual surveys of foreign exchange market activities in April of the selected year since 1986. Exhibit 4.3 displays the aggregate market volume since

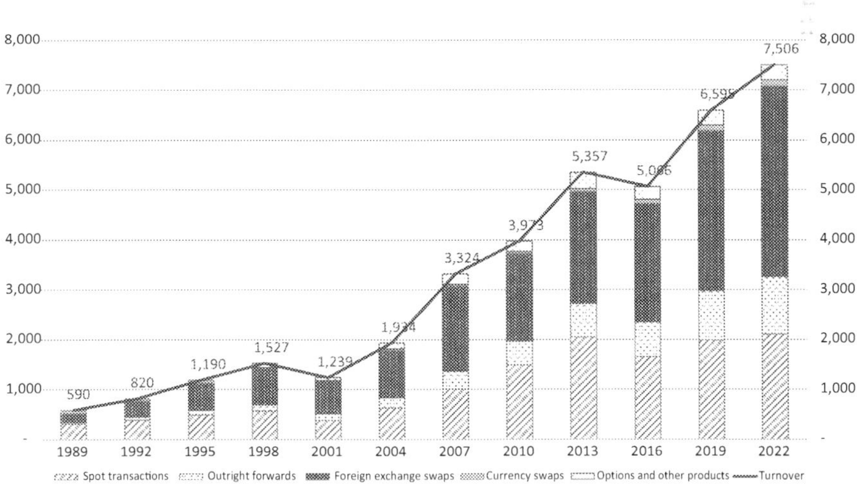

Exhibit 4.3. Foreign exchange market trading volume.

Source: BIS, Central bank survey of foreign exchange and derivatives market activity, 1989–2022.

1989. The foreign exchange market has seen explosive growth since the floating of the major currencies in the early 1970s, reaching an average daily volume of USD 7.5 trillion in April 2022. The aggregate volume of foreign exchange market activities has been growing approximately by 30% in each survey, except for the 2001 and 2016 surveys. The 20% reduction in the market size in 2001 was due mostly to the introduction of the Euro, which eliminated the volume previously attributed to the intra-EMS trading activities (e.g., Franc to Mark and Mark to Lira). The impressive growth continued to 2013 when the total daily trading volume stood at USD 5.4 trillion. In the 2016 survey, a 6% reduction is recorded. The BIS, in its 2016 survey report, suggests that this reduction was mostly due to the USD appreciation against the other major currencies between 2013 and 2016 and that there was actually a modest increase in activities (4%) if the activities in both surveys were valued at constant 2016 exchange rates.

The composition of trading volume is such that outright forwards and swaps are more than double the size of the spot volume, and this has been a growing trend since 1992. This shows that more than half of the foreign exchange volume is motivated by hedging purposes.

The foreign exchange market size is considerably larger than any other financial market segment in the world. For example, the daily average turnover of the global equity market turnover in 2019 was only USD 235 billion from 221 exchanges in 83 countries. There were 43,248 listed companies in total.[2] This is only 3.5% of the size of the aggregate foreign exchange market (or 12% of the spot foreign exchange market in 2019). Moreover, instead of the turnover being spread across a large number of assets, only a handful of major currencies account for the bulk of the market activities. For example, the top four exchange rates (currency pairs) account for 52% of the total market turnover (see Exhibit 4.4, Panel B).

Exhibit 4.4 shows the 10 largest currencies, currency pairs, and market locations between 2001 and 2022. Panel A shows the top currencies, and it can be seen that the USD's share of the foreign exchange market has been stable since 2001 (90% out of a total of 200% in 2001 to 88% in 2022). The distant second was the EUR, with a 31% share in 2022. The JPY and the GBP were ranked 3rd and 4th, respectively, in all surveys, and their shares have also been falling over time. Panel B shows the top currency pairs against the USD. The top exchange rate is the EUR/USD

[2] World Bank, World Development Indicators, 2021.

Rank	2001		2004		2007		2010		2013		2016		2019		2022	
Panel A: Share of foreign exchange turnover by currency (%)																
1	USD	90	USD	88.0	USD	85.6	USD	84.9	USD	87.0	USD	87.6	USD	88.3	USD	88.4
2	EUR	38	EUR	37.4	EUR	37.0	EUR	39.0	EUR	33.4	EUR	31.4	EUR	32.3	EUR	30.5
3	JPY	23	JPY	20.8	JPY	17.2	JPY	19.0	JPY	23.0	JPY	21.6	JPY	16.8	JPY	16.7
4	GBP	13	GBP	16.5	GBP	14.9	GBP	12.9	GBP	11.8	GBP	12.8	GBP	12.8	GBP	12.9
5	CHF	6.1	CHF	6.0	CHF	6.8	AUD	7.6	AUD	8.6	AUD	6.9	AUD	6.8	CNY	7.0
6	CAD	4.5	AUD	6.0	AUD	6.6	CHF	6.3	CHF	5.2	CAD	5.1	CAD	5.0	AUD	6.4
7	AUD	4.2	CAD	4.2	CAD	4.3	CAD	5.3	CAD	4.6	CHF	4.8	CHF	5.0	CAD	6.2
8	SEK	2.6	SEK	2.2	HKD	2.7	HKD	2.4	MXN	2.5	CNY	4.0	CNY	4.3	CHF	5.2
9	HKD	2.3	HKD	1.8	SEK	2.7	SEK	2.2	CNY	2.2	SEK	2.2	HKD	3.5	HKD	2.6
10	NOK	1.5	NOK	1.4	NOK	2.1	NZD	1.6	NZD	2.0	NZD	2.1	NZD	2.1	SGD	2.4
Panel B: Share of foreign exchange turnover by currency pair, against the USD (%)																
1	EUR	30	EUR	28.0	EUR	26.8	EUR	27.7	EUR	24.1	EUR	23.1	EUR	24.0	EUR	22.7
2	JPY	20	JPY	17.0	JPY	13.2	JPY	14.3	JPY	18.3	JPY	17.8	JPY	13.2	JPY	13.5
3	GBP	11	GBP	13.4	GBP	11.6	GBP	9.1	GBP	8.8	GBP	9.3	GBP	9.6	GBP	9.5
4	CHF	5	AUD	5.5	AUD	5.6	AUD	6.3	AUD	6.8	AUD	5.2	AUD	5.4	CNY	6.6
5	AUD	4	CHF	4.3	CHF	4.5	CAD	4.6	CAD	3.7	CAD	4.3	CAD	4.4	CAD	5.5
6	CAD	4	CAD	4.0	CAD	3.8	CHF	4.2	CHF	3.4	CNY	3.8	CNY	4.1	AUD	5.1
7			HKD	0.0	HKD	0.0	HKD	2.1	CNY	2.1	CHF	3.6	CHF	3.5	CHF	3.9
8			KRW	0.0	KRW	0.0	KRW	1.5	HKD	1.3	KRW	1.5	HKD	3.3	HKD	2.4
9			IDR	0.0	IDR	0.0	IDR	0.9	KRW	1.1	HKD	1.5	KRW	1.9	SGD	2.3
10			CNY	0.0	CNY	0.0	CNY	0.8	IDR	0.9	IDR	1.1	IDR	1.7	KRW	1.7
Panel C: Share of foreign exchange turnover by market location (%)																
1	UK	31.2	UK	31.0	UK	34.1	UK	36.7	UK	40.8	UK	36.9	UK	43.1	UK	38.1
2	USA	15.7	USA	19.2	USA	16.6	USA	17.9	USA	18.9	USA	19.5	USA	16.5	USA	19.4
3	Japan	9.1	Japan	8.2	Switzerland	6.1	Japan	6.2	Singapore	5.7	Singapore	7.9	Singapore	7.7	Singapore	9.4
4	Singapore	6.2	Singapore	5.2	Japan	6.0	Singapore	5.3	Japan	5.6	Hong Kong	6.7	Hong Kong	7.6	Hong Kong	7.1
5	Germany	5.5	Germany	4.8	Singapore	5.8	Switzerland	4.9	Hong Kong	4.1	Japan	6.1	Japan	4.5	Japan	4.4
6	Switzerland	4.4	Hong Kong	4.2	Hong Kong	4.4	Hong Kong	4.7	Switzerland	3.2	France	2.8	Switzerland	3.3	Switzerland	3.6
7	Hong Kong	4.1	Australia	4.2	Australia	4.3	Australia	3.8	France	2.8	Switzerland	2.4	France	2.0	France	2.2
8	Australia	3.2	Switzerland	3.3	France	3.0	France	3.0	Australia	2.7	Australia	1.9	China	1.6	Germany	1.9
9	France	3.0	France	2.6	Germany	2.5	Denmark	2.4	Denmark	1.8	Germany	1.8	Germany	1.5	Canada	1.7
10	Canada	2.6	Canada	2.2	Denmark	2.2	Germany	2.2	Netherlands	1.7	Denmark	1.5	Australia	1.4	China	1.6

Exhibit 4.4. Ranking of FX markets: 2001–2022.

Source: BIS, Central bank survey of foreign exchange and derivatives market activity, 2001–2022.

accounting for almost a quarter of the market volume at 22.7%, followed by the JPY/USD at 13.5%. The next two exchange rates held modest at 9.5% and 6.6% of the market, accounted for by the GBP/USD and the CNY/USD, respectively. Although the popularity of the major exchange rates has not changed over time, there is one notable exception. The CNY/USD has been rising in importance since the 2010 survey, accounting for 6.6% in total volume in 2022 compared to a share that did not even register in 2007. Panel C reports the top market locations for foreign exchange trading. The top location is the UK (London) in all surveys, accounting for as much as 38.1% of the total in 2022 despite the Brexit-related concerns causing a dip in 2016. The US market (New York) is a distant second with a 19.4% share. The top two account for as much as 57.6% of the market total. Other major markets are Singapore, Hong Kong, Japan, and Switzerland.

4.2.3. *Lower transaction cost*

The cost of a transaction in the foreign exchange market can be measured by bid–ask spreads. Bid and ask prices are the highest price buyers are willing to pay and the lowest price sellers are willing to sell, respectively, at a given point in time. Foreign exchange market spreads are significantly lower than in any other market. Exhibit 4.5 shows the bid-ask spreads of the top exchange rates and the narrowest spreads on the New York Stock Exchange and the Nasdaq on 31 December 2022. The exchange rate spreads range from 0.8 to 5.2 basis points, while the averages for the US stock markets were 76.7 and 95.2 for NYSE and Nasdaq, respectively.

There are multiple factors that contribute to the much smaller spreads in the foreign exchange market. *First*, the disaggregated OTC market organisation leads to more global competition, which reduces spreads. Unlike centrally organised markets, foreign exchange market spreads do not include fixed cost components necessary to cover operating costs (e.g., clearing charges and brokerage fees). *Second*, the 24-hour trading for major currency pairs and the resulting large volume concentrated on the major currencies (see Exhibit 4.4, Panel B) greatly help narrow the spreads. The high volume of daily turnover reported in Exhibit 4.3 represents a highly liquid market. Unlike other markets where a large number of contracts account for the total volume, the foreign exchange market is dominated by the USD, and the top four exchange rates (Euro, JPY, GBP, and RMB against the USD) account for 52.3% in 2022 (USD 3.9 trillion).

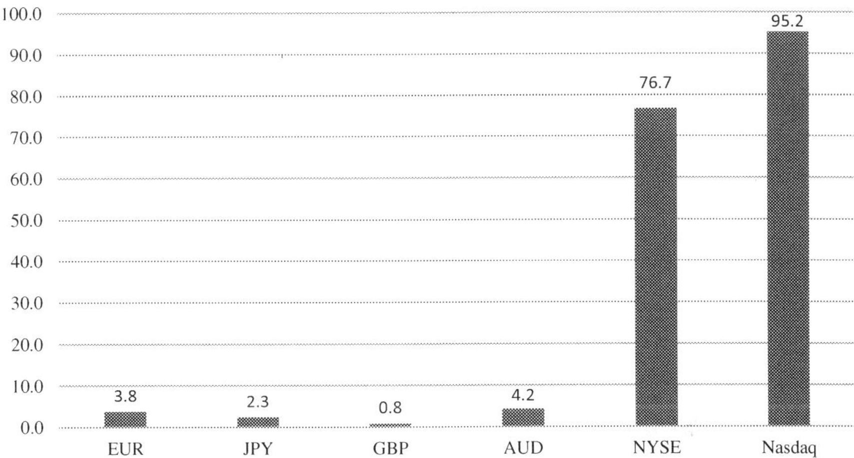

Exhibit 4.5. Bid–ask spread comparisons between foreign exchange and stock markets in 2022 (in basis points).

Source: Foreign exchange bid–ask spreads were calculated from the quotes from Refinitiv Eikon, and the NYSE average spread was taken from NYSE market quality, 2018, https://www.nyse.com/publicdocs/nyse/markets/nyse/NYSE_Market_Quality_infographic.pdf.

Thus, this high liquidity is translated into slimmer spreads. *Third*, the regulation-related costs of transaction are either very low or non-existent due to the difficulty of regulating the cross-border nature of foreign exchange market transactions. However, the international banks participating in the market are subjected to the regulations governing their overall operations, not just their foreign exchange market activities.

4.2.4. *Relatively unregulated operations*

Financial regulation aims to achieve stability and integrity of the financial system by regulating both the financial markets and the participants. The financial market segments organised around centralised trading locations (exchanges with clearing house roles) include stock and derivative markets. Orderly market trading is ensured by imposing exchange-specific rules, such as operating hours, trading mechanisms, price limits, margin requirements, and trading halts. Market participants are regulated via both regulation on their activities (e.g., position limits) and balance sheet positions (e.g., Basel Accord capital adequacy requirements for banks). The regulatory measures aim to control market participants' risk-taking behaviour to avoid defaults that could have negative spillovers to the rest of the financial system.

The foreign exchange market is decentralised (Over The Counter, OTC) with no centrally organised marketplaces where uniform rules can be imposed. Moreover, foreign exchange transactions are typically cross-border in nature, where the buyer and the seller are located in different jurisdictions, making market location-specific regulation of default and settlement risks tricky. As such, the foreign exchange market is unregulated in this respect, although central banks occasionally intervene to preserve order. There are no price limits or trading halts that can be imposed. Importantly, there is no regulation on insider trading, and to the extent that the OTC organisation of the market can lead to information asymmetry, market participants who possess superior information can act on it and end up with a substantial profit. Market manipulation, which is prohibited in any other market, is often observed.

However, regulations on some of the market activities can be imposed to the extent that they can be linked to a market location. For example, the broker market segment of the foreign exchange market somewhat resembles a centralised market arrangement which then can be regulated. Also, foreign exchange derivatives are traded on organised exchanges such as the Chicago Mercantile Exchange (CME) in the US, which Commodity Futures Trading Commission regulates. Regulations at the institutional level can also be imposed that can indirectly control their foreign exchange market activities. Commercial banks, in particular, are required to satisfy capital, liquidity, and operational regulations under the Basel III accord, which limits the extent of overall risk-taking activities.

4.3. Organisation

The foreign exchange market is organised into three market segments: the direct dealing market, where market makers (commercial banks) trade against each other on a reciprocity basis; the broker market, where banks trade via foreign exchange brokers; and the customer market segment, where banks transact with retail customers (financial and non-financial institutions, governments, and individual customers). Each segment has its unique characteristics and contributes to the process of price discovery in the market as a whole. Exhibit 4.6 shows a representation of the three market segments and the changes in their market shares in 2022 compared to

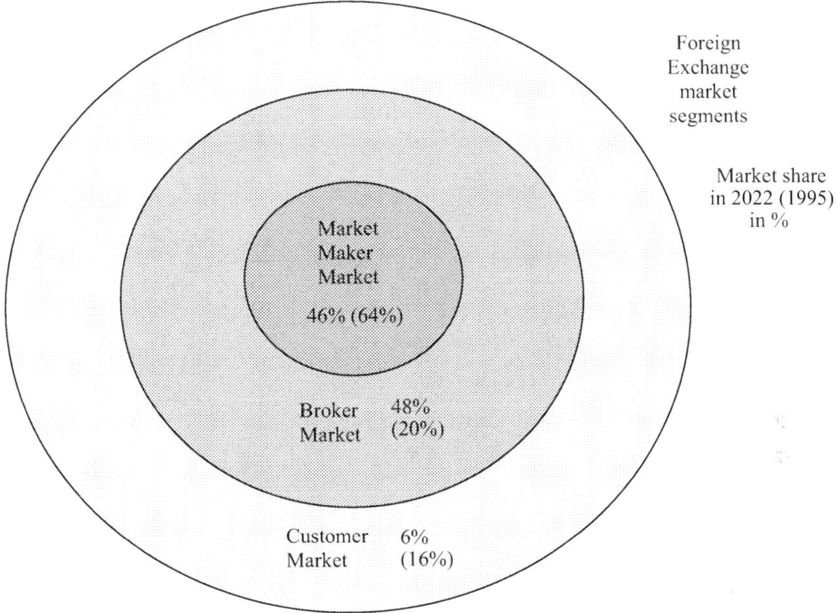

Exhibit 4.6. Foreign exchange market segments and their overall share of the market in 2022.

1995. The market maker segment accounted for 38% of the total market volume in 2022, which is a significant drop from 64% in 1995. The broker market segment has grown substantially from only 20% to 48%, while the customer segment shrunk from 16% to 6%. The notable factor responsible for the growth of the broker market has been the advancement of communication and payment-related technologies that facilitated electronic trades via online broking services. When combined, the maker and broker markets accounted for as much as 94% of the market volume in 2022 (up from 84% in 1995), leaving only 6% of the market for the customer segment.

4.3.1. *Direct market (Market maker market)*

This segment of the market is characterised as a decentralised, continuous trading, and double auction market and is where international banks act as market makers and trade against each other. Unlike centralised markets, such as stock exchanges and futures exchanges, foreign exchange markets are not located in a single geographical location where buyers and sellers congregate. Rather, currency trading is conducted on a bilateral basis between market participants over a communication network (telephone and other electronic means) in a given market environment. However, market participants are located in geographically identifiable locations and trade among each other during the business hours of their regional markets.

This segment of the foreign exchange market is a *double auction* market. The banks participating in the market act as market makers providing liquidity in their specialised currencies by quoting their buying (bid) and selling (ask) prices for a specified trade size in a foreign currency. This is a common characteristic of other types of financial markets, such as interbank money markets, where market makers are expected to provide liquidity when needed. Once quotes are given, market makers must be able to follow through with their quotes, but they would not know beforehand which of the two rates (bid or ask) would be hit. Market-making requires sufficient reserves in both the foreign currencies in which market-making banks deal and bank reserves (i.e., money). Given the size of the market volume in this segment 46% of the market volume or approximately USD 3.5 trillion in 2022, only the large international banks with significant cash and foreign exchange reserves can adequately perform this role.

Exhibit 4.7 shows a typical organisational chart of an international bank's foreign exchange and money market operations. Foreign exchange and money markets trading share common organisational forms: OTC and

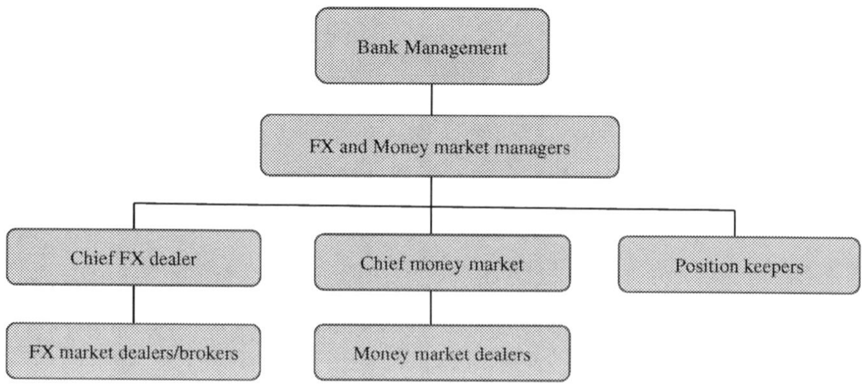

Exhibit 4.7. Organisation of a typical FX/MM department.

continuous trading, where market makers provide liquidity. Foreign exchange transactions can be conducted without money market participation, provided the bank has enough liquidity in domestic and foreign currencies needed to make the market in that exchange rate(s). On other occasions, banks may need to raise credit in either currency to facilitate market-making. For example, a bank that is asked to supply USD 1 million needs to raise this amount via its money market department by issuing a certificate of deposit in the appropriate amount if it does not have enough USD funds in reserve. Thus, this requires a close and similar mode of operation between the international bank's foreign exchange and money market trading desks when acting as a foreign exchange market maker.

4.3.2. *Broker market*

International banks also trade via foreign exchange brokers when they have one-sided needs and timely access to the best price is required. Instead of market-making for a fee income (i.e., spreads), they may wish to exploit an information advantage on exchange rate movements and earn a speculative profit. Alternatively, they may need to balance their inventory of foreign exchange after overselling (or buying) in one currency during market-making. One option is to trade with a market maker, but multiple banks might need to be contacted before an acceptable rate is found. The resulting search cost makes the services provided by brokers invaluable. Brokers located in major money market centres receive limit orders (specific amount and price) from banks and other market participants and work out the best bid and ask prices for each currency at a given moment. These best rates are known as the broker's inside spreads and are released to the market upon request or via online trading and broking platforms. The amounts on either side can differ, e.g., EUR/USD spread of 1.0729–1.0730 for 10 and 11 EUR million indicates that the highest bid rate is from a buyer of EUR 10 million and the lowest sell price is from a seller of EUR 11 million. It is likely that a buyer or a seller might need to engage in more than one transaction to satisfy their desired needs as a result. In short, the broker-based segment of the foreign exchange market is quasi-centralised since interested parties are attracted to brokers located in a specific time zone. It is a continuous and single-auction limit book market.

This segment of the foreign exchange market has seen the most growth in recent years, rising from a 20% share in 1995 to over 48% by

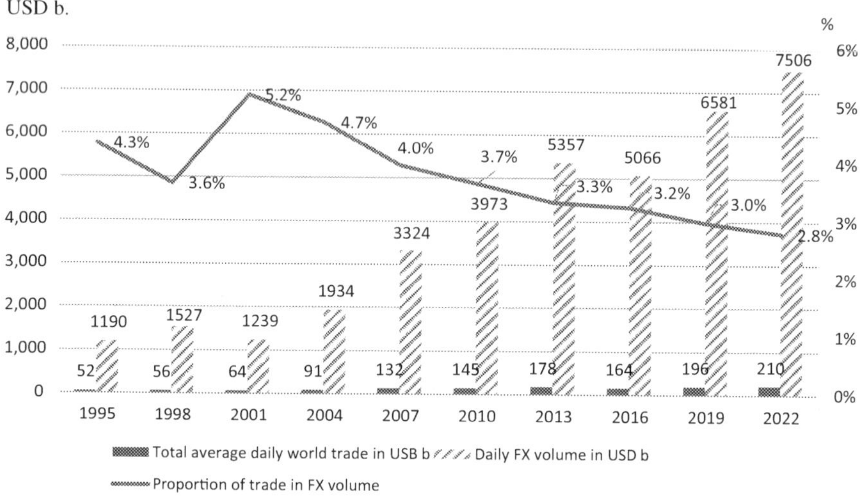

Exhibit 4.8. Daily world trade volume and foreign exchange market turnover in USD billion.

Source: The daily world trade volume is calculated from the annual volume of international trade in goods and services reported in the World Bank's World Development Indicators database. The daily foreign exchange turnover data are obtained from BIS's triannual survey of the foreign exchange market.

2022. Most of this growth is accounted for by the popularity of electronic broking service providers (see Exhibit 4.13).

4.3.3. *Customer market*

Traditionally, the most important reason for trading in foreign exchange has been to facilitate international trade in goods and services. Exporters, importers, and international investors (both financial investments and foreign direct investments) require services to convert between foreign and domestic currencies. These are the end-users of the foreign exchange who engage in economic activities that go beyond the foreign exchange market. The total world trade volume and foreign exchange market turnovers from 1995 are summarised in Exhibit 4.8. The daily volume of international trade, including merchandise and services trades, has increased from USD 52 billion in 1995 to USD 210 billion in 2021, while the foreign exchange market volume rose from USD 1,190 to USD 7,506 billion between 1995 and 2022. The daily world trade in goods and services accounted for a paltry 4.3% of the daily foreign exchange market trading volume in 1995, falling to 2.8% in 2022 (using the 2021 figure for the world's trade). This suggests that almost the entire foreign exchange turnover is accounted for by the transactions that stay within the foreign exchange market with no apparent background economic activities being supported. There are also retail customers who require foreign currencies for international travel, transferring funds to overseas relatives, etc. The customer segment represents a cost centre operation for banks where they need to minimise the costs associated with trading in foreign exchange on behalf of their (non-financial) business customers. Trades initiated by the customers can be fulfilled in either the direct dealer or broker segments of the foreign exchange market.

Although this segment represents only a tiny fraction of the total market volume, as mentioned above, it nonetheless provides the banks with information on economic fundamentals that influence exchange rates. Customer 'order flows' (net positive or negative orders for a currency) are an important source of information for banks as they convey market forces behind the flows. The quality of information content of customer order flows would vary across different banks. Banks that handle non-financial customers of significance (e.g., large multinationals engaging in international trade) would be in a better position to judge an overall trend in the market forces (demand and supply conditions for a given currency) that influence exchange rates leading to a potential information advantage in their trading in the market maker and broker segments of the market.

4.4. Participants

There are various types of participants in the foreign exchange market. These include the end-users of foreign exchange, where foreign currencies are used to finance international trade in goods and services, international investments, international travel and remittance, etc. Business and retail customers interact with their banks to secure or sell foreign currencies to facilitate required transactions. These types of customers accounted for only 6% of counterparties in foreign exchange transactions in 2022, down from 16% in 1995. Exhibit 4.9 shows the market share breakdown among the three types of participants from 1995 to 2022.

The second category of participants is financial institutions that act as market makers and brokers. Together, they accounted for 94% of the

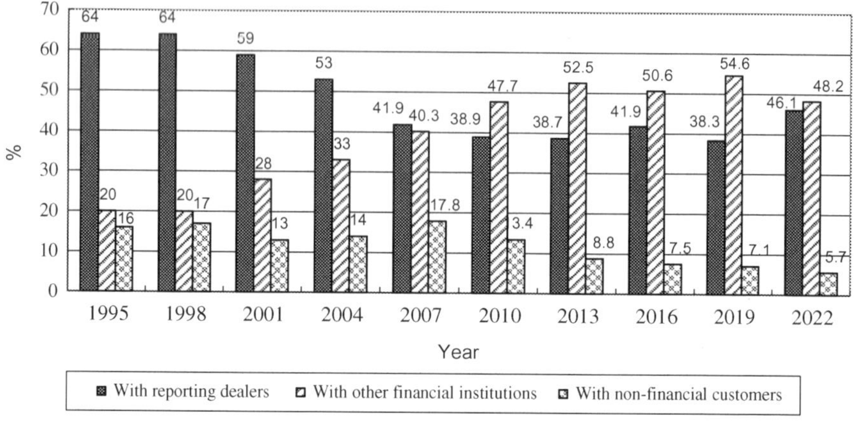

Exhibit 4.9. Foreign exchange turnover by counterparty.

Source: BIS, Central bank survey of foreign exchange and derivatives market activity, 1995–2022.

market volume in 2022 (increased from 84% in 1995). Within this group, the market makers' share dropped from 64% in 1995 to only 46% in 2022, whereas the brokers' stakes increased from 20% to 48% over the same period, which was due mostly to the increasing sophistication and acceptance of electronic broking in the market. Exhibit 4.10 lists the top 10 financial institution counterparties in the market. Panel A shows the leaders of overall market share in spot, forward, swaps, options trading, and in aggregate. The top 10 participants provided 64–92% of market volume across various contracts.

There are several notable features. First, major international banks and bank holding companies dominate the market share, most notably, Deutsche bank, UBS and JP Morgan and UBS. They each maintained on average a 10% or higher market share in recent years in overall trade. Deutsche Bank has been the top liquidity provider for some time (e.g., it was No. 1 in 2007 and on and off in later years), but its share has diminished considerably (from 21% in 2007). Other international banks on the list have also been consistently significant players in the market. *Second*, the emergence of algorithmic trading firms is noteworthy. XTX market is an algorithmic trading company founded in 2015. Its foreign exchange trading volume is ranked fifth in 2022 with a 5.5% market share, which is an impressive growth since its incorporation. Jump Trading, founded in

2022 Rank	Counterparty	Market share (%)	Counterparty	Market share (%)	Counterparty	Market share (%)	Counterparty	Market share (%)
Part A: Overall foreign exchange market counterparty by market share (%)								
	Overall Trades	*63.9*	*Spot/Forward outright*	*68.5*	*Swaps*	*74.0*	*Options*	*91.5*
1	Deutsche Bank	13.7	UBS	10.9	Deutsche Bank	17.8	Deutsche Bank	30.2
2	UBS	9.4	Deutsche Bank	10.6	State Street	10.6	UBS	11.5
3	JPMorgan	8.1	XTX Markets	9.6	Commerzbank	7.5	Goldman Sachs	8.8
4	State Street	6.4	JPMorgan	9.4	UBS	7.3	Bank of America	7.4
5	XTX Markets	5.5	Jump Trading	7.4	Citi	6.4	Barclays	7.2
6	Citi	5.1	Bank of New York Mellon	4.7	JPMorgan	6.4	NatWest	7.1
7	Jump Trading	4.4	Citadel Securities	4.7	Barclays	5.5	BNP Paribas	6.1
8	Commerzbank	3.8	Citi	4.1	BNP Paribas	4.5	JPMorgan	5.9
9	Bank of New York Mellon	3.8	Goldman Sachs	3.9	Bank of America	4.0	Citi	5.2
10	Goldman Sachs	3.7	State Street	3.4	Morgan Stanley	3.9	Morgan Stanley	2.2
Part B: Overall foreign exchange market counterparty in electronic trades by market share (%)								
	Overall electronic trades	*67.8*	*Electronic spot/forward outrights*	*70.9*	*Electronic swaps*	*78.3*	*Electronic options*	*93.8*
1	Deutsche Bank	14.0	UBS	11.7	Deutsche Bank	19.2	Deutsche Bank	33.4
2	UBS	10.6	Deutsche Bank	11.3	Commerzbank	12.4	Citi	9.8
3	JPMorgan	8.9	XTX Markets	10.9	UBS	8.5	BNP Paribas	9.5

(*Continued*)

Exhibit 4.10. Foreign exchange market share ranking.

Source: Compiled from Euromoney, June 2022.

2022 Rank	Counterparty	Market share (%)	Counterparty	Market share (%)	Counterparty	Market share (%)	Counterparty	Market share (%)
4	XTX Markets	7.2	JPMorgan	9.1	JPMorgan	8.4	UBS	9.2
5	Jump Trading	5.8	Jump Trading	8.6	Barclays	7.6	JPMorgan	7.0
6	Commerzbank	5.0	Citadel Securities	5.4	Citi	5.5	Barclays	5.7
7	Citi	4.6	Citi	4.1	Goldman Sachs	4.8	Goldman Sachs	5.4
8	Barclays	4.1	Goldman Sachs	3.7	HSBC	4.6	Morgan Stanley	5.4
9	Goldman Sachs	4.1	HCTech	3.1	BNP Paribas	4.2	Bank of America	5.1
10	Citadel Securities	3.6	Bank of America	3.1	State Street	3.2	NatWest	3.4
Part C: Overall foreign exchange market counterparty in regional markets by market share (%)								
	Americas	*69.9*	*Asia Pacific*	*76.3*	*CEEMEA*	*83.8*	*Western Europe*	*68.8*
1	State Street	17.4	Deutsche Bank	16.0	XTX Markets	19.6	UBS	11.2
2	Deutsche Bank	8.0	JPMorgan	12.8	Deutsche Bank	14.2	Deutsche Bank	10.9
3	Bank of New York Mellon	7.1	UBS	11.2	UBS	12.2	XTX Markets	9.5
4	UBS	6.6	Citi	8.1	JPMorgan	9.6	JPMorgan	9.1
5	Citadel Securities	6.1	Credit Suisse	5.2	Swissquote	6.4	Jump Trading	8.1
6	JPMorgan	5.8	Bank of America	4.9	Credit Suisse	6.2	Citi	4.6
7	Jump Trading	5.2	Barclays	4.9	Goldman Sachs	4.6	Goldman Sachs	4.4
8	Morgan Stanley	5.1	XTX Markets	4.8	UniCredit	4.4	BNP Paribas	4.3
9	XTX Markets	4.4	HSBC	4.6	NatWest	3.4	Bank of New York Mellon	3.6
10	Bank of America	4.3	State Street	3.9	Commerzbank	3.3	Bank of America	3.0

Exhibit 4.10. (*Continued*)

1999, ranked seventh with a 4.4% market share. The two algorithmic traders accounted for 9.9% of the market in overall trade. *Third*, algorithmic trading is concentrated in spot and outright forward transactions, and they are absent in swap and options trading, where more complex structures are involved.

Panel B shows the market share of the participants in electronic trading. The overall picture does not change much from that of Panel A. Not surprisingly, the share of the overall volume for the two algorithmic traders is higher in electronic trading. XTX trading's share is 7.2% compared to its overall share of 5.5%, and Jump trading's share is 5.8% compared to 4.4%.

Panel C reports the top market participants in various market locations. In the Americas and Asia, established international banks dominate. However, in CEEMEA (Central and Eastern Europe, Middle East and Africa), XTM Markets dominates with a 19.6% market share, just ahead of Deutsche bank with a 14.2% share. In Western Europe, the combined share of the two algorithmic traders (XTX Markets and Jump Trading) is as much as 17.6%. This suggests that algorithmic trading is much more established in the emerging market segments and, to a less extent, in Western Europe.

Overall, large international banks and bank holding companies dominate foreign exchange trading, with the emerging importance of algorithmic trading companies concentrating on the spot and outright forward contracts in CEEMEA countries and Western Europe.

The third category of participants in the foreign exchange market is central banks. They act as a banker to their governments and provide foreign exchange services in a similar way that commercial banks service their business and retail customers. *First*, when the government of a country needs to finance infrastructure investments, importation of hardware, etc., that require foreign currency, its central bank is tasked to raise the needed foreign currency. It will tap into the market maker and broker segments as a customer. *Second*, central banks can intervene in the foreign exchange market to keep the exchange rate within a certain range or at a fixed rate. Under a fixed exchange rate system, central banks peg their currency against a major currency (usually the USD) or a basket of currencies by conducting open market operations. When there is an excess supply of (demand for) their currency in the market, the central bank then enters the market to remove this excess supply (demand) in order to maintain the fixed exchange rate. Under floating exchange rate regimes, central bank interventions can still occur. They can conduct occasional intervention transactions in the market with the aim of influencing the trend or volatility of their currency in the market. In most countries, the central bank is independent of government and is tasked with ensuring the stability of its currency in terms of its purchasing power.[3] The external purchasing power of a currency is measured by its exchange rate against other currencies, and achieving its stability is one aim of intervening in the foreign exchange market. Kim and Sheen (2002, 2006) suggest that the Reserve Bank of Australia's main aim was to address the volatility of the AUD movements rather than to influence its trend. However, the Bank of Japan (BOJ) aimed to change the exchange rate trend in the EUR/JPY and USD/JPY exchange rates with their 'lean against the wind' interventions. The BOJ intervened in the market to prevent the JPY from appreciating too much, and the last of this type of intervention was in April 2004. After an absence of nearly 20 years, BOJ intervened on 21 October 2022 to purchase JPY 5.5 trillion (approximately USD 37 billion) in the environment of the JPY depreciating quickly towards 150 per USD.

4.5. Trading Mechanism

Currencies are traded via a number of different methods. In the market maker segment, two dealers trade with each other via direct telephone communications or electronic dealing systems (e.g., Reuters' conversational dealing system and Electronic Broking System). Banks can also trade directly with dealing banks via voice communications or via electronic trading systems. Similarly, in the indirect broker market segment, broking services can be provided for the two parties involved in a transaction over a telephone line or an electronic broking system. The delivery of foreign currency and its corresponding payment in a foreign exchange transaction between two parties (banks) occurs via a correspondent banking relationship. The two banks maintain a demand deposit account with each other and use these accounts to transfer payments. For example, Citibank buys EUR 1 million from Deutsche Bank, and then Citibank credits the equivalent USD amount (USD 1.08 million, at EUR/USD =

---

[3]Many advanced country central banks have an inflation targeting mandate where the monetary policy target is set to achieve a domestic inflation rate within a specific acceptable range (as of 2022, the US Fed, the ECB, England's BOE, and Japan's BOJ all target 2%, whereas Australia's RBA set 2–3% range as acceptable inflation range).

1.08) to the USD account Deutsche Bank maintains with Citibank. Deutsche Bank then credits EUR 1 million to Citibank's Euro account with Deutsche Bank.[4]

4.5.1. *Traditional telephone-based voice trading*

The traditional method of dealing in the foreign exchange market is via bilateral communication networks, with the telephone network playing a vital role. The customer initiates a transaction by placing a call to a market-making bank, and a bid/ask quote given by the market maker in response can be acted upon. Market makers need to provide two-sided quotes and stand ready to perform either side of the transaction. Alternatively, foreign currency transactions could be via a broker. In this case, a broker, who is not obliged to act as a counterparty in a transaction, provides information needed for both parties to facilitate a trade.

4.5.1.1. *Direct market*

The following is an example of a typical market maker-directed transaction. Trade begins with a bank calling another bank (market maker) to obtain a quote on a foreign currency. Assume that HSBC calls Westpac for its quote on the AUD against the USD in the Sydney market.

HSBC: 'Aussie-dollar please'

In the foreign exchange market, the most important currency, the USD, is the price currency against which all other currencies are priced. Cross rates, exchange rates that do not involve the USD, are calculated from the appropriate bilateral rates that involve the USD, which are all kept in line by arbitrage. The first currency mentioned is the foreign currency that is in trade, and the second is the pricing currency (the USD).

Westpac: '45–55'

Since dealers are aware of the magnitudes of current rates, there is no need to quote full rates. Instead, only the last two digits are quoted. In this

[4]These accounts are also referred to as *Nostro* (meaning ours) and *Vostro* (meaning your or theirs) accounts. From the viewpoint of Citibank in the transaction, it pays in the USD to the *Vostro* account of Deutsche Bank and receives the EUR to its *Nostro* account.

case, the bid–ask rates quoted by Westpac are 0.7145–0.7155 USD per one AUD.

HSBC: 'Two mine'

HSBC hits the ask rate of Westpac and buys two million AUD at 0.7155.

Westpac: 'my dollar to Westpac New York'

Now that the price and the amount of trade have been agreed upon by both parties, they need to work out the payment details. Westpac wants its USD payment (1.431 million) for selling AUD 2 million to be deposited with its New York branch (or a Nostro account held at its US correspondent bank).

HSBC: 'my Aussie to HSBC Sydney'

HSBC in return specifies its payment requirement. It wants the AUD 2 million payment to be made to its Sydney branch (or to a corresponding bank in Australia). Payments in a foreign currency must be made in the payment system in which it is a local currency. In this case, the AUD payment must occur through the Reserve Bank Information and Transfer System (RITS), whereas the USD payment must go through the US system (Fedwire or CHIPS). Exhibit 4.11 shows the payment instruction flows in this transaction.

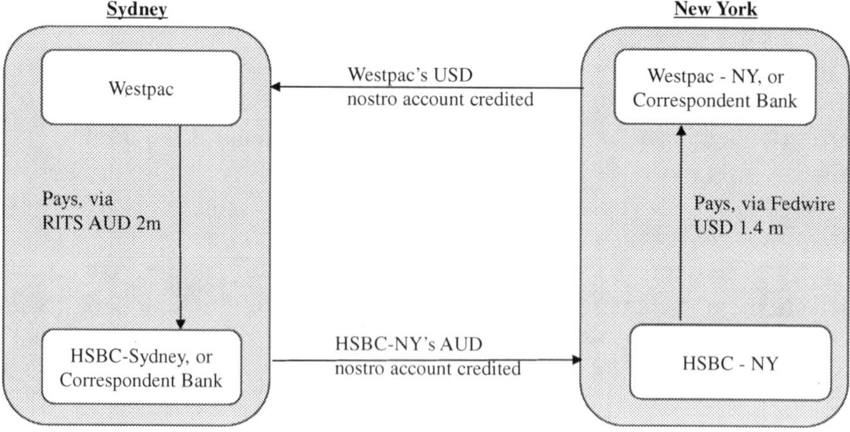

Exhibit 4.11. Direction of payment flows in a foreign exchange transaction.

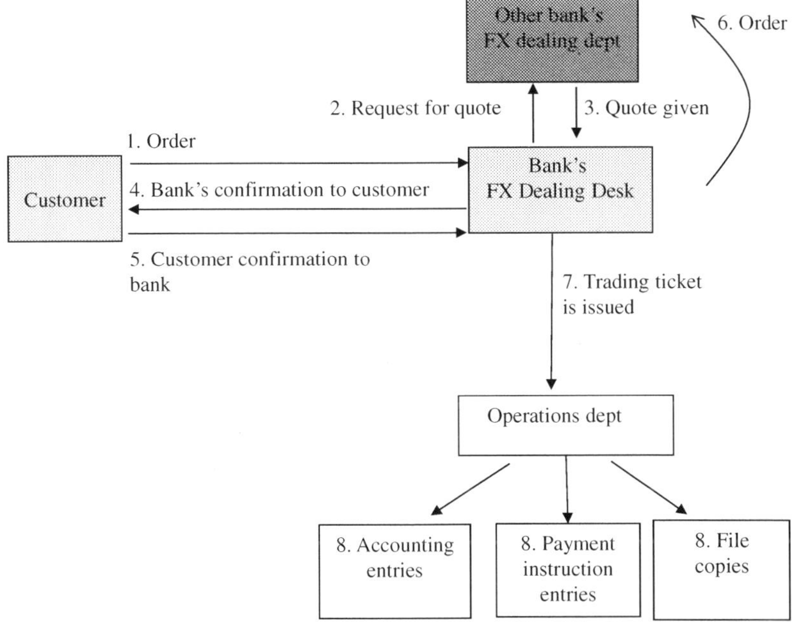

Exhibit 4.12. General case of customer-driven FX trading.

Exhibit 4.12 illustrates the procedures involved in executing a customer-driven foreign currency trade for a dealer bank. Once an order is received from a customer, the bank contacts another bank(s) for a quote on the current price. The given quote is provided to the customer for confirmation, and once it is given, the trade is executed. After this, back office procedures are performed, e.g., creating, filing, and recording a trading ticket for the transaction.

4.5.1.2. *Broker market*

Instead of international banks acting as market makers, some may perform the role of a broker in the foreign exchange market. This requires an efficient network of intelligence-gathering instruments and up-to-the-minute information on the spreads of all quotes in the market. A transaction is initiated when a bank contacts a broker and asks for an inside spread. A typical transaction is described in the following:

HSBC: 'What is Aussie, Please?'

HSBC contacts a broker and asks for a two-way price quotation.

Broker: 'I deal 45–50, two by four'

The best bid price is 0.7145 USD per one AUD for two million AUD, and the best ask is 0.7150 USD for four million AUD. Note here that the bid and ask amounts are not the same, as these come from different dealers in the market.

HSBC: 'I buy at 50, from whom?'

HSBC wishes to buy four million Australian dollars at the price of 0.7150 and requests the identity of the seller.

Broker: 'Westpac, Sydney'

The broker announces that Westpac is the seller. Both parties of the transactions are now aware of the identity of the counterparty, and the bilateral transaction will now commence.

4.5.2. *Electronic trading*

The advancement of communication and payment technologies from the early 1990s, combined with a relatively simple structure of spot foreign exchange transactions, led to the introduction of electronic trading and broking platforms in the foreign exchange market. Heath and Whitelaw (2011) suggest that the introduction of electronic trading significantly impacted the price discovery process and spread market volume away from the traditional liquidity providers (large international banks) by increasing the participation of the non-banks. The participation of non-banks in the direct dealing market effectively blurred the boundaries of the traditional activities of each of the market participants. The non-bank market participants in the electronic trading system include investment and commercial banks, corporate participants, and individual traders. There are several benefits associated with electronic trading. *First*, in most cases, human errors in transcribing, executing, and back-office functions can be eliminated. *Second*, price discovery is straightforward. Trading platforms (Reuters dealing system 3000 and EBS) show quotes from multiple banks (multibank direct trading system) and best bid and ask prices, as well as near (second best, third best, etc.) prices, on one screen. *Third*, trade execution is much quicker and more accurate as all the necessary back-office processes (shown in Exhibit 4.12) are automated.

The first-ever electronic trading system launched was the Reuter's Monitor Dealing Service in 1981, which was replaced by its upgraded Reuters Dealing 2000–2001 service in 1987. This was the electronic equivalent of telephone-based direct trading between two traders, as detailed in Exhibit 4.11. It provided an electronic method of directly connecting money market and foreign exchange market dealers located in many countries (more than 110 countries, according to Reuters). It allowed an electronic version of trade conversation (as per telephone trading). Deal tickets are automatically created upon the conclusion of each trade. The Reuters Dealing 2000–2001 system concentrated on the major Commonwealth currencies (CAD, AUD, HDK, and SGD against the USD and cross rates). In 1992, Reuters Dealing 2000 system was introduced, which included Dealing 2000–2001, the direct trading platform, and Dealing 2000–2002, which was an electronic broking service designed to replace telephone-based broking. In 2000, the 2000 system was replaced by the Dealing 3000, which was bundled with a direct dealing system (known as D1), a broking system (known as D2), and news alert and other information delivery systems that aided in price discovery. In 2013, it was replaced by Thomson Reuters (now Refinitiv) Eikon trading platform.

In a parallel development, Electronic Broking System (EBS) was created in 1993 by a consortium of banks to provide an alternative to the broking part of the Reuters Dealing 2000 system (D2). In 1995, it acquired a rival system Minex which was created by a group of Japanese banks in 1993. The EBS caters for major European currencies (the EUR and the Swiss Franc) and the JPY against the USD and their cross rates. These currency pairs account for the bulk of foreign exchange trading.[5] As each competing platform has currency concentrations, as discussed above, traders' choice of which system to use is dictated by the currency requirements of each trader. For example, for the EUR and the JPY transactions, the EBS system has a much larger volume, and for the GBP, the AUD, and the CAD, the Reuters platform is much more liquid.

Not surprisingly, the advantages of the electronic trading and broking systems in the foreign exchange market contributed to a significant share

---

[5]The combined market share of USD/EUR and USD/JPY exchange rates was 36.2% in 2022, down from 50% in 2001.

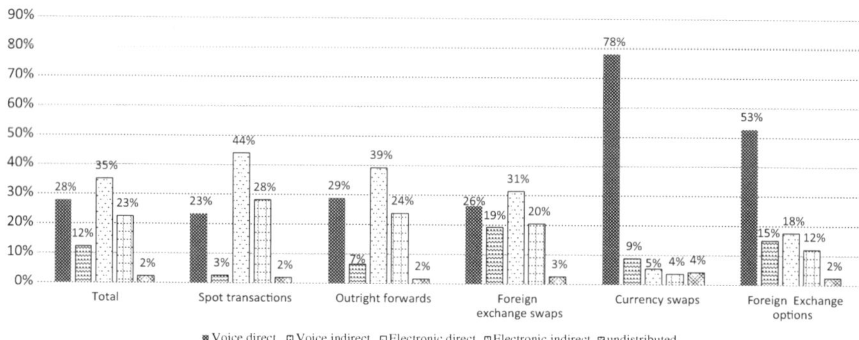

Exhibit 4.13. Foreign exchange market turnover by execution method.

Source: BIS triannual foreign exchange market survey, 2022.

of total trading in the market. Drehmann and Sushko (2022) identifies electrification of trading as a key trend in the foreign exchange market in recent decades. Exhibit 4.13 shows the relative market share of traditional (voice) and electronic execution methods in 2022. The traditional voice execution in the interbank dealer and broker market accounted for 28% (voice direct) and 12% (voice indirect) of the total market volume. Although the combined total of 40% is significantly lower than in the previous years (e.g., 66% in 2007), voice-based trading is still a significant component. Conversely, electronic trading is growing in importance, accounting for 58% (electronic direct and indirect) of the market share due to the emergence of high-frequency algorithmic traders, such as XTX market and Jump Trading (see Exhibit 4.10). Electronic trading is concentrated in spot, outright forward, and foreign exchange swaps (combinations of spot and outright forward contracts entered simultaneously) markets where the trading mechanism is straightforward and can easily be standardised and programmed. Electronic trading accounted for 72%, 63% and 52%, respectively. In the derivative trading segments of currency swaps and options, traditional voice-based trading still dominates, accounting for as much as 87% and 68%, respectively. As these contracts are usually tailor-made to suit client requirements and traded OTC, voice communication methods are still widely used, especially in the voice direct market segment.

4.6. Settlement Risk

Settlement risk, also referred to as Herstatt risk,[6] refers to the risk of non-payment by a counterparty after your payment is made and processed. Hence, it is a counterparty default risk. In addition to the principal risk, there can also be a liquidity risk consideration. If payment from the counterparty is delayed or incomplete, one risks raising the required foreign currency through other channels at additional costs. In the previous example (Exhibit 4.11), assuming the payments are to be made on the same calendar date, Westpac bears the settlement risk as it pays the AUD in Sydney while it will receive the USD payment during the New York market operating hours after the close of business in Sydney. The settlement risk is more pronounced for foreign exchange transactions because local currency settlements are carried out via the payment system operating in that local Real Time Gross Settlement System (RTGS),[7] and the two payment systems involved may not have overlapping business hours. The

[6]The Bankhaus Herstatt, a private German bank, accumulated large foreign exchange trading losses between 1973 and 1974, estimated to be approximately DEM 470 million, while its capital was only DEM 44 million. On 26 June 1974, the German authority forced it into liquidation. Herstatt seized its operation during German business hours on the day (16:30 German time, which was 10:30 EST in the US). Due to the time gap between the German and New York business hours, the USD payments due to its counterparty banks scheduled to be made during the US business hours did not eventuate. The settlement or Herstatt risk arose mainly due to the nature of the netting arrangements adopted by international banks that were used to settle their payment obligations to each other. The deferred (or overnight) settlement system involved banks in international foreign exchange trades allowing overnight receipts and payment obligations of their trades to accumulate. The settlements in net amounts against each counterparty will be initiated the next business day. It is possible that on a given day, a bank's accumulated payment obligation can far exceed its receipts. If this shortfall exceeds the available liquidity the bank has access to, then a default in payment could occur. This has the potential for a chain reaction of subsequent defaults in the domestic and international banking systems. These days, however, most payment systems (domestic and international) are based on a Real Time Gross Settlement (RTGS) system, whereby each payment obligation is met in real-time. So if a bank is short on liquidity, it will default on only one transaction rather than a series of transactions accumulated overnight. This minimises the severity of payment defaults, and the potential of a payment crisis is minimised.

[7]The RTGS systems for the top five currencies in the foreign exchange market are Fedwire in the US, TARGET2 (Trans-European Automated Real-time Gross Settlement Express Transfer Systems) in the Eurozone, BOJ-NET (Bank of Japan Financial Network System)

operating hours of the payment system in each country would normally follow the business hours of their financial system. Exhibit 4.1 shows a considerable gap in business hours between the Asia Pacific and North American countries, for example. As such, there is clearly exposures to settlement risk involving banks in these two regions when they trade with each other.

A recent development that aims to address this issue of foreign exchange settlement risk is the introduction of the Continuous Linked Settlement (CLS) bank, established in September 2002. CLS bank (now CLS Group)[8] was created as an EdgeAct Corporation in New York as a limited-purpose bank regulated by the Federal Reserve. As of March 2023, CLS handles 18 currencies[9] among over 70 members, including all the central banks of the currencies involved and large banks that participate in the foreign exchange market. All member banks participating in the system are required to open a correspondent account with the CLS bank in the participating currencies. CLS bank, in turn, maintains accounts (Exchange Settlement Account) with the participating central banks and would have access to the respective RTGS systems. CLS bank operates between 7 am and 12 pm Central European Time (6 am to 11 am UTC), and all participating currencies' RTGS systems are required to have sufficient overlap in operating hours with the CLS. CLS acts as a clearinghouse that receives payment from both parties in a transaction and pays out only when both payments are cleared. A modified foreign exchange transaction example in Exhibit 4.11 is shown in Exhibit 4.14. Westpac agreed to sell AUD 2 million to HSBC-NY for USD 1.4 million. Westpac and HSBC-NY now pay their obligations to CLS bank, not to each other's correspondent bank, as in the previous example. Once both AUD and USD funds are cleared through to CLS bank via RITS and Fedwire systems to the CLS's accounts with each bank, CLS pays the AUD 2 million to HSBC-Sydney via RITS and USD 1.4 million to Westpac-NY via Fedwire. This Payment versus Payment (PVP)-based clearing ensures that

---

in Japan, CHAPS (Clearing House Automated Payment System) in the UK, and RITS (Reserve Bank Information and Transfer System) in Australia.

[8]https://www.cls-group.com/.

[9]The eighteen participating currencies are the Australian Dollar, Canadian Dollar, Danish Krone, Euro, GB Pound, Hong Kong Dollar, Hungarian Forint, Israeli Shekel, Japanese Yen, Korean Won, Mexican Peso, New Zealand Dollar, Norwegian Krone, Singapore Dollar, South African Rand, Swedish Krona, Swiss Franc, and US Dollar.

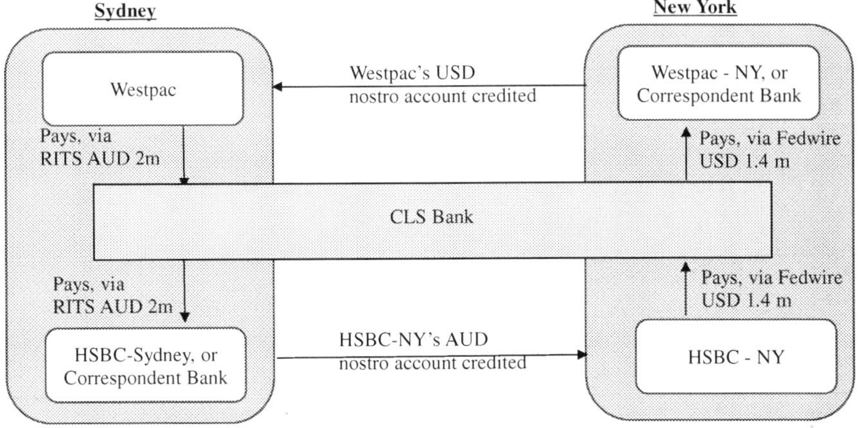

Exhibit 4.14. CLS bank settlement of foreign exchange trades.

if one party defaults on its payment obligation under the transaction, the defaulting party will not receive its corresponding foreign currency payment and the payment already made to CLS by the non-defaulting party will be returned. This process effectively eliminates settlement risk in foreign exchange transactions.

Normally, multiple transactions involving the same participants are netted across the operating hours of CLS. At the end of CLS operating hours, all member accounts with CLS are required to have a zero balance. The average daily trade volume cleared by CLS was USD 1.91 trillion in January 2023, composed of 0.138 in forward, 1.31 in swap and 0.456 in spot transactions.[10]

4.7. Bid–Ask Spread

Bid–ask spreads in the foreign exchange market represent the cost of doing business for market makers who earn spread income for proving liquidity when requested. In general, the higher the volume of trade, i.e., high liquidity, and the lower the underlying market uncertainty, the lower the bid–ask spreads. Foreign exchange transactions are conducted on a non-commission basis in the wholesale market. That is, international

[10] https://www.cls-group.com/news/cls-fx-trading-activity-january-23/.

banks' returns on market-making activities are measured as the difference between their selling (ask) and buying (bid) prices for a currency.[11] This does not, however, represent a main source of income for market makers. Rather, most of their trading-related income is from position-taking (Cheung and Lim, 2000). There are various reasons for the spread: cost recovery, adverse selection, and inventory adjustment needs.

4.7.1. *Cost recovery*

Market makers are required to provide two-sided quotes upon demand and are expected to stand behind them. They do this by having access to inventories of foreign currencies and credit lines, and the cost of providing this *predictable immediacy* is to be covered by charging a spread between buy and sell transactions. From the viewpoint of the customers, the presence of search costs in finding a counterparty for transactions would permit market makers to charge a premium (i.e., spread) for providing liquidity. However, due to the apparent absence of significant entry barriers (apart from sufficient capitalisation) or exit barriers to the foreign exchange market-making business, together with high levels of competition in the market, this premium is expected to be thin enough so as to just cover the costs of providing *immediacy* services in major currencies. It is possible that, under certain circumstances, market makers' spreads are so slim that they do not cover their costs, or there might be instances when market makers quote a single figure to be used either as a bid or an ask price (i.e. a zero spread). This is to attract interest from informed traders who would reveal potential arbitrage information by trading with the market maker. If the market maker receives an order, it will take this as an indicator of a possible direction of price movements in the short term. There is also some anecdotal evidence of market makers paying little attention to cost recovery when setting their spreads. Cheung and Chinn (2001) report that 70% of market makers in the two largest foreign exchange markets, London and New York, follow market conventions rather than recouping potential costs. Important reasons for market conformity included 'to maintain an equitable and reciprocal trading relationship' and 'to secure a good market image for the firm'. An ability to

[11] In the retail market, however, a foreign exchange conversion fee, in addition to the spread, might be applicable.

maintain a slim margin is seen as a sign of the high volume capability of the market maker, and the perception of quality is an essential aspect of market-making.

4.7.2. *Adverse selection*

Traders in the foreign exchange market can be informed or uninformed. Uninformed traders are usually liquidity traders whose main objective is to minimise the cost of a transaction, and, as such, they are willing to pay market makers for providing *predictable immediacy*. Informed traders are keen to exploit their information advantage over other market makers to generate trading profits (Melvin and Norrbin, 2017). Due to the decentralised nature of the foreign exchange market, a perfect market consensus is difficult to achieve, and there can be traders who are better aware of important short-term trends than others. Market makers are generally unable to distinguish between informed and uninformed traders when asked for quotes. The distinct possibility of making a loss against informed traders with arbitrage information may lead the market makers to quote wider spreads than otherwise in order to compensate for this potential loss. However, such losses may be tolerated or even actively sought if the value of the information obtained by trading with informed traders is considered high, as suggested previously.

4.7.3. *Inventory considerations*

One of the costs of providing market-making services is the cost of inventory (interest and exchange rate risks). Market makers may have an imbalance in their currency positions throughout a trading day. That is, they might have a net long or short position in one or more currencies. However, they need to have a balanced position toward the end of a trading day. This requires liquidation of any net long positions and purchase of shortfalls in currencies that are net short. However, a complicating factor for market makers is that although they may desire a liquidation of net long positions in one currency, they cannot refuse to honour their bid quotes if their counterparties desire to sell that currency to them. In such circumstances, they can adjust their spreads to encourage other market makers to buy the currency from them and simultaneously discourage their bid quotes from being hit. This can be accomplished by shifting both bid and ask quotes down sufficiently and increasing the width of the spread to achieve this desired aim. In addition, they may also raise the volume of the bid quote to make it less attractive (Rime, 2003).

References

Bank for International Settlement, Triennial Central Bank Survey of Foreign Exchange and Derivatives Market Activity, 1989–2019. http://www.bis.org/publ/rpfx05.htm.

Bank for International Settlements (March 1996). Settlement Risk in Foreign Exchange Transactions, Basel. http://www.bis.org/publ/cpss17.pdf.

Cheung, Y.-W. and Chinn, M. (2001). Currency traders and exchange rate dynamics: A survey of the US market. *Journal of International Money and Finance*, 20, 439–471.

Drehmann, M. and Sushko, V. (2022), The global foreign exchange market in a higher volatility environment, BIS Quarterly Review, December 2022. https://www.bis.org/publ/qtrpdf/r_qt2212f.pdf.

Eun, C., Resnick, B. and Chuluun, T. (2021). *International Financial Management*, 9th ed., McGrawHill, New York.

Gallardo, P. and Heath, A. (2009). Execution methods in foreign exchange markets, BIS Quarterly Review, March, http://www.bis.org/publ/qtrpdf/r_qt0903h.pdf.

Heath, A. and Whitelaw, J. (2011). Electronic Trading and the Australian Foreign Exchange Market, Reserve Bank of Australia Bulletin, June 2011. https://www.rba.gov.au/publications/bulletin/2011/jun/6.html.

Kim, S.-J. and Sheen, J. (2002). The determinants of foreign exchange intervention by central banks: Evidence from Australia. *Journal of International Money and Finance*, 21(5), 619–649.

Kim, S.-J. and Sheen, J. (2006). Interventions in the Yen-dollar spot market: A story of price, volatility and volume. *Journal of Banking & Finance*, 30(November), 3191–3214.

Melvin M. and Norrbin, S. (2017). *International Money and Finance*, 9th ed., Academic press, London, UK.

Rime, D. (2003). *New Electronic Trading Systems in Foreign Exchange Markets*, Chapter 21 in New Economy Handbook, Elsevier.

Chapter 5

Eurocurrency Market

5.1. Introduction

The interbank money market caters for commercial and investment banks in the financial system to fulfil their short-term borrowing and lending requirements by trading in short-term domestic currency deposits against each other. Similar to the interdealer foreign exchange market, the interbank money market is an over-the-counter market that facilitates trades via market makers and brokers. Commercial banks usually trade on their accounts for profit, and they can also act on behalf of their retail customers on request. For example, if a business customer requests a quick loan that cannot easily be fulfilled by raising deposits, the bank needs to tap into the interbank money market to raise the required amount from another bank. When they trade with their own funds, they aim to achieve balance sheet management objectives (including hedging requirements on their exposures) in terms of currencies, maturities, and interest rate denominations, and also potentially speculate on their expectations of future interest rate and exchange rate movements. Investment banks are also important players in the market. Before the GFC 2007–2009, the business model of investment banks relied heavily on the interbank money market as a source of short-term liquidity to fund higher-yielding investment activities, bypassing more onerous deposits burdened by costly regulatory measures.

The eurocurrency market is an offshore and multi-currency extension of domestic interbank money markets in its core operations. However, there are several distinctive characteristics associated with the eurocurrency market. It is located in offshore money market centre locations that attract international banks to raise and lend funds in major currencies that are not the domestic currency of the market. London has traditionally been the most important location for eurocurrency transactions. Other regional locations such as Frankfurt, Bahrain, Hong Kong, and Singapore also act as a eurocurrency centre. More importantly, the eurocurrency market is where short-term credits in the form of bank deposits in major currencies are traded in locations where they are not the domestic currency. That is, it is a market for bank deposits and loans denominated in currencies that are foreign to the market in which banks trade with each other. For example, a German bank taking a USD-denominated deposit from a US bank in its London branch is a eurodeposit. This USD-denominated eurocurrency deposit is referred to as eurodollar. Other major currencies such as the Euro, the JPY, and the GBP are also used for euro transactions, and they are called euroeuro, euroyen, and europound, respectively. The separation of currency denomination between the instrument and the market is a central characteristic of the eurocurrency market and carries important financial regulation implications. A purpose-built foreign bank branch (or subsidiary) located in a eurocurrency market location and engaging in eurocurrency transactions is called a eurobank.

Exhibits 5.1(A) and 5.1(B) present the pattern of cross-border claims of BIS reporting banks over the recent decades and the proportion of each component of the claims (% market share), respectively. Total cross-border claims stood at USD 35 trillion at the end of 2020, as shown in Panel A of Exhibit 5.1(A), representing over 27 times the size of the 1980 claims. The bulk of the claims is loans and deposits, which account for 63% of all claims (Exhibit 5.1(B)), down from 88% in 1995 (Panel B). Panel C shows the currency denomination breakdown. The most important currency in the cross-border banking market is the USD accounting for 45% of the total claims in 2020, followed by the Euro (31%), the Yen (6%), and the GBP (5%).

In Panel D, the cross-border claims are broken down into those denominated in the domestic currency of the market and those denominated in foreign currencies. Only the latter involves the required currency separation and qualifies as 'euro' instruments. The term 'euro' does not refer to the EUR, the domestic currency in the Eurozone countries. Instead, it is a generic term referring to the presence of the currency separation between the instrument and the market. The share of the USD in the eurocurrency market was 60% in 2020, and it has been stable over the past

	1980	1985	1990	1995	2000	2005	2010	2015	2020
				Panel A: Total cross-border claims					
Total cross-border claims	**1,310**	**2,538**	**6,178**	**7,882**	**10,550**	**20,847**	**29,758**	**27,120**	**35,733**
				Panel B: Total cross-border claims by instruments					
A: Loans and deposits									
US Dollar (USD)				3,260	4,143	7,400	10,948	10,100	11,139
Euro (EUR)				1,610	1,996	4,873	6,865	4,565	6,623
Yen (JPY)				1,319	1,075	814	1,059	667	1,008
UK Pound (GBP)				224	401	979	1,247	1,037	1,200
Swiss Frac (CHF)				235	219	277	370	299	324
All other currencies				314	345	709	1,347	1,531	2,170
All currencies				6,961	8,180	15,052	21,836	18,200	22,464
B: Debt instruments				897	1,943	4,824	5,907	5,792	7,756
C: Other instruments				23	427	971	2,014	2,997	5,355
D: Unallocated				0.010	0.010	0.016	–0.114	132	158
All instruments	**1,310**	**2,538**	**6,178**	**7,882**	**10,550**	**20,847**	**29,758**	**27,120**	**35,733**
				Panel C: Total cross-border claims by currency composition					
US Dollar (USD)	764	1,766	3,326	3,674	5,080	9,243	13,394	13,388	16,140
Euro (EUR)	220	392	1,241	1,945	3,053	7,903	10,672	7,801	11,179
Yen (JPY)	24	144	863	1,382	1,215	1,121	1,491	1,439	2,158
UK Pound (GBP)	36	67	263	247	468	1,192	1,537	1,353	1,693
Swiss Frac (CHF)	64	124	279	258	243	333	477	512	468
All currencies excl. core	202	45	206	377	491	1,055	2,187	2,626	4,096
				Panel D: Total cross-border claims by currency composition and location					
A: Domestic currency									
US Dollar (USD)	173	406	513	527	894	1,830	3,259	2,407	2,915
Euro (EUR)	98	132	389	715	1,968	5,355	7,262	5,185	7,678
Yen (JPY)	17	74	418	625	451	402	735	771	1,103
All other currencies	54	84	232	260	373	893	1,199	1,319	1,811
All currencies	342	695	1,551	2,126	3,687	8,480	12,454	9,683	13,507
B: Foreign currency									
US Dollar (USD)	591	1,360	2,813	3,146	4,186	7,413	10,135	10,981	13,225
Euro (EUR)	122	260	853	1,230	1,086	2,548	3,410	2,616	3,501
Yen (JPY)	7	70	445	757	763	719	756	668	1,055
UK Pound (GBP)	14	29	168	146	265	600	845	769	995
Swiss Frac (CHF)	35	88	162	158	170	249	380	328	337
All currencies excl. core	199	40	186	318	393	838	1,777	1,992	2,925
All currencies	968	1,847	4,628	5,756	6,863	12,367	17,303	17,354	22,037
C: Unallocated		–4.13	–0.22	–0.46	–0.07		0.02	83	189
All currencies and locations	**1,310**	**2,538**	**6,178**	**7,882**	**10,550**	**20,847**	**29,758**	**27,120**	**35,733**

Exhibit 5.1(A) Cross-border positions of BIS reporting banks at end of year, in USD billion.

Note: Deutsche Mark is used as a proxy for the Euro prior to 1999.

Source: BIS locational banking statistics, https://www.bis.org/statistics/about_banking_stats.htm.

	1980	1985	1990	1995	2000	2005	2010	2015	2020
				Panel A: Total cross-border claims					
Total cross-border claims	**1,310**	**2,538**	**6,178**	**7,882**	**10,550**	**20,847**	**29,758**	**27,120**	**35,733**
				Panel B: Total-cross border claims by instruments					
A: Loans and deposits				6,961	8,180	15,052	21,836	18,200	22,464
US Dollar (USD)				47%	51%	49%	50%	55%	50%
Euro (EUR)				23%	24%	32%	31%	25%	29%
Yen (JPY)				19%	13%	5%	5%	4%	4%
UK Pound (GBP)				3%	5%	7%	6%	6%	5%
Swiss Frac (CHF)				3%	3%	2%	2%	2%	1%
All other currencies				5%	4%	5%	6%	8%	10%
All currencies				88%	78%	72%	73%	67%	63%
B: Debt instruments				897	1,943	4,824	5,907	5,792	7,756
				11%	18%	23%	20%	21%	22%
C: Other instruments				23	427	971	2,014	2,997	5,355
				0%	4%	5%	7%	11%	15%
D: Unallocated				0%	0%	0%	0%	0%	0%
All instruments	**1,310**	**2,538**	**6,178**	**7,882**	**10,550**	**20,847**	**29,758**	**27,120**	**35,733**
				Panel C: Total cross-border claims by currency composition					
US Dollar (USD)	58%	70%	54%	47%	48%	44%	45%	49%	45%
Euro (EUR)	17%	15%	20%	25%	29%	38%	36%	29%	31%
Yen (JPY)	2%	6%	14%	18%	12%	5%	5%	5%	6%
UK Pound (GBP)	3%	3%	4%	3%	4%	6%	5%	5%	5%
Swiss Frac (CHF)	5%	5%	5%	3%	2%	2%	2%	2%	1%
All currencies excl. core	15%	2%	3%	5%	5%	5%	7%	10%	11%
				Panel D: Total cross-border claims by currency composition and location					
A: Domestic currency	342	695	1,551	2,126	3,687	8,480	12,454	9,683	13,507
US Dollar (USD)	51%	58%	33%	25%	24%	22%	26%	25%	22%
Euro (EUR)	29%	19%	25%	34%	53%	63%	58%	54%	57%
Yen (JPY)	5%	11%	27%	29%	12%	5%	6%	8%	8%
All other currencies	16%	12%	15%	12%	10%	11%	10%	14%	13%
All currencies	*26%*	*27%*	*25%*	*27%*	*35%*	*41%*	*42%*	*36%*	*38%*
B: Foreign currency	968	1,847	4,628	5,756	6,863	12,367	17,303	17,354	22,037
US Dollar (USD)	61%	74%	61%	55%	61%	60%	59%	63%	60%
Euro (EUR)	13%	14%	18%	21%	16%	21%	20%	15%	16%
Yen (JPY)	1%	4%	10%	13%	11%	6%	4%	4%	5%
UK Pound (GBP)	1%	2%	4%	3%	4%	5%	5%	4%	5%
Swiss Frac (CHF)	4%	5%	4%	3%	2%	2%	2%	2%	2%
All currencies excl. core	21%	2%	4%	6%	6%	7%	10%	11%	13%
All currencies	*74%*	*73%*	*75%*	*73%*	*65%*	*59%*	*58%*	*64%*	*62%*
C: Unallocated	*0%*	*0%*	*0%*	*0%*	*0%*	*0%*	*0%*	*0%*	*1%*
All currencies and locations	**1,310**	**2,538**	**6,178**	**7,882**	**10,550**	**20,847**	**29,758**	**27,120**	**35,733**

Exhibit 5.1(B) Cross-border positions of BIS reporting banks at end of year, % share.

Note: Deutsche Mark is used as a proxy for the Euro prior to 1999.

Source: BIS locational banking statistics, https://www.bis.org/statistics/about_banking_stats.htm.

four decades. The currency Euro was a distant second at 16%, followed by the JPY (5%) and the GBP (5%).

The cross-border claims denominated in domestic currencies are not euro instruments as they are denominated in the currency of the market. However, since the lender is foreign to the market, this part of the cross-border claim is referred to as a 'foreign' claim (e.g., a German bank making USD-denominated loans to US borrowers in the US). In foreign loans, the market share of the EUR was 57%, nearly three times the size of the USD-denominated foreign claims at 22%. In short, international or cross-border claims were made up of euro claims which accounted for 62%, and foreign claims accounted for 38% of the total in 2020. The USD dominated euro claims while the EUR dominated foreign claims. In other words, if banks wish to make loans or borrow in the USD, they mostly do so in the eurodollar market. In contrast, if they need the EUR-denominated transactions, they undertake them directly in the Eurozone markets.

5.2. The Origins and the Sources of Growth of the Eurocurrency Market

The Eurocurrency market traces its origin to the creation of the eurodollar market in the post-Second World War period when the USD became the international trade vehicle currency replacing the GBP. The USD 15 billion Marshall Plan of 1948, aimed at reviving the war-devastated Western Europe, attracted US multinational companies to operate in then a frontier market. These two factors, among others, have contributed to considerable USD funds being circulated outside the US, requiring intermediation and payment services from banks. Judson (2017) reports that as much as 80% of the USD currency (notes and coins) in circulation was outside the US in 2016, an increase from around 13% in 1971. This represents approximately 900 USD billion (60% of 1,500 billion) in 2016 and 25 billion (13% of 189 billion) in 1971.[1] As the USD in circulation outside the US grew, so did the demand for offshore USD intermediation services. US banks already operating in Western Europe, London in particular, in the late 1960s and the 1970s were well placed to offer the required services due to their participation in the USD funds clearing system in the US.

[1] The figures for the USD in circulation were obtained from Money Stock Measures — H.6 Release from the US FRB's website. https://www.federalreserve.gov/releases/h6/current/default.htm.

Other Western European and Japanese banks also became active in the market from the early 1970s.

5.2.1. *The origin of the eurocurrency market*

In addition to the Marshall Plan that encouraged US multinational banks to follow their domestic multinational corporate customers into Western Europe, they also faced push factors that encouraged them to seek opportunities outside the US (see Chapter 2). The restrictive US regulations added significant costs to their domestic operations that they could escape from in their foreign operations. Most notable were Regulation Q and Interest Equalisation Tax. Regulation Q was introduced in 1933 and was a Federal Reserve regulation on capital adequacy requirements for banks operating in the US. Until 2011, Regulation Q prohibited interest payments on demand deposits. Until 1986, it set maximum interest rate payable on other types of deposits, such as savings and Negotiable Order of Withdrawal (NOW) accounts. This regulation applied to banks operating in the US. So, non-US multinational banks that could intermediate in the USD outside the US offered higher deposit rates in the eurodollar market during periods of high USD credit demand. This attracted US depositors seeking higher interest rates to open eurodollar accounts at banks outside the US, which was at the expense of US banks that were effectively prevented from competing with the higher eurodollar deposit rates. In the late 1960s, the interest rate ceiling became binding such that the gap between eurodollar deposit rates and US domestic deposit rates widened, resulting in a burst of market activities in the offshore eurodollar market. As a result, USD deposits flowed to the eurodollar market seeking higher deposit interest rates. Another regulation that led to USD fund outflows into the eurodollar market was the Interest Equalisation Tax during 1963–1974. It was a measure designed to reduce the US balance of payment deficit by imposing levies on the purchase prices of foreign stocks and bonds US residents invested in. The levy was 15% on foreign stocks and up to 22.5% on foreign bonds. An unexpected consequence of this tax was the eurodollar market attracting funds from US investors avoiding the highly taxed foreign investment activities.

Post-Second World War global politics was the main pull factor of USD funds into the offshore money market. The USD became the international trade vehicle currency and the dominant currency in international finance in general. Moreover, commodities such as oil, agriculture, and mineral products are priced in the USD. The strength of the USD due to the US economy was unquestionable. In 1949, the US held approximately 70% of the world's monetary gold, which was more than what was required under the Bretton Woods system of international monetary arrangement (e.g., one ounce of gold was set to convert to 35 USD). The growing tension between the Western and Soviet bloc countries made it hazardous for the countries belonging to the second group and other countries that the US deemed adversarial (e.g., states deemed to support international terrorism) to hold USD assets. As the Cold War intensified, the US government froze USD bank deposits held in domestic branches of US banks of many countries considered to be in conflict with the US. These included Czechoslovakian gold holdings in New York in 1948 and the USD deposits of the British, French, and Egyptian governments during the Suez Canal crisis in 1956. The Soviet bloc countries, therefore, needed to avoid placing their USD funds in the US banking system, where they could be frozen. European banks started to offer USD-denominated deposits outside the US. A French bank with a Telex codename 'eurobank' was active in this space, and the codename became synonymous with eurobanking activities. The crucial premise was that the USD deposits held in banks outside the US jurisdiction were safe from the US authorities' attempts to freeze them.[2] In addition, the sterling crisis of late 1956 and early 1957 spelled the end of the GBP as the international trade vehicle currency. The GBP was the *de facto* international trade vehicle currency until the crisis period, and London was the centre of international

[2]On 7 January 1986, the US authorities tested this premise after terrorist attacks at Rome and Vienna airports that implicated Libya (Rutzke, 1988). They froze the USD 131 million correspondent account of the Bankers Trust (BT)'s London branch owned by Libyan Arab Foreign Bank (LAFB). A presidential executive order was issued to make it illegal for BT or any other US banks to make any payments out of the Libyan account. LAFB sued BT in a UK court, demanding repayment of the remaining balance in the account, and BT put forward a 'eurocurrency defence' for their non-compliance. In essence, the defence relied on the fact that USD payments must be processed through the US payment system which is under full control of the US authorities. As such, the UK court cannot compel BT to process any payments in circumvention of the US executive order. The UK court, however, determined that payments must then be made in London in some other way instead of via the US payment system. BT was ordered to pay LAFB in cash in USD or other currencies in London. This case reinforced that USD deposits in the eurodollar market are beyond the control of the US authorities as long as they are placed outside the US jurisdiction.

finance. However, due to the domestic monetary policy implications, the UK authorities banned the UK banks from providing trade financing in the GBP between non-UK entities (e.g., international trade between two non-UK entities). This almost overnight made the USD the new international vehicle currency, replacing the GBP. As a direct result, the increasing demand for USD credits outside the US led to the creation of the USD credit market outside the jurisdiction of the US.

5.2.2. *The source of growth of the eurocurrency market*

The eurocurrency market has experienced explosive growth since the early years. Exhibit 5.2 shows the market size since 1964, which grew from USD 221 billion to USD 22 trillion by 2021. The dominant component of the eurocurrency market has been the eurodollar market, whose market share hovered around 80% until the early 1980s. Since then, the emerging importance of other currencies, especially the EUR, reduced the dominance of the USD. In 2021, the USD (eurodollar) accounted for 62% of the eurocurrency market, followed by the EUR (euroeuro, 15%), the GBP (europound, 4.3%), and the JPY (euroyen, 3.7%). Exhibit 5.3 shows the share of each major currency in the eurocurrency market in 2021.

The growth of the eurocurrency market can be attributed to various factors. *First*, there was an increasing need for effective global financial

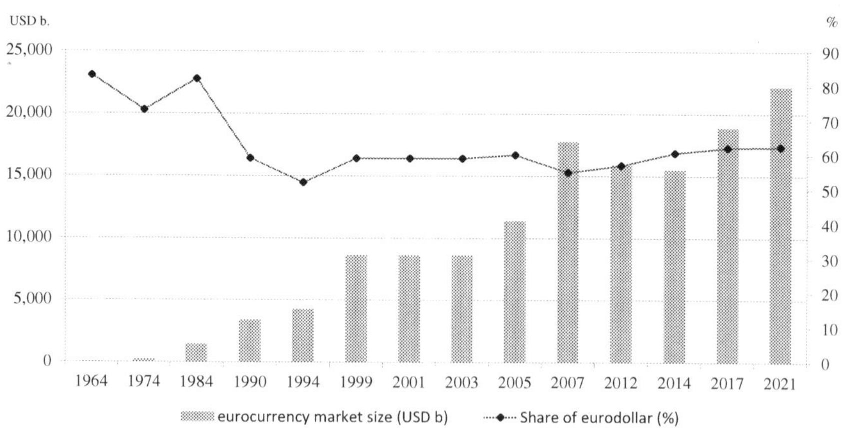

Exhibit 5.2. Size of the eurocurrency market and the share of eurodollar.

Source: BIS locational banking statistics.

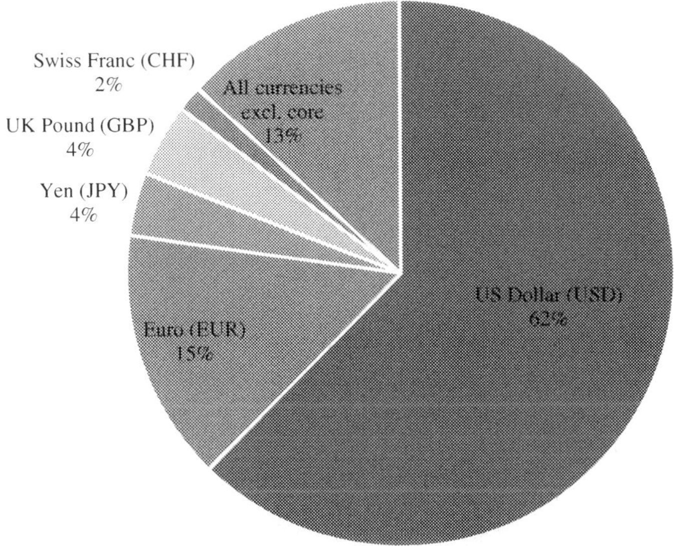

Exhibit 5.3. Currency proportions in eurocurrency markets in December 2021.
Source: BIS locational banking statistics.

intermediation from the early 1970s. The emergence of distinct global savers (OPEC economies in the 1970s, Germany and Japan in the 1980s and 1990s) and borrowers (current account deficit countries; the US, Australia, and developing countries) necessitated efficient global financial intermediation. Also, non-US block countries in the Cold War era needed safe havens for their USD assets which they found in the eurodollar market in the 1960s.

Second, the eurocurrency market is beyond the jurisdiction of any one country and so is free from regulations that limit domestic banks. Since the financial regulator in a country is concerned about ensuring domestic system stability, they concentrate on the stability of price and quantity of their domestic currency. Foreign currency-denominated transactions within their jurisdiction do not have any direct implication on price stability or monetary policy integrity, and as such, there are generally no incentives for imposing regulations on these transactions. The usual reserve requirement does not apply to eurodeposits, so eurobanks can lend the full amount of deposits they receive. There are no interest rate or other lending restrictions. The interest rate ceiling that was binding in the face of rising interest rates in the US in the late 1970s and early 1980s made USD deposits with eurobanks more attractive for US depositors who had access to the eurodollar market. Eurodollar deposits are not subject to deposit insurance, so eurobanks can offer higher deposit rates than US domestic deposit rates. The result is narrower interest rate spreads (e.g., higher deposit rate and lower lending rate) in the eurodollar market compared to the domestic US market. US banks received some support from their government by being allowed to establish the International Banking Facility at home to engage in eurodollar activities without leaving US soil.

Third, the eurocurrency market focuses on the top end of the deposit and loan business, and eurobanks tend to specialise in one or two aspects of the market (in terms of currency, maturity, and amount). As a result, the banks operating in the market can achieve scale economies in their operations.

5.3. Intermediation in the Eurocurrency Market

The eurocurrency market is similar to the foreign exchange market in that it is an OTC market organised around market makers and brokers. The participating banks trade short-term bank time deposits on the 'euro' basis with each other. Market makers provide bid and ask rates (borrowing and lending interest rates) upon request in the direct dealing market segment. In the broker segment of the market, brokers match one-sided bid and ask requests from banks in the market for a fee. Exhibit 5.4 shows the representative bid–ask quotes in the eurocurrency market for major eurocurrencies observed on 5 June 2022.

The bulk of eurocurrency activities centres around borrowing and lending time deposits in various major currencies (the USD, 62% market

	USD		EUR		JPY		GBP		CHF		CAD		AUD	
Duration\Currency	Bid	Ask	Bid	Ask	Bid	Ask	Bid	Ask	Bid	Ask	Bid	Ask	Bid	Ask
Overnight	0.73	0.81	−0.59	−0.38	−0.03	0.01	0.90	1.10	−0.76	−0.38	0.95	1.70	0.18	0.81
Tomorrow next deposit	0.78	1.00	−0.64	−0.55	−0.35	0.02	0.90	1.10	−0.83	−0.68	1.23	1.73	0.40	0.75
Spot week deposit	0.80	1.03	−0.65	−0.44	−0.35	0.03	0.86	1.09	−0.77	−0.62	1.23	1.56	0.68	0.88
1 month	1.19	1.39	−0.59	−0.44	−0.35	0.03	1.03	1.25	−0.80	−0.50	1.30	1.60	0.63	0.93
3 month	1.50	1.63	−0.47	−0.34	−0.23	−0.03	1.36	1.56	−0.60	−0.34	1.50	2.00	1.10	1.40
6 month	2.08	2.28	−0.05	0.10	−0.20	0.06	1.80	2.15	−0.45	−0.15	2.00	2.50	1.70	2.00
9 month	2.32	2.45	0.15	0.30	−0.15	0.15	2.00	2.35	−0.25	0.05	2.60	2.80	2.30	2.55
1 year	2.65	2.78	0.56	0.81	−0.30	0.12	2.13	2.33	−0.06	0.14	2.80	3.05	2.77	3.02

Exhibit 5.4. Eurocurrency deposit rates on 5 June 2022.

Source: Extracted from Refinitiv Eikon on 5 June 2022.

share in 2021) for short-term periods of usually up to 180 days and in amounts starting from USD 1m or its equivalents in other currencies. Trading in eurocurrencies is conducted between banks over both voice and electronic communication methods, and the funds are transferred through credit lines (Nostro and Vostro accounts) they already have with each other. The transfer occurs within the domestic payment system of the currency denomination. All eurodollar transactions are processed via the CHIPS (for netting transactions) or Fedwire (RTGS) system, euroeuro via Target2 system, and euroyen via BOJ-NET. For example, if HSBC purchases a USD 1m eurodollar from (or makes a deposit of USD 1 m. to) Barclays in London, then HSBC instructs one of its New York branches (or other US branch locations) to transfer USD 1m to Barclay's account opened at HSBC via Fedwire.

Exhibit 5.5 shows the role of the eurocurrency market in the intermediating flow of loanable funds between borrowers and lenders located outside the market. A deposit made by an outside depositor is recycled through the eurocurrency market involving one or more (two in this case) eurobanks trading eurocurrency contracts with each other before it is loaned out to an outside borrower. A eurocurrency refers to a time deposit issued by a eurobank in a currency denomination other than the local currency of the issuing market.[3]

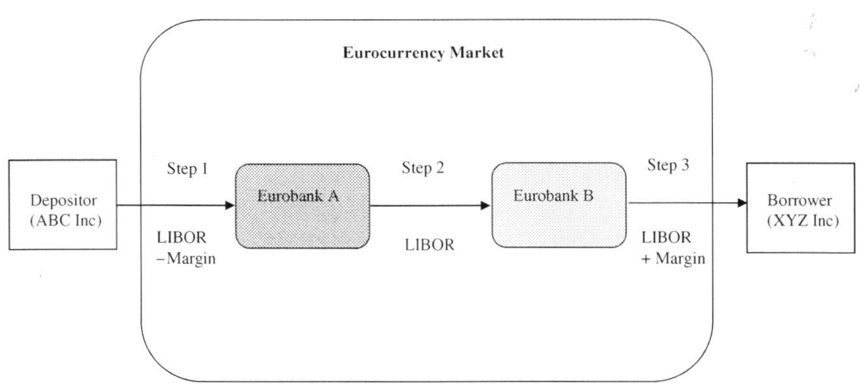

Exhibit 5.5. Operations of the eurocurrency market.

[3]Despite the term 'currency', a eurocurrency is not a currency in the usual sense. A currency is a monetary unit that is legal tender in a country, where it performs the following roles:

Lenders/Depositors are attracted to the eurocurrency market's high deposit rates compared to domestic market counterparts. In Step 1, ABC Inc. places a USD deposit with Eurobank A, via transferring the USD fund from its bank account at a bank in the US to the Eurobank A's correspondent account at a US bank. Eurobank A then needs to find a borrower for the fund and if it has a borrower already lined up, then Step 2 can be skipped. However, Eurobank A generally has a comparative advantage in attracting USD deposits from outside the eurocurrency market. Due to the lack of regulatory protections in the eurocurrency market, depositors prefer large international banks that are highly visible in the market and deemed safer. Eurobank A then aims to find another bank in the market with a competitive advantage in securing borrowers on short notice. Eurobank B has such a competitive advantage and bids for the deposit. In Step 2, Eurobank A places the fund with Eurobank B by transferring the fund to the latter's correspondent bank's account in the US. In Step 3, Eurobank B makes a loan to a borrower, XYZ Inc., attracted to the market's competitive lending interest rates compared to the domestic market counterparts.

Exhibit 5.6 presents the eurocurrency creation process outlined above in a T-Account representation. ABC Inc. is a US company that holds USD 1m of its excess working capital in a time deposit (TD) with a domestic US bank. The balance sheet positions of ABC and its bank are shown in Panel A. The USD 1m is shown as a TD in the asset side of ABC's account, and as a liability in the US bank's account. The second half of Panel A shows the accounts when the TD matures and it is deposited into ABC's demand deposit (DD) account at the US bank. The TD entries are now changed to DD in both accounts.

Suppose that ABC still has no immediate need for the fund and is attracted to the higher deposit interest rate offered by Eurobank A, and decides to place it as a TD (say for one month) at that higher rate. This is shown as Step 1 in Panel B. The ownership of the DD is transferred to Eurobank A from ABC in the liability side of the US bank's account.

---

(1) Medium of exchange: The characteristics of currency are acceptability, standardisation, divisibility, portability, and durability.

(2) Unit of account: Money provides a relative measure of the value of goods and services.

(3) Store of value: Money acts as a store of wealth
(e.g., hard currencies are considered to be solid investments).

Eurocurrency performs only (3).

Panel A: Balance sheet positions before eurodeposit

US Bank

Assets	Liabilities
	$1m TD due to ABC

ABC Inc

Assets	Liabilities
$1m TD with US Bank	

US Bank

Assets	Liabilities
	$1m DD due to ABC

ABC Inc

Assets	Liabilities
$1m DD with US Bank	

Panel B: Step 1 — Deposit with Eurobank A

US Bank

Assets	Liabilities
	$1m DD due to Eurobank A

ABC Inc

Assets	Liabilities
$1m TD with Eurobank A	

Eurobank A

Assets	Liabilities
$1m DD with US Bank	$1m TD due to ABC

Panel C: Step 2 — Eurobank A sells deposit to Eurobank B

US Bank

Assets	Liabilities
	$1m DD due to Eurobank B

ABC Inc

Assets	Liabilities
$1m TD with Eurobank A	

Eurobank A

Assets	Liabilities
$1m TD with Eurobank B	$1m TD due to ABC

Eurobank B

Assets	Liabilities
$1m DD with US Bank	$1m TD due to Eurobank A

Panel D: Step 3 — Eurobank B lends to borrower

US Bank

Assets	Liabilities
	$1m DD due to XYZ Inc.

ABC Inc

Assets	Liabilities
$1m TD with Eurobank A	

Eurobank A

Assets	Liabilities
$1m TD with Eurobank B	$1m TD due to ABC

Eurobank B

Assets	Liabilities
$1m loan to XYZ Inc.	$1m TD due to Eurobank A

XYZ Inc

Assets	Liabilities
$1m DD with US Bank	$1m credit from Eurobank B

Exhibit 5.6. Operations of the eurocurrency market: T-accounts.

Source: Adopted from Eun *et al.* (2021).

ABC's claim is now in TD at Eurobank A. Eurobank A has a liability against ABC but now has the DD transferred to its correspondent account at the US bank. In this step, a eurodollar is created.

In Step 2, Eurobank A places a TD with Eurobank B. The T-account changes from the transfer are shown in Panel C. The DD ownership is now transferred to Eurobank B via the US bank debiting Eurobank A's account and crediting Eurobank B's account. In Step 3, Eurobank B lends USD 1m to a borrower, XYZ Inc, located in the US (Panel D). The payment transfer is again debiting and crediting the accounts held at the US bank by the payer (Eurobank B) and receiver (XYZ) of the fund.

From Steps 1–3, the USD 1m DD held at the US bank has remained in the US banking sector throughout this process. Only its legal ownership has been passed around. Fund transfers in all three steps occur through appropriate accounting entries made to the accounts held at the US bank by the parties involved in these transactions either directly or via correspondent banks who hold accounts at the US bank. The DD has never physically left the US jurisdiction, only the ownership has been transferred from a US entity to foreign banks before coming back to another US entity. This is similar in consequence to a real estate sale to a foreign buyer where the ownership is transferred, but the asset is still housed in the US. As such, the US authorities have full jurisdictional control of the underlying asset and how the fund transfers are processed through its payment system.

In the above example, the end result is that domestic intermediation is replaced by offshore intermediation by two eurobanks due to their competitive advantage over domestic banks in pricing their products. A eurodeposit is created when a eurobank deposits the fund it received from an outside depositor to another Eurobank (e.g., Step 2 in Exhibit 5.5 and Panel B and Exhibit 5.6). A euroloan is then created when Eurobank B loans out the fund it borrowed in the eurocurrency market. The process is summarised in Exhibit 5.7. The red arrows show the direction of fund flows if the domestic banking system intermediated the flows. In this instance, the role of the eurocurrency market is to bypass domestic intermediation. In most other cases, the eurocurrency market intermediates between two international traders and investors, facilitating international capital flows.

Exhibit 5.8 extends the example shown in Exhibit 5.7 by considering the eurocurrency market replacing a domestic banking sector intermediation between a domestic depositor and a foreign borrower. Assume that

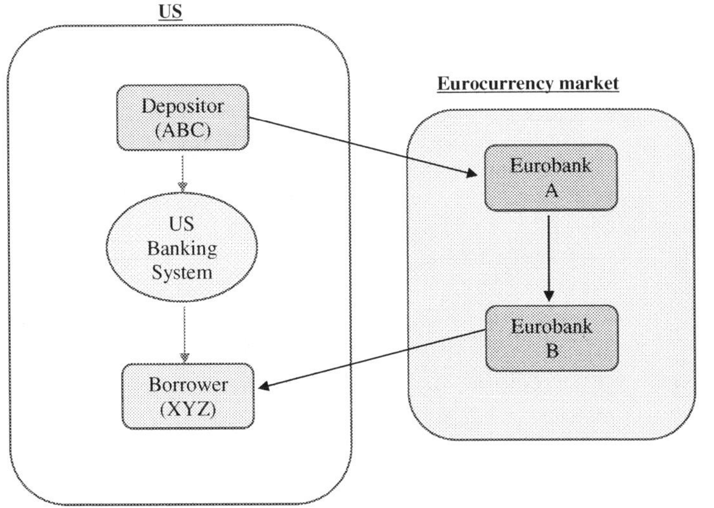

Exhibit 5.7. Eurocurrency markets replacing domestic intermediation.

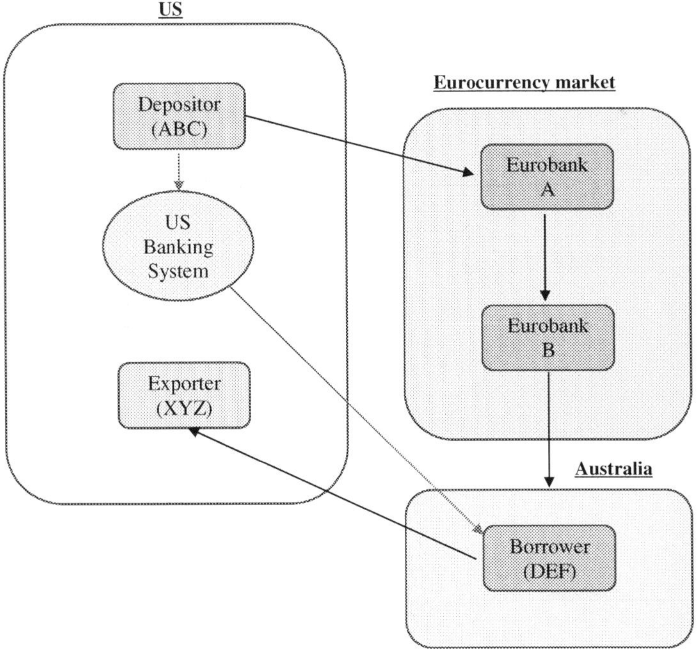

Exhibit 5.8. Eurocurrency markets replacing international capital flows.

the eurodeposit made by ABC Inc is passed onto an Australian borrower, DEF Ltd. DEF receives the USD 1m into its account at a bank operating in the US or the US correspondent bank of its Australian bank. It then uses the fund to pay the invoice of a transaction between it and XYZ Inc, located in the US. At the end of the process, the ownership of the fund is returned to the US banking system. The red arrows show the fund flows (similar to the ownership changes as shown in Exhibit 5.6) in the absence of the eurocurrency market. This requires the Australian borrower to access the US banking system directly. This may pose difficulties as DEF may not be well known in the US as it is in Australia. As such, it may not be able to borrow at all or the full amount, let alone receive an attractive interest rate. Tapping into the eurocurrency market alleviates this issue, as eurobanks are foreign branches of multinational banks that are likely to have a presence in multiple countries, including Australia. If so, they are able to obtain as much information on the borrower from its Australian operation as possible to conduct an adequate risk analysis. As a result, they can charge a much lower interest rate than a domestic US lender by reducing the risk premium component. In extreme cases, some foreign borrowers may not be allowed to do business with US banks due to political reasons, then their only option to raise USD funds is to access the eurodollar market, which is beyond the reach of the US government.

5.4. Functions of Eurocurrency Market

The eurocurrency market is an over-the-counter interbank money market that provides essential services for market participants who are eurobanks and other multinational financial and non-financial corporations. The services provided include eurocurrency intermediation, hedging and position taking, balance sheet management, and regulation cost minimisation.

First, eurobanks channel wholesale funds in major currencies on a 'euro' basis from lenders to eventual borrowers on a global scale. Eurobanks enjoy competitive advantages over domestic banks, such as lower cost of funds due to low or absence of regulation costs and financial innovation. This allows them to intermediate between parties located in the same banking jurisdiction (as in Exhibit 5.7) or across different countries (as in Exhibit 5.8), thereby replacing intermediation by the domestic banking system.

Second, eurobanks provide hedging facilities to each other and to other (mostly financial) institutions. For example, a eurobank with funding needs in the USD and expects a future rise in eurodollar interest rates would borrow eurodollars now to lock in a fixed rate for the term. In addition, over-the-counter derivatives on eurocurrencies, which essentially have the same characteristics as interest rate derivatives traded in domestic money markets, are on offer mostly for hedging purposes. A eurobank can combine cash and futures positions to hedge against unforeseen future interest rate movements. Other forms of interest rate derivatives used include interest rate options, swaps, caps, and floors provided over the counter.

Third, the balance sheet adjustment needs of financial institutions may be fulfilled by trading in eurocurrencies. Eurobanks with unbalanced positions in terms of currency positions (currency mismatch), duration (maturity mismatch), and interest rate denomination (basis mismatch) between assets and liabilities are exposed to risks arising from these balance sheet exposures. They face deteriorating profitability if unfavourable market movements occur. For example, a eurobank with most of its liabilities in the USD and assets mostly in the EUR is exposed to exchange rate risk if the EUR depreciates against the USD. Trading in appropriate eurocurrency contracts (e.g., buying eurodollar financed by selling euroeuro contracts) can reduce this exposure.

Fourth, the eurocurrency market offers both financial and non-financial institutions opportunities to avoid regulation-induced costs. Eurobanks have been able to offer their customers attractive interest rates (higher deposit rates and lower lending rates) compared to domestic banks. Domestic banks are subject to various regulatory measures designed to achieve safety in the relevant domestic banking market, but these regulations add to the costs of providing intermediation services. These include reserve ratios on deposits, deposit insurance premiums, liquidity requirements, exposure limits, and other operational regulations. Due to their multi-jurisdictional status, eurobanks are exempt from most of these constraints when they engage in eurocurrency transactions, allowing them to offer narrower interest rate spreads than their domestic bank counterparts.

5.5. Eurobank Operations

Eurobanks source most of their funds from the eurocurrency market on a short-term basis and hold assets that are also short term. On the liability side, they fund their operations by issuing call money, time deposits, certificates of deposits (CD), floating-rate notes, and bonds. On the asset side, there are loans to other banks and non-bank customers. The liabilities vary in maturities, marketability, and currency denominations. Call money is a deposit with no specific maturity date and is repayable upon notice from the depositor. Depending on the account, repayment may take up to seven days. The most important instrument is a time deposit with fixed maturity date on which the principal and interest (based on LIBOR) are paid. It is usually short term (up to six months, but mostly 90 days), and the interest rate is determined through negotiation between the parties. Although early redemption is possible, it is uncommon since most holders value reputation. When a eurobank buys a time deposit from another eurobank, it becomes the legal owner of the demand deposit of the same amount with a bank located in the country of the currency denomination (a US bank in the case of a eurodollar deposit), as mentioned in Section 4.3. Negotiable CDs are certificates for time deposits that have secondary markets. If the holder of a CD requires payment before maturity, it can be sold in the secondary market at its current price, which is equal to the discounted price from the face value at the going interest rate. Due to the transferability feature and the resulting market liquidity, a negotiable CD is popular with non-bank lenders. However, interest rates on a CD tend to be lower than comparable time deposits because of this additional flexibility. Banks may prefer to issue CDs in their own right to raise funds because interest rates on CDs are lower than on-time deposits of comparable terms and conditions and the circulation of their CDs increases the visibility of the issuing bank in the secondary market. Floating rate notes and bonds issued on a euro basis (i.e., euronotes and eurobonds) are of longer maturities, and secondary markets usually exist. They are usually in bearer form to guarantee the anonymity of ownership and are usually unrated. Other forms of innovation also emanated from the Eurobond market as changes in national regulation and investor preferences evolved (Smith, Walter and DeLong, 2012).

There are broadly two types of lenders in the eurocurrency market: those from the outside and those from the inside the market. The former (non-bank depositors) include multinational corporations, government entities, and (wealthy) individual investors, and funds from these sources represent initial injections into the eurocurrency market (eurodeposits). However, funds from these sources account for only 22% (in 1999) of the total and tend to be short term in nature, usually for placing short-term surplus funds. Large eurobanks have a comparative advantage in attracting funds from outside depositors due to their franchise value and perceived safety in terms of default, liquidity and currency risks. They often receive deposits without matching borrowers from outside the eurocurrency market. They will pass the deposit onto other (smaller) eurobanks who have clients with immediate funding needs or onto those who are prepared to take a position. When a deposit is being passed on, a margin is added that is typically very small to make negligible profits, if any. Also, eurobanks needing to unload eurocurrencies will be a source of funds for other eurobanks. Eurobanks trade in the eurocurrency market for the following motivations: inventory adjustment purposes, the need to be in the market to keep up their appearance (i.e., the perception of being an active player in the market), and information gathering on market conditions (getting the feel of the market by trading), and to take a position based on interest rate expectations.

Assets of eurobanks are mostly loans they make to other participants in the market and commercial customers who have access to the market (i.e., multinational corporations). The former comprises other eurobanks and banks in major financial centres. These loans arise from trading in time deposits. Bid and ask quotes on eurocurrencies are provided by eurobanks acting as market makers. A bid rate is a price that the quoting bank is willing to pay for a eurocurrency deposit (i.e., a time deposit with specific maturity and face value). The ask (sell) rate is its lending interest rate in that currency. Eurobanks that request quotes for liquidity reasons are usually small eurobanks with a comparative disadvantage in attracting deposits from non-bank depositors or those who currently have loan requests that need to be granted on short notice. Position-taking regarding future interest rate movements is also a motive.

Loans to non-banks are credits extended to eventual borrowers who represent the final resting place for eurodeposits. Loans to non-banks are generally longer term, have relatively higher default risk, and are offered on a roll-over basis, usually with a revolving credit facility (which is a set amount of loan that can be drawn in multiple steps within a specified period). Borrowers in this category include multinational corporations, sovereign entities, and wealthy individuals. Due to the large size of eurocurrency loans, they are usually syndicated. Lending banks form a syndicate of lenders that contribute a portion of the aggregate loan and perform a designated role in the syndicate. Lending banks share the tasks of originating, funding and monitoring roles across the syndicate members. By participating in multiple loan syndicates, lenders minimise the credit risk of their loan portfolios compared to concentrating on a smaller number of borrowers. The syndication process leads to lower overall interest costs for the borrower since the lenders can charge a lower risk premium due to the reduction of credit risk uncertainty from better quality information about the borrower provided by syndicate members. Moreover, lenders will be in a much better position to assess the aggregate amount of loans the borrower is seeking in the market by having multiple information sources. International loan syndication is discussed in Chapter 6.

5.6. Loan Pricing

The interest rate on a eurocurrency loan is based on London Inter-Bank Offer Rate (LIBOR), which is the interest rate banks operating in the eurocurrency market are willing to lend to other banks in the market, assuming no counterparty default risk. LIBORs on the USD and other major currencies are used as a benchmark interest rate for each currency and credit maturity not only in the London market where they are set but also in the domestic money market of the currency denomination.

5.6.1. *ICE LIBOR*

From February 2014, InterContinental Exchange (ICE) Benchmark Administration (IBA) assumed the responsibility of administering the calculation and publication of LIBOR, known as ICE LIBOR. LIBOR for each of the currencies and maturities observed on 3 June 2022 is shown in Exhibit 5.9.

As of 1 January 2022, the USD LIBOR is determined using the traditional method of polling banks participating in the London interbank money market to produce an average lending (offer) rate, published at 11:55 am London time each day. A panel of banks (panel banks)[4] makes

---

[4]The panel banks are large multinational banks participating in wholesale and unsecured funding markets in the USD. The current panel banks as of June 2022 are Bank of America N.A. (London Branch), JPMorgan Chase Bank, N.A. (London Branch), Barclays Bank plc, Lloyds Bank plc, Citibank N.A. (London Branch), MUFG Bank, Ltd, Cooperative Rabobank U.A., Royal Bank of Canada, Crédit Agricole Corporate & Investment Bank, SMBC Bank International plc, Credit Suisse AG (London Branch), the Norinchukin Bank,

	USD LIBOR	EUR EURIBOR	JPY LIBOR	GBP LIBOR
Overnight	0.8191	—	—	—
Spot week	—	−0.5660	—	—
1 month	1.1197	−0.5380	−0.0555	1.1248
2 month	—	—	—	—
3 month	1.6260	−0.3280	−0.0190	1.4184
6 month	2.1093	−0.0080	0.0326	1.8742
1 year	2.7754	0.4860	—	—

Exhibit 5.9. LIBOR for major currencies on 3 June 2022 % pa.

Notes: From 1 January 2022, ICE reports LIBOR on only three currencies, USD, JPY and GBP, on the maturities shown above collected at 11:55 am UTC. https://www.theice.com/iba/libor.

The EMMI EURIBOR is the interbank offer rate based on the average interest rates a panel of European banks can borrow from each other and is reported at 2 pm UTC by the European Money Market Institute (EMMI). https://www.emmi-benchmarks.eu/.

Source: Extracted from Refitiv Eikon on 5 June 2022.

their transactions-based and -derived submissions in their USD activities each day. The overnight and one-year maturities for the USD will be dropped from 30 June 2023. The calculation of LIBOR for the GBP and the JPY has changed over to a synthetic method that does not consider current market conditions or panel banks' input. So, as of 1 January 2022, LIBOR is set for only three currencies, the USD, the JPY, and the GBP, across maturities ranging from overnight to one year. Before 1 January 2022, LIBOR was set daily for the EUR, the CHF, and the other three major currencies across seven maturities, resulting in 35 individual rates applicable for each business day.

5.6.2. *BBA LIBOR*

Before the ICE Benchmark Association took over the role of setting LIBORs in 2014, the British Bankers' Association (BBA) was responsible

Deutsche Bank AG (London Branch), UBS AG, and HSBC Bank plc. https://www.theice.com/iba/libor.

for daily LIBOR setting since 1986 when it first took this role. Each day, a panel of 6 to 18 banks operating in the London interbank market reported their actual or expected borrowing interest rates across ten currencies over fifteen maturities at 11 am in London. There were 150 currency and maturity combinations in total.[5] The submitted rates for each of the 150 interest rates were processed by first discarding the top 25% and the bottom 25% of submissions and then calculating the average for the day for each interest rate using the middle 50% of submissions. BBA LIBOR was used as a reference rate to set other interest rates and to price financial derivatives and transactions around the world. A rough estimate of the size of the financial transactions influenced by LIBOR in 2012 was USD 800 trillion, roughly 12 times the world's GDP in that year (Economist, 2012). The growth in international banking centres in many locations saw a commensurate rise in the popularity of alternative benchmark rates at various money market centres around the world, e.g., HIBOR in Hong Kong, SIBOR in Singapore, and PIBOR in Paris. The applicable margin above LIBOR charged to the outside (of the eurocurrency market) borrowers depended on general market conditions, specific liquidity conditions of the lending eurobank, and the specific risk characteristics of the borrower.

One of the crucial failure points in this arrangement was the extensive coverage of currency and maturity combinations totalling 150. In some currency and maturity combinations (other than the most popular USD 1- and 3-month rates), actual traded interest rates may not be available at the time of submission each day, forcing the panel banks to resort to their expected borrowing rates. That is, they would use their previous borrowing rates, which could be many days old. This requires the same market conditions relevant for those old rates to continue to hold or speculate on what the borrowing rate could be under the current market conditions. This often led to inaccuracies at best and outright falsification at worst, leading to potentially significant distortions in published LIBORs. This weakness in calculating LIBOR was actively exploited by multiple banks individually and by collusion leading to significant distortions in published LIBORs for many years.

---

[5]The 10 currencies were the US Dollar (USD), the Euro (EUR), the British Pound Sterling (GBP), the Japanese Yen (JPY), the Swiss Franc (CHF), the Australian Dollar (AUD), the Canadian Dollar (CAD), the New Zealand Dollar (NZD), the Danish Krone (DKK), and the Swedish Krona (SEK). The maturities covered were 1 day, 1 and 2 weeks; 1 through to 12 months, 15 in total.

5.6.3. *LIBOR scandal*

In June 2012, the vulnerability of the LIBOR setting procedures to fraud became public. Some banks in the reference panel that determine daily LIBORs actively manipulated their submissions to achieve higher or lower averages than otherwise for private benefit. Since a panel bank can report an estimate instead of an actual borrowing interest rate, it is possible that what is submitted and the actual rate at which the bank borrows can diverge significantly. Banks can be tempted to under or over-report their estimated cost of borrowing for specific currency and maturity combinations. *First,* since the BBA published an individual bank's submissions at the same time as the daily LIBOR fix for all 150 currency and maturity combinations, which is an average of all submissions in the middle 50%, the market can speculate on the relative strength or weakness of the submitting banks. If a bank is consistently submitting a higher interest rate than its peers, the market may suspect that the bank might be experiencing difficulties in securing funding in the market. As such, a bank currently experiencing financial difficulties might try to avoid unnecessary attention from its peers and regulators by deliberately under-reporting its LIBOR submissions in the hopes that its financial health is interpreted to be stronger than it actually is. *Second,* a bank may choose to under or over-report its submissions in the hope that the LIBOR is impacted accordingly to benefit the positions taken in other trading departments in the bank. For example, a bank that benefits when a lower LIBOR is set has the incentive to under-report its true borrowing cost. If the bank has net short positions or has immediate funding needs in a particular currency and maturity combination, then a lower applicable LIBOR would reduce its funding costs. By submitting a low enough rate (but not too low to raise suspicion) individually or in collusion with other banks to be included in the bottom 25% to be discarded, a bank can effectively lower the average of the middle 50% and hence a lower LIBOR for the day. This is clearly in direct conflict of interest for the submitting bank. On the other hand, a bank that benefits with a higher LIBOR would deliberately submit a high enough rate designed to be included in the top 25% to be discarded, hence raising the resulting average of the middle 50%. These types of manipulation occurred by multiple banks coordinating with each other to submit higher or lower interest rate submissions at the same time to increase the effectiveness of the rate manipulation. The communication among colluding banks was usually via telephone so as not to leave any trace. However, on some occasions, emails were used for this purpose, and they were later used against the colluding banks in legal proceedings. UBS, Deutsche Bank, and Barclays were implicated in compromising emails, among others.[6]

The LIBOR scandal was widespread, involving banking offices worldwide. While the immediate target of the investigation was the money market traders, the fines issued to offending banks suggest, at the very least systemic problems with banks' target-based incentives and corporate control systems. It is reported that the LIBOR fixing had been in place for many decades and that the UK regulator had been aware of this issue for some time. For example, it was reported (Economist, 2012) that Barclays had successfully manipulated LIBORs by submitting higher rates than it could borrow during the credit boom period of 2005–2007, so traders could make profits on derivative positions (cross-currency swaps). This raised some concerns about its stability and prompted the Bank of England to contact Barclays in late October 2008, resulting in subsequent lower submissions. Then, during the GFC, Barclays was reported to have submitted lower interest rates than it could borrow at, to make its risk position and credit profile appear stronger than it really was. Regulatory authorities investigated Barclays and 15 other global financial institutions in the UK, the US, and elsewhere for conspiring to manipulate LIBOR rates from 2003 (McBride, 2016). In June–July 2012, Barclays agreed to pay fines of GBP 290 million (USD 450 million) to the UK and the US authorities. The benchmark rate was meant to provide a base for unsecured international lending, including corporate and government borrowers. Banks used BBA LIBOR to set other international commercial loans (corporate and retail). However, instead of reflecting the real costs of lending (borrowing), banks were found to have manipulated the rates they submitted by making them higher (or lower) to profit from their trading positions.

The consequences of the LIBOR scandal are three-fold. *First*, many international banks implicated in the LIBOR manipulations were fined by the UK and US authorities. International banks have paid over USD9 billion in fines as a result of LIBOR-related prosecutions from the US and European regulatory bodies. Barclays alone paid over USD 435 million in July 2012 to the US and the UK authorities, and they agreed to pay a further USD 100 million to 44 US states for its role in manipulating the dollar-denominated LIBOR rates. UBS paid USD 1.5 billion in penalties in 2012 after prosecution led by the US Commodities and Futures Trading

[6]The transcript of such an email chain showing banks colluding with each other was published in a newspaper article (Treanor, 2015).

Commission. Deutsche Bank paid a total of USD 3.5 billion in fines, including 2.5 billion in a single settlement. In addition, European banks implicated were also fined by the European Commission, in total EUR 1.7 billion.

Second, as a direct consequence of the hefty fines, many top managements in some of the banks involved were forced to resign. The Chairman and the CEO of Barclays resigned as a direct result of Barclays' involvement in the scandal. In addition, the resignation of Société Générale's CEO in March 2018 was believed to be a result of the LIBOR scandal investigations by the US Justice Department (Laurent, 2018).

Third, the unwieldy and flawed system of the BBA LIBOR setting was replaced in 2014 by ICE BBA with a much smaller set of currency and maturity combinations. A total of 150 currency and maturity combinations was replaced by a total of 35 under the ICE LIBOR system in 2015. Five currencies were covered (the USD, the GBP, the EUR, the JPY, and the CHF) across seven maturities (overnight, 1 week, 1, 2, 3, 6, and 12 months). This was further reduced to only three currencies (the USD, the GBP, and the JPY) over much-reduced maturities (overnight, 1, 3, 6, and 12 months for the USD and only 1, 3, and 6 months for the others), resulting in only 11 currency and maturity combinations.

5.7. Interest Rate Linkages in the Eurocurrency Market

Eurocurrency interest rates (both deposit and lending) are subject to arbitrage forces that ensure comparable interest rates are equalised under ideal conditions. Within-currency arbitrage applies between on- and off-shore markets, and assuming efficient financial markets, the nature of interest rate linkage is predictable given current information and transaction costs. For example, domestic US and eurodollar interest rates for the same maturity are kept in line by arbitrage activities. If a eurodollar interest rate is higher than the corresponding onshore interest rate, other things being equal, funds will flow out of the domestic market into the offshore eurocurrency market. The increase in demand for funds in the domestic market will raise the domestic interest rate, while the increasing supply in the eurodollar market will lower the interest rate in the offshore market until interest rate equalisation is achieved. Arbitrage in the reverse direction (raising funds in the eurocurrency market and supplying them in the domestic market) results if the domestic interest rate is higher after factoring in transaction costs and other imperfections. The linkage between two eurocurrency markets in different currencies is via the covered interest rate parity. The interest rate differential between two currencies is kept in line by an expected exchange rate movement over the relevant maturity that will offset the current interest rate differential.

5.7.1. *Eurocurrency and domestic interest rates*

Domestic and euro interest rates are linked through the process of interest rate arbitrage within that currency. Due to market imperfections, transaction costs, and different market characteristics, interest rate equalisation between onshore and offshore money markets does not usually occur. Instead, there are differences between the two market prices that remain even after arbitrageurs have done their work. These differences reflect those market imperfections and apply equally to both deposit and lending interest rates. In general, eurocurrency interest rate spreads (or margins) between deposit and lending (or bid and ask) rates tend to be smaller than corresponding domestic interest rate spreads for the same maturity and credit size. That is, eurocurrency lending rates tend to be smaller, and deposit rates higher than corresponding domestic interest rate counterparts.

Exhibit 5.10 illustrates the differences at both ends that are not arbitraged away due to transaction costs and other market frictions. There is a positive difference between the two lending rates and the two deposit rates; these differences are equilibrium differences that cannot be arbitraged away. If the current interest rate differentials are higher than suggested by the equilibrium differences, there would be appropriate arbitrage transactions that will restore equilibrium.

Eurocurrency lending rates are set lower than the corresponding domestic rates to attract large financial institutions, multinational corporations, and governments. These important borrowers can access multiple sources of funds, and they can be price sensitive as a result. In addition, eurobanks have the incentive to service them as doing so can add to their credentials. However, domestic lending rates may not adequately reflect actual funding costs since banks can mask them by cross-subsidising the cost of the loan by charging higher fees on other products. Thus, domestic lending rates may not be directly comparable to eurocurrency market lending rates. Eurocurrency deposit rates, in general, are higher than the corresponding domestic deposit rates. This may be due to two factors: *First,* assuming that most of the USD deposits are from US depositors, eurobank deposits represent higher-risk investments due to lack of

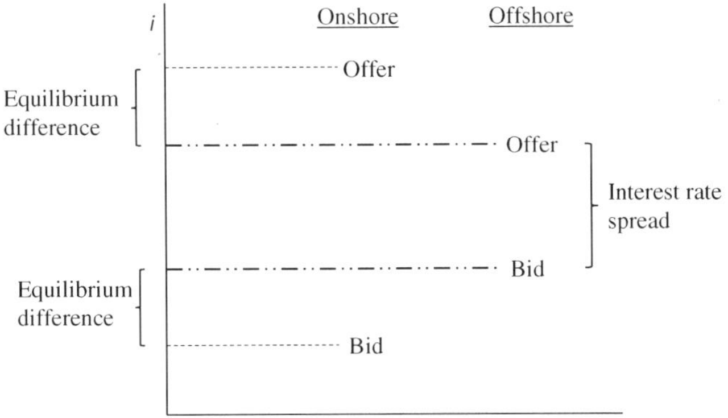

Exhibit 5.10. Interest rate spreads in on- and offshore money markets.

regulation protection, and so they need to be compensated by receiving higher returns for riskier eurodeposits (the higher price of risk view). The higher risk may be due to the removal of currency convertibility for non-residents, the lack of explicit or implicit deposit protection, the lack of a lender of last resort facility, the unregulated nature of bank operations, and a perceived higher probability of non-performance (political risk) due to the involvement of more than one jurisdiction in the process. *Second,* no-arbitrage conditions between the onshore and offshore USD deposit rates can exist with divergent interest rates due to extra costs associated with domestic (onshore) deposits (the cost of regulation view). The extra costs of domestic deposits include a reserve requirement,[7] deposit insurance costs,[8] and government taxes.

Dufey and Giddy (1994) argue that, unless unusual risks or exchange controls are present, the higher eurodeposit rate is mostly accounted for by the regulation cost of domestic deposits. This claim is supported by

[7]Most advanced economies abolished a formal central bank reserve requirement in the 1980s, and the US in March 2020, and instead rely on individual banks' prudent management of liquidity risk. The latest Basel III requirement also addresses the liquidity risk consideration of commercial banks.

[8]Compulsory deposit insurance exists in many countries. For example, in the US, deposits up to USD 250,000 are covered by the FDIC program. In the Eurozone, deposits up to EUR 100,000 are covered, and the administering insurance organisations vary across jurisdictions. For example, in Germany, separate insurance providers exist for private, public banks, and brokerage companies. In France, it is provided by Fonds de Garantie des Dépôts.

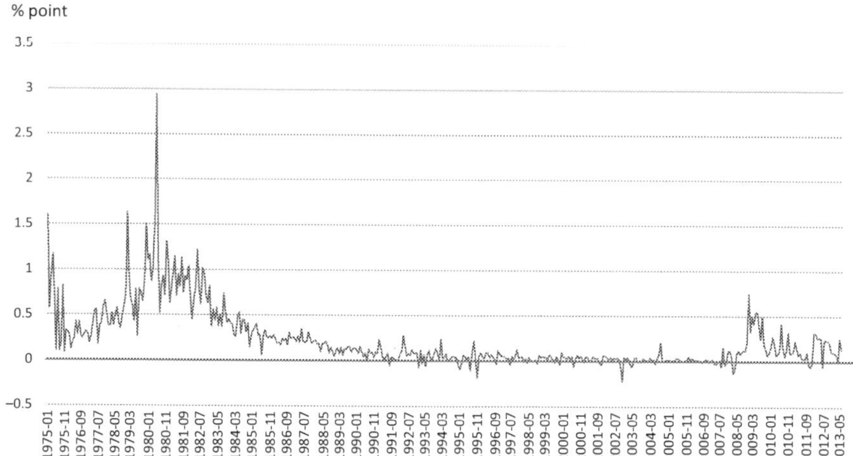

Exhibit 5.11. Three-month eurodollar deposit and US CD rates: Differential (% points).

Source: Constructed from the three-month US certificate of deposit (CD) and the eurocurrency deposit rates extracted from Refinitiv Eikon Datastream database. The CD rates were discontinued in June 2013.

the narrowing gap between the onshore and offshore interest rates after the financial deregulation from the early 1980s. Exhibit 5.11 shows the interest rate differential between the three-month US Certificate of Deposit (CD) rate traded in the secondary market and the eurodollar rates. The US CD interest rate was considered to be the closest to the eurodollar deposit rate in terms of liquidity and low transaction costs. A positive difference between the two represents the premium eurodollar deposit rate needs to include to attract wholesale depositors. In the 1970s and early 1980s, a relatively large interest differential of up to three percentage points existed. However, it started to fall in the early 1980s to zero in early 1990. The period of higher eurodollar deposit rates coincides with the period of binding financial sector regulation in the US and other major economies.

As the banking system entered the era of deregulation from 1981 in the US, the regulation-induced premium in the eurodollar interest rates started to disappear. That is, the cost disadvantage in the US money market due to the regulatory compliance cost was becoming much less, leading to domestic US banks being able to match eurodollar interest rates. This observation clearly supports the regulation cost view of the equilibrium difference in the deposit rates. However, there is also some support for the higher price of risk view during the recent periods of high global instability. The GFC and the Eurozone debt crisis periods clearly show an elevated interest rate gap of 0.745 percentage points in December 2008. In short, although the positive interest difference between the eurodollar and the US CD interest rate was mostly due to the cost of regulation when it existed, there is also some evidence of a higher price of risk view of the differences.

5.7.2. *Covered interest rate arbitrage in the eurocurrency market*

The arbitrage condition that binds the various currency segments of the eurocurreny market is the covered interest rate parity (CIRP). The idea is that the currency with a lower interest rate is expected to appreciate against the currency with a higher interest rate over the funding period. The rate of appreciation of the lower interest rate currency (funding currency) will be the same as the interest rate difference between the two currencies so that the cost advantage of the funding currency is wiped out by the appreciation over the holding period of the eurocurrency. The JPY has traditionally been the lowest-cost funding currency in the eurocurrency market. In order to prevent continual carry trade from the JPY to other major currencies, it needs to appreciate by the same rate as the interest rate differential against other higher interest rate currencies.

For example, for simplicity, if one could borrow and lend at the same interest rate and if the euroyen interest rate for the three-month maturity was 2% per annum, while the eurodollar interest rate was 3% per annum, then to prevent a carry trade, the JPY must appreciate by 1% over the three-month period. This means that borrowing in the JPY at the lower cost and investing in the eurodollar at the higher interest rate will not lead to a profitable trade. This is because the benefit of the lower interest rate will be cancelled out by the higher cost of buying back the JPY at maturity. In short, the CIRP connects interest rates across various eurocurrency interest rates. That is, the interest rates of various currencies in the eurocurrency market are linked to each other through both foreign exchange and the eurocurrency markets.

Exhibit 5.12 shows inter and intra-eurocurrency interest rate linkages. For each of the three major currencies in the market, within-currency arbitrage binds onshore and offshore markets, and intra-eurocurrency arbitrage via CIRP ensures that the three pairs of major currency segments in the eurocurrency market do not deviate from equilibrium.

5.8. Safety Concerns of the Eurocurrency Market

The eurodollar market was established to provide USD-denominated intermediation outside the US, and London became the most important location of eurodollar and other eurocurrency activities. Since the location of eurodollar transactions falls outside the reach of the US jurisdiction, the US authorities do not have sway over the eurodollar market in terms of financial regulation or other controls on market activities. The UK court's decision in 1986 on the case of Lybian Arab Foreign Bank (LAFB) vs BT reinforced this view that the US government had no jurisdiction over the London market even if eurodollar transactions were ultimately based on USD deposits housed in the US banking system. The so-called 'eurocurrency defence' was not accepted as a valid reason for not fulfilling its obligations to the client, Rutzke (1988). This was certainly a boon for the eurodollar market participants who aimed to keep their USD deposits safe and the US corporations who wished to avoid US financial regulation. However, the US authorities may be concerned about the potential negative spillover impact of eurodollar market operations on the domestic US financial system. Dufey and Giddy (1994) list three areas of potential concerns, and these are (1) the potential impact on the effectiveness of the domestic monetary policy, (2) the danger posed by the eurodollar market on the domestic financial system safety, and (3) possible interference of credit allocation objective in the US. The following three sections summarise each of these points and provide discussions.

5.8.1. *Effectiveness of domestic monetary policy*

The monetary authority of a country (the Central bank) is charged with ensuring the stability of domestic currency in terms of its domestic purchasing power (i.e., inflation target) and external purchasing power (stable exchange rate). In its domestic aim of price stability, the central bank sets intermediate targets (monetary aggregates and/or interest rates) to achieve the desired ultimate inflation target. The intermediate targets are controlled via open market operations or directly setting policy interest rates. The emergence of the eurocurrency market may raise some concerns for the monetary authority in its aim to maintain effective

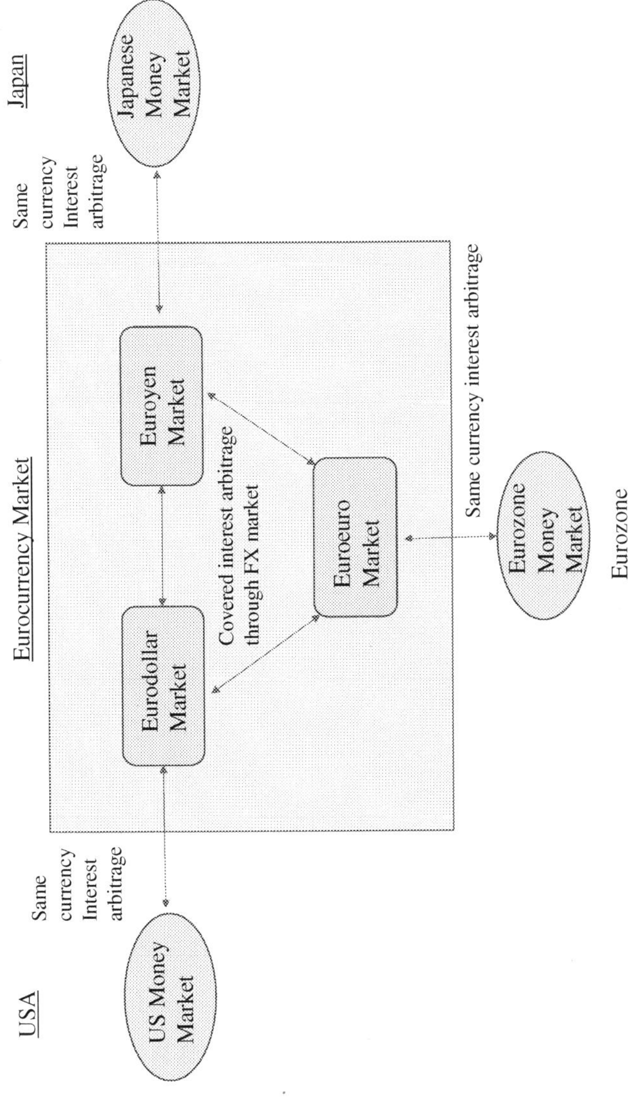

Exhibit 5.12. Interest rate linkages in the eurocurrency market.

control of these intermediate monetary policy targets. This is due to the nature of the eurocurrency market that it escapes costly domestic regulations and is beyond the control of domestic monetary authorities. As such, eurobanks can escape regulation-related costs associated with extending credits to domestic borrowers, as illustrated in Exhibit 5.7.

However, despite the concerns, the eurocurrency market is unlikely to interfere with domestic policy aims as the domestic monetary authority can maintain full control of the intermediate targets of the monetary policy. *First,* the central bank has control over its money base, and the money supply can be controlled by adjusting money base levels. Eurocurrency deposits are held as time deposits at domestic banks, as illustrated in Exhibit 5.6, and when a eurodollar is traded, only the ownership of the domestic deposit in the US, that the eurocurrency is based on is, being traded via account entry adjustments in the US banking system. This implies that when the central bank initiates a tight monetary policy by reducing the domestic money base, total (both internal and external) money and credit supply will shrink. Even with a growing eurocurrency presence, the domestic monetary authorities will retain ultimate control over the monetary aggregates.

Second, the policy interest rate (Fed fund rate in the US, Deposit facility and Main Refinancing operation rates for ECB, BOE base rate for the UK, etc.) can be cut or raised to achieve desired outcomes in impacting domestic economic activities and inflation rate. Once domestic interest rates, especially short maturities, are adjusted to the change in the policy rate, arbitrage capital flows between onshore and offshore money markets will ensure equilibrium is restored between the two markets. This will mainly lead to the external market adjusting to the new domestic interest rate levels. That is, the domestic monetary authority will still control primary interest rates on domestic currency loans and the eurocurrency rate via arbitrage.

However, there can be some added complications in accurately estimating the impact of monetary policy via targeting monetary aggregates as the lack of reserve requirement in the eurocurrency market adds some complications to this effort. Therefore, fine-tuning short-term economic activities or inflation is made more difficult as the monetary aggregate is an intermediate target. Fortunately, monetary aggregate targeting has given way to interest rate targeting from the early 1980s in the advanced economies where the eurocurrency market is of concern. Moreover, reserve ratios on deposits have been dismantled in major economies in recent decades, rendering this potential issue irrelevant. As such, it is difficult to argue that having a eurocurrency market in one's currency outside its financial and legal jurisdiction could jeopardise monetary policy effectiveness.

5.8.2. *Eurocurrency market and financial market safety*

The growth of the eurocurrency market caused some concern regarding the effectiveness of regulation aimed at fostering financial stability. The traditional measures injecting safety nets such as deposit insurance, reserve ratio, a lender of last resort facility, and regulations on lending activities are largely absent in the eurocurrency market. Due to the absence of these safety measures, depositors' protection is absent, and any failure of eurobanks must be fully absorbed by the depositors. Moreover, the credit creation process in the eurocurrency market is beyond the control of the domestic authorities, and hence malicious inflationary pressures from the eurocurrency credit creation and the resulting imported inflation could lead to a potential weakening of the value of the currency and the domestic economy. These concerns are discussed in the following.

Liquidity risk refers to the possibility of banks not being able to meet unusually large deposit outflows. In the worst possible case, a run on the bank could result in a collapse of the whole financial system. Eurocurrencies are time deposits, so a liquidity rush is mostly irrelevant. Also, at maturity, a eurocurrency is paid out as a demand deposit held at a bank located in the financial system of the currency (i.e., a USD deposit in the US), which is under full control by the authorities. Therefore, if there is a liquidity rush, it will be purely domestic in nature. This implies that if the central bank can handle liquidity crises in a domestic economy, the liquidity risk emanating from the eurocurrency market can also be handled.

Due to the nature of eurobank operations, they are not subject to any single government's regulation, and the government of the offshore market has no financial or otherwise incentive to regulate the eurobanking activities within its jurisdiction. However, eurobanks are foreign branches of multinational banks that are subject to the prudential regulatory measures of the home jurisdiction as a consolidated entity. Consolidated operations of multinational banks that include domestic and foreign (including eurobank) activities are subject to Basel capital accords (I, II, and now III) which compel banks to adhere to the prudential regulatory measures in capital adequacy, liquidity, and operational risk. In particular, the capital adequacy requirement (CAR) is vital since various types of capital act as a safeguard against insolvency caused by unusually high bad loan write-offs. All eurobanks (and domestic banks also) are subject to the CAR. In general, it can be concluded that the eurocurrency market is as safe as the domestic banking system in this regard, and so there is no obvious link between domestic financial instability and the growth of the eurocurrency market.

5.8.3. *Eurocurrency market and credit allocation*

In economies where efficient credit allocation is not possible through the market due to financial market underdevelopment and the general lack of efficient market mechanisms, policymakers tend to use the domestic banking system to effect desired credit allocation. Credit allocation controls aim to direct funds to strategic industry borrowers and encourage bank lending to specific areas of the economy. In the absence of an efficient market mechanism, policymakers may use financial intermediaries to achieve the desirable credit allocation aims by providing incentives through regulations for banks to lend to desired borrowers in strategic sectors. It should be noted, however, that any imposition of regulation, incentives, moral suasion, etc. will lead to suboptimal credit allocation for the banks. There will be inevitable capital flights to offshore markets to escape these restrictions, so the credit allocation policy may not achieve its aim. This appears to be a valid concern for those countries with underdeveloped financial markets that require government intervention to achieve credit allocation aims. However, they are unlikely to have offshore demand for their domestic currency-denominated credits. Only the advanced economies whose currencies are in demand in offshore markets have eurocurrency markets in their currencies, and effecting desired credit allocation outcomes has never been one of their objectives in recent decades. Therefore, it is unlikely that the eurocurrency market will interfere with domestic credit allocation policies.

5.8.4. *Types of control on the eurocurrency market*

The governments of offshore financial centres hosting eurocurrency activities may decide to introduce controls on offshore financial activities. However, international banks can easily shift their offshore banking activities to other locations if costly regulation is introduced in the current location. Thus, the imposition of regulation on eurocurrency activities will be ineffective, especially for those locations that international banks use as booking centres without a substantial presence. In addition, the host government has no incentive to introduce regulation on eurobanking activities as they have no implication for domestic monetary stability as they only involve foreign currency transactions mostly between foreign banks (as opposed to involving the domestic currency of the host country), and there are substantial financial and non-financial benefits associated with being an offshore financial centre.

Alternatively, the host government may consider tightening (or even eliminating) the non-resident convertibility of the domestic currency to control eurobanking activities that could impact the domestic financial system. However, this is a drastic step and may lead to an isolation of the economy from the global financial community.

As shown in Exhibit 5.9, intermediation in the eurocurrency market involves taking deposits from outside the market and lending them to a borrower also located outside the market. Two or more banks can be involved in this intermediation flow. During this process, the asset being traded is a time deposit located in the domestic banking system of the currency, and only the ownership of the deposit is transferred via accounting entries in the ledgers of the domestic banking system. In the case of a eurodollar, ownership transfer is through the US payment system, Fedwire or CHIPS. Since no physical movement of any asset is involved, and the actual deposit is housed domestically, domestic authorities can seize the asset if called for and make it an offence to effect actual payment to controlled entities. For example, the US government has frozen financial assets held by foreign entities or governments at banks operating in the US. Eurocurrencies are similar in spirit to real estate, where although the ownership can be transferred to foreign entities, the underlying asset does not physically move. Thus, the US authorities can freeze the USD deposits owned by foreign entities if appropriate, and the eurodollar transactions based on the deposits will not proceed.

References

BIS (2022). International Banking Statistics: Locational Banking Statistics. https://www.bis.org/statistics/bankstats.htm.

Dufey, G. and Giddy, I. (1994). *The International Money Market*, 2nd ed., Prentice Hall, New Jersey. Chapter 6: Lending Techniques in the International Money Market, pp. 237–280.

Economist (2012), The LIBOR scandal: The rotten heart of finance, July 2012. http://www.economist.com/node/21558281.

Eun, C., Resnick, B. and Chuluun, T. (2021). *International Financial Management*, 9th ed., McGrawHill, New York.

Judson, R. (2017). The death of cash? Not so fast: Demand for US currency at home and abroad, 1990–2016. Paper presented at the Deutsche Bundesbank International Cash Conference 2017, War on Cash: Is There a Future for Cash? Island of Mainau, Germany, 26 April. https://www.econstor.eu/bitstream/10419/162910/1/Judson.pdf.

Laurent, L. (2018, 15 March). Libor Scandal Gets Older and Uglier for Banks. Retrieved 7 May 2018, from https://www.bloomberg.com/opinion/articles/2018-03-15/libor-scandal-gets-even-uglier-and-costlier-for-banks#xj4y7vzkg.

McBride, J. (2016). Understanding the Libor Scandal. Council for Foreign Relations. Retrieved 7 May 2018, from https://www.cfr.org/backgrounder/understanding-libor-scandal.

Melvin M. and Norrbin, S. (2017). *International Money and Finance*, 9th ed., Academic press, London, UK.

Rutzke, C. R. (1988). The Libyan Asset Freeze and Its Application to Foreign Government Deposits in Overseas Branches of United States Banks: Libyan Arab Foreign Bank v. Bankers Trust Co. *American University International Law Review*, 3(1), 241–282. https://digitalcommons.wcl.american.edu/auilr/vol3/iss1/6/.

Smith, R. C., Walter, I. and DeLong, G. (2012), *Global Banking*, Third Ed, Oxford University Press, New York.

Treanor, J. (2015). Libor-rigging emails lift lid on City culture, The Guardian, 24 April 2015. https://www.theguardian.com/business/2015/apr/23/libor-rigging-emails-regulators-banks-misconduct.

Chapter 6

International Loan Syndication

6.1. Introduction

International loans tend to be significantly large and subject to additional risks (political, currency, regulation, country, etc.) compared to domestic loans, and as such, they are usually syndicated.[1] In loan syndication, multiple lenders (banks and institutional investors) make up a syndicate to fund a borrower. Each lender in the syndicate contributes a portion of the loan and may also perform a designated management or administration role that earns them fee income on top of interest income. A loan syndicate is formed by one or more lead banks when the borrower (or issuer) requests a syndicated loan. The lead bank performs a role similar to the traditional investment banking role of arranging for the issuer (borrower) to raise capital from the investor communities. The lead bank is the book runner responsible for soliciting interest from the international bank and investor communities to complete a book-building process. After collating all offers (e.g., a bank offers 10m at LIBOR+25bp and 15m at LIBOR+30bp) from interested parties, the lead bank determines an equilibrium price and announces it to the lenders. Various roles within the syndicate are shared (co-manager, agent, co-agent, etc.) with different compensation structures (fee income share) depending on the pledged amount and the significance of the administration role. In essence, there

[1]The average deal size in the international loan syndication market in 2021 was USD 521 million. See Exhibit 6.2.

are broadly two types of lenders in a syndicate: The first is the senior lender group, which engineers origination, conducts the required credit risk analysis and other administrative tasks, and provides the bulk of the funding required. The second is a group of junior lenders who are not required to perform any role within the syndicate other than to provide funding.

Borrowers in loan syndications are large corporations or sovereigns with varying risk structures. Loans to investment-grade borrowers are relatively simple in their structure, as there is no real need to factor in extensive safety measures in case of a default. On the other hand, for loans to speculative-grade borrowers (also known as leveraged borrowers) with an external credit rating of BB and below, the structure of a loan syndicate is more complicated as there are additional requirements such as extra monitoring roles to be performed, stronger loan covenants, collateral requirements, and matching of interest payments to cash flows. In addition, the lead arranger is expected to perform much more extensive risk analysis and monitoring roles and contribute a larger share of the loan.

One of the most important aspects of loan syndication is that it helps address information asymmetry between the borrower and the lenders much more effectively than the traditional case of one lender extending the loan. The existence of information asymmetry between the borrower and the lender creates adverse selection and moral hazard concerns, inevitably leading to inefficient resource allocation. The degree of information asymmetry is reduced in loan syndicates if the lead bank has a good reputation (history of previously successful lead bank role in loan syndicates, ranked high in the lead bank league table, see Exhibit 6.3), and the borrower has a good credit standing (previously accessed the market with good standing) and has transparency (a large public company with good independent credit ratings). If the borrower is not transparent (i.e., private company, not rated by independent rating agencies, and not previously in the syndication market), the required monitoring and due diligence level are much higher. As a result, the lead bank is required to hold a larger share of the loan to convey confidence in the borrower to the rest of the syndicate to show that it has more 'skin in the game'. There is usually more than one bank in the lead bank group, and the banks included in the group generally have more information about the borrower (i.e., banks local to the borrower) to reduce the level of information asymmetry.

6.2. Recent Developments in International Loan Syndication

Exhibit 6.1 shows the growth of the global loan syndication market since 2009. The loan volume has grown from USD 1.8 trillion in 2009 to 5.4 trillion by 2021. At the same time, the average value per deal has increased from USD 336 million to 521 million over the same period. Although the growth has been steady across the years, there was a significant drop in the volume to USD 3.49 trillion in 2020 due to the depressed economic activities brought on by the global COVID-19 Pandemic. It rebounded swiftly in 2021 with a 55% increase in activity.

Exhibit 6.2 provides further details on the market activities with the breakdown in terms of the borrower's regional location. Panel A reports the syndication volume by region. The bulk of the syndication activities is concentrated in the North American region, accounting for 64% of the global volume, followed by Europe (17.7%), Asia-Pacific (10.5%), and AMECA (Africa Middle East Central Asia, 2.4%). The US borrowers account for the bulk of the market in the Americas and globally, and their

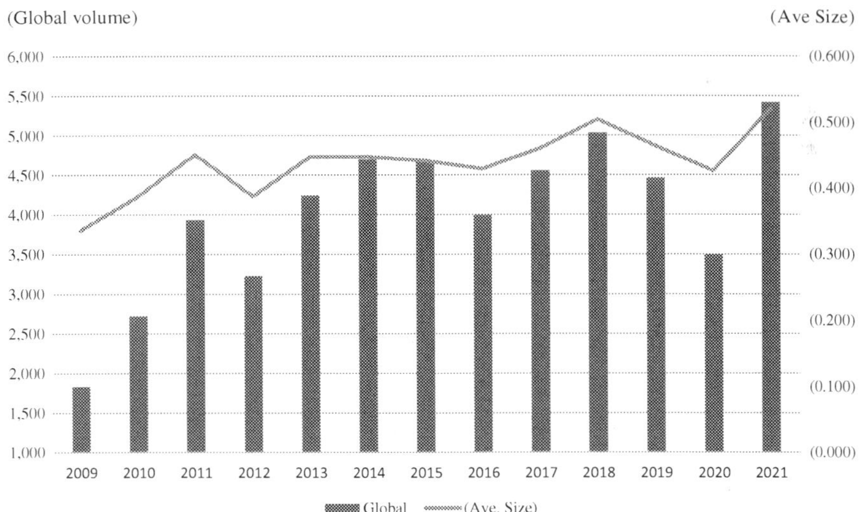

Exhibit 6.1. Global syndicated loan volume and average value per deal, 2009–2021 in USD b.

Source: Refinitiv Thomson Reuters Global Syndicated Loans Review, 2009–2021.

	2009	2010	2011	2012	2013	2014	2015	2016	2017	2018	2019	2020	2021
Panel A: Syndicated loan volume by global regions, in USD b. and average size per deal													
Global	**1,830**	**2,719**	**3,934**	**3,227**	**4,240**	**4,691**	**4,662**	**3,991**	**4,551**	**5,035**	**4,460**	**3,496**	**5,416**
(Ave. Size)	(0.336)	(0.387)	(0.450)	(0.387)	(0.447)	(0.448)	(0.441)	(0.429)	(0.460)	(0.504)	(0.464)	(0.426)	(0.521)
Americas	694	1,222	2,124	1,830	2,534	2,640	2,622	2,321	2,936	3,237	2,740	1,905	3,527
(Ave. Size)	(0.359)	(0.410)	(0.512)	(0.449)	(0.538)	(0.533)	(0.543)	(0.553)	(0.588)	(0.640)	(0.580)	(0.518)	(0.639)
(% of global total)	(35.5%)	(44.1%)	(52.9%)	(55.5%)	(59.0%)	(54.9%)	(54.9%)	(57.2%)	(63.6%)	(63.2%)	(59.9%)	(53.8%)	(64.1%)
North America	651	1,199	2,082	1,789	2,503	2,577	2,560	2,284	2,893	3,180	2,669	1,881	3,474
(Ave. Size)	(0.348)	(0.412)	(0.513)	(0.446)	(0.543)	(0.538)	(0.549)	(0.560)	(0.593)	(0.644)	(0.583)	(0.522)	(0.643)
USA	*579*	*1,089*	*1,913*	*1,626*	*2,309*	*2,340*	*2,342*	*2,091*	*2,658*	*2,912*	*2,411*	*1,750*	*3,147*
(Ave. Size)	*(0.351)*	*(0.422)*	*(0.519)*	*(0.441)*	*(0.546)*	*(0.546)*	*(0.564)*	*(0.576)*	*(0.612)*	*(0.668)*	*(0.607)*	*(0.548)*	*(0.665)*
(% of global total)	*(31.7%)*	*(40.1%)*	*(48.6%)*	*(50.4%)*	*(54.5%)*	*(49.9%)*	*(50.2%)*	*(52.4%)*	*(58.4%)*	*(57.8%)*	*(54.1%)*	*(50.0%)*	*(58.1%)*
Latin America	43.6	21.5	38.4	39.0	29.7	56.0	55.3	33.7	35.0	54.6	69.4	21.9	49.0
(Ave. Size)	(0.670)	(0.359)	(0.499)	(0.582)	(0.337)	(0.361)	(0.381)	(0.288)	(0.373)	(0.471)	(0.507)	(0.295)	(0.495)
Caribbean	0.327	1.739	3.611	1.662	1.300	7.158	7.067	4.153	7.743	2.915	1.832	1.704	3.389
(Ave. Size)	(0.164)	(0.217)	(0.301)	(0.415)	(0.260)	(0.895)	(0.471)	(0.692)	(0.516)	(0.416)	(0.305)	(0.341)	(0.339)
Europe	608	818	1,018	648	837	1,114	1,094	812	816	915	891	776	961
(Ave. Size)	(0.665)	(0.751)	(0.696)	(0.575)	(0.644)	(0.693)	(0.591)	(0.547)	(0.607)	(0.623)	(0.597)	(0.638)	(0.709)
(% of global total)	(33.3%)	(30.1%)	(25.9%)	(20.1%)	(19.7%)	(23.8%)	(23.5%)	(20.4%)	(17.9%)	(18.2%)	(20.0%)	(22.2%)	(17.7%)
Western Europe	564	762	923	574	738	1,049	1,023	745	768	866	835	736	901
(Ave. Size)	(0.684)	(0.788)	(0.707)	(0.574)	(0.628)	(0.703)	(0.604)	(0.547)	(0.615)	(0.628)	(0.600)	(0.651)	(0.707)
Eastern Europe	44.6	56.6	94.6	74.2	99.4	65.0	71.0	67.2	48.0	48.8	56.6	39.9	60.0
(Ave. Size)	(0.495)	(0.460)	(0.602)	(0.580)	(0.789)	(0.565)	(0.449)	(0.546)	(0.505)	(0.542)	(0.566)	(0.470)	(0.741)
Africa/ME/Central Asia	56.5	70.1	63.7	74.0	90.9	86.7	166.0	123.2	77.0	135.4	93.6	97.9	129.5
(Ave. Size)	(0.601)	(0.723)	(0.545)	(0.560)	(0.598)	(0.549)	(0.725)	(0.800)	(0.675)	(0.717)	(0.574)	(0.759)	(0.776)
(% of global total)	(3.1%)	(2.6%)	(1.6%)	(2.3%)	(2.1%)	(1.8%)	(3.6%)	(3.1%)	(1.7%)	(2.7%)	(2.1%)	(2.8%)	(2.4%)
Middle East	38.0	45.5	38.4	43.2	57.3	54.2	114.6	80.0	46.7	96.5	63.8	65.4	99.4
(Ave. Size)	(0.791)	(0.843)	(0.600)	(0.664)	(0.666)	(0.623)	(0.996)	(0.879)	(0.865)	(1.096)	(0.887)	(1.258)	(1.242)
Africa	18.18	22.06	22.75	27.38	32.56	29.05	43.56	36.30	26.23	25.38	27.89	31.24	29.03
(Ave. Size)	(0.433)	(0.566)	(0.517)	(0.442)	(0.543)	(0.476)	(0.440)	(0.626)	(0.514)	(0.334)	(0.324)	(0.416)	(0.341)
Central Asia	0.391	2.554	2.546	3.441	1.023	3.483	7.870	6.935	4.038	38.962	1.892	1.300	1.150
(Ave. Size)	(0.098)	(0.639)	(0.283)	(0.688)	(0.171)	(0.348)	(0.525)	(1.387)	(0.067)	(0.386)	(0.378)	(0.650)	(0.575)
Asia-Pacific (ex Japan)	221.3	355.8	419.8	352.7	502.7	629.0	554.7	497.9	493.3	514.5	496.6	460.5	570.7
(Ave. Size)	(0.263)	(0.296)	(0.322)	(0.293)	(0.335)	(0.338)	(0.336)	(0.338)	(0.332)	(0.375)	(0.340)	(0.330)	(0.365)
(% of global total)	(12.1%)	(13.1%)	(10.7%)	(10.9%)	(11.9%)	(13.4%)	(11.9%)	(12.5%)	(10.8%)	(10.2%)	(11.1%)	(13.2%)	(10.5%)
Japan	249.2	252.1	308.7	322.1	275.5	220.3	225.8	235.8	228.5	232.6	237.5	257.5	228.7
(Ave. Size)	(0.150)	(0.153)	(0.181)	(0.179)	(0.148)	(0.113)	(0.110)	(0.117)	(0.114)	(0.120)	(0.132)	(0.141)	(0.123)
	(13.6%)	(9.3%)	(7.8%)	(10.0%)	(6.5%)	(4.7%)	(4.8%)	(5.9%)	(5.0%)	(4.6%)	(5.3%)	(7.4%)	(4.2%)
Panel B: Syndicated loan volume by global regions, in USD b. and average size per deal													
Developed Countries	1,521	2,288	3,434	2,777	3,630	3,999	3,901	3,346	3,980	4,380	3,819	2,954	4,727
(Ave. Size)	(0.338)	(0.400)	(0.468)	(0.396)	(0.459)	(0.471)	(0.451)	(0.438)	(0.475)	(0.517)	(0.479)	(0.439)	(0.538)
(% of global total)	(83.1%)	(84.1%)	(87.3%)	(86.1%)	(85.6%)	(85.3%)	(83.7%)	(83.8%)	(87.5%)	(87.0%)	(85.6%)	(84.5%)	(87.3%)
Developing Countries	274.3	367.3	408.3	370.9	492.1	544.8	626.3	499.8	414.7	492.4	457.2	405.1	496.6
(Ave. Size)	(0.324)	(0.323)	(0.338)	(0.329)	(0.362)	(0.317)	(0.380)	(0.348)	(0.331)	(0.399)	(0.343)	(0.333)	(0.386)
(% of global total)	(15.0%)	(13.5%)	(10.4%)	(11.5%)	(11.6%)	(11.6%)	(13.4%)	(12.5%)	(9.1%)	(9.8%)	(10.3%)	(11.6%)	(9.2%)
Offshore Centres	34.9	63.9	91.2	78.5	117.8	147.0	135.0	145.2	156.2	162.3	183.1	137.9	192.8
(Ave. Size)	(0.360)	(0.382)	(0.490)	(0.374)	(0.483)	(0.482)	(0.456)	(0.588)	(0.535)	(0.527)	(0.570)	(0.475)	(0.515)
(% of global total)	(1.9%)	(2.3%)	(2.3%)	(2.4%)	(2.8%)	(3.1%)	(2.9%)	(3.6%)	(3.4%)	(3.2%)	(4.1%)	(3.9%)	(3.6%)

Exhibit 6.2. Global syndicated loan — 2009–2021, in USD b.

Source: Refinitiv Thomson Reuters Global Syndicated Loans Review, 2019–2021. https://www.refinitiv.com/en/products/deals-intelligence/syndicated-loans.

global market share has risen from 32% in 2009 to 58% by 2021. However, the average size of the deal is the largest among the borrowers in AMECA, USD 776 million, which is much larger than the global average of USD 521 million. In particular, Loans to the Middle East averaged

1.2 trillion in 2021. This suggests that while loans to borrowers in the Americas and Europe were much more frequent, loans to Middle Eastern borrowers were much less frequent but considerably larger when loan deals were struck.

Panel B reports the syndication volume disaggregated into developed, developing, and offshore centre borrowers. Developed market borrowers dominate the syndication market, and their market share ranges from 83% to 87% across the period. The borrowers from developing countries accounted for only 9.2% in 2021, a substantial reduction from 15% in 2009. The offshore centre location's share has been steady and achieved only 3.6% in 2021.

Exhibit 6.3 lists the top 10 book runners (lead banks) of international syndicated loans. In Panel A, global bookrunners are shown. The US banks in the top 10 list arranged 33% of the global syndicated loans, followed by the Japanese banks (9.7%) and the European banks (6.1%). The top three banks in 2021, BOA, JPMorgan, and Citi, have consistently ranked in the top spots for decades. JPMorgan has been the clear top bookrunner in the early 2000s, with the other two fighting for the number two spot. Since 2009, Citi has been consistently in the number three spot, and since 2014, JPMorgan and BOA have been switching places between the top and the second places.

In Panels B through D, regional top 10 book runners are shown for the Americas, the EMEA, and the Asia Pacific (ex-Japan). It is noticeable that the banks dominating the business in each region are headquartered in the same region as the borrowers. US banks dominate in the Americas, European banks dominate in the EMEA region, and Chinese banks dominate in the Asia Pacific (ex-Japan) region. It is not surprising that regional banks are active in syndicated loans to the borrowers in their own region as they have an information advantage on the borrowers compared to the lenders from other regions (see Section 4.2). Moreover, US banks are also active in the EMEA region, and traditionally developing market-focused UK bank, Standard Chartered Bank, and the Asia Pacific market-focused bank, HSBC, are also strongly present in the Asia Pacific region.

In short, the trends in the global loan syndication market that have been observed in recent decades are summarised as follows. First, the global loan syndication market has been growing, despite the recent drop due to the Pandemic in 2020, which is fully reversed in 2021, achieving a global volume of USD 5.4 trillion. Second, the market is dominated by developed market borrowers in North America and Western Europe. In

	Headquarter Country	Rank 2021	Rank 2020	Proceeds USD m	No. of Deals	Market Share (%)	
	Panel A: Global loans bookrunners						
BofA Securities Inc	USA	1	2	488,005	1723	9.9	1.8
JPMorgan	USA	2	1	442,984	1516	9	0.2
Citi	USA	3	3	277,974	779	5.7	–0.3
Wells Fargo & Co	USA	4	5	263,266	1138	5.4	1
Mizuho Financial Group	Japan	5	4	176,525	865	3.6	–1.3
Mitsubishi UFJ Financial Group	Japan	6	6	166,915	1221	3.4	–0.7
Goldman Sachs & Co	USA	7	11	154,086	564	3.1	0.7
Barclays	UK	8	9	152,282	623	3.1	0.5
BNP Paribas SA	France	9	8	145,899	613	3	–1
Sumitomo Mitsui Finl Grp Inc	Japan	10	7	133,849	978	2.7	–1.4
	Panel B: Americas loans bookrunners						
BofA Securities Inc	USA	1	1	449,741	1636	12.8	0.2
JPMorgan	USA	2	2	405,073	1417	11.5	–0.6
Wells Fargo & Co	USA	3	4	260,587	1123	7.4	0.3
Citi	USA	4	3	243,119	675	6.9	–1.2
Goldman Sachs & Co	USA	5	6	135,512	512	3.9	0.6
Barclays	UK	6	5	129,273	563	3.7	0.2
RBC Capital Markets	Canada	7	8	127,938	563	3.6	0.8
BMO Capital Markets	Canada	8	13	101,762	589	2.9	0.5
Mitsubishi UFJ Financial Group	Japan	9	9	93,045	470	2.6	–0.1
US Bancorp	USA	10	11	92,533	524	2.6	0.1
	Panel C: EMEA loans bookrunners						
BNP Paribas SA	France	1	1	65,142	273	8.2	–3.8
Societe Generale	France	2	4	54,403	154	6.8	1.9
Credit Agricole CIB	France	3	2	50,802	245	6.4	–0.7
Deutsche Bank	Germany	4	10	37,879	134	4.8	1.1
JPMorgan	USA	5	3	36,714	115	4.6	–1.8
BofA Securities Inc	USA	6	17	35,858	106	4.5	2.5
ING	The Netherlands	7	12	31,058	136	3.9	1.1
UniCredit	Italy	8	6	30,005	164	3.8	–0.9
Citi	USA	9	8	29,050	95	3.7	–0.3
HSBC Holdings PLC	UK	10	5	27,100	123	3.4	–1.5
	Panel D: Asia (ex Japan) loans bookrunners						
Bank of China Ltd	China	1	1	65,668	294	20.8	–3.2
Agricultural Bank of China	China	2	12	18,469	39	5.9	3.5
Standard Chartered PLC	UK	3	4	13,884	76	4.4	0.5
China Merchants Bank	China	4	3	13,286	37	4.2	0.2
China Construction Bank	China	5	5	11,637	47	3.7	0.2
HSBC Holdings PLC	UK	6	8	11,506	83	3.6	0.8
Industrial & Comm Bank China	China	7	2	8,949	35	2.8	–2
DBS Group Holdings	Singapore	8	6	8,875	52	2.8	–0.5
CITIC	Hong Kong	9	11	8,588	55	2.7	0.2
Sumitomo Mitsui Finl Grp Inc	Japan	10	7	8,433	57	2.7	–0.2

Exhibit 6.3. Top 10 bookrunners in global loan syndication — 2021.

Source: Refinitiv Thomson Reuters Global Syndicated Loans Review, 2021.

particular, US borrowers dominate the global market accounting for 87% of the market share in 2021. Third, whereas developed market deals are much more frequent than in other regions, resulting in larger overall size and market share, deals involving Middle Eastern country borrowers are much higher in average size, easily outstripping all others. Their average size is more than twice as large at USD 1.2 trillion as the global volume of USD 521 million in 2021 and similarly in 2009 (791 m compared to 336 m). Fourth, each region's top bookrunners of loan syndicates are headquartered in the same region as their borrowers. Moreover, USA banks are also strongly present in the EMEA region.

6.3. Syndication Process

Loan syndication is very similar in process to international debt underwriting or a large initial public offering of equity in terms of one or more underwriters intermediating between the capital market and corporations wishing to raise capital. There are three main participants, the issuer (of debt or equity) or borrower, a group of arrangers (mostly investment banks for equity and bond offerings and large commercial banks for loan syndication), and a group of investors (lenders) in the primary market. There is a large overlap in the skill set required for successful fundraising, a full subscription of the security issues (debt securities or syndicated loans). These include the capacity to conduct a thorough analysis of the issuer's (borrower's) characteristics, such as the standing of the borrower/issuer in the market, its business model, proposed cash flows from funding, and credit risk. Moreover, the arrangers are expected to show a good understanding of the market conditions and have a good reputation for successfully completing similar deals in the past. What follows are typical steps of international loan syndication, illustrated in Exhibit 6.4.

Assume that a company in the mining industry, ABC mining, wishes to raise USB 1 billion to finance an expansion of its operations. If the company is of good international standing and has successfully tapped into the international loan syndication market previously, multiple banks will offer their services to act as lead managers. Offers are invited from large international banks, and they can be via open bidding, select bidding, or selecting from a panel of pre-determined lenders. The role of a lead manager is attractive for participating banks since they receive the most significant portion of the fee income in the lending group. More

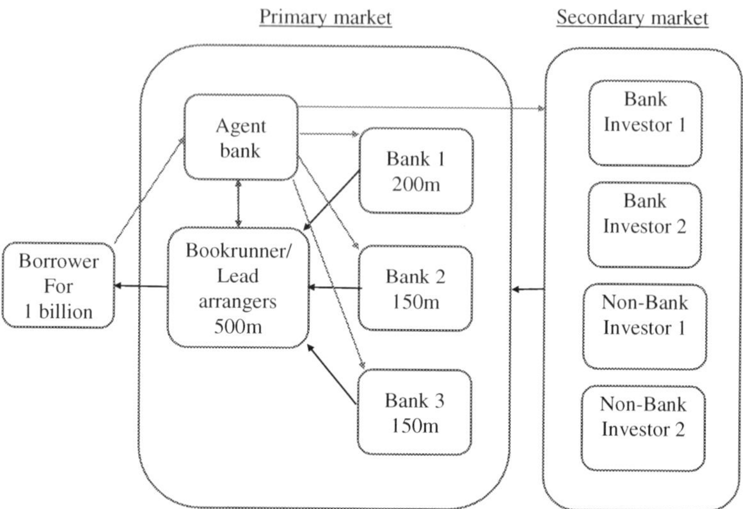

Exhibit 6.4. Loan syndication process.

importantly, banks enjoy the prestige associated with being the lead manager as this may lead to future business from the same borrower, referral business from other banks, and enhanced reputation amongst its investors (shareholders and other stakeholders), especially if the syndication size is substantial and there is good media coverage of the loan issue in the markets. In addition, international banks of good standing are on the lookout for such opportunities by relying on their foreign branches and correspondent banks for intelligence on potential borrowers that require syndication. In addition, they may also receive referrals from other units in their organisation, banks that are not yet ready to act as lead managers, and investment banks that advise their clients on loan syndications.

Upon solicitation of syndication, invited banks submit syndication proposals. In the proposal, they specify the required information about the proposed syndication. This includes the share of the management bank in the syndication, the terms of the loan, the amount to be provided by each participating bank, drawdown conditions, price (margin over LIBOR), market flex clause, and expiration of the offer. The bidding banks must estimate the most likely market responses to eventual syndication, as failure to achieve a full subscription from participating banks would be costly. Hence, the information in the proposal must be carefully researched and finalised.

One bank (or a group of banks) will receive a mandate to form a syndicate of lenders. A mandate can be either unrestricted or restricted in terms of the types and locations of banks to include (or exclude) and other specified conditions. Unconditional mandates would be preferable for the winning bank as these afford the most flexibility for the lead bank. The determinants of a successful mandate include price, reputation, and management ability to organise successful syndicates.

Once a mandate is given, the lead manager pledges to fund half the required amount, 500 million, and then will attempt to form a syndicate to fund the remaining 500 million. This is done via email or telephone in the first instance and followed by formal correspondence. If the loan amount is particularly large, the lead manager will solicit other banks to join the management group. Lead banks share the responsibility of managing the syndicate, such as the preparation and distribution of information memorandum, keeping records of syndication responses from potential participants, negotiating loan agreements, arranging the signing of the agreements, handling publicity (publication of tombstones), and performing agency functions. A typical structure of participants includes the lead manager or a group of lead managers, co-managers, participants, and agents. In general, lead managers (also known as bookrunners) are selected for their ability to manage successful loan syndication, and they may not necessarily have expertise in the area of business the borrower is in. As such, the lead arranger seeks banks that are knowledgeable in the industry, in this case, the mining industry, and also are located in the same country as the borrower to assess the borrower's credit risk more accurately and better manage the risk. The three banks in the syndicate must provide the specialised skills that the lead arranger lacks. For example, Bank 1 specialises in the mining industry, Bank 2 is located in the same country as the borrower and preferably has dealt with them previously, and Bank 3 is a large multinational bank with extensive experience in loan syndications as both lead arranger and a participating bank. Bank 1 and bank 2 will provide the borrower and industry-specific risk analysis, and Bank 3 will assume further supporting roles. In addition, one of the lead arrangers can act as an agent bank that handles the necessary communications among all the participants. The arrows going from right to left indicate the flow of funds supplied to the borrower. The arrows running from left to right show the process of interest and relevant fee payments and the eventual repayment of the loan. It should be noted that all five banks involved are individually contracted to provide their allocated portion of the loan amount under the

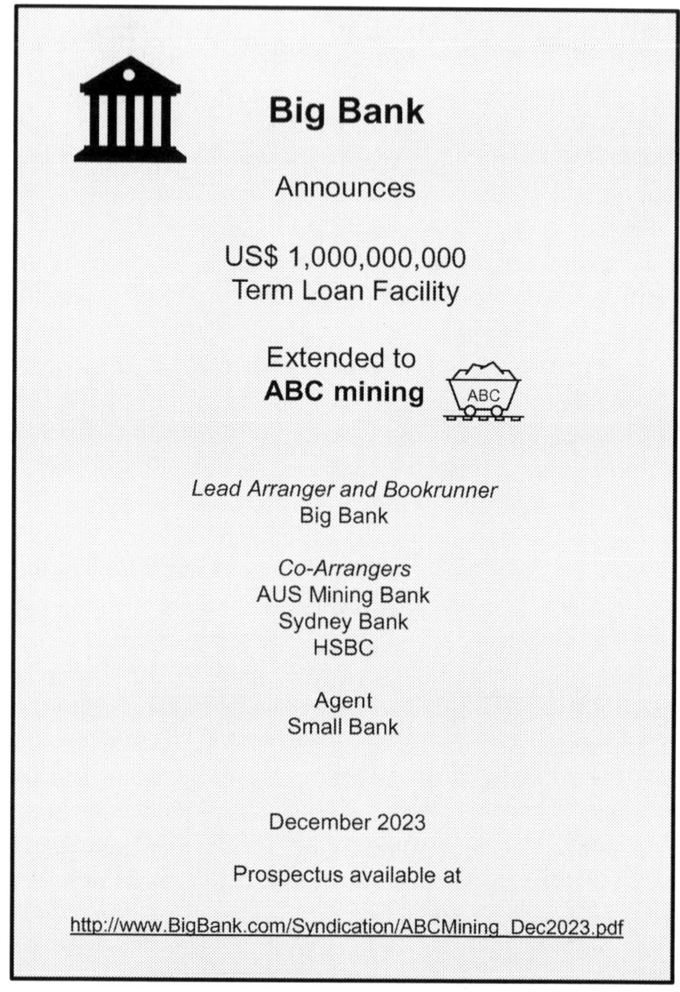

Exhibit 6.5. A tombstone of a loan syndication.

same terms and conditions specified in the syndication documents. However, all communications and fund flows are via the Agent bank for efficiency. If any of the three banks in the second group wishes to liquidate their position in the syndicate, there is a secondary market for syndicated loans where banks and non-bank investors are willing to take over their position (see Section 6.8).

Once the syndicate is formed and the necessary duties are allocated among the participating banks, the syndicate might release a tombstone. A tombstone is a written advertisement of the successful formation of loan syndication (or IPO or bond issuance involving multiple participants) detailing the borrower, participating banks, and their role, loan amount, and conditions. The purpose of a tombstone is to enhance the visibility of the syndicated loan and the participating banks and to solicit future interests from prospective banks, investors, and borrowers. Exhibit 6.5 shows an example of a tombstone in this loan syndication. The lead arranger, Big Bank, together with an agent bank and three co-arrangers, arranged a USD 1 billion term loan to ABC mining. Upon placing this tombstone in all relevant media outlets, potential borrowers and lenders may approach the named banks for future business.

6.4. Benefits of Loan Syndication

6.4.1. *Benefits of loan syndication for borrowers and lenders*

There are three steps in financial intermediation that banks need to perform. The *First* step is origination, where the lender is required to secure a borrower. Traditionally, an extensive network of branches was necessary for a commercial bank to attract borrowers successfully. In this step, the lender performs credit risk analysis on loan applicants to select borrowers that satisfy the lender's minimum credit quality requirements. Credit scoring and other methods can be used to determine suitable borrowers. The *Second* step is to secure funding for the loan. The most important source of funding for a commercial bank is deposits. Other forms of liabilities, such as loans from other banks and bond issuance, can also fund loan origination. The *Third* step is to monitor the borrower's loan usage to ensure adherence to the loan covenants. Also, periodic credit assessment of the borrower throughout the loan period is required to assess the time-varying risk characteristics of the borrower. In loan syndication, the lead managers perform all three steps to varying degrees depending on the borrower's risk profile. However, other participating banks can perform only some of the steps to exploit their comparative advantage. For example, smaller participating banks can rely on the lead bank for origination (step 1) and loan monitoring (step 3) and only provide partial funding for the loan (step 2). Other banks may provide administration functions liaising between the borrower and the lenders in addition to providing partial funding without being part of the origination step. Loan syndication, therefore, allows participating banks to specialise in the steps they have a comparative advantage in to achieve overall efficiency in the loan syndication, and this results in benefits going to both the lenders and the borrower.

The lenders benefit from participating in loan syndication. *First*, they achieve loan portfolio diversification. Instead of holding one USD 1 billion loan asset against one borrower, they can potentially pledge to lend USD 100m each in ten loan syndicates, achieving loan portfolio diversification. *Second*, the banks in a syndicate, especially smaller ones, can access those borrowers they normally would not have access to (i.e., sovereign or large MNC borrowers with high credit ratings). Once contact with the borrower through syndication is established, they can hope to do further business with the borrower in the future. *Third*, better information gathering and sharing can result in lower information asymmetry. *Fourth*, syndication lowers loan default probability due to the enhanced penalty faced by the borrower should there be a default. Multiple banks can blacklist the borrower, making access to the international loan market difficult. *Fifth*, there is potential for loan trading and associated derivative (credit derivatives) business (securitisation and secondary market trading) that contribute to the liquidity of the syndicated loan portfolios.

Loan syndication provides some of the benefits of both relationship and transaction borrowing for the borrower (Greenbaum, *et al.*, 2019). The borrower in loan syndication benefits from the process because a larger amount of borrowing is possible, and the cost of borrowing is lower than if only one bank is providing the fund. The first point is obvious, whereas the second requires more explanation. The cost of borrowing is lower because the lenders in the syndicate better understand the borrower's credit risk. Continuing with the example of the borrower wishing to raise USD 1 billion, one option for the borrower is to contact as many lenders as possible to raise the 1 billion required, for example, 10 banks for 100 million each. In this case, all 10 banks must perform all three steps of financial intermediation identified above. More importantly, it is likely that each bank is aware of the borrower contacting multiple banks, but they may not be aware of the total amount of the borrowing involved or the conditions of each loan. As such, the lending banks must price this additional risk in the lending cost offered to the borrower to compensate for the information asymmetry and higher administration costs of the loans. On the other hand, if a syndicate is formed comprising of banks with various expertise and outreach (e.g., banks with a prior business relationship with the borrower, located in the same country/region as the borrower), information asymmetry can be reduced. The syndicate is then in a much better position to assess the borrower's overall risk much more effectively. These considerations will result in lower loan spreads applicable to the borrower (i.e., a margin above LIBOR). The cost of borrowing is also lower under syndication due to the more liquid nature of the loan. Banks participating in the syndicate can liquidate the lending portfolio by various means (e.g., via secondary markets and securitisation via CLO, Collateralised Loan Obligation), and this added liquidity allows for lower margins.

6.4.2. *Asymmetric information and loan syndication*

The existence of asymmetric information between the lender and the borrower significantly impacts how a loan contract is constructed. The wider the information gap (especially concerning the willingness to repay on the part of the borrower), the higher the perceived risk for the lender. This results in a higher lending rate, tighter loan conditions such as onerous loan covenants, more frequent audits on loan usage, and collateral requirements. At its extreme, information asymmetry will lead to an adverse selection problem, and the lender will extend no loans. There are a number of ways that this problem can be addressed. A better credit risk assessment involves not only hard information, such as the borrower's financial reports, statements, analyst reports, industry assessments, and the macro environment but also soft information, such as the social connection of the borrower's CEO and the borrower's potential alternative sources of finance. As the lender obtains better information on the borrower (both hard and soft) and develops skills in using this information to predict the likelihood of the borrower's default accurately, the adverse selection problem may be avoided.

Loan syndication can help in this regard as the lenders in the syndicate share information they have on the borrower. Some participating banks may have done business with the current borrower previously and are familiar with the borrower's and its industry's business models and conditions. Other participating banks may have come from the same country as the borrower. As a result, the syndicate will possess much better overall information on the borrower's risk profile than any one lender can obtain on their own. This then leads to a lower information gap and hence a lower lending rate and less stringent loan conditions benefiting both the lenders and the borrower, as discussed in the previous section.

Information asymmetry also determines the syndicate structure. Since loan use monitoring efforts by the lead manager in a syndicate are not readily observable, there is a moral hazard problem with the lead manager, especially when the borrower is of lower credit quality (i.e., a leveraged borrower). Sufi (2017) finds that in an environment where there is wider information asymmetry which requires more intense monitoring and due diligence but the lead manager's monitoring activities are not easily observable, the loan syndicate structure tends to be that (1) the lead managers hold larger shares of the loan than otherwise, (2) the loan syndicate is more concentrated (i.e., a fewer number of participating banks), (3) participant banks are sought from the same region as the borrower or having a previous lending relationship with the borrower, and (4) the lead managers need to have a good reputation (e.g., previous experience of being a successful lead manager).

6.5. Types of Syndication

The form of loan syndication that provides the maximum protection for the borrower is *fully committed syndication (or underwritten syndication)*, where the lead arranger of the syndicate gives a commitment to the borrower before the syndicate is formed. This implies that the borrower is guaranteed to raise the loan amount agreed upon. The lead arranger then tries to form a syndicate of lenders to raise the full amount of the committed loan. If the lead manager is not successfully generating enough interest among investors, it is required to provide the shortfall out of its own balance sheet. The lead manager can then sell the additional loan portions later if desired. Thus, the lead arranger in a fully committed syndicate faces exposure to the loan and must be able to absorb any shortfalls, which requires a substantial balance sheet. In addition to facing an unexpectedly large share of the loan share in the syndicate, the lead arranger in undersubscribed syndication would also suffer reputation damage. On the other hand, if the lead arranger is generating more interest from the market than the required amount at the proposed lending spread, the borrower may not be happy as this indicates the interest rate was set higher than what was necessary to achieve full subscription. Thus, a successful lead arranger must be an effective and efficient investment banker in the first instance and be able to judge the market sentiments, the borrower's standing in the market, etc., to achieve full subscription. Moreover, it must have a large balance sheet in case there is a need to provide a larger share of the loan than ideal. Underwritten syndication is used by the lead arranger to increase the chance of obtaining mandates. Also, underwritten syndication has more lucrative fees for lead arrangers due to additional risk. Underwritten syndication is the most popular form of loan syndication in continental Europe. This reflects the role banks play in the financial system, where they take a more active role in corporate governance for their corporate borrowers. So, when their customers require syndicated loans, they normally treat this as an extension of their relationship with them and attempt to provide full commitment.

In contrast, in a *best-effort-based syndicate*, the lead manager is not called upon to guarantee the full amount of the loan. They commit to underwrite a smaller amount than the entire loan amount and attempt to achieve a full subscription in the market by securing enough interest from the market. If the loan is undersubscribed, syndication will not proceed unless the borrower is willing to take a smaller loan than required or agree to change the loan conditions (e.g., market flex conditions in the syndication) to make it more attractive to investors (i.e., higher all-in spreads). The syndication is cancelled if the loan cannot be fully subscribed at the conditions acceptable to the borrower and they do not agree to take the lower amount. This type of syndication relies more on the market conditions and the lead arranger's expertise in judging the market's risk appetite. If the borrower is of higher risk (companies that are small, unlisted, and young), then best-effort syndication is preferred as it requires less risk to be taken by the lead arranger. This form of syndication is popular in the US where banks take more of a market-oriented relationship with their corporate clients, and so syndication requires more of an investment bank mindset that relies on the market than their own funding sources.

Club deal is syndication with relatively small amounts of less than USD 150 million, in general, and pre-marketed to lenders that already have relationships (or in the same lending club) and know each other well. An interesting feature is that although there is an arranger, the funding is equally spread across the lenders in the club, and the speed of execution of syndication is usually much quicker due to the familiarity of the club members and the exclusivity. Another feature of club deal loan syndication is that while other forms of loan syndicates are temporary and disband when the loan reaches maturity or is cancelled, club syndicates are likely to continue beyond one syndication as they are based on longer-term relations among trusted member banks.

Participation syndication is where the borrower has a fiduciary relationship only with the lead arranger. The lead arranger originates the loan on either underwritten or best-effort basis and acts as the sole counterparty to the borrower. This process involves a large and well-known bank originating a loan and then selling portions of the loan to other participating banks once the deal is closed. The originating bank sells only the rights of the cash flow from the loan in portions (e.g., 10% to Bank A, 20% to Bank B, another 20% to Bank C, and retains the remaining 50% of the loan) and keeps the relationship with the borrower. The borrower and the participating banks only have a relationship with the originating bank, and not with each other. Cash and information flows between the borrower and the participating banks are via the originating bank.

From the discussions above, it can be summarised that the essential characteristics of a lead bank include the following: (i) a substantial deposit base (i.e., a large and healthy balance sheet) or an ability to generate funds to fill any gap in financing (most relevant in underwritten syndication), (ii) expertise in credit risk analysis, and (iii) expertise in the traditional investment banking activities (more valuable in best-effort syndications).

6.6. Types of Syndication Loan Facilities

Syndicated loan types are similar to domestic loans and vary in complexity and usefulness to the borrower. *Term loans* are standard loan contracts that require periodic payments of interest, amortisation, and a final payment of the remaining principal at maturity. In most cases, lending banks prefer maturities of less than five years, although longer maturities are possible in exceptional cases where the borrower is well known to the lenders with a successful past business relationship and the lenders have lending expertise in the borrower's business and the industry. Hasan *et al.* (2021) report that for the period 1998–2016, the average maturity of the loan in the syndication market was 50 months (or 4.1 years), with the average amount of USD 178 million provided by 10.25 lenders in the syndicate. There are three methods of repayment. Amortisation payment is the payment of equal amounts on a regular basis across the loan period, resulting in a zero balance after the last payment. Bullet repayment requires only one payment of the full amount at maturity. A balloon repayment schedule involves small and regular repayments throughout the period leaving one large repayment amount at maturity. Fight (2004) suggests that the amortisation method is the most popular, and the other two are used mostly in special circumstances.

Revolving facilities allow the borrower to borrow, repay, and then re-borrow at the end of the interest period (e.g., month) but within the facility period. They are usually extended to investment-grade borrowers (i.e., borrowers with credit ratings at or above BBB issued by major credit rating agencies). They are also referred to as 364-day facilities as they often run for 364 days due to higher capital requirements for lending banks if the maturity goes beyond one year (Standard & Poors, 2019). Commitment fees apply for the unused amounts of the facility. Revolving credits can allow multi-currency borrowing and can be turned into term loans at a given date of conversion. Also, at maturity, revolving facilities can be reset and rolled over for the same maturity. This is known as an evergreen option. This option is relevant when the loan is to finance working capital, and whether to roll over to the next period is determined at annual reviews. Sufficient notice is required to be given (1–2 years) to the borrower if the facility is to be cancelled.

Letters of credit can be provided by a syndicate of banks to the borrower involved in international trade (both export and import letters of credit). The syndicate banks are responsible for the payment guarantee of the trade amount and are required to pay the obligation should the borrower defaults.

Special purpose facilities are used for the borrower to finance specific investments. For example, acquisition facilities are used to acquire other businesses in an M&A deal, equipment facilities are for financing equipment purchases, and CAPEX facilities are to fund capital investments. Although these investments are long term in nature, requiring matching maturities, arranging long-term finances such as bond or equity issuance usually takes a substantial amount of time, especially if the market conditions are not benign. To take advantage of emerging opportunities quickly, the borrower can approach their banks for a short-term loan facility, such as a 364-day facility. The repayment of the facility can be made from the proceeds of later bond or equity issuance.

Exhibit 6.6 presents the breakdown of the loan syndication amount in 2016 by syndication type and loan facility. Panel A shows the breakdown by syndication type. Eighty-six percent of the market (USD 3.7 trillion) is accounted for by syndicated loans covering underwritten, best-effort and

	USD billion	% of total
Panel A: Amount of syndication by type		
Syndication (Underwritten, Best-Effort, Participation)	3,659.747	86.25%
Club Deal	503.882	11.87%
Private Placement	13.870	0.33%
Bilateral	28.564	0.67%
Sole Lender	1.389	0.03%
Undisclosed (Loan)	33.165	0.78%
Undisclosed (Bond)	2.600	0.06%
Syndication (Bond)	0.034	0.00%
Total	*4,243.251*	*100.00%*
Panel B: Amount of syndication by facility		
364-Day Facility	246.023	5.80%
Islamic Finance (Ijara and Murabaha)	14.979	0.35%
Notes and Bonds (FRN, NIF and Schuldschein)	13.062	0.31%
Revolver/Line < 1 Yr.	17.865	0.42%
Revolver/Line >= 1 Yr.	1,524.790	35.93%
Revolver/Term Loan	18.842	0.44%
Special purpose facilities (Acquisition, CAPEX, Construction	10.875	0.26%
Term loan, A-D, F-I, delay draw	1,871.954	44.12%
Trade credit (Bonding, export, LC)	37.870	0.89%
Others	486.946	11.48%
Total	*4,243.207*	*100.00%*

Exhibit 6.6. Loan syndication amount by syndication type and facility — 2016 USD b. and %.

Source: Compiled from syndicated loan data for 2016, obtained from Dealscan database.

participation syndications. The distant second is Club deal which accounts for 12% (USD 503 billion). Other types of funding in the syndication market are negligible in comparison. Panel B shows the breakdown by loan facilities. The largest share of the market is accounted for by term loans in various forms (44% or USD 1.87 trillion). The close second is revolving loans, with a maturity greater than one year, holding a 36% share or USD 1.52 trillion. Out of the three types of revolvers, the other two types of revolvers were negligible. The other notable facility is the 364-day facility which accounts for 5.8% or 246 billion. In short, the loan syndication market was dominated by the three syndication types (underwritten, best-effort, and participation) in 2016. The two equally important facility types were term loans and revolving credit of more than one year of maturity.

6.7. Loan Pricing

Syndicated loans are typically priced in terms of LIBOR. To this floating base, a spread (margin) is added, which can be changed during the life of the loan. The interest rate is regularly adjusted throughout the life of the loan, typically every three or six months. It is also possible that borrowers combine the loan with various derivative products to limit the rise in the cost of borrowings, such as interest rate caps, floors, and collar options. As the loans are based on floating interest rates, they can usually be repaid early without penalty. These early repayments generally occur at interest payment (base adjustment) dates. The spread or margin is mainly determined by the perceived credit risk of the borrower, which essentially measures the degree of uncertainty the lenders face and are unable to resolve fully. The senior members of the syndicate are responsible for assessing and pricing this risk by utilising their credit risk expertise and also by referring to the third-party credit rating of the borrower.

In addition to the spread added to LIBOR, the borrower needs to pay a long list of fees for various services provided by the syndicate banks, which are shared among them according to a pre-determined formula. In general, the lead arranger receives the largest share of the fee income, followed by other senior members of the syndicate that also perform management duties. In general, the fee income is one of the most attractive aspects of joining a loan syndicate for senior syndicate members, as the fee can amount to as much as 10% of the loan amount in some cases. On the other hand, junior members of the syndicate without management or administration roles are drawn to the syndicate by the interest income and the opportunity to have a relationship with the multinational or sovereign borrower that would otherwise be impossible.

There are three different types of fees: upfront, annual, and one-off fees for optional services (Gadanecz, 2004). Front-end fees are payable by the borrower at the start of syndication before the borrowed funds are released. *Arrangement fee* is paid to the lead arrangers for originating the loan and putting the syndication together. A fixed percentage (e.g., 1%) of the total amount of the loan is set aside as the management fee, which will be shared among the senior group of banks that perform management duties. The lead manager withholds a portion for itself (called *praecipuum*), and the remainder is distributed among other senior banks according to the level of services provided by each bank. *Underwriting fee* is paid to those member banks that perform underwriting duties. Underwriting requires a

	Upfront fees
Arrangement fee	Paid to lead arrangers for organising syndication. It is a fixed percentage of loan amount and shared around the senior syndicate banks after the lead arrangers taker their share (called praecipuum).
Underwriting fee	Paid to member banks acting as underwriters.
Participation fee	Paid to all the banks in the syndicate contributing to funding. Fees are paid according to the contribution tiers, e.g., 50 basis points for 10 million, 100 basis points for 20 million, 150 basis points for 40 millions, and above.
Legal Fee	Paid to law firm providing legal advices when constructing the syndicate structure and syndication documents.
	Annual fees
Agent fee	Paid to the bank acting as the agent for the syndicate.
Facility fee	Paid to member banks for providing the loan facility whether it is fully used or not.
Commitment fee	Fee paid on unused loan commitments. Commitment and facility fees are not charged together. If one is charged, the other is not.
Utilisation fee	Fee payable if utilisation of facility is above pre-determined level (e.g., 50%) of credit line.
	One-off fees
Prepayment fee	Payable when the borrower repays the loan earlier than maturity.
Cancellation fee	Payable when the borrower cancels the credit line facility before maturity.

Exhibit 6.7. Structure of syndication fees.

Source: Gadanecz (2004), and Berg *et al.* (2016).

commitment to deliver promised amount of funds irrespective of whether they are able to fund it from their own balance sheets or find willing investors. Some or all of the senior members of the syndicate perform this role to a varying degree. *Participation fee* is paid to all banks contributing to the loan amount and is proportional to the contributed amount. *Legal fee* is paid to the law firm that provides legal services when constructing the syndicate's structure and producing legal documents. It is a usual practice to specify aggregate upfront fees in the contract rather than specifying the fee distribution among syndicate members and the spreads. The resulting all-inclusive spreads are presented to the borrower. It is up to the lead arrangers to work out the optimal proportion of the aggregate upfront fees among the syndicate members. The lead managers end up with the largest fee amongst the syndicate participants, as they will collect arrangement, underwriting, and participation fees. Senior member banks will collect smaller portions of these fees, and junior member banks without management responsibilities will only collect participation fees.

An annual fee is payable throughout the life of the loan on a yearly basis. *Agent fee* is paid to the agent bank for performing administration duties, such as processing interest payment distribution and providing information to the member banks to protect their rights. It is not shared with other member banks but instead fully retained by the agent bank. The agent bank has a contractual obligation to both the syndicate banks and the borrower. *Facility fee* is charged to the borrower for the provision of the loan facility, whether it is used or not. *Commitment fee* is applicable to the unused portion of the loan amount. It is more common in credit lines where the borrower may not fully utilise the full amount of the facility. For term loans, commitment fees are levied when the drawdown dates are not explicitly set. Commitment fees are an alternative to facility fees in credit lines as one replaces the other (Berg *et al.*, 2016).

One-off fees include a cancellation fee and a prepayment fee. The former is applicable in credit line loans where the borrower cancels the facility before maturity, and the latter is a penalty for early repayment in term loans. A summary of the syndication fees is presented in Exhibit 6.7.

6.8. Transferability of Syndicated Loans

Lenders in a loan syndicate can sell off their stakes in one of two ways, assignment and participation. *Assignment* is where a lender in a syndicate relinquishes all rights, with the borrower's consent, to the payments of interest and principal (and the credit risk, too) to another party by formally selling the loan contract. The borrower may not consent to assignment unless they are in default, in which case the borrower's consent in selling the portion of the loan held by the lender is not required. *Assignment with novation* represents a stronger form of assignment in that a new contract is drawn between the new lender and the borrower, in addition to the above. The existing rights and obligations between the selling bank and the borrower are cancelled, and the new lender assumes the rights and obligations under the same conditions as the previous arrangement. The syndication document usually sets a minimum amount (USD 5 million, Standard & Poors, 2019) that can be assigned. Moreover, an assignment fee, normally USD 3,500, can be reduced or even waived if the assignment is to another syndicate member via trading with the arranger.

Another method of selling off all or part of the stake of a lender in a syndicate is *participation*. The lead arranger sells a portion of the loan (to be more specific, a proportion of the cash flows from the loan) to a participating bank after a syndicate has been formed. The participating bank holds a claim only against the selling bank, the lead arranger, and it does not have a direct link to the borrower. The selling bank retains the role of the lender to the borrower, and the participating bank has only derivative rights rather than the right to the part of the loan directly. Unlike assignment, participation does not require the borrower's consent, there is no minimum amount required or fees, as the seller fully retains the fiduciary relationship with the borrower. If the selling bank defaults on transferring cash flows from that portion of the loan, the participating bank must wait until the bankruptcy process of the selling bank is completed to see whether there is any asset left to recoup. In the example shown in Exhibit 6.4, the arranger who originated the loan of USD 1 billion completes the syndication contract with the borrower for the full amount and then attempts to find participants, three in this case, who would buy a 50% right in aggregate to the loan's cash flows. The three participants invest 200, 150, and 150 m, respectively, and their claims are against the arranger (specifically, 50% of the arranger's share), and they do not have a direct claim on the loan or have contractual rights against the borrower.

The secondary market for syndication loans has developed since the early 1980s following various episodes of international sovereign debt defaults. In the mid-1990s, two standard-setting bodies were established to aid the trading of loans. The Loan Market Association (LMA) was established in 1996 to cater to the EMEA region's syndicated loan market participants (Campbell and Weaver, 2013). Loan Syndications and Trading Association (LSTA) was established in 1995 in the US for a similar purpose for the US syndication market participants. Both organisations provide documentation to standardise the process of loan trading, which greatly assists both buyers and sellers in the secondary loan market. Different sets of procedure documents exist depending on the types of loan sales: par trade vs distressed loan trade; the asset being traded is a debt (loan) vs act as a claim; whether the sale is via assignment or sub-participation, etc. The traders are encouraged to use the procedure documents of LMA and LSTA as templates for trading negotiation, which might require modifications of terms and conditions to suit individual trade requirements. Due to the standardisation of secondary market trading procedures for syndicated loans, liquidating one's position in a syndicate became quicker and more straightforward. One important consequence is that one of the hurdles of joining loan syndication as a lender is removed. That is, if the lender can easily liquidate their loan position instead of being stuck with the loan until maturity or selling at a loss, they may not hesitate to join the syndicate, making the lead arranger's job of forming a syndicate easier. If the seller wishes to sell a portfolio of loans, then the negotiation is more complex, and custom-made solutions are required for the sale negotiations instead of relying on the standardised loan sale and trading procedures by the two standard-setting bodies.

References

Altunbas, Y., Gadanecz, B., and Kara, A. (2006). *Syndicated Loans A Hybrid of Relationship Lending and Publicly Traded Debt.* Palgrave Macmillan, New York.

Berg, T., Saunders, A., and Steffen, S. (2016). The total cost of corporate borrowing in the loan market: Don't ignore the fees. *The Journal of Finance*, LXXI(3), 1357–1392.

Campbell, M. and Weaver, Ch. (2013). *Syndicated Lending Practice and Documentation*, 6th ed., Euromoney Institutional Investor PLC, London.

Fight, A. (2004). *Syndicated Lending*. Elsevier, Amsterdam.

Gadanecz, B. (2004). The syndicated loan market: Structure, development and implications. *BIS Quarterly Review*, December 2004. https://www.bis.org/publ/qtrpdf/r_qt0412g.pdf.

Greenbaum, S., Thakor, A., and Boot, A. (2019). *Special Topics in Credit: Syndicated Loans, Loan Sales, and Project Finance in Contemporary Financial Intermediation*, 4th ed., Academic Press, London, UK.

Hasan, I., Kim, S.-J., Politsidis, P., and Wu, E. (2021). Loan syndication under Basel II: How do firm credit ratings affect the cost of credit? *Journal of International Financial Markets, Institutions and Money*, 72, 101331.

Refinitiv Thomson Reuters, Global Syndicated Loans Review, 2010 to 2021. https://www.refinitiv.com/en/products/deals-intelligence/syndicated-loans.

Standard & Poors (2019). A Syndicated Loan Primer. https://www.spglobal.com/marketintelligence/en/documents/lcd-primer-leveraged-loans_ltr.pdf.

Sufi, A. (2017). Information asymmetry and financing arrangements: Evidence from syndicated loans. *The Journal of Finance*, LXII, 2.

Part 2

International Financial Crisis and Secret Money

Chapter 7

International Banking Crisis

7.1. Introduction

The financial system in an economy aims to effect an efficient transfer of funds from net savers to net borrowers by prioritising the deployment of scarce financial resources to the most productive use. The aim is to achieve a result that the system benefits due to the additional economic activities and the resulting income generated for all involved. The various segments of the financial system perform this role via intermediated and direct fund flows between net savers and net investors. The banking system brings together borrowers and lenders who rely on banks for intermediating between them and perform necessary risk management roles (credit risk analysis on the borrowers and deposit protection for the depositors). Debt and equity markets (and the derivatives' markets based on them) allow companies to raise funds directly in the respective markets where investors assume the counterparty risk. The well-known adverse selection and moral hazard issues are under control as long as the level of uncertainty in the economy is at a manageable level and the investors' risk appetite remains healthy. In times of high levels of uncertainty in the economy, information asymmetry is high enough to cause severe adverse selection and moral hazard problems. Consequently, economic activities will shrink due to a compromised financial system at best and a total collapse of the system (market failure) at worst.

A financial crisis is composed of market failures in various segments of the financial system. *First*, a banking crisis refers to the banking sector in a financial system that is not effectively performing its functions, leading to a system-wide reduction (or even a collapse) in economic activities. When banks in a financial system experience a sudden drop in the value of their assets (both loan portfolios and other security holdings) relative to the liability side of their balance sheets, their ability to make new loans and maintain existing assets is compromised. The resulting reduction in bank intermediation will significantly impact economies over-reliant on bank credit for economic activities. Developing countries with under-developed financial markets and the bank-focused financial systems of continental Europe and Japan in the advanced countries belong to this group. Despite advances in the banking sector (technological and regulatory), banks remain sensitive today to panics and runs as in the last century (Allen *et al.*, 2009). *Second*, a currency crisis is where the value of a country's currency against a hard currency such as the USD or the EUR falls sharply due to various factors (speculative currency attacks, rapid correction of currency mispricing, etc.). The resulting inflationary pressure and increase in the domestic currency value of foreign currency-denominated liabilities of banks and other companies in the country can lead to corporate insolvencies. Moreover, if the central bank attempts to defend its currency by raising domestic interest rates to discourage short-selling of the currency, domestic economic activities will contract and add to the recessionary effect of the currency crisis. *Third*, a stock market crisis is where a sharp downward correction of stock prices, usually following a collapse of a speculative bubble, leads to a collapse of asset values. Hedge funds, pension funds, and other investment management firms will experience a sudden and rapid reduction in their asset value that can potentially cause fund runs and other liquidity drains. *Fourth*, a sovereign debt crisis is when a country's government (sovereign) is unable to service its foreign currency-denominated liabilities, which can be due to either solvency or liquidity-related difficulties.

In some cases, more than one type of crisis can occur concurrently. For example, the Asian financial crisis of 1997–1999 involved currency, stock, and banking crises. The Global Financial Crisis 2007–2009 saw countries experience both stock market and banking crises (the US, Ireland, the UK, etc.). The Eurozone debt crisis of 2009–2011 involved banking, stock, and sovereign debt crises.

	Banking	Currency	Sovereign
		1971 to 2017	
All countries	*151*	*239*	*75*
Advanced countries	25	13	2
(share of total)	(17%)	(5%)	(3%)
Developing countries	126	226	73
(share of total)	(83%)	(95%)	(97%)
		1971 to 2006	
All countries	*122*	*204*	*63*
Advanced countries	8	12	0
(share of total)	(7%)	(6%)	(0%)
Developing countries	114	192	63
(share of total)	(93%)	(94%)	(100%)
		2007 to 2017	
All countries	*29*	*35*	*12*
Advanced countries	17	1	2
(share of total)	(59%)	(3%)	(17%)
Developing countries	12	34	10
(share of total)	(41%)	(97%)	(83%)

Exhibit 7.1. Number of financial crises, 1976–2017.

Source: Author's calculation using Table 7.1 in Laeven and Valencia (2018).

7.1.1. *Frequency and impact of financial crises*

The international financial system has witnessed numerous crises over recent decades with varying severities and multitudes of causes. Exhibit 7.1 summarises three types of financial crises that have occurred since 1971, as reported in Laeven and Valencia (2018). There were 151 banking crises for the whole period, and the vast majority (126 or 83%) occurred in developing countries. Currency crises were much more frequent (239 in total), but the number of sovereign crisis cases was much smaller in comparison (75). The latter two types of crises were also much more likely to occur in developing countries, accounting for 95% and 97% of the total. From 1971 to 2006, the dominance of developing countries is also visible, where all three types of crises dominate, with over 90% of occurrences in all three types of crises. However, in the later period of crises, 2007–2017, there were more advanced country banking crises (17 vs. 12) which reflect the GFC's impact where advanced country banks had direct involvements via their investment in CDOs based on US subprime mortgage loans. On the other hand, there was only one incidence of a currency crisis (Iceland in 2008) and two episodes of sovereign crises (Cyprus in 2011 and Greece in 2009) in the recent crisis period in the advanced countries.

So, financial crises were much more common in developing countries, and this is likely due to the underdevelopment of the general economic and financial sectors in developing countries. Moreover, the adoption of a less flexible exchange rate system that does not correctly reflect market forces and the strength (or weakness) of the economic conditions likely resulted in insufficient foreign currency reserve holding. These structural weaknesses of developing countries resulted in currency and banking crises occurring much more frequently than in advanced countries. These characteristics are discussed in Chapter 8.

The impact of a financial crisis can vary depending on the overall role banks play in the economy. The impact of a banking crisis ranges from a mostly contained event where small- to medium-sized firms cannot borrow from their banks to a full-blown system-wide crisis where the whole financial system fails to function. The nature of the banking crisis also varies, ranging from those that arise from illiquid but otherwise solvent banks in the system and those that are caused by a more fundamental problem related to bank insolvencies. The crisis caused by illiquidity is mostly short term in nature and can usually be addressed relatively effectively by the government by injecting liquidity into the banking system and providing further protection for depositors to avoid bank runs. Official interventions can help liquidity-induced banking crises via established channels, such as emergency loans at penalty rates, increasing central bank discount windows, repurchase agreements, and nationalisation of troubled commercial banks. Such actions reduce the level of uncertainty in the system. However, many more fundamental remedies are required for those banking systems experiencing structural deficiencies arising from bad investment decisions (i.e., solvency issues). These measures involve both asset-side adjustments, such as the purchase of bad assets by the government and liability-side assistance, such as capital injection and preferential share purchase of banks by the US government in 2008.[1]

[1] For example, the USD 700 billion rescue package passed house approval in October 2008 in the US was designed to absorb non-performing asset holdings (Collateralized Debt

7.1.2. *Definition of a banking crisis*

A narrow definition of a banking crisis is where a series of financial losses and the collapse of asset values, both financial and non-financial, threaten the integrity of the banking system, requiring government interventions to protect failing institutions. If this strict definition is used, such crisis episodes have been relatively scarce in developed countries. Recent crisis episodes include the US subprime crisis that led to the Global Financial Crisis, the banking crises in Spain in the 1980s, Scandinavia and Japan in the 1990s, and the Eurozone crisis stemming from the sovereign debt crisis involving some of the member countries in the Eurozone — from Greece in 2009 and to Cyprus in 2011. In developing countries, there have been many more banking sector problems in recent decades. These include the Asian financial crises of 1997–1998, the Russian episode of 1998, and the Argentinean crisis of 1998. If a definition of a banking crisis is widened to include the incidences of isolated banking sector difficulties, the savings and loan crisis in the US during the mid-1980s and the severe losses of many financial institutions in Australia in the late 1980s and early 1990s would also qualify.

Schwartz (1987) separates financial crises into 'real' and 'pseudo' crises. The former is associated with a fear that the payment system is unavailable at any price due to a paralysed banking system that is unable to perform the payment system function, leading to a flight to liquidity (cash and near-cash). The liquidity drain due to deposit outflows can lead to a credit squeeze which may result in a recession if it spreads system-wide. Preventing a potential crisis requires decisive action by monetary authorities to inject liquidity into the banking system. For example, a central bank can issue a deposit guarantee for the banks in its jurisdiction in the place of (or in addition to) deposit insurance and open up borrowing facilities for banks to ease their liquidity drain. This will decrease the probability of bank runs as depositors are guaranteed the availability of

Obligations or CDOs) of US banks, allowing them to resume making loans using the increased liquidity. This is similar to the Resolution Trust Corporation solution in the late 1980s in the US that was set up to absorb the assets of failing Savings and Loan institutions. Similarly, some of the countries during the Asian Financial Crisis set up government-owned and operated Asset Management Companies (AMCs) that were designed to liquidate the bad assets of troubled banks. These measures are designed to inject both liquidity and capital back into the banking system.

liquidity upon demand provided by the central bank that has the power to generate (i.e., print) money.[2] A pseudo crisis does not lead to a system-wide crisis, but rather involves a decline in asset values in many sectors stemming from unusually large cases of mistaken or miscalculated investments.

In general, broadly two theories of banking crisis are suggested in the academic literature. The *first* explanation is to do with the uncertain needs of economic agents of future consumption. With the constraint of costly liquidation of longer-term investments, agents desire to withdraw liquidity. Also, the anticipation of similar action by other agents would cause more withdrawals leading to an eventual banking panic. This explanation is self-fulfilling and random in nature. The *second* explanation relates to the anticipation of an economic downturn whereby economic agents withdraw liquidity in anticipation of the liquidity problems of the banks in the system due to falling asset prices. This is not random and, to some extent, predictable.

7.2. Information Asymmetry and Banks — Adverse Selection and Moral Hazard

Information Asymmetry (IA) is present in an imperfect world where business transactions take place. The parties involved in a transaction are unsure about each other's true default risk, which can only be approximated with given (imperfect) information. Each party always has more information about its own default characteristics, which introduces suboptimality due to the need to compensate for the uncertainty, leading to higher transaction costs. A direct consequence of information asymmetry is *Adverse Selection (AS),* which occurs before the transaction, where the party with the most to lose has no option but to impose a high-risk premium before conducting the transaction. This leads to only undesirable counterparties being drawn to the transactions with an incentive to engage

[2]During the GFC period, various central banks initiated this step. Ireland provided guarantees for all liabilities (i.e., deposits) of six Irish banks via legislation. This was followed by EU finance ministers announcing on 7 October 2008 that they would raise the minimum bank deposit guarantee from EUR 20,000 to 50,000 across 27 EU countries. In 2018, the Australian government introduced Financial Claims Scheme to protect deposits up to AUD 1 million, later reduced to AUD 0.25 million in 2012.

in high-risk activities to compensate for the higher cost. This is known as *Moral Hazard (MH)*, which occurs after the transaction.

7.2.1. *Information asymmetry and the financial markets*

In application to financial intermediation, the two parties in a transaction are the borrower and the lender (bank). The counterparty default risk needs to be correctly identified and managed, which is difficult if information asymmetry exists. The borrower can default on their loan, and the default likelihood is better understood by the borrower. The lender can respond to the information asymmetry by recalling the loan early or changing other loan conditions within the allowable limit stipulated under the loan contract if the borrower's credit quality is deteriorating. This will disrupt the borrower's liquidity management at best and may cause bankruptcy at worst.

The borrower's default risk (in relation to the willingness to repay) repay is best understood by the borrower, and there is an information gap between the borrower and the lending bank in favour of the former. Risk analysis of borrower default requires collecting quantifiable and non-quantifiable information to estimate the likelihood of default and the expected damage on occurrence. Quantifiable information helps determine the borrower's *capacity* to repay the loan. For publicly listed borrowers, quantifiable or quantitative information includes accounting reports submitted to the stock exchange, analyst reports on the company and the industry, and ratings and outlooks supplied by credit rating agencies. For private companies that are large enough to require audits by outside audition firms, such reports can be used in addition to the borrower's own reports and projections. Qualitative information addresses the borrower's *willingness* to repay. For example, the borrower with an incentive to default is unlikely to disclose their intention to the lender when applying for a loan. For example, a pharmaceutical company facing bankruptcy due to an imminent failure of the product it has been developing for years has the incentive to gloss over this important fact when applying for more loans to tie them over until the next product comes through. An individual borrower who intends to permanently leave their country for another with no extradition treaty would hide the true purpose of the loan when they apply for a loan. The willingness to repay is not easily observable, so the lender is more likely to be in the dark and at an information disadvantage.

The lender will then require a risk premium on their lending rate and also more collateral or outside guarantors.[3] In an extreme case where the lender cannot assess the credit risk of any borrower (e.g., during the periods of near or complete market failure), they apply the maximum lending interest rate possible to every borrower or, even worse, do not lend to anyone at all. The outcome is likely to be that good-quality borrowers with productive uses are discouraged from borrowing, while high-risk borrowers remain who are more likely to be unconcerned about the high interest rate as their intended use for the fund is for projects of high risk and potentially high return with a low probability of success. The lender will then end up with a borrower pool consisting only of high-risk borrowers who are more likely to default. This is known as *adverse selection.* Once risky borrowers receive loans, they tend to undertake higher-risk projects with lower probabilities of success but with high payoffs if the risk-taking pays off. This is because, in the unlikely event that the higher-risk projects are successful, the borrower would benefit, and the bank will be able to recoup the loan, but if the projects fail, the costs may not be borne by the borrower (e.g., personal and corporate bankruptcy protection and the existence of outside guarantors). This then leads the borrower to take higher risks with the borrowed funds increasing the likelihood of default on the loans. This is *moral hazard.* In addition to the asymmetric incentive structure of the borrower, moral hazard could also be a concern for the lending bank. As large banks (often referred to as Too Big to Fail (TBTF) or systemically important banks) often enjoy safety nets provided by the government, they may take higher than the prudent level of risks in their investment activities (including loans). Gains from such risky investments are internalised (via higher payoffs to managers and shareholders), whereas costs from defaults are absorbed externally (via government bailouts). This asymmetric incentive fosters higher risk-taking behaviour by BTBF banks, a moral hazard problem for the bank regulator.

---

[3] In some emerging market economies, individual lending officers of a bank were personally liable for damage should there be a default on the loans they approved. As such, it was a standard practice to require collaterals whose value was in access of the loan amount or in the absence of such, personal guarantors with such collaterals were required before loans were granted. This was the most critical failing of emerging market banking systems where the lending institutions were unwilling and incapable of conducting credit risk analysis or taking risks due to information asymmetry.

Other segments of the financial system suffer in a similar way when information asymmetry is high. In the corporate bond market, information asymmetry is relevant if bond issuers know their risk better than the investors, which is normally the case. In the presence of high costs of obtaining information on the quality of the issuers, investors who are unsure about the quality of the companies issuing bonds are willing to pay a lower price for the bonds than otherwise (hence receiving a higher bond rate). This will lead to only higher-risk companies willing to issue bonds in the market, creating a similar adverse selection problem as discussed above for the bank facing asymmetric information. Equity issuance will also suffer from the same problem if asymmetric information exists between the company and the potential equity investors. In an insurance transaction context, an adverse selection problem occurs if the insurer cannot determine the risk of an individual applicant/policyholder and charges the same maximum premium for everyone, irrespective of the heterogeneous risk characteristics which the insurer cannot decipher. This practice of charging a uniformly high premium drives out good risk customers, and only the highest risk (unhealthy customers who are more likely to lodge a claim) customers will remain. Once the high-risk policyholders obtain insurance protection, moral hazard occurs when the policyholders act in a way to increase the likelihood of the insured event occurring. For example, fire insurance on a house can lead the owner to be less vigilant in removing fire hazards around the house, leading to a higher likelihood of fire.

During financial crisis periods when the degree of information uncertainty is at its highest, the resulting information asymmetry leads to inefficient (financial) resource allocations due to adverse selection and moral hazard problems.

7.2.2. *Measures to address adverse selection problem*

Information asymmetry due to uncertainty leads to adverse selection and moral hazard problems in the financial system, resulting in, at best, suboptimal outcomes of financial transactions and, at worst, a series of defaults in the financial system. Alternatively, investors and depositors may decide not to invest at all as they may not be capable of managing the high risk. The result is a severely compromised financial system (or even market failure) that may lead to economic collapse. Therefore, information asymmetry must be addressed effectively to encourage investors and borrowers to engage in productive transactions. The methods addressing the information gap between both parties in a transaction include financial intermediaries, third parties providing further information on credit risk, government regulation ensuring up-to-date and verifiable information, a big data analysis on the borrower's credit risk, and third-party guarantees or collaterals. Each of these methods is discussed in the following sections.

7.2.2.1. *Financial intermediaries*

Asymmetric information is at its greatest for individual lenders who are incapable of conducting counterparty default risk analysis. Without a specialised risk assessor conducting the risk analysis for the investor, they are likely to abstain from the loan market. This problem may be addressed by financial intermediation. A deposit-taking financial institution accepts deposits and invests the resulting pool of funds in various forms of (financial) assets. A larger number of smaller and short-term (at call and short-term term deposits) deposits are transformed into a smaller number of loans that are longer-term, less liquid, and larger in size. The intermediary takes a fiduciary relationship with both side of its balance sheet participants (depositors and borrowers). It has legal obligations to depositors to guarantee the deposits, which are in turn also guaranteed by either compulsory deposit insurance or the lender of last resort facility provided by the government. The depositors do not have any relationship with the borrowers, nor do they have any legal claims against them. As such, there is no need for the depositors to perform credit risk analysis on the borrowers. The intermediary has legal claims against the loans extended to the borrowers and is responsible for conducting the necessary credit risk analyses on the borrowers to avoid lending to high-risk borrowers. Conducting effective credit risk analysis requires specialised skills that the individual depositors and investors do not usually possess, so it makes sense for the intermediary to specialise in this task and earn an interest rate spread (i.e., interest income). It is more economical to have a small number of financial intermediaries to develop the necessary skills in risk analysis and facilitate the flow of funds by accepting the role of fiduciary responsibilities against both the borrowers and the depositors. This form of financial flow is suitable for those economies (i.e., emerging market

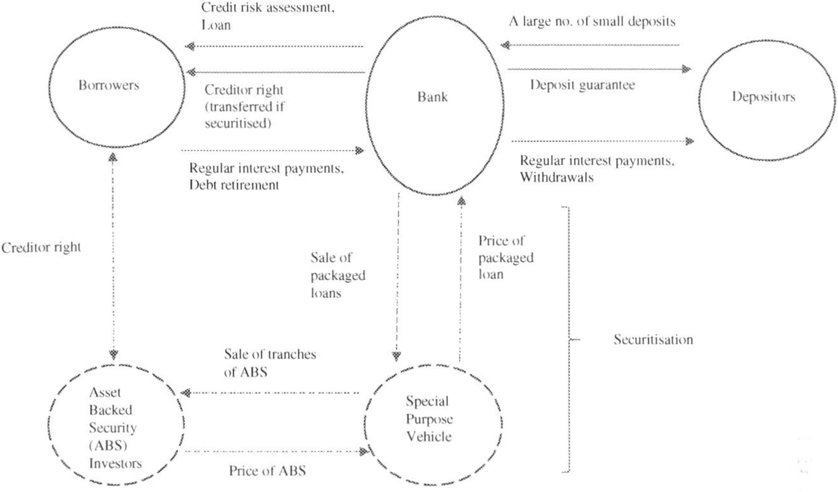

Exhibit 7.2. Financial flows with an intermediary.

economies) that have yet to fully develop non-bank financial segments. It is also suitable for those financial systems where banks play more critical roles in corporate governance (i.e., bank-focused systems, such as Japan and Western European economies).

Exhibit 7.2 depicts the intermediary's relationships with its customers on either side of its balance sheet. The arrows connecting the entities represent the flow of funds and the associated fiduciary relationships. As the banking system in major economies started to deregulate from the early 1980s, these relationship-based flows began to change towards more transactional-based flows as the banks sought to minimise credit exposures and explore other fee-based income sources. The bottom half of Exhibit 7.2 depicts a typical securitisation channel where an existing loan portfolio of the originating bank is securitised. The broken arrows represent the flows of funds and the associated transactions. The intermediaries originate the loans to the borrowers, and then the loans are packaged and sold to investors via Special Purpose Vehicles (i.e., a legal entity set up to facilitate the sale of the packaged loans). Once the shares in the Asset-Backed Securities (ABS) backed by the cash flows of the packaged loans are sold, so is the credit risk associated with the loans relieving the originator of the risk. The process of securitisation is discussed in more detail in Chapter 9.

7.2.2.2. *Third-party information providers and secondary market*

The fund flows directly from the investor to the issuer of financial securities in the debt market. Debt market investors can directly observe who the issuer is and can potentially assess the credit quality of the security and the issuer by using available information supplied by the issuer and from other sources. Asymmetric information problems, however, can prevent investors from purchasing the security issue as they may not be confident in their ability to assess the default risk given the supplied information. At its extreme, no investor would purchase the security issue. A third-party information provider can be involved to alleviate the information asymmetry.

Exhibit 7.3 shows a direct relationship between the investors and the issuers of a financial instrument. Instead of relying on a bank loan, firms can choose to fund their projects by raising the necessary capital by issuing and selling debt obligations directly to the investors in the market. The instruments can take many forms and maturities (notes, bonds, promissory notes, etc.), and there can be a secondary market for these instruments. The

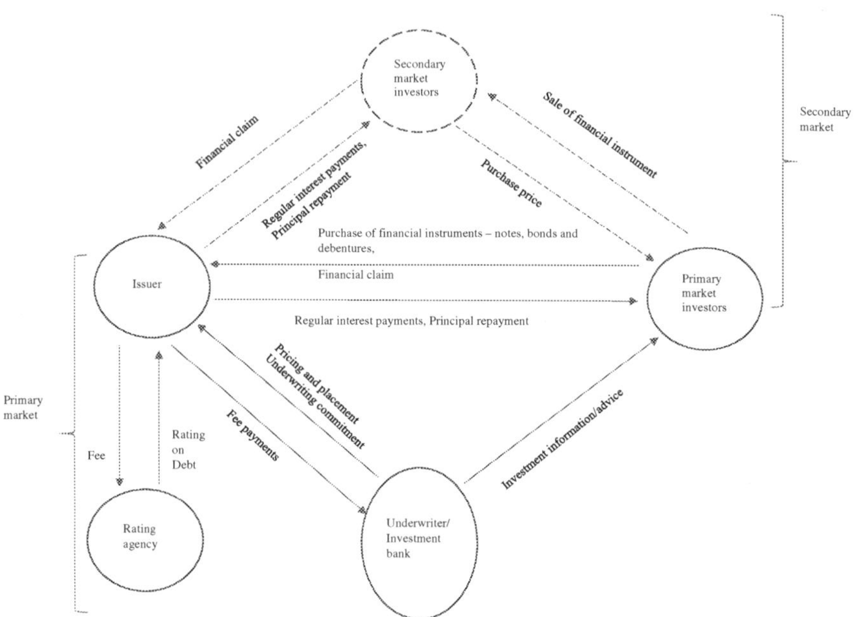

Exhibit 7.3. Financial flows via capital market.

issuer is usually guided by one or more investment banks depending on the size of the debt, and the lead investment bank (if there are more than one) underwrites the debt issuance and arrange for a rating assessment by a credit rating agency (or two). The main investment bank (if there are more than one underwriter) is responsible for assessing the market for the appropriate interest rate to apply on the debt issuance and other aspects of bringing the debt to the market. The investors are responsible for conducting the credit risk analysis on the issuer. Institutional investors perform their own assessment of the risk involved. However, individual investors who lack such expertise rely on the reputation of the issuer and the rating associated with the debt issue. Once the market fully absorbs the debt issuance, a secondary market develops that allows trading of the debt (shown in broken lines in Exhibit 7.3). The existence of the secondary market for the security provides an easy way of exiting out of the investment in the security, provided enough liquidity exists in the market. An easy exit from the investment thus provides additional protection for investors and acts as a way to counteract information asymmetry.

Major global credit rating agencies (CRAs), Standard & Poor's, Moodys and Fitch, and local agencies provide credit ratings on the debt instruments of companies, such as corporate bonds, preferred stock, CDS, and other debt issuance. In addition, they also provide entity ratings that indicate the company's credit risk as a whole. This contributes to understanding the borrowing company's default risk for institutional and individual lenders who lack the necessary knowledge of the borrowers' risk profiles. Moreover, since Basel II, the ratings of corporate bonds and the borrowers are baked directly into the capital requirements for banks. Although outside ratings could have a positive impact on reducing information asymmetry, there are also known issues. Rating shopping is one such issue. Companies wishing to raise funds by issuing bonds approach multiple CRAs for a rating, and the CRAs compete with each other to gain the borrower's business by providing more favourable ratings than without such competition, resulting in rating inflation. As such, a company's entity rating and security ratings can be misleading under such circumstances, leading to investors paying unnecessarily high prices for the securities due to the inflated ratings. Indeed, many AAA ratings were issued even to the senior tranches of Collateral Debt Obligations (CDOs) based subprime mortgages in the US. The resulting US subprime crisis led to the global financial crisis of 2007–2009.

7.2.2.3. *Government regulation*

Government regulation can also play an important role. Financial regulators in each country provide guidance to the financial institutions in their countries. Deposit-taking institutions are strictly supervised to meet capital, liquidity, and other operational safety measures under Basel III, which limits the nature of risk-taking by banks on their asset-side (loan and security investments) and liability-side (capital requirement and liability maturity matching) operations. Securities market operations are regulated by relevant authorities to ensure accurate and timely release of information by the security issuers. In the US, the Securities and Exchange Commission (SEC) ensure that reputable accounting firms independently audit companies wishing to raise funds via issuing debt securities or stocks. Independent audits will ensure that the companies strictly adhere to the information disclosure requirement on their operations and follow required accounting and reporting principles, Any company not satisfying these requirements will be delisted from the stock exchanges if they are already listed, or the security issuance will not be approved. Therefore, investors can be assured that any company that satisfies the listing and disclosure requirements imposed by the regulator can be deemed to be of investable quality. Other countries have their equivalents to SEC. The European Securities and Markets Authority (ESMA) handles that task for the EU countries, Financial Conduct Authority (FCA) is for the UK, Financial Services Agency (FSA) is for Japan, and the Australian Securities and Investment Commission (ASIC) is for Australia. However, there have been cases where spectacular failure of oversights has occurred. In the US, the Enron collapse in 2001 implicated the accounting firm Arthur Anderson which was indicted for accounting fraud. A telecommunication firm Worldcom was found to have manipulated its accounting records to hide its losses before filing for bankruptcy in 2002. These examples show that even the financial system with strong government regulatory oversight can still experience stunning failures.

7.2.2.4. *Collaterals and third-party guarantees*

Collaterals and third-party guarantees can reduce adverse selection problems for the lender as the loss due to borrower default can be mitigated. Borrowers who can put up an asset as collateral are more likely to be granted a loan. However, the lender must be able to verify that the asset used as collateral can be secured and its market value does not depreciate when it is liquidated upon default by the borrower. One of the causes of the US subprime crisis in 2007 was the excessive loans granted to subprime borrowers who put up the houses they purchased using their loans. Lenders were confident that the value of the mortgaged asset would hold up even when they foreclosed on the asset and put it for sale when the borrower defaulted. However, as the housing boom dissipated, they discovered that the value of the collateral was significantly less than the amount of the loan.

Third-party guarantees can also encourage lenders to engage with the borrowers, as the loss from loan defaults can be mitigated if a guarantor is required to step in. A developing country's government often provides a loan guarantee for corporate borrowers when they tap into the international banking market. The lenders then look to the government in case of default, and to the extent that the government can provide loan payments or some alternative compensations, they are likely to lend to the borrower with their government's guarantee.

7.2.2.5. *FinTech*

One of the recent developments in the financial markets, irrespective of development status, is FinTech (or Financial Technologies) which poses significant challenges for established financial institutions. Commercial banks, especially in developing countries, have traditionally concentrated on serving customers they can easily reach via an established network. The nationwide branch network was required to harness grassroots-level business in various business centre locations. Potential customers located in the regions where commercial banks do not have a presence could not be served. Also, those segments of the customer base that are considered to be of high risk are also neglected even when they are located nearby a bank branch. Information asymmetry is at its highest for customers in a distant location and is considered a higher risk.

However, the advancement of communication and information technology since the early 2000s allowed banks to assess customers in remote locations. Internet banking started to be used by banks to reduce the overall costs of providing account services by standardising information collection and risk analysis via a Web-based interface. Initially, advanced countries with wide Internet adoption benefited from emerging technologies. Big data technology based on the Web provided information relevant to conducting credit analysis on previously unbanked customers. These include information collection on potential customers from their Internet activities such as Internet transaction records, social media activities, Web browsing habits, and identified social networks of the customers. Using these data mining techniques, banks and other lenders can obtain crucial information on potential customers' economic and social activity preferences that could be used to determine their credit quality. From the early 2010s, the broad adoption of smartphones intensified the data collection on customer behaviour which helped to reduce the information gap relevant to credit risk analysis. More importantly, developing countries that previously were not benefiting from the Web-based FinTechs due to the lack of landline Internet infrastructure rapidly adopted mobile-based Internet activities. In addition to the traditional Internet activities of potential customers that have mostly migrated to mobile platforms, additional data emerged that proved useful. The collection and processing of data on many potential customers' mobile-based activities can be used to produce a general economic and social profile of customers, which will be helpful in predicting future defaults and thus reduce information asymmetry.

7.3. Credit Booms, Asset Bubbles, and Financial Market Crashes

If not addressed, information asymmetry leading to adverse selection can lead to the borrower being unable to secure funding from the lender, as discussed in the previous section. Dell'ariccia and Marquex (2006) provide a theoretical explanation as to how a reduction in information asymmetry from collecting private information on the borrower could lead to lower lending standards. They argue that lower lending standard leads to greater aggregate loan surplus and potential financial instability. Excessive lending in the economy is the opposite to the outcome of an adverse selection problem. Banking crises are usually preceded by credit booms and asset and real estate price bubbles.

During boom periods, lenders may observe fewer loan defaults as their borrowers seem to be doing well, and the market value of collaterals tends to stay above the loan amount. Lenders seek to expand their loan portfolios to take advantage of the increasing demand for credit in the expanding economy. Thakor (2015) suggests that lenders overestimate their risk assessment skills and underestimate the profitable outcomes due to luck, resulting in investing more in risky assets (loans). When it is revealed that the profitable outcome was mostly driven by luck, investors withdraw funds, and a banking crisis follows. In addition, the excess inflow of deposits into the banking system (often uncontrolled) would often lead to a relaxation of lending standards to recycle the excess deposit. For example, emerging market economies receive foreign capital inflows upon liberalisation of their financial systems when the banking sector asset activities have yet to diversify (i.e., heavy reliance on lending as asset side operations).

Another example is the growth of eurodollar deposits originating from OPEC's rapidly rising oil revenues following the first oil price shock in the early 1970s. Eurobanks had no option but to relax their lending standards to loan out the excessive deposits they received. The resulting credit growth in an economy beyond its productive capacity is bound to spill over to speculative investments such as real estate and stock markets, leading to asset inflation. In its extreme, credit booms will lead to speculative bubbles in the financial markets distorting the credit allocation channel in the economy.

Alternatively, official interest rates kept arbitrarily low for a sustained period could lead to lending booms. For example, the US lending boom in the early 2000s was a result of a rapid and sustained period of policy interest rate cuts from 2001 that created a fertile ground for financial bubbles in the economy and eventually contributed to the subprime crisis in 2007. Speculative bubbles in financial markets have been the case of history repeating itself, from the stock market bubble in the run-up to the 1929 stock market crash in the US that led to the Great Depression to the financial market bubbles that led to the Global Financial Crisis that broke out when Lehman Brothers filed for bankruptcy on 15 September 2008.

A financial (or economic) bubble is a situation where financial assets are continually traded at inflated prices well above the levels suggested by fundamentals. Financial assets such as stocks and debt instruments are priced in terms of expected future cash flows. If current market prices do not reflect the equilibrium values due to excess demand for the assets brought on by factors other than fundamentals, then there are bubbles in the market. Also known as a rational speculative bubble, market participants may be aware of the gap between the fundamentals-based prices and the current market prices of financial assets. However, it is rational for them to perpetuate the uptrend as long as it is likely to continue. This herding behaviour often results from overreliance on technical analysis that leads to a 'self-fulfilling prophecy' and over-optimistic outlook of the future (e.g., 'Irrational exuberance' as coined by the former chairman of the US Federal Reserve Board, Alan Greenspan). Financial institutions, especially commercial banks and rating agencies, have been mostly reactive to market developments instead of being proactive. The results were that they helped fuel the bubble by continuing to supply the funds needed for financial speculation and issuing high enough ratings for assets mostly based on the current market characteristics. During bubble periods, banks may be unable to distinguish between good and bad risk (fundamentally sound or otherwise) borrowers since they all tend to run what appear to be profitable operations. Bubbles usually develop in tandem among various segments of the economy, namely the stock, credit, and real estate markets. Two representative examples of lending booms leading to a crisis are in the US in 2007 (subprime mortgage crisis) and in Japan (stock and real estate market bubble collapse in 1991 and the banking crisis in the late 1990s).

7.4. Banking Crisis Following Deregulation

There is an accepted view that financial markets contribute significantly to economic developments in emerging economies. As economies move through the transition to achieve the status of being developed, so do the national financial markets. There are stages that each of the developed financial systems has undergone from an early stage of economic and financial development. Exhibit 7.4 outlines the four stages of financial market development. The *first* stage in the development of the financial system is to regulate the system, as the market has yet to develop the necessary market mechanism to achieve efficient resource allocation. The regulated banking sector is usually inefficient as it is protected, and there is little competition. Due to the important functions the banking sector performs, commercial banks are regulated by appropriate government bodies, usually central banks. The types of regulations typically include (1) legal (entry into the banking sector is strictly regulated), (2) price (deposit and lending rates being fixed), (3) quantity (restrictions on annual loan growth), and (4) quality (restrictions on the types of borrowers permitted/not permitted to service) and operational regulations. As a result of these regulations, the banking sector is protected from outside entries, and the government provides implicit and explicit protections. This results in

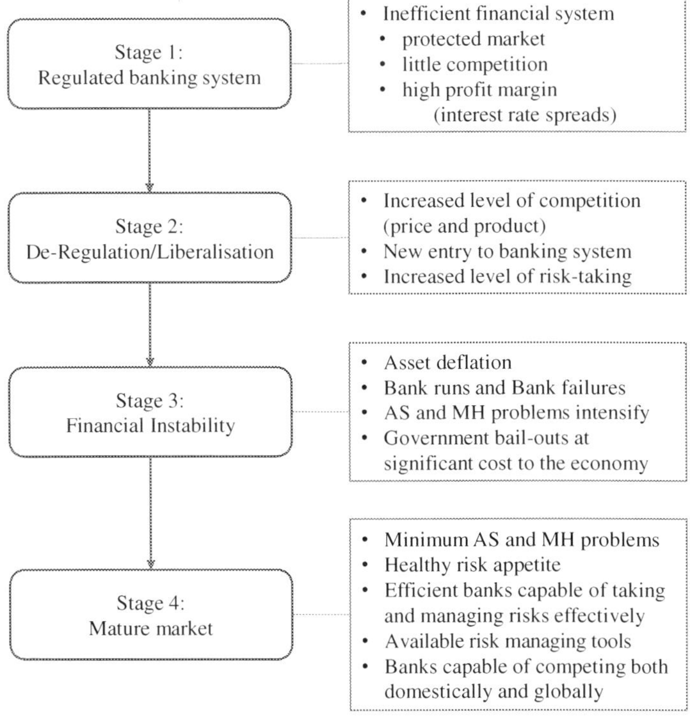

Exhibit 7.4. Stages of financial market development.

the banking sector being inefficient in terms of the standard performance measures, such as cost-to-income ratio and NPL ratio, and there is generally no incentive to innovate as there is no meaningful competition in the sector. The range of products offered is limited, and the costs of services are higher compared to deregulated markets.

The *second* stage is where deregulation and liberalisation take place. The financial system, in general, and the banking sector, in particular, undergo a process of deregulation. The first and most important indication that deregulation is in place is the entry of new banks from other financial market segments or foreign banks. At the same time, various types of regulations are dismantled and are replaced with a series of self-regulatory or prudential measures — most importantly, liquidity and capital ratio requirements. The process of deregulation started in the early to mid-1980s for most advanced countries and from the early to mid-1990s for some of the developing countries. One of the most important tools of prudential regulation is the BIS's Capital Adequacy Ratio requirement which requires at least 8% of risk-adjusted assets of banks to be held in capital in its first version, Basel I, which was introduced in 1998 and adopted in G10 countries in 1992. Banks in the deregulated environment are allowed to compete against each other and provide non-banking services as well. At the beginning of this stage, due to the limited ability of banks to compete on products (i.e., financial engineering), they focus on price competition. They would also take additional risks (in terms of asset and liability diversifications) to compensate for the lower income due to competition. Both customer and product dimension expansions would result.

The *third* stage of financial market development is the period of consolidation under financial instability. As a direct consequence of increased competition, brought on by deregulation, that led to banks taking higher risks without a commensurate and simultaneous increase in the capacity to manage them, NPL ratios would rise, and some banks would face eventual bankruptcies, resulting in higher systemic risk. There is a potential for the banking sector to be paralysed and market failures to occur. However, with prompt and decisive actions by the authorities, bank failures could be contained, possibly with bank rescues, and a system-wide crisis could be averted. In the US, the process of financial deregulation in the early 1980s saw an increase in deposit protection from USD 40,000 to 100,000 in 1980 and thrift institutions (Savings and Loan) were allowed to make commercial loans up to 10% of assets and offer new accounts to compete with money market funds. This encouraged risk-taking activities that thrifts could not manage, which contributed to the Savings and Loan crisis in the 1980s that resulted in a total cost of USD 132 billion in taxpayers' money to resolve (Sherman, 2009). In Australia, the deregulation of the financial sector started in the mid-1980s and resulted in credit growth beyond lenders' risk management capacity. In the 1990s, State Bank of Victoria and the State Bank of South Australia collapsed and were later taken over by the Commonwealth Bank of Australia and Advance Bank, respectively. In the same year, Pyramid group of building societies collapsed after experiencing bank runs they could not control.

In the *fourth* and final stage, after the weak banks are weeded out in stage three, the banking sector is left only with efficient competitors capable of surviving competitive market dynamics. In this stage, the adverse effects of adverse selection and moral hazard problems are at their minimum, and the lenders' risk appetite is strong, resulting in healthy levels of intermediation of loanable funds through the system. Banks left standing are capable of competing with both domestic and foreign banks operating in the domestic banking system. The risk assessment skills have reached a sufficiently high level that warrants investing in higher-yielding assets, and the higher risks associated with such assets can be managed by judicious use of risk-transferring tools available in the financial system.

7.5. Consequences of a Banking Crisis

In the case of 'real' banking sector crises, the fundamental functions of the banking sector are compromised, leading to a system-wide breakdown of financial activities. In essence, banking crises add to the systemic risk, as any reduction in lending activity adversely affects economic activity in the economy, especially in emerging economies that are over-reliant on bank credits. Lending cutbacks by troubled banks would lead to a credit crunch for small-to-medium-sized companies that may not have alternative sources of finance. In addition, there is a possibility of a negative spillover effect on other countries' banking systems. The integration of advanced financial systems from the early 1980s through deregulation and the liberalisation of many developing country financial markets from the early 1990s allowed financial instabilities in one system to spread to others via common investors, bilateral trade and foreign direct investments, etc. Multinational banks operating across many countries may be forced to adjust their global investment portfolios away from countries with similar characteristics during a crisis in one of the countries. This is because if a country is undergoing a banking crisis, countries with similar characteristics (in the same region, have the same financial market development stage, country risk, etc.) are likely to experience similar levels of capital outflow and subsequent domestic liquidity drain, as the common lenders withdraw from the epicentre of the crisis and from the countries with a similar risk profile.

7.5.1. *Resolution of a banking crisis*

Given that commercial banks can fail for many reasons, it would be difficult to decide whether the government should provide a helping hand without clearly identifying the cause of the failure to avoid misusing taxpayers' money. Broadly, there are two reasons paths to a bank insolvency. *First*, a bank becomes technically bankrupt when a series of asset write-offs (and write-downs) reduce the bank's capital to zero or even negative. This is an inevitable result of bad investment decisions (e.g., mortgage loans when house prices are falling), leading to potential insolvency if not addressed effectively. *Second*, despite prudent lending practices, some banks may still become insolvent if they cannot handle sudden increases in liquidity demands during bank runs, for instance. If troubled banks cannot raise liquidity from other sources (e.g., borrowing from other banks in the interbank money market or borrowing from the government via a repurchase agreement), they will be forced to liquidate their assets (illiquid but otherwise performing) at fire sale prices. This will directly result in reducing the bank's balance sheet much more than the amount of the liquidity outflow, and the banks with insufficient capital will become technically insolvent. In both of these cases, the outcome is the same: some portion of their assets will evaporate, and they need sufficient capital to remain solvent. In response to bank insolvencies, a critical issue is recapitalising the bank's capital base either through the market (private solution) or the government's rescue programs (public solution).

If insolvency is due to ineffective liquidity management, then as long as the bank's investment practices are sound and the issues associated with moral hazard are not considered detrimental, various rescue options should be considered. *First*, existing shareholders may provide more capital, and the stock market may be tapped into for additional capital raising (either tier 1 equity capital, such as shares, or tier 2 capital, such as convertible notes). However, this may not be practical in an environment of financial instability that causes liquidity drains that require immediate action. Moreover, the market participants may not have enough risk appetite to come to the bank's rescue on their own without protection (from the government). *Second*, if private sector solutions are not practical, then the government must be involved, which can be in many different forms. The government can provide payment protection to private sector lenders and equity investors to allow troubled banks to raise much-needed equity capital and liquidity. They can also directly extend liquidity via repurchase agreements, provide a deposit guarantee to prevent further liquidity drains, and act as a Lender of Last Resort (LOLR). In short, the role of the government is crucial in preventing illiquid but otherwise healthy banks from becoming insolvent due to market-based solutions being unavailable.

On the other hand, if the cause of the bank insolvency is due to mismanagement, such as excessive risk-taking and other general operational mistakes, then there is a moral hazard argument against providing assistance to the troubled bank. The core of the argument is that for privately owned banks, when risk-taking pays off, the benefits are enjoyed by the owners and the management, while if they get into trouble due to excessive risk-taking leading to unrecoverable losses, their losses are covered using the taxpayer's money. The government effectively underwrites the management's risk-taking activities, so the government covers the losses while the management and the shareholders enjoy the benefits. The asymmetric incentive structure in the case of government rescue provides incentives for the bank to continue with the risky strategies. Therefore, a troubled bank's shareholders and management should be held accountable, and the bank should be subjected to market forces and be allowed to fail. For example, The US government allowed Lehman Brothers to fail in 2008, which was the second largest investment bank at the time, after many brokered private sector rescue attempts failed. However, the Too Big To Fail (TBTF) argument applies to large banks and other financial institutions with enough clout in the economy that, if allowed to fail, can have system-wide consequences and the economy as a whole can experience market failure. The US government decided to rescue AIG (American International Group) in 2008 by putting up USD 85 billion of the taxpayer's money since its collapse would cause not only a default on its commitments on CDSs sold to banks but also the general insurance protection sold to many other non-finance industry customers as well. If left to market forces, AIG would have collapsed, and many facets of the US economic activities would have been paralysed without suitable insurance protection. After the GFC, international efforts were directed at identifying those TBTF banks that are systemically important. The Financial Stability Board (FSB) started to publish the list of Globally Systematically Important Financial Institutions (G-SIFIs) that require special attention from the regulator of their headquartered countries. In addition, each country also designates its domestic market counterparts in Domestically Systematically Important Financial Institutions (D-SIFIs).

If allowing troubled banks to fail is not an option, the government can consider several options. Market-based solutions involve troubled banks merging with or being purchased by healthy banks or non-bank financial institutions. As healthy banks would not wish to purchase or merge with a failing bank unless there is a net benefit of doing so (e.g., non-overlapping customers, products or geographical market coverage), attractive incentives must be provided by the government as in the case of the US government orchestrating mergers between banks during the height of the GFC. For example, Bank of America purchased Merrill Lynch for USD 50 billion in 2008, and JPMorgan took over Bear Stern for USD 1.4 b. also in 2008 to save it from a certain collapse. In general, acquirers must be more longer-term oriented and have access to liquidity to weather the storm so that they can afford to sit on the illiquid assets of the failing banks until market values recover sufficiently. In some of the cases in the past banking crisis episodes, private equity capital firms or private wealth funds with a longer time horizon with their investments have actively participated in purchasing some or all of the troubled banks' assets. Puri *et al.* (2021) find that private equity firms played a role in stabilising the banking crisis by investing in troubled bank assets during the Global Financial Crisis period.

If it is impractical to find an acquirer for a troubled bank, the government can nationalise it and turn it into a bridge bank which can be returned to the private hands later. For example, the UK government nationalised Northern Rock on 17 February 2008, after the now infamous run on the bank at its branches. Virgin Money was selected by the UK government to purchase Northern Rock for GBP 747 million, and it did so on 1 January 2012. Governments can also set up asset management companies (AMCs) to purchase troubled assets from troubled banks so as to improve their balance sheets. The mandate of an AMC would be to purchase troubled assets to restructure and liquidate them as quickly as possible or when their market values recover sufficiently. AMCs are not under the same level of liquidity constraint as the troubled banks, so they can wait out the market volatility and liquidate the assets when the market restores order to achieve higher sale proceeds. Klingebiel (2000) suggests that there is mixed evidence of effectiveness in this approach. AMCs established in Spain and the US achieved their objectives of asset liquidation. However, those in Mexico and the Philippines were not so fortunate as politically motivated loans and fraudulent assets were transferred to them which were difficult to liquidate. Exhibit 7.5 outlines the process of crisis resolution discussed above.

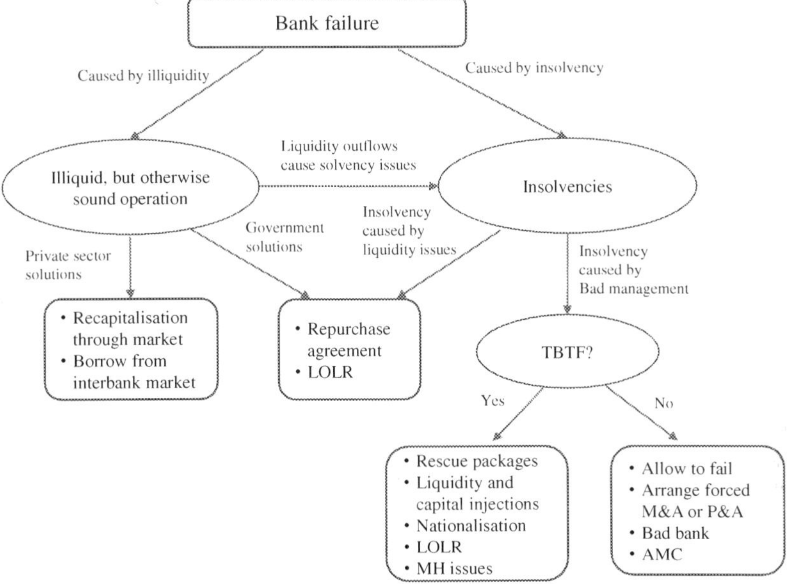

Exhibit 7.5. Process of banking crisis resolution.

7.5.2. *Cost of a banking crisis resolution*

Given the harmful effect of a banking crisis on the economy, the government of a country experiencing a banking crisis cannot afford to rely entirely on market forces to resolve the crisis. As discussed in the previous section, liquidity injection and the provision of deposit guarantees for troubled banks are required to combat the liquidity drain-induced panic in the banking system. Avoiding bank runs and the negative spillover effects of bank collapses should be a top priority. Recapitalisation of troubled banks is also required once the liquidity crisis is averted. The cost of a banking crisis can be measured in terms of the amount of the taxpayers' money used to inject liquidity and recapitalise troubled banks, and the amount of economic output lost due to the crisis (De Grauwe, 2008, Claessens and Kose, 2013, Miline and Wood, 2003). The former is a direct fiscal cost that can easily be measured, however, the latter is not directly observable but can only be approximated by calculating the deviation of actual GDP growth of the economy from the projected growth without the

Averages	Duration of Crisis	Output Loss (Actual - Trend GDP)	Fiscal Cost			Liquidity Provision		Peak NPLs
	in years	% of trend GDP	% of GDP	Net % of GDP	% of Financial Sector Assets	Peak	Liquidity Support	% of total loans
				1971 – 2017				
All countries	*3.1*	*43.5*	*13.0*	*10.6*	*29.4*	*33.7*	*19.2*	*29.3*
Advanced countries	3.8	38.7	9.0	5.1	5.3	14.5	10.8	15.6
Developing countries	3.0	29.1	14.2	12.5	38.2	37.4	21.0	33.3
				1971 – 2006				
All countries	*3.0*	*43.9*	*14.6*	*13.6*	*40.3*	*37.5*	*20.4*	*33.4*
Advanced countries	3.5	35.2	5.7	4.4	8.1	9.9	4.9	17.4
Developing countries	2.9	29.8	15.4	14.4	43.8	39.2	21.4	35.2
				2007 – 2017				
All countries	*3.7*	*41.9*	*9.7*	*6.3*	*7.3*	*18.5*	*15.0*	*17.7*
Advanced countries	3.9	39.9	10.5	5.3	4.0	16.7	13.6	14.8
Developing countries	3.2	22.2	8.3	6.7	12.3	20.9	17.1	21.8

Exhibit 7.6. Costs of banking crisis resolution, 1971–2017.

Source: Average costs were calculated using Table 2 in Laeven and Valencia (2018).

crisis. Hoggarth *et al.* (2002) estimates the output loss for banking crises up to the 1990s were roughly 15–20% of annual GDP for developing countries and 10–15% for advanced countries. Direct costs include the costs of resolving the crisis, such as using public funds for rescuing failing banks (for recapitalisation, USD 700 billion for the US's subprime crisis)[4] and the opportunity costs of such funds. Such uses of public funds involve opportunity costs and create a moral hazard problem.[5] The resulting financial crisis and adverse selection problems would lead to inefficient resource allocation. Indirect costs are losses incurred due to depressed economic activities during crises, and the IMF measures these as the

[4]The Troubled Asset Relief Program (TARP) in the US was initially authorised with USD 700 billion. However, it was reduced to 475 billion by the Dodd–Frank Wall Street Reform and Consumer Protection Act.

[5]The moral hazard problem is relevant if an asymmetric payoff from investments exists. Banks which invest in high risk assets (lending to risky projects) benefit when investments perform but do not pay the costs when default occurs if monetary authorities provide implicit/explicit guarantee. This will create incentives for banks to engage in higher risk investment activities than otherwise, leading to potentially higher costs of resolution when they face difficulties.

difference between GDP growth trends (assuming no crises) and actual growth during crises.

Exhibit 7.6 shows these two types of costs as well as other related statistics. For the whole period covering 1971–2017 and for all countries, a banking crisis lasted, on average 3.1 years in the sample. The output loss, measured by the difference between actual and projected GDPs, was as much as 43.5%. Direct fiscal costs were 13% of GDP (gross) overall and 10.6% net of recovered amounts, and 29% of financial sector assets were involved during the rescue. Liquidity provision measures the ratio of central bank claims on the banks in the country and liquidity support from the treasury to total deposits and liabilities to non-residents. At its peak, as much as 33.7% of bank assets were rescued by the central bank, and 19.2% of liabilities to non-residents were supported. On average, NPLs reached 29% of total loans.

Rather unexpectedly, advanced countries experienced a slightly longer crisis period of 3.8 years, and the output loss is larger at 38.7% of the GDP loss compared to 3 and 29.1%, respectively, for developing countries. As seen in Exhibit 7.1, banking crises were much less frequent in advanced countries, but when they experienced one, they lasted longer and had a larger GDP loss. On the other hand, in developing countries, direct costs of banking crisis resolution, government liquidity commitments, and Non-Performing Loan (NPL) ratios are much higher. When comparing the earlier crisis period to the later one, crises lasted slightly longer, and the costs were generally higher for advanced countries in the later crisis period, reflecting the higher number of advanced countries experiencing a banking crisis during the GFC, as shown in Exhibit 7.1. On the other hand, the costs were much higher in the earlier period for developing countries.

7.5.3. *Preventative measures and policies*

As discussed in the previous section and shown in Exhibit 7.6, the cost of a banking crisis can be high, incurring direct fiscal costs with corresponding opportunity costs leading to output loss for the entire economy. Especially for developing countries, the cost of a banking crisis can cripple their economies as they rely more on the banking sector and their financial systems are underdeveloped. When a country experiences a banking crisis, an established process of resolution, as indicated in Exhibit 7.5, can help devise early and swift responses to the crisis to minimise the cost to the economy and the financial system. However, ideally, a better outcome is to prevent an outbreak of a crisis as much as possible. There are such preventative measures. *First*, an effective risk analysis is vital. By accurately assessing the default risk characteristics of the borrower, the lender can avoid a build-up of NPLs. *Second*, banks should maintain adequate levels of liquidity and capital buffers to prevent liquidity-induced insolvencies. Basel III includes both capital and liquidity requirements, among others which should improve the safety of bank operations. Currently, its adoption is limited to advanced countries, and the full implementation has been postponed repeatedly, with the latest deadline being 1 January 2023. *Third*, at the system level, the regulators and policymakers should aim to achieve a reduction in information asymmetry as much as possible to avoid the resulting adverse selection and moral hazard problems. *Fourth*, regulatory measures should be geared toward identifying and addressing potential weaknesses in the system. Identifying and designating systemically important institutions (TBTF institutions) for special regulatory attention can mitigate excessive risk-taking. Regular stress testing can potentially help identify banks that are at risk of illiquidity or insolvency.

In general, the safer a bank gets in terms of its operations by having higher liquidity and capital buffers, the lower its overall profitability. The inherent opportunity cost associated with ensuring safety during periods of market tranquillity may be considered unnecessarily restrictive as the bank can miss out on some potential profit opportunities. Therefore, there is a trade-off between ensuring safety in operations and profitability from risk-taking activities. However, the perceived safety of the bank's operation due to extra liquidity and capital buffers can potentially provide a competitive advantage in minimising funding costs. This is because depositors and other banks in the interbank money market may require a lower risk premium due to the lower perceived risk.

References

Allen, F., Babus, A. and Carletti, E. (2009). Financial Crises: Theory and Evidence. http://finance.wharton.upenn.edu/~allenf/download/Vita/ARFE-Crises-08June09-final.pdf.

Claessens, S. and Kose, M. A. (2013). Financial Crises: Explanations, Types, and Implications, IMF Working Paper, WP/13/28. https://www.imf.org/en/Publications/WP/Issues/2016/12/31/Financial-Crises-Explanations-Types-and-Implications-40283.

De Grauwe, P. (2008). The Banking Crisis: Causes, Consequences and Remedies. http://aei.pitt.edu/11706/1/1758.pdf.

Dell'ariccia, G. and Marquex, R. (2006). Lending booms and lending standards. *The Journal of Finance*, LXI(5), 2511–2546.

Goldstein, M. and Turner, P. (1996). Banking Crises in Emerging Economies: Origin and Policy Options. BIS Economic Papers, No. 46. http://www.bis.org/publ/econ46.pdf.

Hoggarth, G., Reidhill, J. and Sinclare, P. (2003). Resolution of Banking Crisis: A Review. Bank of England Financial Stability Report.

Hoggarth, G., Reis, R. and Saporta, V. (2002, May). Costs of banking system instability: Some empirical evidence. *Journal of Banking and Finance*, 26(5), 825–855.

Klingebiel, D. (2000). The Use of Management Companies in the Resolution of Banking Crisis. World Bank Policy Research Working Paper 2284.

Miline, A. and Wood, G. (2003). International banking crises, Chapter 15 of *Handbook of International Banking*, Mullineux, A. W. and Murinde, V. (eds.), Edward Elgar, UK.

Laeven, L. and Valencia, F. (2018). Systemic Banking Crises Revisited, IMF Working Paper WP/18/206. https://www.imf.org/en/Publications/WP/Issues/2018/09/14/Systemic-Banking-Crises-Revisited-46232.

Puri, M., Ross, E. and Ma, S. (2021). Private Equity and Financial Stability: Evidence from Failed Bank Resolution in the Crisis. FDIC Center for Financial Research Paper No. 2021-04. https://ssrn.com/abstract=3901997 or http://dx.doi.org/10.2139/ssrn.3901997.

Schwartz, A. J. (1987). *Money in Historical Perspective* (Chapter 11 Real and Pseudo financial crises), University of Chicago Press, Chicago, USA.

Sherman, M. (2009). A Short History of Financial Deregulation in the United States. Center for Economic and Policy Research, Washington, DC.

Thakor, A. (2015). Lending booms, smart bankers, and financial crises. *American Economic Review: Paper and Proceedings*, 105(5), 305–309.

Chapter 8

Banking Crisis in Emerging Economies

8.1. Introduction

A banking crisis is one of the consequences of extreme information asymmetry, which renders the financial system inoperable. As discussed in Chapter 7, banking crises are more likely to occur in emerging market countries with underdeveloped financial systems than in advanced countries. The cost of crisis resolution is also substantially higher, as measured by the direct fiscal cost governments must incur to rescue the failing banking system. Although the elevated level of asymmetric information leading to the collapse of financial transactions ultimately sits at the centre of banking crises in both emerging and advanced countries, the route to the asymmetric information and hence the root causes of the banking crisis are different between the two groups of countries. In this chapter and Chapter 9, discussions on this issue are presented.

8.2. The Nature of a Banking Crisis in Emerging Economies

By the very nature of financial intermediation, commercial banks are exposed to various mismatches between their assets and liabilities. Their liabilities are shorter term, less liquid and in a much larger number of smaller denominations than the assets these liabilities fund. For example, to fund one USD 1 million loan to a company for 10 years, a bank will take a much larger number of retail deposits ranging from hundreds of dollars to thousands each in the form of on-call savings and term deposits. When some of the deposits are withdrawn, they need to be replaced with additional deposits or borrowing from other sources. During the duration of the loan, the bank needs to make these liability adjustments regularly, even at a daily frequency. The financial intermediation service and the resulting asset transformation function commercial banks perform are invaluable for the economy, and the banks receive interest rate spreads as compensation for the risk-taking.

Moreover, a currency mismatch can be typical of an emerging market country's banking system. Due to an insufficient pool of loanable funds, emerging market country banks are often required to access international money markets to fund their corporate customers. Since they cannot raise funds in their own currencies, they are forced to borrow in hard currencies (the USD or the EUR). The foreign currency funds are then converted into domestic currencies before making loans to domestic corporate borrowers. If the domestic currency depreciates against the funding foreign currency, then larger amounts of domestic currency income are needed to service and repay the appreciating foreign currency loans, putting pressure on their profitability and solvency. Exhibit 8.1 shows the nature of balance sheet mismatches emerging market country banks typically face.

Financial intermediation requires banks to create mismatches that expose them to liquidity, credit, and currency risks. When the level of uncertainty in the system is high, and risk appetite evaporates, the banks' ability to manage defaulting borrowers, liquidity drain, deposits, and other funding sources in the market is put to the test. In emerging market countries, banks have not generally attained the level of competency required to manage various risks arising from balance sheet mismatches. Moreover, markets do not exist for effective risk transfer vehicles, such as interest rate derivatives, credit derivatives, and other necessary market mechanisms. Due to these vulnerabilities, banking panics would spread to the economy during times of a sharp rise in systemic risk. Banking crises occur when most banks in a country are experiencing financial difficulties and are unable to make new loans. This explains why the incidences of a banking crisis are much more frequent (83% of all recorded banking

	Assets	**Liability**
Duration:	Long-term	Short-term
Size denomination:	larger denomination	Smaller denomination
Liquidity:	Less liquid	Liquid
Currency denomination:	Soft currency	Hard currency

Exhibit 8.1. Balance sheet mismatches of emerging market country commercial banks.

crises occurred in emerging market countries for the period 1971–2017, see Exhibit 7.1), and the direct cost of crisis resolution is much higher (Hoggarth *et al.*, 2002).

A multitude of factors can potentially spark events that eventually lead to a banking crisis in emerging market countries. Given the nature of financial underdevelopment, emerging market countries are ill-equipped to handle an outbreak of a financial crisis. Before the breakout of a crisis, an underdeveloped financial system is held together with a heavily protected banking system with no credible alternatives, a less than freely floating exchange rate regime vulnerable to speculative attacks, and banks being inefficient in assessing investment risks (loans and financial and non-financial investments). When events occur that intensify the level of adverse selection and moral hazard problems, inadequately supervised and poorly managed banks are likely to be under immense pressure from the fast-depreciating assets due to loan defaults and asset deflation which can eventually lead to a full-blown banking crisis. The negative effects of a banking crisis are stronger and more severe in developing countries as a result of these factors (Allen *et al.*, 2009, Hoggarth *et al.*, 2002, and Laeven and Valencia, 2018).

Exhibit 8.2 outlines a sequence of a banking crisis in emerging market countries. Macroeconomic shocks emanating from external or internal sources can test the strength of the financial system. Global factors such as supply shocks and sudden and sharp increases in the cost of funding for international banking activities can ultimately cause a financial crisis in an emerging market country. Internal factors include macroeconomic mismanagement that leads to external and internal deficits with the corresponding depreciation pressures on the domestic currency (Mishkin, 2013). When these factors become difficult to manage effectively, the banks in the system will experience depreciation of the market value of their assets. Their financial investments will lose value along with the general asset deflation in the system, and the health of their loan portfolios may also be in doubt as the borrowers' repayment capacity is deteriorating. The combination of falling asset values, and hence the market value of any collaterals for existing loans, and the rising probability of loan defaults with the subsequent rise in NPLs add to the level of uncertainty in the system. Increasing degrees of asymmetric information problem and their subsequent deterioration into adverse selection and moral hazard problems can lead to the loss of confidence in the banking system, leading to depositors seeking to withdraw their deposits in the absence of credible government deposit guarantees. Bank runs will ensue, leading to some banks in the system being unable to satisfy the increasing liquidity

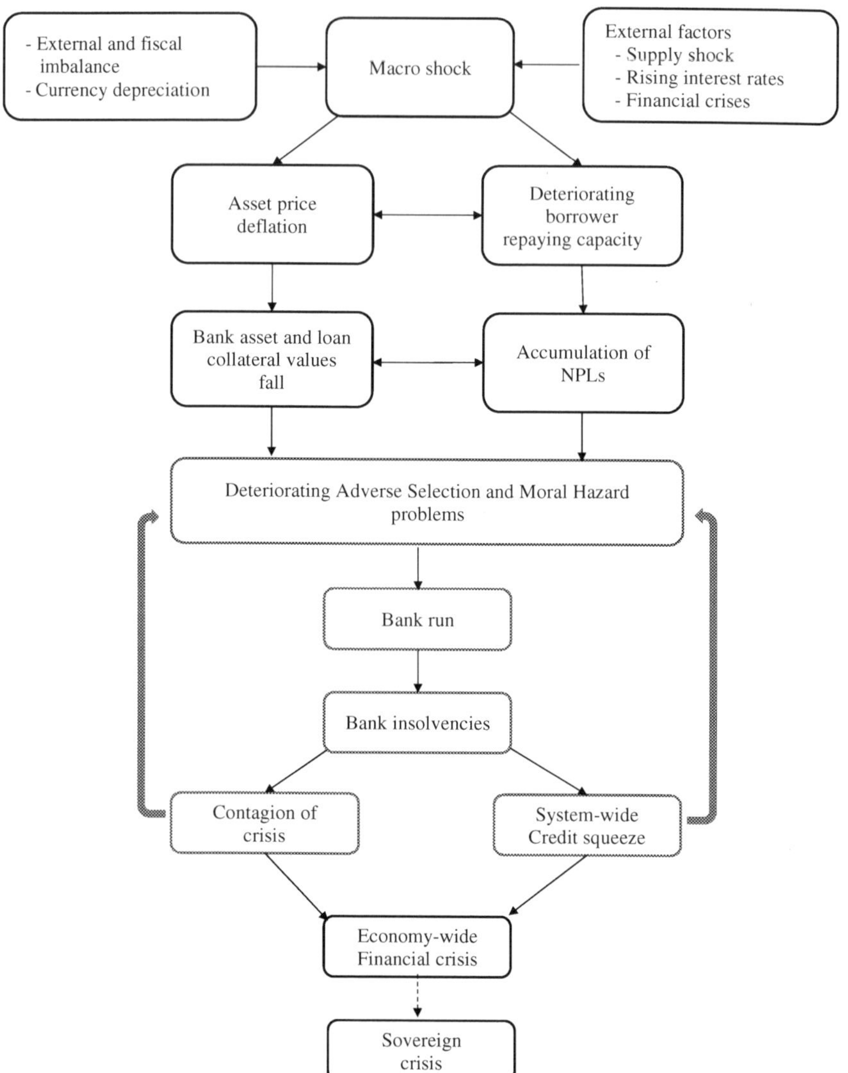

Exhibit 8.2. Anatomy of an emerging economy banking crisis.

outflows. Banks will then be forced to raise liquidity by selling off their existing assets that can still be sold or by borrowing from the market, however unlikely, or from the government. If all efforts fail, those banks who are unsuccessful in getting replacement liquidity will fail and become insolvent, which will further deteriorate the already heightened adverse selection and moral hazard problems and destroy investor risk appetite. This will lead to a system-wide credit squeeze where no borrower is funded, irrespective of prior credit quality. Moreover, there will be spillovers to other countries with similar characteristics that may also experience liquidity drains and credit squeeze as foreign lenders withdraw from emerging market countries with similar risk characteristics. Finally, if the government of a troubled banking system and depreciating currency runs out of foreign currency reserves to defend their currency and tools to contain domestic system failure, a sovereign debt crisis can follow from a banking crisis.

8.3. Contributing Factors to a Banking Crisis: Micro Factors

Factors contributing to a banking crisis in emerging economies are rooted in the underdevelopment of financial markets and inadequate supervision of bank risk-taking (Goldstein and Turner, 1996). In this section, these factors are discussed in detail.

8.3.1. *Inefficient risk management*

The essence of banking is in credit risk management. As discussed earlier, commercial banks are exposed to various mismatches in their balance sheets. These include mismatches between assets and liabilities in terms of currency denomination, duration, interest rate base, and liquidity. Vulnerability to liquidity and currency risks is higher in emerging market banks because of the lack of access to long-term liabilities and market instruments for liquidity transformation used for hedging. In addition, banks in some emerging market countries are unable to find sufficient funds that their borrowers require, and this forced them to raise funds in hard currencies (usually the USD) in the international banking market, although the domestic assets using the fund are denominated in the domestic currency. The resulting currency mismatch can cause harm when the domestic currency depreciates rapidly due to external shocks. Moreover, some emerging market borrowers concentrated on short-term their USD borrowing, although they needed longer-term funds. This was because international banks were reluctant to extend long-term credits due to the higher risk of emerging market borrowers or charged higher interest rates if they agreed to lend long-term. This was one of the difficulties faced by some of the Korean banks in the run-up to the financial crisis in 1997. Banks in Turkey also made the same mistake of borrowing short-term foreign currencies to facilitate longer-term domestic lira loans, which contributed to the financial crisis in 1994.

In the absence of rapid development in fundamental risk management skills of emerging market banks and readily available risk-shifting tools, holding excess liquidity and capital over and above the level advanced country banks are required to hold under Basel III is one of the only methods to achieve safety in operation in emerging market banking systems. Holding excess tier-one capital beyond the minimal Capital Adequacy Ratio (CAR) requirement will go a long way to reduce its dependence on outside party's help in times of trouble, and this will be seen positively by the market. In addition, a generous liquidity buffer is required. The development of a debt market is important in this regard for banks to invest in liquid assets such as government securities and money market instruments that are highly liquid. Banks should avoid heavy reliance on short-term foreign currency borrowing to finance longer-term domestic assets to reduce currency mismatches. Instead, the government should pursue the development of broader and longer-term domestic debt markets. In addition, sufficient foreign currency reserves would provide a buffer against potential speculative attacks on the domestic currency. Foreign currency reserves are composed of bank deposits in reserve currencies (the USD, the EUR, and the JPY), gold reserves, the IMF's Special Drawing Rights (SDRs), and reserves with the IMF.[1] In July 2022, the top five countries in terms of their foreign reserves were China (the equivalent of USD 3.5 trillion), Japan (1.4 trillion), Switzerland (964 billion), India (576 billion) and Russia (576 billion).

8.3.2. *Moral hazards: Distorted incentives, government ownership, and connected lending*

The existence of asymmetric incentives leads to excessive risk-taking behaviour by banks. This is especially true when bank owners have small stakes in the bank or bank managers carry very little personal responsibility for the risks they take. In some of the emerging markets, these agency

[1] Statistica (2023) Foreign exchange reserves in selected countries and territories across the world as of September 24, 2022. https://www.statista.com/statistics/247231/currency-reserves-of-selected-countries/.

and moral hazard problems are more severe as the ownership structures of banks are very narrow and are often a part of a larger business structure (a conglomerate). In such circumstances, those banks mainly serve their the conglomerate customers. As such, there would be little diversification of loan portfolios, and the survival of the banks are assured by cross-subsidisation guarantees from their conglomerate owners. In general, bank owners (shareholders) benefit most when the banks' risk-taking activities pay off, so they should be the ones losing the most in times of restructuring. That is, the government should not automatically recapitalise privately owned banks to avoid the moral hazard problem, and this will lead to owners appointing capable managers to minimise financial difficulties and reduce the agency problems. Thus, the level of bank capital acts as a source of good governance as well as a cushion against loan write-offs (and write-downs). Increasing the level of bank capital is vital in injecting confidence in the banks and bank shareholders paying the price of restructuring, further reducing moral hard and agency problems.

Moral hazard problems also exist for depositors. The existence of government bailouts and other guarantees would lessen the need for depositors to monitor banks' risk-taking behaviour, and they will pay little attention to the creditworthiness of banks as long as their deposits are protected. There are currently 97 countries in the world that have some form of national deposit insurance facility.[2] Most of these countries that have introduced state-run deposit insurance schemes have done so mostly after a significant crisis event, such as the GFC. For example, in the EU, all except France (introduced in 1999) and Malta (in 2003) introduced a deposit insurance scheme after 2008. For countries with a compulsory deposit insurance scheme, the same lack of vigilance on the part of depositors is observed. To encourage appropriate incentives, it may be necessary to consider (1) partial insurance rather than full insurance so that depositors will not be fully protected, encouraging them to monitor banks' risk-taking, (2) risk-weighted insurance, where the cost of insurance depends on the level and the types of investment risks that the bank takes, and (3) deposit insurance through mutual liability, such as bank bail-ins that require partial deposit loss.

---

[2]As of March 2023, the International Association of Deposit Insurers (IADI) currently has membership from 99 members across 97 countries. https://www.iadi.org/en/about-iadi/deposit-insurance-systems/deposit-insurance-systems-governing-statutes/.

In some emerging market countries, most commercial banks are state-owned and operated and are run effectively as quasi-fiscal agencies based on political criteria with no regard for commercial principles. This undermines their solvency and the soundness of other better-run banks in the sector. China and India are two examples where their top commercial banks are government owned. The top four banks in China by total assets (ICBC, BOC, ABC, and CCB), which are also highly ranked globally, are state-owned. In India, there is a long list of public sector banks that are ranked highly in terms of operating performance. For example, the State Bank of India (SBI) is one of the most profitable banks in India, ranked second most profitable in 2021 after Housing Development Finance Corporation (HDFC) bank. Other countries own specific purpose banks, such as export–import bank agencies and bridge banks which are a short-term solution to failed privately owned banks. The market mechanism may not govern the lending decisions of state-owned banks, but instead, they can be made on policy grounds without any regard for the profitability or the solvency considerations of the lending banks, as they are unlikely to fail. In some countries, even privately owned banks could not escape government-directed policy loans to allocate funds to desired industries and firms. At an early stage of economic development, the necessary market forces that will guide the flow of funds via the price mechanism are weak, rendering efficient resource allocation difficult. Under such a circumstance, active government involvement ensures that key sectors of the economy receive priority funds from the banking sector. This can be achieved by state ownership of key commercial banks and applying appropriate regulations to those banks to make 'policy loans' to key segments of the economy. Also, the government can use moral suasion against privately owned banks to get them to comply with its wishes. For example, successive Korean governments used the banking sector to prioritise funds for industries and companies deemed essential in their five-year economic and social development plans, which started in 1962 and lasted until 1996.

Inevitably, efficiency loss will result beyond a certain point in economic and financial market development due to resource misallocation, leading to NPL accumulations in banks. More importantly, the banking sector will be denied the opportunity to become competitive and will remain inefficient and uncompetitive, with little incentive to compete and innovate. Not surprisingly, countries with high government bank ownership tend to have less efficient banking sectors that have higher NPLs.

When banking crises occur, the government will be obliged to bail out failing banks, and the rescue costs will have both direct and opportunity costs. Ideally, the government-directed credit allocation should seize once the financial system and the economy have developed sufficient levels of sophistication. If this is not the case, measures to reduce moral hazard problems should be introduced. Appropriate policy measures include enhancing the transparency of government involvement in the banking sector to better communicate with the market, corporatisation or privatisation of government-owned banks to expose state-owned banks to market forces, and sharing the burden of policy loans across all banks if there is a continued need for policy loans.

8.3.3. *Weakness in accounting and legal framework*

A company's accounting reports are an important source of information that helps investors decide whether to invest in that company's debt or equity issuance. They convey current and past company performance trends and, together with independently obtained forward-looking information on the company's future prospects, help investors, creditors, regulators, and other stakeholders make correct assessments of the company. For commercial banks, externally imposed additional safety measures are also reported, such as capital adequacy ratios, NPLs, and loan provision ratios. The accuracy of disclosed accounting information is paramount in correctly conveying the company's prospects. However, accounting disclosure and external audit requirements vary across countries, and so does the accuracy of their accounting reports.

A less stringent requirement on the classification of NPLs can lead to an unwanted accumulation of NPLs. Typically, NPLs are defined as those loans with repayments in arrears for 90 days or more. In some countries, NPLs are based on non-payment only and not on the borrowers' continuing credit risk analysis. In principle, banks must carry out a credit risk analysis on their borrowers on a continuing basis to detect any possibility of a loan default caused by deterioration in the borrower's loan servicing capacity. If the relevant definition of NPL is based solely on the non-payment of loans, by the time a loan is classified as NPL, it is likely too late for the bank to initiate any pre-emptive measure to avoid eventual defaults. For example, if a bank is made aware of the difficulties faced by one of its borrowers that subsequently misses a regular interest payment, it may not choose to report the loan as not performing until the 90-day period is up to avoid higher funding costs in the inter-bank money market due to the higher NPL ratio if the loan is classified as non-performing. Thus, lenient disclosure requirements prevent timely reporting of NPLs, and failure to report high-risk-taking activities contributes to the accumulation of NPLs. In short, understating NPLs will result from weakness in accounting reporting standards. Moreover, there can be a collusion between banks and failing borrowers in the case of connected lending to disguise the extent of NPLs through loan restructuring, which further undermines the accuracy of the accounting records of banks.

A weak requirement on loan loss provisioning is also responsible for banking sector problems. Loan loss provisions (the portion of a loan portfolio set aside in liquid assets to cover contingencies, which varies between 10 and 30%) act as a safety buffer against the adverse effects of loan defaults on the solvency of banks. Due to the opportunity cost involved, too high a provision rate would drag the bank profitability down. On the other hand, too low a provisioning would not shield banks from insolvency should there be an unusually severe level of defaults.

Moreover, weak and ineffective supervision by regulators would allow unsafe lending practices to go unchecked. If the types of regulation and relevant laws preventing financial fraud, taking higher risks, etc. can be relatively easily avoided, the bank owners and managers would be incentivised to avoid costly regulations. In addition, government-affiliated banking sector supervisors may have an incentive not to reveal the full extent of the banking sector problems to avoid criticism.

In short, there are inevitable consequences of weak and ineffective accounting and legal frameworks. Troubled banks can appear healthy by under-reporting NPLs, over-reporting loan provisioning and restructuring problem loans, and other means. Inaccurate health assessments due to these weaknesses make it difficult for troubled banks to receive pre-emptive support from the government as much-needed remedies for the ailing banking sector are neither sought nor seem to be justified. It will be too late when the government notices that they might be in difficulties. Therefore, it is necessary to toughen NPL classification, increase NPL provisioning, initiate and enforce public disclosure requirements of bank performance and the risk characteristics of bank operations, and improve the bank supervisor's ability to implement stricter regulatory measures outlined.

8.4. Contributing Factors to a Banking Crisis: Macro Factors

The macro factors that contribute to a banking crisis in emerging market countries point to system-wide mismanagement, such as inadequate preparations for financial market liberalisation that allow uncontrollable foreign capital inflows, the resulting lending booms, and domestic macroeconomic mismanagement, among others.

8.4.1. *Inadequate preparation for financial liberalisation*

Financial sector deregulation in the advanced economies started in the early 1980s, which was followed by emerging market liberalisation and globalisation in the late 1980s and early 1990s. Market liberalisation refers to the process of dismantling existing restrictions in the system to allow the participation of previously prohibited entities. For example, opening up the banking system to allow non-banks to accept deposits, banks to invest in financial assets other than loan portfolios, etc. Market globalisation refers to the process of opening up domestic financial markets to foreign participants and, at the same time, allowing domestic banks to operate freely in foreign markets. For both advanced and emerging market economies, but especially for the latter, the processes of deregulation, liberalisation, and globalisation initially lead to a more volatile financial environment. This is due to the availability of previously inaccessible investment outlets and to more risk-taking due to increased competition within the banking sector (De Grauwe, 2008, Miline and Wood, 2003). A natural consequence of this is to observe increased levels of instability in the financial market, which is a process that all newly deregulated financial systems go through. Advanced countries that experience financial instability are generally better equipped to handle banking sector difficulties than emerging market economies.

In emerging market countries, it is vital that liberalisation proceeds in a manner that allows local market participants, such as banks, non-bank financial institutions, and regulators, to keep pace with the introduction of new financial products, processes, and more internal and external competition. In general, liberalising a previously protected banking sector would result in (1) higher volatility of domestic interest rates, (2) rapid credit expansions shortly after liberalisation due partly to higher domestic real interest rates and also due to capital inflows (if globalisation occurs at the same time, that might lead to a lending boom), (3) intensified competitive pressures which would lead to excessive risk-taking (liberal use of off-shore derivative products, etc.). In addition, inadequate preparations on the part of the financial supervisors to oversee new developments would exacerbate the banking sector difficulties. Also, sudden withdrawals of foreign capital due to loss of confidence, etc. expose domestic banks to unforeseen liquidity risks. Therefore, the preconditions for financial liberalisation are (1) a sufficient degree of competitiveness in the local financial markets (banking sector in particular), (2) carrying out a fit-and-proper test on new entrants to the banking sector, and (3) supervisors well equipped to handle more complex and new banking activities. It is essential to ensure that the globalisation of the domestic banking system occurs after the process of liberalisation is satisfactorily completed so that domestic banks can compete effectively with incoming foreign banks when the market is opened up to foreign entrants. That is, globalisation should occur after the banking system reaches close to stage four in the development stage (Chapter 7).

However, if globalisation occurs when domestic banks are not yet ready to compete with each other, let alone global banks, the inevitable financial instability will be greatly exacerbated. Korea is a good example to show what not to do in this regard. The Korean government started liberalising (and globalising) the Korean financial system in the early 1990s while maintaining a relatively fixed exchange rate system with no real efforts to develop system efficiency. The sudden increase in freedom for banks and non-bank financial institutions to access foreign markets allowed credit growth mainly from the USD-denominated borrowing in the international money market to fuel the insatiable appetite of Chaebols (Korean conglomerates) to expand their businesses domestically that could not be fully funded from the domestic capital market. The combination of the currency mismatch of the Korean financial institutions (especially short-term borrowing by finance companies that were incapable of managing their currency and liquidity risks effectively), the ineffectiveness and incompetency of the financial regulators, and uncontrolled inflows of short-term foreign capital all contributed to a lending boom that eventually unfolded into a series of corporate collapses and a banking sector distress. As such excessive and uncontrolled credit growth is one of the important predictors of a banking crisis (Claessens and Kose, 2013). The system-wide crisis in 1997 covered multiple areas — currency, banking, and stock markets — although Korea quickly recovered in a few years. By

1999, most macroeconomic measures and financial system indexes returned to the pre-1997 levels. The Korean experience is a valuable lesson for emerging market countries on what to avoid in financial system liberalisation and globalisation. However, if globalisation needs to occur before the system fully achieves stage four status, it is crucial to initiate policy measures to slow the rate of capital inflows and the speed of financial engineering. This will allow supervisors to catch up with new developments and provide effective supervision and system safety.

8.4.2. *Macroeconomic volatility and exchange rate regime*

Crises of confidence in the banking sector may arise due to external factors. Even efficient and properly supervised banking systems could face crisis episodes if the macroeconomic environments under which they operate become hostile and adverse selection and moral hazard problems become uncontrollable. This scenario is depicted in Exhibit 8.2 as a possible starting point in the outbreak of a financial crisis in an emerging market country. Macroeconomic policy mismanagement can lead to the following exposures: vulnerability to external shocks and macroeconomic volatilities such as uncontrolled lending booms and sudden reversals; sudden slowdown in the growth of the economy or exports; loss of an export market; sharp changes in exchange rates and interest rates; asset price and real estate price bubbles that develop and burst; and inflation volatility. These will adversely affect the borrowers' capacity to repay their loans, and the performance of other bank assets will also deteriorate, leading to a loss of confidence in the banking system.

Volatilities originating from foreign sources are mostly beyond the control of domestic authorities. However, governments should adopt policies that reduce volatilities originating domestically and maintain a stable economic environment. Monetary policies should be aimed at maintaining low rates of interest rate while keeping inflation under control. Fiscal policies should aim to balance the government budget, if appropriate. In addition, financial market policies should aim to achieve a mature banking sector capable of effectively managing risks through better risk identification and risk reduction through diversification of activities and the vehicles for risk transfer (e.g., derivatives and insurance) and liquidity enhancement (e.g., securitisation).

Another source of macroeconomic vulnerability is a country's exchange rate system. A flexible exchange rate system, in its various guises, allows market forces to determine the value of a country's currency against those of others. Given that market forces are difficult to predict accurately, exchange rates are also largely unpredictable, especially for longer-term horizons. The uncertainties surrounding the future values of a currency encourage international traders to seek protection from their banks and the market. For example, an exporter who receives a foreign currency payment in one month's time may wish to lock in a domestic currency equivalent to avoid the foreign currency depreciating by the time of payment receipt. Banks can provide over-the-counter forward or options contracts to sell the foreign currency, or the exporter can directly purchase an appropriate option at a derivative exchange (e.g., Chicago Mercantile Exchange in the US). In emerging market countries, neither of these options might be practical due to banks being unable to provide such protection and the non-existence of organised derivative trading. Often, the government of an emerging market country provides blanket foreign exchange protection by fixing the exchange rate, which will eliminate the need to hedge the foreign exchange risk. This is an optimal choice until the economy and the financial system develop a fully (or managed) floating exchange rate system that can provide a cushion against external shocks. However, there are significant downsides to fixed exchange rate systems. Economic mismanagement that leads to fiscal deficits, high inflation and interest rates, the loss of domestic competitiveness, and external imbalance requires constant government intervention to prop up the value of the domestic currency under the fixed level of the exchange rate, foreign reserves permitting. Continuing to keep the exchange rate at the current level via intervention rather than devaluing the currency will inevitably lead to an exhaustion of foreign currency reserves and a much larger eventual devaluation or even a forced floating of the currency due to speculative currency attacks. In the meantime, the real appreciation of the currency[3] will deteriorate the external

[3]Under a fixed exchange rate regime, the two countries involved in the arrangement must follow the same monetary policy stance. The weaker of the two economies cannot have an independent monetary policy that results in a significant deviation of the inflation rate, nominal interest rates, etc., from its counterpart without risking abrupt adjustment to the fixed exchange rate level. For example, assume that the Australian dollar is fixed at parity against the US dollar (i.e., 1 AUD = 1 USD) and the two economies are at equilibrium with 0% inflation. The Australian central bank (RBA) now carries out monetary policy easing, ultimately leading to an annual inflation of 10%. Purchasing power parity (PPP) condition

competitiveness of export-oriented emerging market economies, further adding pressure on the economy, and may trigger a banking crisis, as seen in Exhibit 8.2. Once again, economic mismanagement and underdeveloped market mechanisms will invariably expose the financial system to volatility, and there will come a point when the higher level of volatility in the system cannot be sustained. A banking crisis and an overall financial crisis will result. Hence, in this case, allowing some degree of nominal flexibility in exchange rate movements would partially shield the local economy from external shocks.

8.4.3. *Lending booms and bubbles*

Seemingly uncontrolled lending by banks can be due to the influx of large deposits that cannot be fully absorbed by existing borrowers or to a significant and continued rise in loan demands during the expansion phase of a business cycle. The former can arise from a sudden rise in the level of liquidity and risk appetite in the system. For example, during the two oil price shocks in the 1970s, OPEC economies amassed a fortune in oil revenue, which they deposited to eurobanks, funding increased international loans. The latter can be due to low-interest rates and the euphoria in the investment community during asset and real estate market boom periods where bank loans finance investments in these speculative markets. Moreover, the process of deregulation and globalization forces banks to undertake unfamiliar competition and exposes bank balance sheets to bubbles and crashes (De Grauwe, 2008, Miline and Wood, 2003). For emerging market countries, lending booms usually follow financial deregulation and market liberalisation of the closed and regulated banking sector. The liberalisation of a previously isolated banking sector is likely to lead to capital inflows if foreign investors see value in investing in the

---

suggests that the value of the AUD must fall by 10% over the one-year period. This implies that the AUD should be worth only 0.90 USD, but if the Australian government wishes to keep the fixed rate at parity, the AUD is overvalued by 10% at the current exchange rate. In other words, the AUD has appreciated in real terms with all the consequences of external economic performances associated with appreciating domestic currency. Even worse, RBA's foreign currency reserve (USD assets) will dry up if speculators determine that this situation is unsustainable and create a continued excess supply of the AUD, which the RBA needs to remove by selling the USD against the AUD.

country when they open up.[4] The increased capital inflows following liberalisation are likely to exceed the volume of liquidity that the underdeveloped financial market could absorb due to the lack of diversified investment options available in the country. The inevitable relaxation of lending controls can end up with the total credit extended in the economy well in excess of the level that is required for sustaining the current projected level of economic growth. Inevitably, excess credit would end up in speculative segments of the economy, such as stock and real estate markets, and also in emerging segments, such as cryptocurrencies, which have the potential of leading to excess capacity in the real economy due to overinvestment. Thus, excess demand for financial assets created by lending booms would ultimately lead to speculative bubbles in the financial markets. During boom periods, it is difficult to distinguish between good and bad credit risks, and so higher loan volumes provide an appearance of profitable lending activities for banks. However, when a sharp decline in asset prices eventuates (bubble bursting), NPLs of banks will accumulate as the market values of their collateral decline. Thus, sharp falls in asset prices are a good indicator of an impending banking crisis.

Sterilisation of capital inflows following liberalisation is one of the measures to discourage lending booms. Dismantling capital controls is usually associated with capital inflows, which can be a source of a lending boom unless effective sterilisation measures are in place. Sterilisation is the practice of a government issuing domestic currency-denominated government bonds and securities to absorb excess liquidity introduced by foreigners' inward capital investments. For example, if a US investor brings in USD 100 million into an emerging market country, say Mexico, that has just opened up to foreign investment, it will first be converted to an equivalent amount in the domestic currency (2.08 MXN billion at 20.86 MXN per USD) via the foreign exchange market. The foreign

---

[4]Many emerging market financial sectors were not accessible by multinational financial institutions even though potentially significant profitable opportunities existed due to the higher economic growth rates in some countries. The combination of sustained higher economic growth rates and reliance on bank credits for corporate financing in many emerging market countries provided an attractive alternative to the overcrowded and less profitable intermediation markets in advanced economies. Upon liberalisation of emerging market country banking sectors, multinational banks entered these markets, leading to substantial capital inflows, which in most cases were concentrated in speculative segments of the economy and ultimately led to lending booms.

investor then has the local currency fund to invest in the economy. This represents an increase in the money base by the same amount, which will have a multiplier impact if left unchanged. So, the initial USD 100 million injections into the economy will increase the domestic money supply by 20.8 MXN billion if the money multiplier is 10. Unless the money supply increase is consistent with the monetary policy stance at the time, the government will try to remove the extra money base by issuing government bonds to the tune of 2.08 MXN billion to remove the increase in the bank reserve as a result of the USD 100 m inflow. The result is no aggregate impact on the money base and the money supply. However, although the overall amount of credit availability remains unchanged, the nature of credit allocation will be altered to the extent that the foreign investor may exhibit different investment preferences and patterns. For example, the foreign investor may prefer to invest only in stock markets, and then there would be a net flow of loanable funds from the capital market to the stock market. This may complicate the government's efforts to influence the credit allocation process. The sterilisation process will work in reverse for capital outflows. Without the government's bond market intervention, capital outflows triggered by a fall in confidence by foreign investors will lead to a falling money base. This will have a negative multiplier effect that could cause a banking crisis due to a sudden fall in credit supply. The government should then buy enough bonds to inject sufficient liquidity into the system to maintain a constant money base. The effectiveness of sterilisation, however, depends on the depth of government debt markets, which, unfortunately, is lacking in most emerging market countries. Therefore, complete sterilisation of foreign capital inflow may not be possible or practical.

Alternatively, the government can raise reserve requirements to absorb excess liquidity from capital inflows. However, this adversely affects both well-run and weak banks as a whole and is inappropriate under a deregulated environment.

8.4.4. *Contagion of a financial crisis*

As emerging market economies open up and foreign investors participate in domestic intermediation, linkages among emerging market countries will develop via the common foreign investors and lenders across many emerging market countries. For example, if advanced country banks and investors decide to invest in Mexico and Argentina in the Americas,

Poland and Hungary in Eastern Europe, and Thailand and Malaysia in South East Asia as these markets open up, these emerging markets will experience increased market co-movements, especially during turbulent times. When foreign banks and investors withdraw some or all of their investments from one emerging market region due to the fear of a market downturn, they are also likely to withdraw from other emerging market regions with similar characteristics so that they can run to safety in the traditional safe-haven countries in the US, Western Europe, and Japan. When this occurs, the emerging markets from which the advanced market lenders are exiting will simultaneously experience a liquidity drain and a rapid asset price deflation. Therefore, due to financial integration, a banking crisis in one country may spill over to others in the same region via the common lenders and investors reacting by exiting from multiple markets simultaneously. For example, during the 1997 Asian Financial Crisis, the five countries involved, namely Korea, Malaysia, Indonesia, Thailand, and the Philippines, simultaneously experienced rapid capital outflows, a fall in currency values, and collapsing stock and banking markets. There were insignificant trade and financial linkages among these countries at the time. However, all were in varying stages of liberalisation, allowing foreign capital inflows, and were put into a vulnerable situation when rapid capital outflows occurred due to the evaporation of foreign investors' and lenders' risk appetite in emerging markets in general.

Once a financial system is liberalised, it is challenging to return to the pre-liberalised state of prohibiting direct foreign investor participation. Therefore, the only practical option for the government of a newly liberalised financial system to ensure system safety from the vagaries of international capital movements is to push through the process of market development and deepening. When the stage four level of development is reached, banks and other financial institutions are mature in their operations and risk management with access to risk-transferring tools in the system. Moreover, the government debt market would have been developed to effectively sterilise the unwanted impact of international capital flows on the integrity of the domestic monetary policy.

References

Allen, F., Babus, A. and Carletti, E. (2009). Financial crises: Theory and evidence. http://finance.wharton.upenn.edu/~allenf/download/Vita/ARFE-Crises-08June09-final.pdf.

Claessens, S. and Kose, M. A. (2013). Financial crises: Explanations, types, and implications. IMF Working Paper, WP/13/28. https://www.imf.org/en/Publications/WP/Issues/2016/12/31/Financial-Crises-Explanations-Types-and-Implications-40283.

De Grauwe, P. (2008). The banking crisis: Causes, consequences and remedies. https://www.ceps.eu/ceps-publications/banking-crisis-causes-consequences-and-remedies/.

Goldstein, M. and Turner, P. (1996). Banking crises in emerging economies: Origin and policy options, BIS Economic Papers, No. 46. http://www.bis.org/publ/econ46.pdf.

Hoggarth, G., Reis, R. and Saporta, V. (2002). Costs of banking system instability: Some empirical evidence. *Journal of Banking and Finance*, 26(5), 825–855.

Laeven, L. and Valencia, F. (2018). Systemic banking crises revisited, IMF Working Paper WP/18/206. https://www.imf.org/en/Publications/WP/Issues/2018/09/14/Systemic-Banking-Crises-Revisited-46232.

Miline, A. and Wood, G. (2003). International banking crises, Chapter 15 of *Handbook of International Banking*, Mullineux, A. W. and Murinde, V. (eds.), Edward Elgar, UK.

Mishkin, F. (2019). *The Economics of Money, Banking and Financial Markets*. 12th ed., Pearson, Harlow, UK.

Chapter 9

Banking Crisis in Advanced Economies

9.1. Introduction

Banking crises that occurred in advanced economies in the late 1980s and the early 1990s share common characteristics with those observed in emerging market crises. In both cases, banks were generally incapable of competing effectively with each other and risk management skills were lacking in general. This was mainly due to the underdevelopment of the financial and economic system in emerging markets and the lack of competition under strictly regulated financial systems in advanced economies. When ill-prepared banks face increased competition as a result of financial and economic system liberalisation or are suddenly plunged into a deregulated environment, they are incentivised to take unmanageable risks (De Grauwe, 2008, Miline and Wood, 2003). However, recent crises in the advanced economies, including the Global Financial Crisis (GFC), were unique to the characteristics of the advanced financial system. In general, the common factor for all types of banking crises is ineffective management of bank risk-taking activities. Discussions on these cases are presented in this chapter.

9.2. Crisis Following Banking Sector Deregulation

With the banking sector at its core, the financial system allocates loanable funds to individuals and businesses from investors and depositors. Banks perform irreplaceable roles in the system, such as credit creation, being a conduit for monetary policy and being the main contributor to the payment system. Since banks must perform these roles without disruption for the soundness of the economy, the government needs to ensure that the environment under which banks operate is stable and that banks are free from fear of collapse. One way to achieve this aim is to regulate the banking sector to ensure its safety. First and foremost, entry regulation is imposed where entry into the banking industry is determined not by market forces but by government regulation. Preventing entry into the banking industry by non-banks effectively reduces the level of competition that the entry of new and more efficient players could bring. Price regulation (for example, Regulation Q in the US to set maximum interest rates that banks can charge) is where the regulator sets both deposit and lending interest rates in the so-called belt and brace regulation. Quantity regulation aims to control credit growth as a part of monetary control in the era of monetary targeting. Banks are not allowed to increase credit growth beyond a designated rate in each period. Quality and operational regulation are for controlling the quality of bank borrowers and the types of loans that banks can make. For example, in Australia, commercial banks were not allowed to make loans to individuals for any purpose other than mortgage loans in the regulated financial system of the 1970s and early to mid-1980s. Individual borrowers were directed to non-bank lenders for non-mortgage loans, such as vacation loans and car finances, typically at much higher interest rates. In addition, banks were regulated to keep minimum levels of their loan portfolios in certain types of loans.

If various types of regulations have the desired effect, the banking sector is without excessive risk-taking and no unnecessary competition among banks, making bank failure and crisis unlikely. However, due to the competition and innovation-limiting regulations, the banking sector, under strict regulation, may be more vulnerable to system-wide instability as they transition to a deregulated environment where banks face competition.

The process of economic and financial deregulation in the advanced economies has its roots in the floating of major currencies in March 1973, when the Bretton Woods system of the fixed exchange rate was abandoned. Instead of the USD fixing its value against gold (USD 35 per ounce of gold) and other currencies fixing against the USD, major currencies began to freely float against each other. The currencies of developing countries were still adhering to a fixed rate system with a peg to the USD or a basket of trade-weighted currencies. The floating of currencies exposed international traders to foreign exchange rate risk in their international transactions, and they looked to their banks to provide hedging services for the exposures. Effective hedging of foreign exchange exposures requires banks and other market participants to offset the risk they absorb from their clients by taking the opposite position of the exposure. Easy access with minimum cost is required to the foreign exchange market and the money markets in the two currencies involved in the foreign exchange exposure. Under a regulated financial system, however, foreign banks' access to national money markets was not as easy or cost-effective as domestic banks in the system.

Moreover, the development of the offshore eurocurrency market in London attracted multinational banks and their clients that were drawn to the lack of regulation on eurocurrency activities imposed by the UK government (as discussed in Chapter 5). Much of the financial engineering originated or flourished in the offshore markets as multinational banks via their foreign branches (known as eurobanks) freely compete with each other and deliver financial innovation. For example, various foreign exchange and interest rate derivatives owe their popularity to the eurocurrency market. By comparison, banks operating only in the domestic markets under a regulated financial environment were effectively prevented from competing with each other, let alone engaging in financial engineering. They were at a competitive disadvantage compared to multinational banks with access to offshore markets. Some governments created vehicles to allow their domestic banks' much-needed support to be more competitive in specific product areas. For example, the US government allowed their banks to establish an International Banking Facility (IBF) within their domestic operation as a separate accounting entity, allowing international banking activities without binding domestic regulations. Moreover, US banks were allowed to set up Edge Act corporations as separate legal entities to allow international banking activities free from domestic regulation. The Australian government's version of the US's IBF was Offshore Banking Unit (OBU) which allowed tax concessions for Australian banks that conduct offshore banking activities if they go through their OBUs.[1] The supply shock events in the 1970s, the two oil price shocks, which led to higher levels of inflation, put pressure on banks

[1] The Australian government announced on 13 September 2021 that the concessional tax rate of 10% on OBU income will be removed from the 2023/2024 income year for banks that operate an OBU.

and thrift institutions in the US that were under the binding interest rate regulation, Regulation Q.

The factors outlined above and others contributed to the financial sector deregulation in the early 1980s in advanced economies. As briefly discussed in Chapter 7, a period of financial instability will follow as banks explore their newfound freedom and take on new products and customer types in different market locations and segments. Invariably, the additional risk-taking can lead to accumulating losses from new activities as banks are not fully equipped to take on unfamiliar risks (Claessens and Kose, 2013, De Grauwe, 2008). At its worst, banks may lose the confidence of their depositors, leading to a potential bank run.

9.2.1. *Savings and loan crisis in the US*

The US started the process of financial deregulation in the early 1980s. Initially, the focus was on the Savings and Loan (S&L) industry as they experienced a string of failures following a combination of binding interest rate regulation, high inflation, and high real interest rate environment (FDIC, 1997). S&Ls are similar to building societies in the British commonwealth countries, where the primary aim is to provide mortgage loans to individual borrowers funded by deposits, often from the same pool of borrowers. Some share similar characteristics to credit unions, where they are operated as member-owned and operated financial intermediaries. Their deposits were guaranteed by the Federal Savings and Loan Insurance Corporation (FSLIC), similar to FDIC providing protection for commercial banks. There were approximately 4,000 S&Ls in 1980, with assets up to USD 604 billion (Federal Deposit Insurance Corporation (FDIC), 1997) protected by the FSLIC. S&Ls were regulated to offer fixed and low-interest rates for mortgage loans to encourage home ownership. To provide an edge for S&Ls in attracting deposits, they were allowed to pay as much as 25 basis points over what commercial banks could pay. This was because, under Regulation Q in the US, S&Ls could only offer savings accounts to their customers, unlike commercial banks that could also offer check accounts and raise funds from non-deposit sources. The late 1970s' inflation environment and the ensuing high-interest rate policies of the US government created a balance sheet mismatch for S&Ls where they faced increasing deposit rates but were bound by fixed lending rates. This situation led to a situation of low or even negative interest rate margins, which led to some S&Ls failing by the early 1980s. The removal of the interest rate ceiling under Regulation Q in 1980 put even more pressure on the S&L in attracting deposits as the 25 basis point advantage became ineffective.[2] Depositors were lured away to money market funds that offered higher interest rates. There were 11, 34, and 73 S&L collapses in 1980, 1981, and 1982, respectively (FDIC, 1997), with a total cost of USD 3.5 billion to the FSLIC. This is in contrast to only 143 failures costing only USD 306 million during the 45-year period from 1945 to 1979. In order to provide some support to the S&L industry, from 1982, they were allowed to make up to 10% of their assets in commercial loans and offer accounts with high-interest rates to compete against money market funds.[3]

Although these measures were to provide S&Ls with the ability to compete effectively against banks, the newfound ability to compete for deposits and new investment possibilities posed a significant risk to their already strained balance sheets. Some offered above-market interest rates to attract deposits, and the inflow of deposits into the S&L industry between 1982 and 1985 allowed a rapid expansion of their balance sheets, further intensifying the balance sheet mismatches they already had (i.e., rising cost of short-term deposits funding long-term mortgage loans with interest rates that could not rise at the same rate or not rising at all). Moreover, the freedom to make commercial loans attracted borrowers investing in commercial properties. Sherman (2009) reports that S&Ls' assets in home mortgage loans fell from 78% in 1981 to 56% in 1986. The deregulation of the S&L industry encouraged more risk-taking in commercial loans leading to an overheated real estate market. This also resulted in increasing their balance sheet mismatches due to the rising short-term funding costs (e.g., higher deposit rates paid and offered accounts similar to money market instruments) that funded the long-term real estate sector loans. The resulting combination of excessive risk-taking in new types of investments without appropriate risk management skills and moral hazard (FSLIC covers failures) led to the now infamous S&L crisis that formally lasted until 1995. Between 1980 and 1988, there were 4,337 insolvent S&Ls with a combined asset of USD 2.2 billion, and a total of 563 eventually failed, bankrupting FSLIC itself in 1988. The FSLIC's reserves turned from only 4.6 million to –6.3 million in 1986, –13 million in 1987, and –75 million in 1988 when it failed (FDIC,

[2]Depository Institutions Deregulation and Monetary Control Act (DIDMCA) of 1980. https://www.federalreservehistory.org/essays/monetary-control-act-of-1980.

[3]Garn-St. Germain Act of 1982.

1997). The efforts to resolve the S&L crisis started in 1989 when the Resolution of Trust Corporation (RTC) was created to wind down failed S&Ls that FDLIC had taken control of.[4] The RTC was wound down in 1995, indicating an official end of the S&L crisis that started more than a decade earlier. In aggregate, the cost of the crisis resolution was over USD 160 billion, of which 132 billion was from federal taxpayers (FDIC, 1997). It was the government policymaker's failure as much as the S&Ls' uncontrolled risk-taking behaviour. The government's response of deregulating the S&L industry in 1980 and 1982 following an initial wave of failures was ill-timed, and safety measures to limit risk-taking by S&Ls were largely absent.

The S&L crisis in the US is a typical case of a stage-three financial crisis (Exhibit 7.4). The S&Ls were depository institutions in a newly deregulated industry and were not yet mature enough to take on additional risk. Yet, they expanded their business into unfamiliar risk territories in part due to the explicit or implied guarantees of survival and suffered the inevitable consequences of failure. The government's responses of introducing a series of policy measures to resolve the crisis eventually restored order, however, not before high fiscal costs were incurred mostly at the taxpayers' expense, raising further moral hazard concerns.

9.2.2. *Australian banking crisis in the early 1990s*

The Australian financial system experienced a period of turbulence in the late 1980s and the early 1990s following the financial deregulation from the mid-1980s (Fitz-Gibbon and Gizycki, 2001). The Australian financial market deregulation started with the Australian Dollar (AUD) floating in December 1983. This was soon followed by the deregulation of the banking sector by allowing both domestic and foreign bank entries and the relaxation of price, quantity, and operational controls imposed on banks. Both saving banks and building societies (similar to the US's S&L) started to access investment options they previously did not have access to (e.g., non-mortgage loans and business customers). Coming from a regulation era where banks were effectively regulated in all aspects of their operations, the freedom to pursue both the asset and liability side operations that

[4]This was a part of the Financial Institutions Reform, Recovery, and Enforcement Act of 1989 (FIRREA). https://www.ojp.gov/ncjrs/virtual-library/abstracts/firrea-financial-institutions-reform-recovery-and-enforcement-act.

opened up to them inevitably led to credit growth, as in the case of the US S&L deregulation experience. Moreover, increased competition among banks motivated them to engage in a price competition as their ability to compete on other fronts had not been developed yet. The resulting aggressive competition that necessitated high risk-taking and uncontrolled lending by banks inevitably worsened the balance sheet positions of some of the banks and building societies due to mounting non-performing loans. Even large and well-established banks such as Westpac were on the verge of collapse by the early 1990s. However, it was the smaller banks and building societies that eventually succumbed to the pressure and collapsed.

The State Bank of Victoria collapsed in 1990 with losses of AUD 1.5 billion. It was eventually sold to the Commonwealth Bank of Australia for AUD 2 billion in 1991. The State Bank of South Australia collapsed in 1991. In the late 1980s and early 1990s, it completed a string of acquisitions to build up the size of its operations. It merged with the Savings Bank of South Australia in 1984 and purchased an insurance company in 1988 and a building society in 1990. It collapsed in 1991, and the accumulation of non-performing assets in, mostly corporate and property loans, was identified as the direct cause of the collapse. The portion of assets that were still performing was sold to Advance Bank in 1992. As both state banks were state-owned, depositors were protected by the respective state governments. However, the state governments were not so fortunate as the Labor governments in the two states were brought down in subsequent elections.

In addition, there were runs on the Farrow group of building societies, made up of the Pyramid, the Geelong, and the countrywide building societies, that led to their collapse in 1990 with a debt of more than AUD 2 billion (equivalent to USD 1.54 billion). Once again, aggressive lending to property-related projects following the deregulation in the 1980s led to unrecoverable losses and accumulated non-performing loans. The government of the state of Victoria paid the unsecured depositors, and the Reserve Bank of Australia put out a statement indicating that this was an isolated case and that other building societies were sound, which appeared to have calmed the market.

9.2.3. *Banking crises in Sweden, Norway, and Finland*

Other advanced economies sharing similar post-deregulation financial crisis episodes include three Nordic countries of Sweden, Finland,

and Norway (Drees and Pazarbasioglu, 1998, Honkapohja, 2009). In Sweden, lending growth in the 1980s caused a real estate sector and financial market bubble, which inevitably collapsed. The deregulation had its root in 1985 when the government abolished the quantity control of commercial bank lending. The previous credit rationing at given interest rates that held demand in the housing sector in check was abolished with an expected result in the housing sector. Both bank lending growth and house prices started to grow rapidly from 1985 until the collapse of the boom in 1991. The lending growth between 1985 and 1990 averaged around 17% per annum, and the house price index rose from around 92 in 1985 to its peak of over 195 in 1990, an increase of 112% over a six-year period (Jonung, 2009). When the banking sector collapsed after the real-estate bubble burst in 1990, a severe credit crunch followed until 1993, plunging the whole economy into a bust cycle. The government guaranteed the bank deposits in all the banks in the country and assumed the bad debt of banks in return for a partial nationalisation of the troubled banks. The bad debts were later sold in the market to recoup some of the costs. The total cost of the bailout was estimated to be around 4% of GDP, excluding the cost recovery from the sale of bad assets assumed from troubled banks.

In Norway, quantity and price regulations on banks were removed in 1984 and 1985. The lending boom that ensued resulted in average loan growth of 20% per annum between December 1984 and September 1986 (Vale, 2004). The extra liquidity was largely absorbed into both residential and commercial real estate markets. Following the devaluation of the Krone after the oil price hikes in 1985, signs started to emerge in the banking sector in 1988 when smaller banks started to fail. The full-scale banking crisis was averted by coordinated support that resulted in the troubled banks merging with sound ones. However, the continued volatility of the Kroner due to external factors such as the reunification of Germany and higher interest rates squeezed the profitability of existing corporate borrowers. Eventually, several large banks collapsed over the period from 1991 to 1992, paralysing financial intermediation in the economy. The government stepped in and largely nationalised the troubled banks as private sector re-capitalisation efforts were insufficient to avert a full-scale crisis. The direct cost of the government bailout was around 2% of GDP, which was much smaller than in the case of Sweden, which experienced its banking crisis around the same time and with the same core contributing factors.

Finland also shares a similar experience of deregulation leading to credit expansion and higher risk-taking. Deregulation of the Finnish financial sector started in the early 1980s, with more meaningful deregulation processes occurring in the second half of the 1980s (Nyberg and Vihriälä, 1993). From 1985 all controls on interest rates such as lending rates, foreign bank access to the money market, not allowing floating rates on loans, etc. were removed. At the same time, the financial system was liberalised. This was largely concentrated on removing restrictions on international capital movements allowing foreigners to bring capital into the country and allowing domestic residents to invest in foreign markets. Since Finland maintained relatively high-interest rates compared to comparable countries, removing restrictions to access the Finish financial sector led to significant capital inflows. Nyberg and Vihriälä (1993) report that at its peak in 1988, bank lending grew by 30%. Together with benign external factors that improved the external positions of the economy, the lending boom significantly increased economic activities. The resulting rise in liquidity eventually flowed to both stock and real estate markets, creating asset inflation. The government authorities attempted to rein in the liquidity boom by tightening monetary policy in early 1989. In addition, the reserve ratio was raised to control bank lending, and the currency, Markka, was allowed to revalue. Both measures raised short-term interest rates towards the end of 1989. These measures made foreign currency borrowing attractive. When the Soviet Union started to dissolve in the late 1980s, Finland's export income decreased significantly due to an increase in external uncertainty. This triggered concern as the external debt had grown considerably by that time. By 1990, several banks that were managed inefficiently during the boom period showed signs of weakness and started to require overnight debt from the central bank to cover their liquidity positions. The government responded by providing interest-free loans to banks that require liquidity. In addition, they also nationalised troubled banks and liquidated the assets of failed banks using a bad bank method. In the end, the direct cost of crisis resolution was about 50 billion Markka (equivalent to USD 1 billion and roughly 0.7% of GDP of USD136 billion in 1990).

9.3. Banking Crisis Due to Financial Innovation

Advanced economies, in general, have gone through financial deregulation from the early to mid-1980s and experienced similar effects as described in the previous section. The common consequences of deregulation include rapid credit growth, expanded loans to finance stock and real estate market investments, and higher risk-taking activities by both banks and their borrowers. The inevitable accumulation of non-performing loans threatened the soundness of their banking sectors. Once the crisis has been overcome and order restored, the banking system is transformed into stage 4 (Exhibit 7.4) in the financial development scale, characterised as efficient, competitive, and open to financial innovation and new competition.

Commercial banks in advanced economies have expanded their operations into various segments of the financial services sector, leading to a continuous stream of financial engineering products, both product and process related. This process of broadening banking activities has its regulatory implications, however. For example, commercial banks have been subjected to the strict capital regime of Basel's capital accord when it was first introduced in 1988 and adopted in 1992 in most developed countries. However, the financial market segments commercial banks have been venturing into, such as funds management, investment banking, and other capital market operations, were not generally subjected to this rule. Therefore, increasing proportions of commercial banks' activities beyond the traditional commercial banking activities, together with the increasing complexities of their asset and liability side operations, made it increasingly challenging to ensure adequate levels of supervision. In particular, the process of financial engineering greatly helped banks not only to manage their risks but also to take additional risks. For example, the application of securitisation techniques to the portfolio of both existing and new loans allowed banks to improve the liquidity of their otherwise illiquid long-term loan assets. Moreover, credit derivatives such as credit default swaps act as insurance against loan and other asset defaults. These financial innovations have greatly assisted banks in risk management. However, they also provide challenges as the product complexities increase the difficulties of accurately assessing their risk (Mishkin, 2013). Financial regulators are usually one or more steps behind financial innovations than those they supervise and often react to market events instead of pre-emptively managing the risk-taking activities of banks. Uncontrolled and ill-understood risk-taking behaviour in the financial market due to the complexities of the newly engineered financial products could lead to ineffective supervision and an eventual financial crisis, as witnessed in the US and other advanced countries during the GFC period.

9.3.1. *Securitisation*

Securitisation is one of the most important innovations in the deregulated financial market. It is a process of bundling illiquid assets into marketable securities with the underlying assets as collaterals for investors. The income streams of the underlying assets fund the interest payments of the new securities. The process of securitisation involves three distinct phases, and these are (1) pooling of assets with regular cash flows, (2) delinking of the credit risk of the collateral asset pool from that of the originator, and (3) tranching of liabilities that are backed by the asset pool (Fender and Mitchel, 2009).

New or existing tangible or intangible assets with constant income streams can be pooled together to create an asset base against which additional layers of securities can be created and marketed, known as Asset-Backed Securities (ABS). A Mortgage-Backed Security (MBS) is an example of an ABS, backed by a pool of mortgage loans. Banks can securitise a part of their existing loan portfolios, or alternatively, they can originate loans to securitise them (originate to distribute). The securitisation process allows mortgage loan originators to fund their loan portfolios without having to fulfil all the functions necessary for financial intermediation. Originators are typically loan brokers who originate loans financed entirely by securitisation. ABSs can be created by setting up Special Purpose Vehicles (SPV), which are called Collateralised Debt Obligations (CDO). When loan portfolios are used to create an ABS via SPV, it is referred to as Collateralised Loan Obligations (CLO). The emergence of the origination business in the domestic financial system dates back to late 1980 when the capital market funded mortgage loan market started to gain popularity with the advent of securitisation tools.

Exhibit 9.1 depicts a typical set-up in a more complex arrangement where CLOs are created. The originating bank makes loans to ten borrowers secured by the acquired assets (e.g., homes or other properties) as collateral against the loans. The lender can also be an institution that performs the origination function only, such as a mortgage originator. These ten loans can be packaged as a pool of loans to be securitised. Alternatively, existing loans can also be packaged for securitisation. Normally, loans sharing similar characteristics are included in a securitisation package, such as the same type of loan and mortgage loans to the same geographical area, similar maturity and loan conditions.

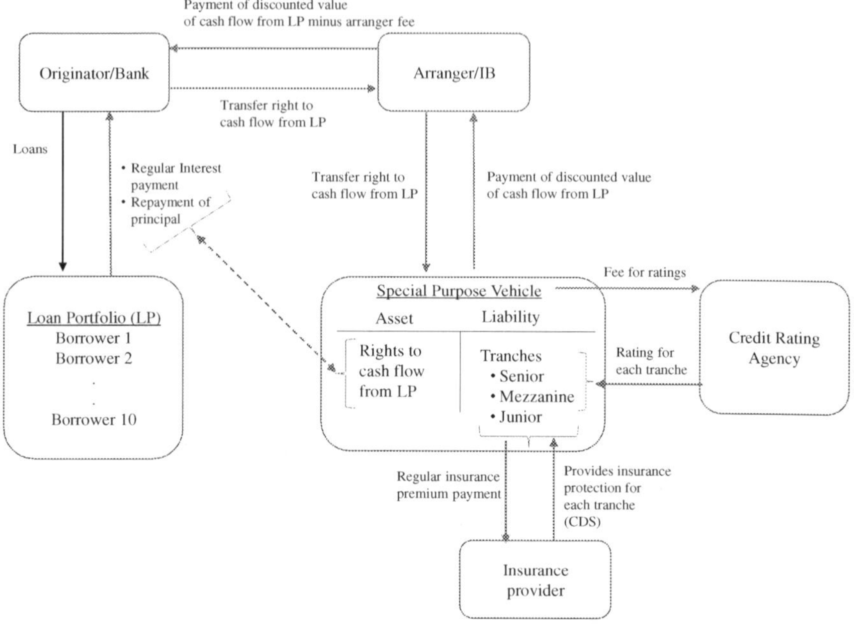

Exhibit 9.1. Securitisation process of loan portfolio.

Source: Author, adapted from Fender and Mitchel (2009).

The arranger (an outside party such as an investment bank or a different department of the originating bank) creates an SPV, or also called Special Purpose Entity (SPE), to securitise the pool of selected loans. An SPV is a separate legal entity created to isolate financial risk arising from the pool of loans that the bank holds or creates. The arranger then raises enough funds via the SPV to purchase the loan pool from the bank. At this point, the originator transfers the credit risk of the loans as well as the rights to the cash flows from the loan pool to the investors of the assets issued by the SPV.

The SPV is funded by the sale of the entity's securities (or equities) in tranches. The holders of the senior tranches are guaranteed to receive a fixed rate of return, say 8% p.a., for the duration of the security. The cash flows the SPV vehicle receives from the arranger are used first to pay these interest payments to senior tranche holders. The Mezzanine tranche holders receive their interest payments next, and the rate of return is set higher than the senior tranche, say 10% p.a. Finally, the remaining interest income is distributed to the junior tranche holders and, depending on the rate of defaults of the underlying loans, the return can vary in a wide range of returns (0% to significantly higher than the rate of return for the other tranche holders, say 20%).

The tranches are rated by outside rating agencies (Moodys, S&P, Fitch, etc.) so that they can be marketed to domestic and international investors. Due to the complex layers of the SPVs in their structure, the rating agencies 'may have been encouraged to rate highly complex products for which little or no historical performance data existed' (Fender and Mitchel, 2009).

Finally, tranche holders may seek protection against default by purchasing insurance in the form of Credit Default Swaps (CDS) provided by an insurance company in return for regular premium payments. The role CDS played in the US subprime mortgage crisis is discussed later in the chapter.

Exhibit 9.2 shows the trends of ABS issuance and outstanding amount in the US between 1990 and 2021 for different types of ABS, namely Automobile loans, CDO and CLO, Credit card debt, equipment loans, and other debt. In Panel A, ABS issuance is shown. There has been a growing trend since 1990, which was accelerated in 2005 and peaked in 2007. The ABS issuance grew by 2.4 times between 2004 (USD 330 m.) and 2007 (796 m.) This spectacular growth was due to CDO/CLO issuance growth, which rose nearly four times over the same period (from USD 124 to 490 m.). The ABS issuance (both in total and CDO/CLO) dropped in 2008 to only 27% of its size in 2007, and the drop in CDO/CLO issuance is single handily responsible for this collapse. The ABS issuance started to recover in 2012 as the US financial system began to return to the pre-GFC level of activities.

In Panel B, outstanding ABS over the same period is shown. The same general pattern is shown with a rapid rise between 2005 and 2007, then a downtrend until 2012 before recovery is shown. As can be seen, ABS, CDO/CLO in particular, played a significant role in the creation and then the bursting of the housing sector bubble in the US, leading to the GFC. The later sections provide further details on the background of the crisis.

9.3.2. *Credit default swap*

A CDS is an insurance product against the default of a debt instrument or a company for the debt holder. For example, if an investor holds bonds issued by a company, then they can purchase a CDS contract against the default by the company on the bonds. If default occurs, the bond investor is compensated by the CDS seller. Regular payments of CDS premium measured

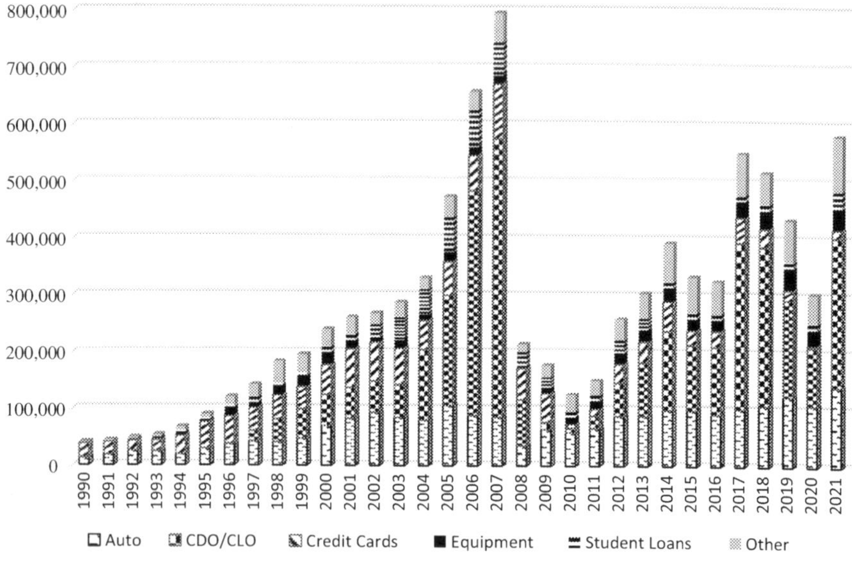

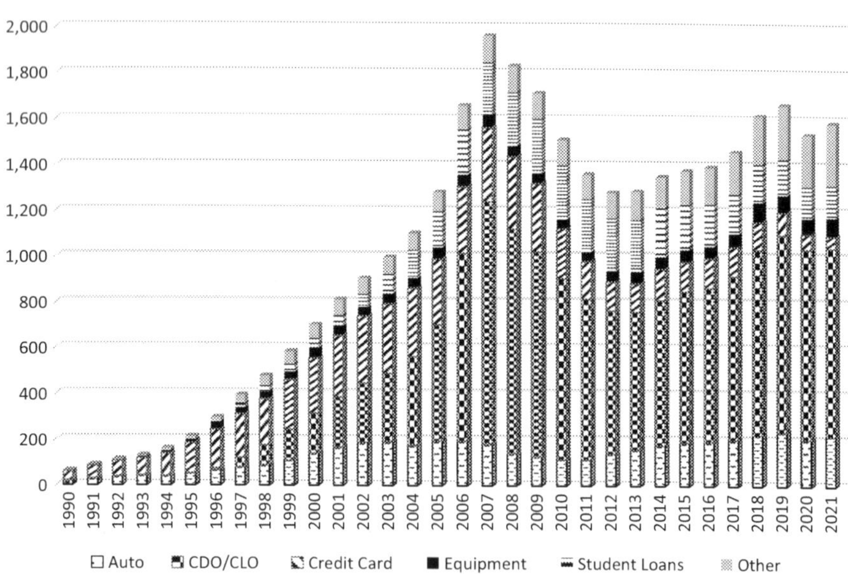

Exhibit 9.2. Asset-Backed Security issuance and outstanding in the US, 1990–2021.

Source: Constructed using data from SIFMA's (Securities Industry and Financial Markets Association) US Asset Backed Securities Statistics. https://www.sifma.org/resources/archive/research/statistics/.

in basis points throughout the life of the bonds is the income flow for the CDS seller. Normally, a buyer of a CDS on bonds would have exposure to the underlying bonds, so if the bond holding is valued at USD 1 million, then the CDS contract would compensate for the loss, and the annual premium, say, five basis points amounts to USD 500. If there are 10 million dollars' worth of bonds in issuance and all bondholders purchased the same CDS protection, the CDS sellers have the total exposure equal to the underlying amount of USD 10 million. In this instance, the risk of default is completely transferred to the CDS sellers, and there is no change in the aggregate amount of risk from the USD 10 million bonds in the system. The CDS, in this case, is referred to as a covered CDS. As a result, there should be no overall increase in the risk exposure of the CDS seller from engaging in the CDS market since the default risk of the bonds is simply transferred from one party to another within the system. Clearly, there are benefits for both parties involved in the transaction and for the efficiency of the financial system. The CDS buyer effectively transfers the default risk to a third party and is fully covered if a default occurs. This has the positive effect of encouraging the investor to be more active in the bond market and stimulating the overall market activities. The CDS seller is typically an insurance company that is well versed in taking on the risk from customers and squaring it off in a pool of assets with offsetting default characteristics.

An uncovered or naked CDS is where the CDS buyer does not have exposure to the underlying asset. If an investor buys a CDS protection for the USD 1 million bonds in the previous example without holding the bonds, this will have negative consequences on a number of fronts. Since the CDS buyer benefits only when the issuing company defaults on the bonds and loses the premium payments if the default does not occur, they have the incentive to see default occurs, creating a perverse incentive and moral hazard. For example, the CDS buyer could proactively cause a default by the company by spreading rumours about the company's financial troubles, smearing the reputation of the company management, etc., that are designed to create a negative perception about the health of the company. Moreover, naked CDSs increase the overall risk in the system. For example, in addition to the 10 USD 1 million CDS contracts, if there are ten speculators with naked CDSs for USD 1 million each, the total exposure for the system becomes USD 20 million, although the aggregate default exposure of the underlying assets is only USD 10 million. An argument can be made about naked CDSs improving the CDS market efficiency by aiding the price discovery process in a similar vein to the argument for short selling. However, the negatives of naked CDSs may significantly outweigh the potential benefits, as the world has witnessed in the events of the US subprime crisis. The role naked CDSs played was to increase the overall risk exposure beyond what the CDS sellers could manage.

Although most of the CDS sellers are insurance companies, others may also be involved, such as investment banks that are relatively unregulated. Moreover, although CDSs function like an insurance product, they were not regulated as such, as sellers had no requirement to maintain reserves to the same level as regulated insurance products. This was one of the factors that allowed CDS sellers such as AIG to greatly extend their exposure with devastating consequences during the subprime crisis period. Non-insurance company CDS sellers typically manage the risks of CDS by diversifying into CDSs based on assets of offsetting characteristics and opposite positions on the underlying assets. However, this strategy has proven to be ineffective in the environment of system-wide instability as evidenced by multiple failures of investment bank CDS sellers during the US subprime crisis.

Exhibit 9.3 shows CDS volumes and maturity concentrations in the global market for the period 2004–2021. The overall pattern of outstanding CDS volume is similar to that of the outstanding volume of ABS in the US market shown in Panel B of Exhibit 9.2. A similar pattern observed

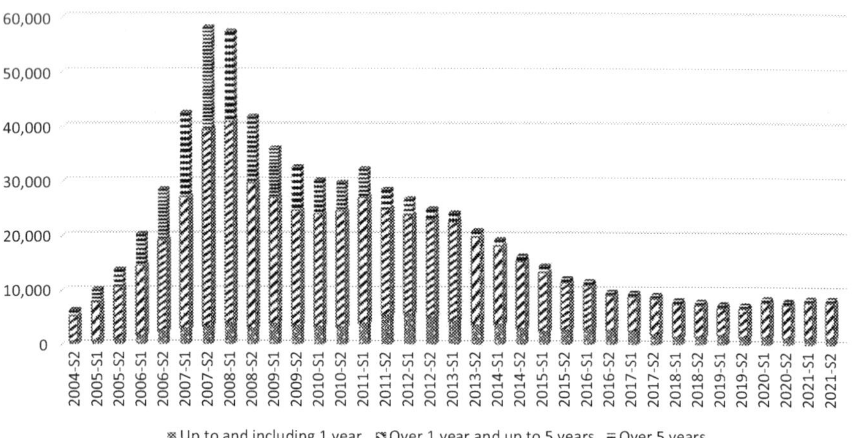

Exhibit 9.3. CDS Notional Outstanding by maturity, USD b. (all sectors, all countries).

Source: Constructed from BIS's OTC derivatives outstanding. https://www.bis.org/statistics/derstats.htm?m=2071.

is the rapid growth from 2004 with its peak in 2007 (over USD 60 USD trillion) before falling sharply. Although the ABS market in the US recovered quickly, the global CDS market continued to struggle, and by the second half of 2016, the global volume had returned to the 2005 level, at just under USD 10 trillion. Also, it is shown that the CDS market is dominated by the medium-term maturities of 1–5 years, accounting for over 70% throughout the period. In the second half of 2021, CDS with less than one year accounted for 14% of the total, while the shares of 1–5 years and five years were 78% and 8%, respectively.

9.3.3. *The US subprime crisis and the Global Financial Crisis*

The GFC 2007–2009 was the most severe financial and economic crisis since the great depression of 1929. It was sparked by the collapse of the bubble in the US housing market, which led to massive defaults on the CDOs created on mortgage loans. Due to the widespread creation of CDOs by US investment banks and subsequent investments by the US and international investors located throughout Europe, once the underlying assets backing CDOs defaulted, the multiplier effects of CDO defaults resonated across many national boundaries. The spread of the crisis was quick, and the devastation it caused to the investors was unprecedented. So was the scale of rescue packages many governments desperately provided to avert national and international financial meltdown.

There were multiple factors that contributed to the US subprime crisis and, subsequently, the GFC. The record low-interest rates in the US following the 9/11 terrorist attack in 2001 resulted in easy credit conditions and a lending boom in the US, creating a housing sector boom fuelled by low mortgage loan rates. From an international investor's viewpoint, low interest rates on the US government securities made them unattractive despite their safe haven status. They began to seek alternative US dollar-denominated assets, which were largely met by Wall Street supplying them with higher yielding CDOs based on mortgage loans. However, neither the mortgage origination industry that provided mortgage loans to be packaged into CDOs nor the investment banking industry that created and sold CDOs to investors were subjected to any effective regulation. The unregulated mortgage industry was dominated by small- to medium-sized mortgage originators who often made 'liar' loans to subprime customers who borrowed beyond their ability to repay, and so the default was inevitable. The investment banks purchased mortgage loans and MBSs to create CDOs to sell to investors who assumed the risk of default and made their decisions mainly on the inflated ratings of the major credit rating agencies. This section highlights the events that led to the US subprime crisis and the government's responses.

9.3.3.1. *Mechanics of MBS and CDO*

In the US, to encourage home ownership by mortgage loans, government agencies were created to purchase and manage mortgage loans made by banks and S&Ls. By buying the loans from the mortgage originators and freeing them from the credit risk of those loans, lenders can make more loans with the proceeds of the loan sales, and the new loans can also be sold off to the agencies. The first such agency created was Fannie Mae (its formal name is Federal National Mortgage Association, FNMA) which was created in 1938 to provide stable funding for housing. Initially, it was only allowed to buy mortgages issued by another government agency, Federal Housing Administration (FHA), and the loans guaranteed by Veterans Administration (VA). Two years after being privatised in 1968, it was also allowed to buy conventional mortgages, such as mortgage loans made by commercial banks. During the deregulation era of the 1980s, it started to issue MBSs in the US and international capital markets to provide even more liquidity in the mortgage loan market. For decades following the start of the MBS business, Fannie Mae dominated this market. Fannie Mae concentrated on government agency-related mortgages and those issued by large banks, so mortgage loans made by smaller banks and S&Ls missed out due to their perceived higher risk associated with less efficient risk assessments. Freddie Mac (the formal name is Federal Home Loan Mortgage Corporation, FHLMC) was created to fill this gap in 1970, and it was privatised later in 1989. Both Fannie Mae and Freddie Mac (FM^2) operate in a similar manner. They buy mortgage loans from lenders and either hold the loan portfolios or package them as MBS and sell them to capital market investors. The bank lenders are then freed from the credit risk of the existing loans and can make more loans from the loan sale. The role FM^2 played was to transfer the credit risk of loan portfolios from banks to allow more loans and to increase the liquidity of the secondary market for mortgage loans. They supported the secondary mortgage market in order to stimulate the primary mortgage loans market.

Together they controlled the multi-trillion dollar MBS market in the US and dictated strict conditions on mortgage loans they bought. To sell their mortgage loans, bank lenders and other mortgage originators were required to apply these stringent lending standards to minimise loan defaults. They investigated the borrower's ability to repay via checking in the borrower (job security, current assets, character, credit history, history of tax returns, etc.). The credit risk analysis is labour and time-intensive and used to take up to 90 days per application. Anyone other than prime applicants, who can afford down payments on the loan and showed the capacity to repay, would be denied a loan. Therefore, the sub-prime loan market did not exist during the period when FM^2 were dominant in the industry. The MBS was popular with institutional investors because of the relatively high yields and low risk, and this was made possible by the sound lending decisions by the mortgage originators that kept loan defaults to a minimum and the buoyant housing sector since 2001, thanks to the low-interest rate environment. Also, the healthy and stable growth in the US housing sector helped the attractiveness of MBS to investors. The housing prices in the US traditionally had shown steady growth for many decades and were consistent with household income growth. In moderately rising housing markets, lenders face little risk as loan defaults can be handled by the foreclosure sales of affected properties that would bring in sufficient funds to cover the loan defaults. Investment banks also participated in the MBS market which went one step further and created Collateralised Debt Obligations (CDO), a collection of (senior) tranches of different MBSs. The share of Wall Street in the MBS market was minimal until late 2002.

9.3.3.2. *The housing market bubble and subprime mortgage*

In the wake of the dot-com bubble collapse in 2000 and the 9/11 terrorist attack in 2001, the US fell into a recession. To stimulate economic growth, the US Federal Reserve lowered the policy interest rates (Fed Funds target rate) in quick succession to 1% by 25 June, 2003, from 6.5% in January 2001, which was a level that had not been seen since the 1950s. Exhibit 9.4 shows the Federal funds' target interest for the period 2000–2022. To stimulate economic growth, the Fed chose to maintain an environment of lower interest rates for much longer than had historically been the case in prior recessions. It was not until 30 June 2004 that the Fed reversed the policy stance by raising the rate by 25 basis points.

This ultra-low-interest rate environment in the early 2000s led to three main outcomes that contributed to the subprime mortgage crisis later in

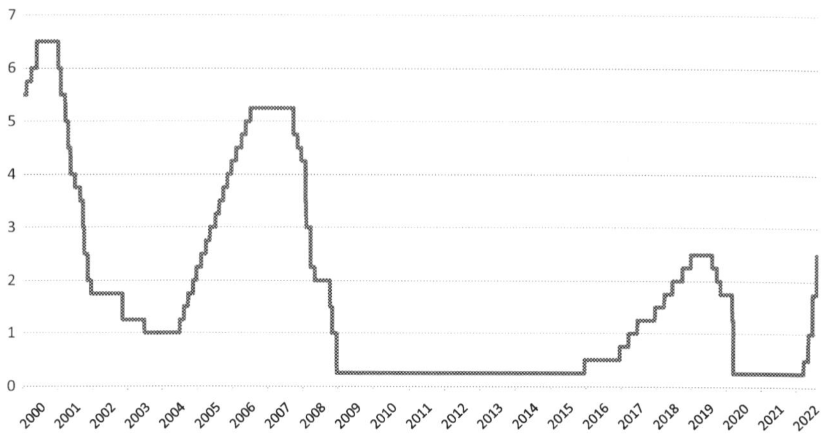

Exhibit 9.4. US Federal funds target rate 2000–2022.

Source: US Fed reserve, FRB of St Louis, https://fred.stlouisfed.org. Federal fund target rate until 15 December 2008, the upper range of Fed target afterwards.

the decade and subsequently led to the global financial crisis in 2007–2009. *First*, international investors who had traditionally invested in safe US Treasury securities found that the yields on these securities became too low for them even though the assets still fulfilled the safe haven asset role. These investors were typically pension funds, insurance companies, sovereign wealth funds, mutual funds, etc., that manage globally diversified assets with specific mandates in terms of the asset compositions in their portfolios. This led to surplus capital seeking safe investment alternatives with higher yields than the US government securities. *Second*, the low-interest rates allowed the banking sector to borrow cheaply and increase its total leverage. The cheap cost of funds for banks translated into a larger volume of loans to home buyers and property investors, leading to a surge in housing investment. *Third*, the increasing demand for higher-yielding but still perceived as safe assets on the one hand and the increasing mortgage loans to the booming housing sector on the other led to the growth of the US mortgage-backed CDOs to cater to those investors craving for higher-yielding USD-denominated securities.

Investments in the US housing sector were rising along with the stock market during the late 1990s, and property prices started to increase on a real, after-inflation basis. The cheap and seemingly abundant credit allowed an ever-increasing number of families to refinance their existing mortgages, expand their property asset portfolios, or enter the property market for the first time. Many families obtained their loans through mortgage brokers, who took a commission for connecting household borrowers with large lending institutions or through mortgage originators. In most cases, these lenders then on-sold these mortgages to FM^2 and, to a lesser extent, investment bankers on Wall Street, and also took a fee for doing so. In the absence of a significant yield on government securities, Wall Street realised that the market appetite for safe, higher-yielding investments could be filled with investments derived from mortgage payments and was drooling on the prospects of further MBS business. Historically, default rates on residential mortgages in the US were very low, so investments based on these mortgages were also deemed safe.

An MBS is an example of how FM^2 and investment bankers were able to structure these mortgages into an investment product. As discussed in the previous section on securitisation, FM^2 and investment banks act as arrangers in the process. They purchase a large number of mortgages from banks and other lenders of mortgage loans, pool them into a package, an MBS, and sell portions to investors via SPVs. By combining large numbers of mortgages together, the potential default of any one loan (or a small subset of loans) would have a minor impact on the value of the pool of mortgages. Investment banks could also take one additional step by combining a slice from each of many MBSs and then creating yet another packaged security, a CDO. CDOs are structured in tranches which are ranked based on their risk characteristics. The junior tranche is the riskiest but offers the highest return rate. In the event of a sufficient number of defaults in the mortgages that back the CDO, the junior tranche no longer receives their income, whereas the more senior tranches are continued to be paid. The most senior tranche of a CDO is the safest but offers the lowest rate of return. In order to achieve a AAA rating for the senior tranche from the various rating agencies, the arranger would insure the senior tranche against some of the default risk in the underlying securities with CDSs. Furthermore, in the event of a default by a borrower, the original lender would foreclose on the loan, offer it up for auction, and recover its value. The senior tranches are then marketed to the same investors looking for a safe alternative to investing in the low-yielding US Treasury securities. Given the insurance protection, the low rate of historical defaults in the US, and a AAA rating, this marketing strategy proved very popular with these investors, and the demand for such investments grew rapidly. However, this increase in demand soon outstripped the supply of quality (or prime) mortgages that were available for purchase and subsequent pooling into MBSs and CDOs.

The role of the investment banks was relatively unimportant compared to the volume of MBSs generated by FM^2. However, during the period 2003–2004, both of these companies were involved in damaging accounting scandals that led to the departures of their top management, leaving them paralysed and largely withdrawn from the market. Their demise in the MBS market presented a golden opportunity for Wall Street investment banks. They took over the rein and started to dominate the MBS and CDO markets. New mortgage originators and brokers saw substantial unmet demands for mortgage loans from subprime borrowers. The new breed of mortgage originators did not wish to abide by the stringent lending guidelines set by FM^2 and found investment banks easy buyers of their mortgage loans. They started to aggressively target subprime borrowers, and the normal process of credit analysis was completely ignored in most cases. The so-called 'liar loans' were issued to borrowers who had no or insufficient income and bad credit scores. Borrowers were required only to state their income (stated income rather than verified income), and often mortgage lenders overstated the applicants' income on the paperwork without their knowledge. Loans were issued to people without a deposit, proof of income, or other documents normally required for a loan application to be accepted. Despite being of much lower quality and much higher default risk, these low-quality (or subprime) loans were still bought by Wall Street investment banks. The mortgage originators' lending activities were unregulated, so there were no measures in place to discourage unsafe subprime lending.

The investment banks structuring CDOs based on subprime loans knew that house prices in the US had historically risen and assumed this would continue. If some of the mortgage loans underlying CDOs default, the lending bank would foreclose on the loan and auction the property off to recover its value. It was believed that, due to the property market boom, the value recovered from the auctioned property could potentially exceed the value of the loan. This further reduced the risk of the process, which encouraged Wall Street to seek more mortgage assets to pool into CDOs, lenders to make more subprime loans, and mortgage brokers to find more subprime loan applicants. Each of these parties profited from the fees they took at different stages of the process. As the mortgage loans to subprime borrowers increased rapidly, so did the excess demand for houses, which resulted in a further sharp rise in house prices in the US. In Panel A of Exhibit 9.5, the median household income index and the US housing price index, both at 100 in 2000, are shown. Until 2000, both indexes rose at the same pace, suggesting that house prices rose along with the median income. However, since 2000, the gap between the two started to widen and peaked in 2006 before narrowing. This suggests that the housing

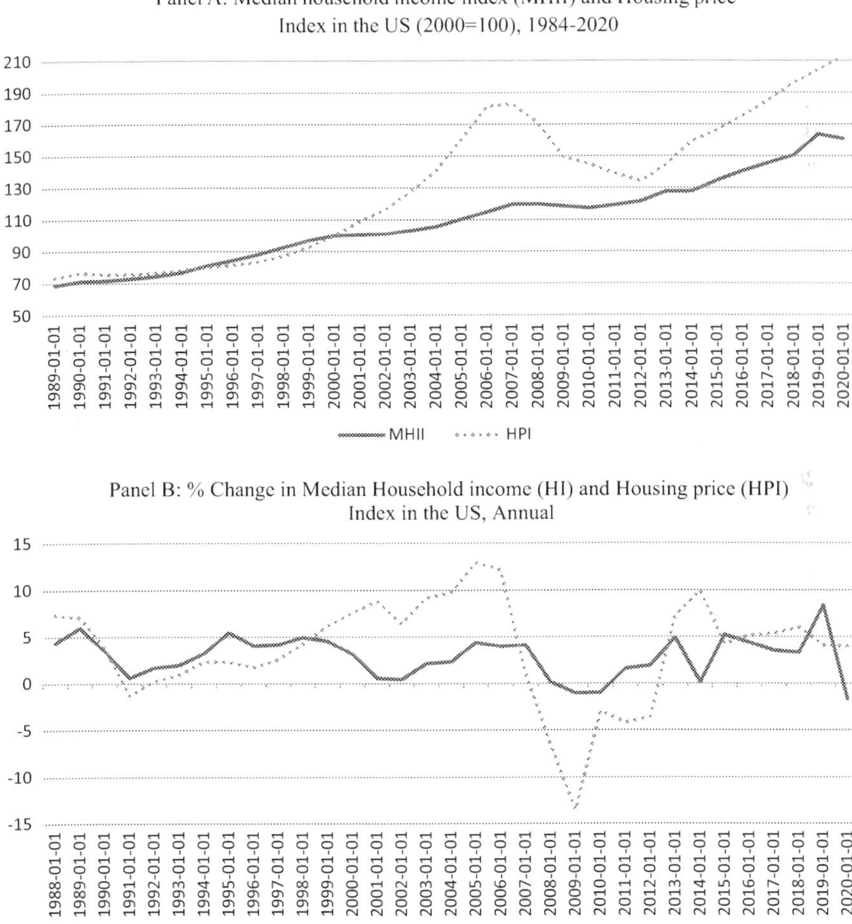

Exhibit 9.5. US household income and house price index.

Source: FRB of St Louis, https://fred.stlouisfed.org.

boom in the early 2000s was mainly caused by the easy availability of mortgage loans, not by rising household income. Panel B shows the annual growth rates of the housing price index and the median income.

This process was helped by credit rating agencies, who competitively lowered their standards for issuing their top ratings. Most of the CDOs issued by investment banks received the top rating despite being based on subprime mortgages, as long as they were senior tranches in the CDOs. However, senior tranche investors can also be wiped out if the majority of the loans backing the CDOs default in the environment of a housing market meltdown as events unfolded.

The prospect of continuously rising housing prices and Wall Street's appetite for mortgages, regardless of the underlying risks, led to homeowners' excessive use of home equity lines of credit. Mortgage borrowers regularly refinanced their loans, and increasing home equity due to rising house prices allowed them to withdraw funds against the value of their houses. Homeowners borrowed a total of USD 349 billion in 2006 against their home equity, effectively using their homes as an ATM to fund their consumption spending (Aladangady and O'Flaherty, 2020).

Exhibit 9.6 summarises the process leading to the creation of the housing sector bubble in the US, which eventually collapsed in 2008 during the GFC. The rapid and deep cuts to the policy interest rate to counteract the economic shocks in the early 2000s led to a period of rapid loan growth. Combined with the demise of the government agencies in the MBS market, the lack of regulation in the mortgage origination, CDO and CDS markets eventually led to predatory lending to subprime customers. This created the development of the housing sector bubble, as shown in the last step.

9.3.3.3. *The subprime mortgage crisis*

During the subprime mortgage boom, many families, who would not normally qualify for a mortgage loan, were granted generous housing loans. Moreover, the underwriting standards for subprime mortgages in the securitisation phase fell to a very low standard (Mishkin, 2013). Inevitably, some of the mortgage loan borrowers began to default on their mortgages and walked away from the properties, leaving their lenders to pick up the pieces. The lending banks foreclosed on the loans as intended and placed the properties up for auction. However, given the large number of properties appearing on the market simultaneously, the supply exceeded the

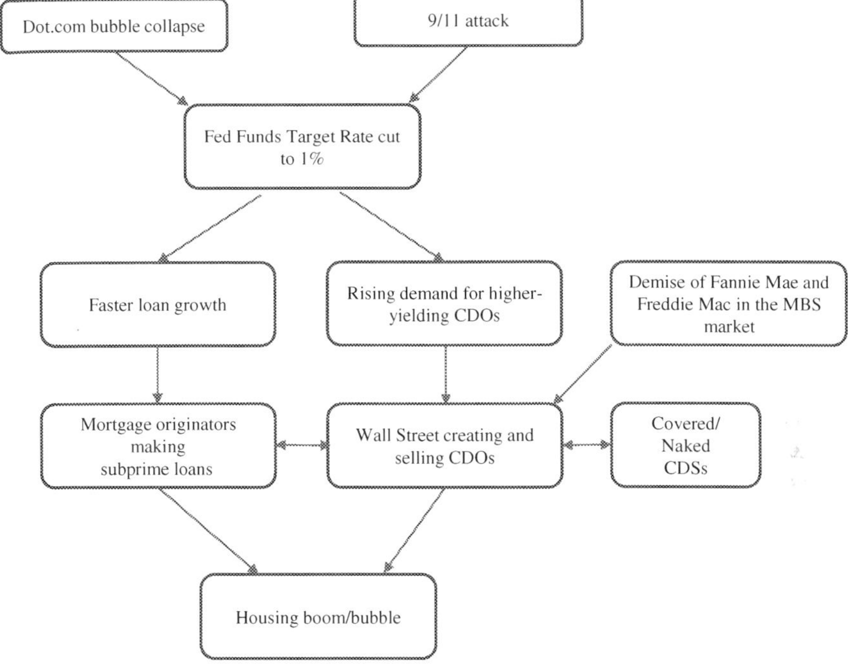

Exhibit 9.6. Process leading to the housing bubble in the US.

demand, and the market values of these properties consequently began to fall. There was a sufficient excess supply that the investment banks holding the CDOs based on these properties as collaterals were unable to recover the full value of the mortgages that backed them, which wiped out not only the junior tranches but, in some cases, eventually the senior tranche investors as well. As more subprime borrowers defaulted, the housing market slump grew, leading to even larger losses for the CDO investors, who are the ultimate bearer of credit risk.

Mortgage defaults spread from those who could not pay their mortgage payments to those who were financially capable of doing so. The borrowers of these mortgages may have taken out a mortgage of several hundred thousand USD in order to purchase their houses and properties. Although still able to meet repayments, the value of their property may have dropped below the balance of the loan they owe due to the collapsing housing market. Rather than continuing to pay down the loan, they had the incentive to default and walk away from the commitment. This further exacerbated the mortgage market's problems, helping to turn a slump into a crash and leading to massive write-downs on the value of the CDO investments by investors. Upon realising their past CDO purchases were souring, the investors stopped investing in CDOs and were looking to unload their portfolio of CDOs before it was too late. This left many investment banks with a pool of mortgages they could not sell to other investors. As noted earlier, some of the CDO creators highly leveraged themselves in order to purchase mortgages in the first instance. However, the increasing default rates and the decreasing property values led to a situation whereby it became questionable whether the banks still holding these CDOs would be able to make the payment on the loans they had taken out. Fear increased within the financial sector, and banks ceased lending to each other because their counterparty bank might default. As banks hoarded cash and ceased to lend to each other, lending to non-financial corporations also slowed. This, in turn, led to a credit crunch and eventually the Global Financial Crisis when the US subprime crisis spread to other financial systems via the international CDO investment connection.

Another contributor to the crisis is the accounting requirement of marking to market assets. This required necessary adjustments of asset values to reflect current market values. Banks holding CDOs as investments were forced to reduce the value of their CDO holdings on their balance sheets as the market values of houses that formed the asset packages collapsed. This led to a sharp reduction in the capital adequacy ratios of many banks, putting them at risk of insolvency.

As noted previously, the senior tranche of a mortgage-backed CDO was usually insured to some extent against default through CDS. Although acting as a credit risk protection for the holder of the mortgage security, a CDS also allows speculative positions to be taken on the credit market, which further facilitated the spread of the subprime mortgage crisis. The writer of a CDS essentially bets that there will be no default and that they will continue to receive their regular premium income from the holder of the CDS. For a given mortgage with a face value of USD 200,000, there is no limit to the potential amount of insurance that has been written covering this contract in the presence of naked CDS. This permits bets to be placed on the mortgage market that are many times in excess of the value of the underlying securities. Firms that wrote many such contracts, such as American International Group (AIG) and Lehman Brothers, did so in the belief that the premiums received from the contracts written across a broad range of underlying mortgage securities would be sufficient to cover the required payouts in the event that some number of those securities defaulted. However, as default rates climbed systematically across the entire US housing market, the premiums became inadequate to cover the payouts. From September to December 2008, AIG's collateral postings against counterparties amounted to USD 22.4 billion, which it could not honour.[5] Among other failures, this led to the bankruptcy of Lehman Brothers and the government takeover of AIG, which further exacerbated the lack of confidence within the financial markets and threatened a system collapse. AIG, the largest insurance company in the US, wrote a substantial portion of the CDS on the US subprime mortgage-based CDOs and was taken over by the US federal government in September 2008 with a USD 85 billion rescue package which resulted in the government owning 79.9% of the company. This effectively prevented the negative spillover effects on the general US economy upon the collapse of the AIG. On the other side of the equation, some hedge funds directly benefited from the housing market's collapse by investing heavily in CDSs on CDOs. They were able to collect the difference between the market values and the full face values of the underlying mortgages as a cash settlement.

Exhibit 9.7 shows the process of the US subprime crisis that emanated from the housing market bubble that had its origin in the aggressive interest cuts in the early 2000s.

9.3.3.4. *Lessons to be learned*

The most important failure point of the system in the run-up to the subprime crisis was the lack of understanding of the underlying risk of the financial engineering products, CDOs and CDSs. Even the former chairman of the US Federal Reserve, Alan Greenspan, admitted that he did not have a full understanding of the risks involved in a CDO.

In addition, the two most important players in the process were unregulated. The Wall Street investment banks, which effectively replaced FM^2 in 2004 as the buyer of most mortgages, did not enforce the same level of stringent requirement on the mortgages they bought because they were able to transfer the risk of defaults to investors of CDOs and there were unmet demands for the CDOs in domestic and international markets.

[5]https://www.reuters.com/article/financial-aig-cds-idUSN1546073920090315.

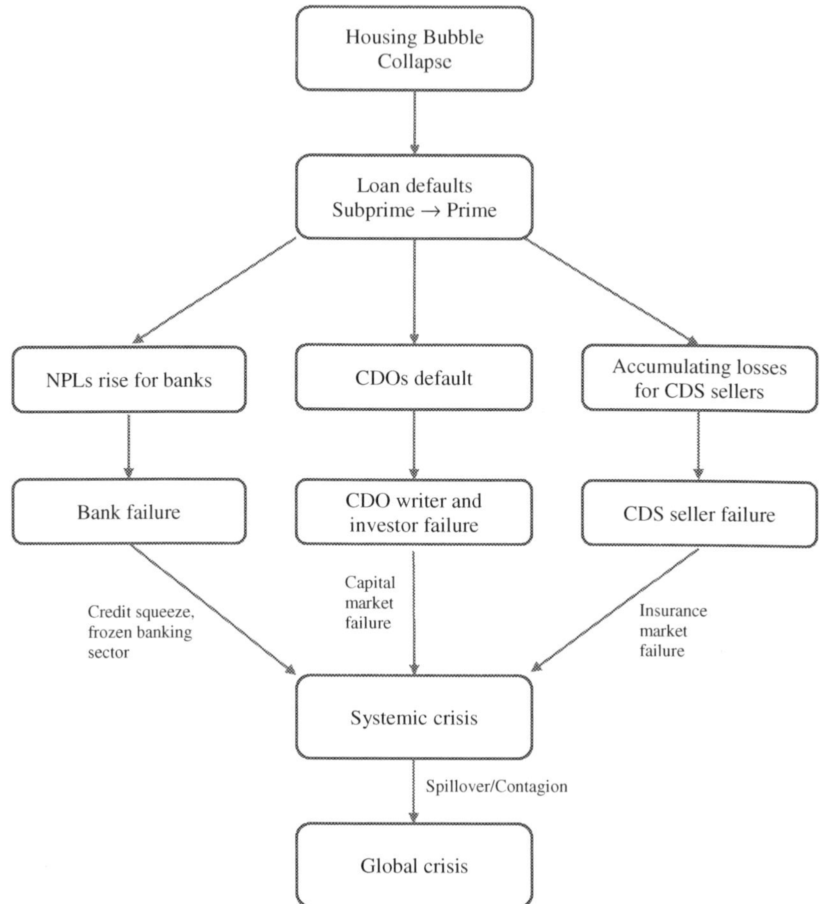

Exhibit 9.7. Process of the US subprime crisis.

Mortgage originators practised indiscriminate lending, and Wall Street investment banks purchased these mortgages to satisfy the need for more CDOs without due diligence. As long as CDOs were created and sold to investors, investment banks and mortgage originators enjoyed the fee income, and the credit risks were entirely borne by the CDO investors. The CDS market was also unregulated. A CDS is essentially an insurance product. However, instead of the usual 30% asset backing required for the contingent event, CDS sellers set aside only 3–5% so that the sellers can issue more CDSs, given current cash reserves.

During boom periods of low-interest rates, easy credit availability, booming economic conditions and financial markets, it is difficult to distinguish the good risk from the bad. However, the toxic combination of the increasingly complex nature of the MBS and CDO markets, the increasing demand for such products and the unregulated nature of the markets involved, including the mortgage origination market, led to excessive risk-taking by all participants involved. However, all of these excessive and aggressive mortgage lending to subprime borrowers and thus the creation of the housing bubble could have been avoided had there been strong and explicit regulation on mortgage lending. Introduction and enforcement of the ability to pay principle, which requires a careful credit risk analysis instead of relying on applicants' stated income, would have prevented the creation of the bubble in the first place. This highlights the need for an effective regulation that controls uncontrollable human greed.

9.3.3.5. *Government responses*

The US government attempted to avert a system-wide collapse by adopting conventional and unconventional monetary policy measures. It provided rescue packages to the failing institutions considered to be systematically important and to all commercial banks. It also orchestrated the consolidation of the investment banking industry by forcing M&As between commercial and investment banks.

One of the first responses of the US Federal Reserve (US Fed) was to immediately switch to expansionary monetary policy as they had done previously in response to major crisis events. On 18 September 2017, the target policy rate was cut by 50 basis points to 4.75%, which was soon followed by successive cuts to reach a historic low of 0.25% by 16 December 2008. Such rapid and aggressive rate cuts, from 5.25% to 0.25% just over a 12-month period, are indicative of the desperation shown by the US Fed to avert what could potentially be a much more severe financial crisis than the Great Depression of 1929. The unprecedented low-interest rate environment continued until 16 December 2015, when the pattern of 25 basis point interest rate hikes started (Exhibit 9.4).

Cutting the policy rate to stimulate lending in the banking sector usually works as intended. However, despite the historically low policy rates, financial intermediation is unlikely to occur at any interest rate without addressing the low or even non-existent risk appetite in the credit market and the information asymmetry at its highest. As witnessed in the post-banking crisis period in Japan, cutting the policy interest rate to zero and holding it at that level for some periods failed to encourage credit growth. During the peak of the GFC, multiple cuts in policy interest rates failed to stimulate economic activities in the major economies as banks, as a conduit of monetary policy transmission mechanism, refrained from extending loans due to extreme levels of risk. Also, business investment levels failed to respond to the interest rate cuts due partly to the lack of supply of loanable funds (i.e., banks were not lending) and partly to a lack of risk appetite.

As an alternative, the US Fed, among other central banks (e.g., ECB, BOE in addition to the BOJ), initiated the process of purchasing long-term government bonds and other financial assets from banks and other financial institutions, thereby directly increasing the money base in the economy. The aim of this policy, known as Quantitative Easing (QE), was two-fold. *First*, by absorbing the US securities and even non-performing MBSs from liquidity-strapped banks, their balance sheets would improve to the point where they could start lending again. *Second*, the excess demand created in the long-term capital market from QE will lower medium to long-term interest rates, potentially tempting corporations to make investments. In the US, QE started in December 2008, and the US Fed supplied liquidity to the economy by purchasing financial assets (MBS, Treasury securities, and other debts) from banks and government agencies (especially Fannie Mae). As a result of the successive quantitative easing programs, the US money base increased from USD 1.26 trillion in November 2008 to USD 3.88 trillion in April 2014 (see Panel A in Exhibit 9.8) and then to 6.1 trillion by April 2022, a total of USD 4.7 trillion increase in the money base over the period. The unwinding of QE from April 2022 caused the money base to reverse course and fall.

There were three phases of quantitative easing in the US before COVID-19, namely QE1, QE2, and QE3.[6] The *first* phase, QE1, was from December 2008 to March 2010. In March 2009, the Fed purchased agency debt from Freddie Mac, Fannie Mae (USD 175 billion), and Ginnie Mae (USD 200 billion). In addition, it bought MBSs from banks (USD 1.25 trillion) and a further USD 300 billion in long-term Treasury securities. The *second* phase, QE2, was from November 2010 to June 2011. As the

[6]During the COVID-19 outbreak period, the US Fed re-activated its asset purchasing program of monthly purchases of USD 80 billion agency debt and USD 40 billion MBSs. This can be referred to as QE4.

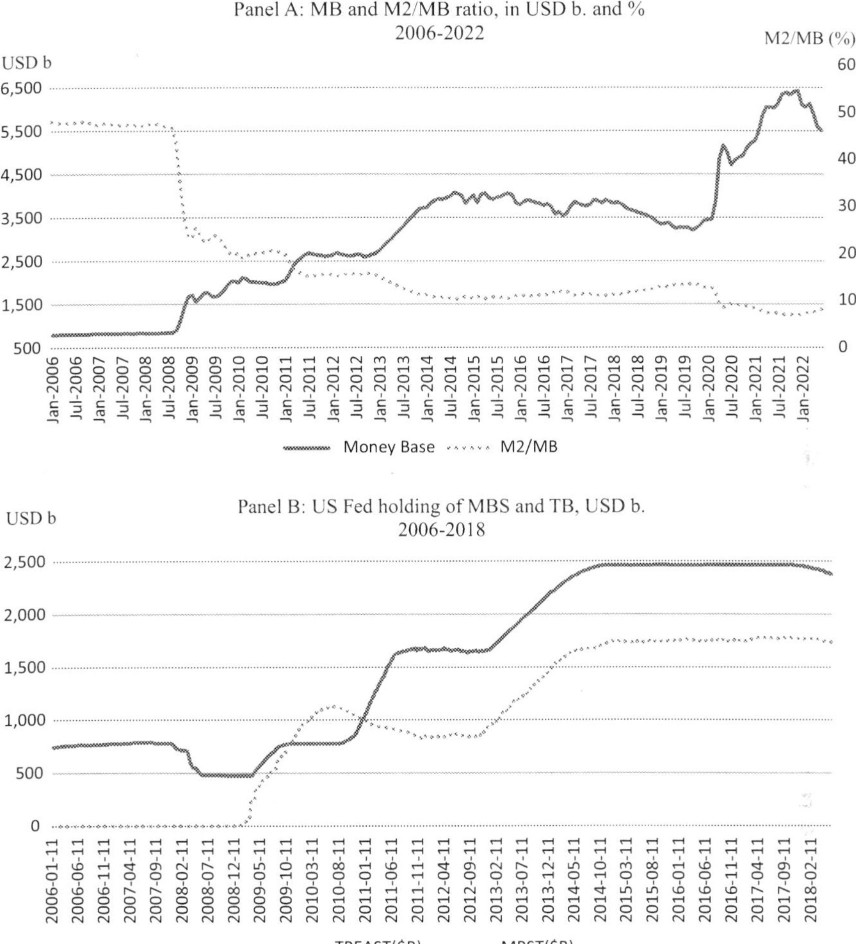

Exhibit 9.8. The impacts of US Fed's QE on monetary aggregates and Fed asset holdings.

Source: FRB of St Louis.

output and employment targets were not fully met, the asset-buying program continued. In November 2010, the Fed announced that a further injection of USD 600 billion would be made to buy Treasury securities by the end of June 2011, USD 75 billion per month for eight months until June 2011. The *final* phase, QE3, was between September 2012 and

October 2014. The third round of QE was announced on 13 September 2012 as a USD 40 billion per month program of bond purchasing, in addition to the Fed's commitment to maintaining a near-zero policy rate at least through to 2015. This monthly injection amount was increased to USD 85 billion on 12 December 2012.

Exhibit 9.8 shows the movements of US monetary aggregates and the US Fed's asset holdings during the three phases of quantitative easing. In Panel A, the movements of the money base (MB) and the ratio between M2 and the money base are shown. There has been a rapid increase in the money base from November 2008, before the first phase of QE started, to January 2015, when QE3 was concluded. The money base was increased by 4.4 times (USD 909 to 4,017 billion) over the three QE periods. However, the M2/MB ratio, which is representative of the extent of credit creation in the economy, has dropped from 27.56 to 10.38 over the same period suggesting that the increased monetary injection did not lead to desired levels of credit creation hoped for. Panel B shows the movements of the Fed's holdings of mortgage-backed securities and Treasury securities. As a direct result of the three phases of QE, the Fed's holding of US securities has increased from USD 476 billion in November 2008 to USD 2.5 trillion by January 2015. The Fed's holding of MBSs has gone from zero to USD 1.7 trillion over the same period. Traditionally, the Fed holds only government securities as a part of its open market operations. However, the start of QE1 in 2008 resulted in a rapid increase in the Fed's holding of MBSs purchased from financial institutions (both banks and non-banks). The Fed's MBS and US Treasury holdings peaked in January 2015 at USD 1.7 and 2.5 trillion, respectively, and have been maintained at those levels.

Exhibit 9.9 shows the US economic performance surrounding the crisis and how it responded to the three phases of QEs. The immediate target of QEs was to lower long-term interest rates via *the operation twist* to stimulate investments over long-term horizons. Panel A shows a negative time trend in the 10-year Treasury bill yield, which is a direct consequence of the Fed's rapid and sustained purchase of US treasuries. The share market also responded to QEs as the rapid liquidity injection removed the fear of impending market collapse. Panel B shows a dip in the DJIA from 2008 to 2009, but it quickly rebounded and returned to a pre-crisis level by 2012. As a result of the Fed purchasing both private (MBS) and government securities from financial institutions (both banks and non-banks, e.g., pension funds), they needed to look for alternative long-term investment

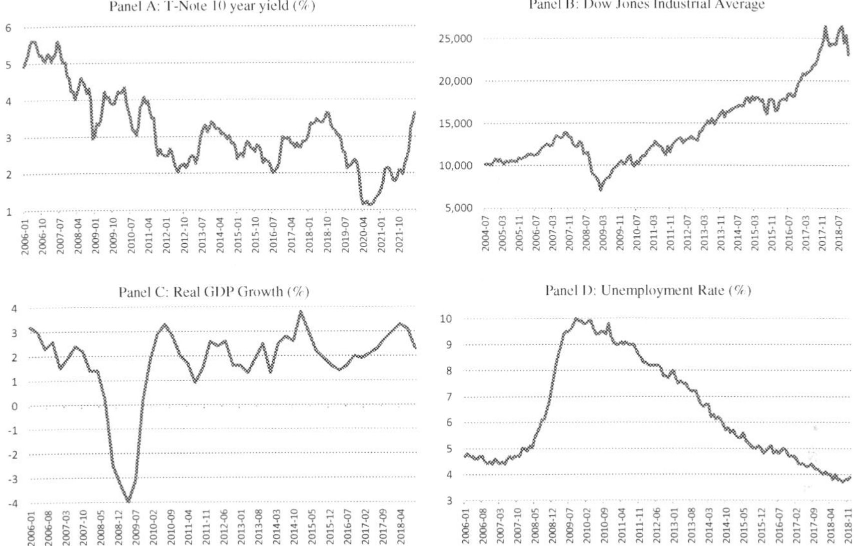

Exhibit 9.9. The impact of US Fed's QE on the financial market and economic indicators.

Source: FRB of St Louis.

vehicles in the environment of low long-term interest rates. This led to the increased demand for higher yield securities, including equities leading to steady improvements in the US share market.

The impact on the economic indicators has also been positive. The real GDP growth rate quickly rebounded by early 2010 to the pre-crisis level of around 3% after hitting the lowest point of –4% in the first quarter of 2009 (Panel C). The growth rate has fluctuated around 2% since then, representing one of the best economic performances in the advanced countries following the GFC. The unemployment rate peaked at 10% in October 2009 and steadily declined to reach 4.1% by February 2018 (Panel D). The housing price index (S&P/Case-Shiller U.S. National Home Price Index) reached its lowest point of 134 since the outbreak of the GFC in February 2012 and started to recover to reach 196 by December 2017, which is higher than the pre-GFC peak of 185 reached in July 2006 (Panel A, Exhibit 9.5).

Both financial and economic indicators suggest that the US economy has benefited from the series of quantitative easing measures. Equally, however, there are some concerns that the recovery was based on shaky grounds. *First*, it appears that most of the recovery in the financial markets was due mostly to searching-for-yield type of investments. Although the performance measures of US banks significantly improved and loans extended rose, the amount of credit creation as measured by the changes in the M2/MB ratio was more than halved between 2007 and 2022. The ratio has fallen from 43.63 in September 2008 to 8.12 in June 2022 despite a six-fold increase in the money base. This indicates that the increased liquidity was largely directed to financial investments leading to asset price movements.

9.3.3.6. *Re-regulation and subsequent partial deregulation since the subprime crisis*

It is clear that regulators could not keep pace with the newly developing financial technologies with potentially unquantifiable risks. There were growing calls for regulation on those that contributed to the subprime crisis, namely banks and mortgage originators, investment banks, CDS sellers, and credit rating agencies. The outcome was the *Dodd–Frank Wall Street Reform and Consumer Protection Act of 2010* (known as the Dodd–Frank Act), which was the most significant piece of financial regulation in the US since the 1930s. The Dodd–Frank Act created 225 new rules across 11 agencies. It was enacted under the Obama Administration in 2010, named after Senator Christopher J. Dodd and Representative Barney Frank, Dodd–Frank, who tabled the Bill.[7]

The part of the Act that addresses the banking sector and the financial system is the establishment of *the Financial Stability Oversight Council* (FSOC) chaired by the Treasury Secretary to oversee the entire industry, including systemically important financial institutions. It aims to identify and regulate systemic risk. Banks with assets of more than USD 50 billion were classified as too big to fail and would be regulated by the Fed, which involves higher reserve and capital requirements, in addition to the capital adequacy ratio. In addition, large banks must provide an orderly plan to

[7]The Dodd–Frank Wall Street Reform and Consumer Protection Act of 2010. https://www.cftc.gov/sites/default/files/idc/groups/public/@swaps/documents/file/hr4173_enrolledbill.pdf.

unwind their operations in case of financial insolvency to avoid a costly taxpayer-funded bailout.

Under the Volker rule that came into effect in April 2014, banks are not allowed to own, invest or sponsor hedge funds, private equity funds or operate any propriety trading for profit. This effectively reinstated a limited form of Glass–Stegall 1933, which was removed in 1999 by the Gramm–Leach–Bliley Act (GLBA). However, in March 2018, the Senate changes exempted banks with less than $10 billion in assets.

CDS and other potentially risky derivative products are now to be regulated by the SEC or the Commodity Futures Trading Commission (CFTC). A clearinghouse is required for swap transactions to reduce counterparty default risk and enhance market transparency. The Volker rule also includes a provision for regulating financial companies when they trade in derivatives. Its aim is to prevent too big to fail banks from taking a high level of risk that could have a negative impact on the whole system.

Credit Rating Agencies (CRA) have also failed in their duties to ensure ratings on securities that reflect their underlying default risks during the run-up to the subprime crisis. The overly complicated structure of higher-level CDOs (so-called CDO^2 and CDO^3 and so on that are based on CDOs) made it difficult to assess their risk characteristics and the distance between these assets and the mortgage loans they are ultimately based on. The Office of Credit Rating within the Securities and Exchange Commission (SEC)[8] was established to ensure that CRAs provide unbiased and reliable credit ratings on financial assets, derivatives, and business entities.

Mortgage originators operated without restraint since the demise of Fannie Mae and Freddie Mac in the early 2000s. They organised loans, for immediate sale to their investment bank partners, to even those borrowers who had no apparent means of repayment and hence default was an obvious outcome of the loans. They and their investment bank partners successfully shifted the credit risk, and so the cost of default, of the mortgage loans to the investors of CDOs. The Act aims to protect consumers from these predatory practices of mortgage originators. Consumer Financial Protection Bureau (CFPB) was created for this purpose. It is tasked with protecting consumers from predatory lending, such as those that contributed to the subprime crisis by unregulated mortgage brokers. It aims to prevent mortgage originators from exploiting their customers by

---

[8] https://www.sec.gov/page/ocr-section-landing.

steering them towards high-cost (both high interest and other hidden costs) mortgage alternatives that generate higher fee income for them. CFPB also aims to oversee other consumer finance products, such as credit and debit cards and payday loans.

Despite the underlying circumstances of the introduction of the Act, there were criticisms that eventually led to *The Economic Growth, Regulatory Relief, and Consumer Protection Act 2018*[9] being introduced that materially weakened the Act in two ways. It raised the threshold of banks becoming classified as *too big to fail* from USD 50 billion to 250 billion. Second, it eliminated small banks with less than USD 10 billion in assets from the Volker rule. Taken together, these changes rolled back some of the important safety measures introduced by the Dodd–Frank Act. One needs to be reminded that smaller banks can also cause system-wide instability if risky derivative instruments, such as naked CDSs, are used without foresight. Reinhart and Rogoff (2009) wisely warn that short memories allow repeated crises.

On 10 March 2023, Silicon Valley Bank (SVB) collapsed, forcing the US government to hose down the fear of a 2018-style financial meltdown by temporarily raising the deposit protection limit of USD 250,000 to protect depositors with above threshold amounts. The main weak point of the SVB operation was its reliance on government bonds and other securities as their investments instead of loans. It had total assets of USD 209 billion as at 31 December 2022, which was invested into 73 billion in loans and 125 billion in investments, including Treasury bills and other securities.[10] The ratio of loans to total assets was only 35% which was far lower than the aggregate US commercial banking sector average of 52%, and the financial investment portfolio accounted for 60% of its assets (against the industry average of 24%).[11] SVB's concentration in financial securities made it vulnerable to the high-interest rate environment from 2022, leading to the fast depreciation of its assets. The inevitable bank runs led to the intervention by the US government. Two days after the collapse of SVB, Signature Bank collapsed on 12 March. As of 31 December 2022, it had USD110 billion in total assets.[12] Another major

---

[9]https://www.congress.gov/bill/115th-congress/senate-bill/2155.

[10]https://ir.svb.com/financials/annual-reports-and-proxies/default.aspx.

[11]https://www.federalreserve.gov/releases/h8/.

[12]https://www.federalreserve.gov/releases/lbr/current/.

bank collapsed shortly after that. On 1 May 2023, First Republic Bank, with total assets of USD 213 billion as at 31 December 2022, was compelled to sell out to JP Morgan for a mere USD 10.6 billion. Raising the TBTF threshold from USD 50 to 250 billion allowed these banks' vulnerability to go unnoticed until it was too late. The Federal Reserve admitted on 28 April 2023 that it failed to take proactive measures to prevent the SVB collapse (Smialek, 2023). Therefore, the potential negative consequence of raising the threshold voiced at the time of the introduction of the EGRRCP Act in 2018 became a reality.

References

Aladangady, A. and O'Flaherty, P. (2020). How Much Does Home Equity Extraction Matter for Spending? FEDS Notes, 1 May 2020, Board of Governors of the Federal Reserve System. https://www.federalreserve.gov/econres/notes/feds-notes/how-much-does-home-equity-extraction-matter-for-spending-20200501.html.

Claessens, S. and Kose, M. A. (2013). Financial Crises: Explanations, Types, and Implications, IMF Working Paper, WP/13/28. https://www.imf.org/en/Publications/WP/Issues/2016/12/31/Financial-Crises-Explanations-Types-and-Implications-40283.

De Grauwe, P. (2008). The Banking Crisis: Causes, Consequences and Remedies. https://www.ceps.eu/ceps-publications/banking-crisis-causes-consequences-and-remedies/.

Drees, B. and Pazarbasioglu, C. (1998). The Nordic Banking Crisis: Pitfalls in Financial Liberalization, International Monetary Fund Occasional Papers, 20 April 1998.

Federal Deposit Insurance Corporation (FDIC, 1997). History of the Eighties: Lessons for the Future. Vol. 1, An Examination of the Banking Crises of the 1980s and Early 1990s. Washington, DC: FDIC. https://www.fdic.gov/bank/historical/history/vol1.html.

Fender, I. and Mitchel, J. (2009). The future of securitisation: How to align incentives? BIS Quarterly Review, September, pp. 27–58. http://www.bis.org/publ/qtrpdf/r_qt0909e.pdf.

Fitz-Gibbon, B. and Gizycki, M. (2001). A History of Last-Resort Lending and Other Support for Troubled Financial Institutions in Australia, Reserve Bank of Australia discussion paper, RDP 2001–07. https://www.rba.gov.au/publications/rdp/2001/pdf/rdp2001-07.pdf.

Honkapohja, S. (2009). The 1990's financial crises in Nordic countries, Bank of Finland Research Discussion Papers, No. 5/2009, ISBN 978-952-462-491-6,

Bank of Finland, Helsinki. https://nbn-resolving.de/urn:NBN:fi:bof-20140807103.

Jonung, L. (2009). Financial Crisis and Crisis Management in Sweden: Lessons for Today, Asian Development Bank Institute Working Paper Series, No. 165, November 2009. https://www.adb.org/sites/default/files/publication/156020/adbi-wp165.pdf.

Miline, A. and Wood, G. (2003). International banking crises, *Handbook of International Banking*, Mullineux, A. W. and Murinde, V. (eds.), Edward Elgar, UK.

Mishkin, F. (2019). *The Economics of Money, Banking and Financial Markets*. 12th ed., Pearson, Harlow, UK.

Nyberg, P. and Vihriälä, V. (1993). The Finnish Banking Crisis and its Handling, Bank of Finland Discussion Papers, No. 8/1993, ISBN 951-686-370-1, Bank of Finland, Helsinki. https://nbn-resolving.de/urn:NBN:fi:bof-201808011834.

Reinhart, C. and Rogoff, K. (2009). *This Time is Different: Eight Centuries of Financial Folly*. Princeton University Press, Princeton, NJ.

Sherman, M. (2009). A Short History of Financial Deregulation in the United States, Center for Economic and Policy Research, July 2009. https://www.cepr.net/documents/publications/dereg-timeline-2009-07.pdf.

Smialek, J. (2023). Fed slams its own oversight of silicon valley bank in post-mortem, *The New York Times*, 28 April 2023. https://www.nytimes.com/2023/04/28/business/economy/fed-silicon-valley-bank-failure-review.html.

Vale, B. (2004). The Norwegian Banking Crisis, in The Norwegian Banking Crisis, Thorvald G. Moe, Jon A. Solheim and Bent Vale (eds.), Norges banks Occasional papers, No. 33. https://www.norges-bank.no/contentassets/ed5dd397dce345338046a22c7e07f959/hele_heftet.pdf?v=03/09/2017122240&ft=.pdf.

Chapter 10

Country Risk Analysis

10.1. Introduction

International banks lend to national governments or sovereigns and corporate borrowers from various countries. The total cross-border claims of BIS reporting banks have grown exponentially over the last few decades, from USD 687 billion in 1977 to USD 35.8 trillion by 2022, an impressive growth by a factor of 57 (Panel A, Exhibit 1.1). The USD and the EUR together accounted for 77% of the currency denomination of the cross-border claims in Q1 2022. Exhibit 10.1 shows the cross-border claims of BIS reporting banks against public sector borrowers in major currencies from 2013 to 2022. The borrowers include national governments and sub-national and other government bodies, and the claims include all types of instruments, including loans, debt, and other instruments.

The aggregate claim as of Q1 2022 was USD 1.5 trillion (total claims against all borrowers was USD 35.8 trillion, Panel A, Exhibit 1.1), which grew from USD 646 billion in Q4 2013, a more than two-fold increase. Interestingly, the EUR dominates the cross-border lending to governments accounting for as much as 77% (USD 498 b) of the total in Q4 2013, while the USD debt's share was only 13% (USD 82 b.). This suggests that cross-border bank flows to governments within the Eurozone dominated the 2010s following the Eurozone debt crisis. Although the debt in the EUR was stable over the period, the USD-denominated instruments grew over the recent period, and the relative shares reflect this trend. The share of the EUR fell to 37%, and that of the USD debt rose to 49% by Q1 2022. The USD-denominated bank flows to governments rose from USD 82

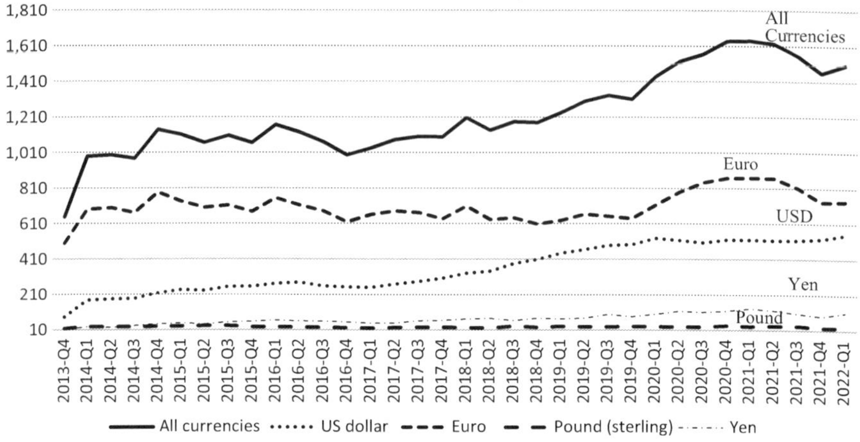

Exhibit 10.1. Cross-border claims of BIS reporting banks against general governments, USD b, Q4 2013–Q1 2022.

Source: BIS locational statistics, https://www.bis.org/statistics/bankstats.htm.

billion in Q4 2013 to USD 1.5 trillion in Q1 2022, an impressive growth by a factor of close to 7. However, there was a noticeable pause in the overall growth from Q2 2020, which coincided with the outbreak of the COVID-19 pandemic. This drop in bank claims against governments was mostly due to the EUR-denominated debt, as the USD claims were stable over the same period.

Unlike loans to corporate borrowers, loans to government borrowers, especially sovereign governments, entail a different level of risk as it is not possible to pursue a course of legal action against a defaulting sovereign. Although sovereigns have the option to default on their loans with no immediate consequences, several factors may discourage this course of action. To the extent that a sovereign's reputation matters in many aspects of international negotiations (government to government, NGOs, and multinational corporations), there is a clear incentive for the sovereign to work out its problems with its creditors to maintain some perception of its 'willingness' to repay. Moreover, a default will have longer-term consequences of locking the sovereign, other government borrowers it usually guarantees and possibly corporate borrowers from the country out of the international loan and capital markets. Flores (2016) reports that defaulting sovereigns were locked out of the global loan market for about 10 years, for the defaults occurred between 1926 and 1975. Sovereigns that cannot borrow from foreign lenders are unable to finance current account deficits and therefore forgo opportunities for economic development. This is especially distressing for developing countries relying heavily on foreign capital and technologies for economic development.

However, despite the potential negative consequences, there have been numerous episodes of sovereign defaults in recent history. Correa and Sapriza (2014) identify the following as contributing factors to a sovereign debt crisis. *First*, political factors or risks (e.g., corruption and government instability) can potentially undermine efficient resource allocation in the economy. *Second*, when the government's fiscal position is weakened due to an economic downturn, its ability to service its external debt obligation is negatively impacted. *Third*, terms of trade fluctuations can be a significant contributing factor. Some countries are over-reliant on a narrow range of natural resources (mineral and agricultural products) whose prices are determined in international markets and denominated in the USD. The fluctuating global demand and supply conditions have a direct impact on the ability of the governments of these countries to service their loan obligations. *Fourth*, a sovereign debt crisis is related to currency mismatches between the sovereign's debt denomination and the source of revenue. Local currency devaluations can put the government in a difficult position if the foreign currency repayment is financed by local currency revenues (i.e., tax revenues and other local currency-denominated income from the domestic economy).

There have been broadly two periods of major sovereign debt events involving multiple countries: the early 1980s and the 2010s. In both cases, lending booms preceded the crises. Spurs to the growth of international lending began in the early 1970s, immediately following the first oil price crisis in 1973 when the market price of crude oil jumped from USD 3 to 12 per barrel following political and military tensions in the Middle East. The approximate amount of current account surplus of OPEC member countries between 1974 and 1981 was around USD 450 billion, and more than 90% of this was accounted for by the Middle East and North African member states. The surplus countries deposited the 'petrodollars' to international banks operating in offshore locations as they lacked domestic capital markets capable of absorbing such a large influx of foreign currency funds. The deposited funds were then recycled mostly as loans to developing country borrowers as the market in advanced countries was soft due to the economic downturn caused by the oil price shock. Over time, continued inflows of petrodollars started to overwhelm the international banking market, and the need to match increasing inflows with demands for funds inevitably led to the relaxation of minimum lending standards, eventually leading to the deterioration of asset quality of many lending banks.

More recently, debt-ridden Eurozone periphery countries revealed their inability to service their external debt obligations. Specifically, Greece defaulted on its external debt in 2012, and many other countries faced repayment difficulties. These include Greece, Italy, Ireland, Portugal, and Spain. Rescue packages were quickly organised to address the affected sovereigns' liquidity and solvency problems. They were debt write-offs by German and French banks that owned the vast majority of assets issued by the governments (especially the Greek government) involved and rescue funds provided by a special purpose vehicle set up by the Eurozone governments (and the ECB) and the European Union. The involvement of the European Commission and the IMF completed the 'troika' of international organisations involved in resolving the crisis. The crisis spilled over to Cyprus in early 2013, and the Greek government was judged to be in default in 2012 after a 53% debt write-off by private lenders and defaulted on a USD 1.7 billion IMF loan repayment in June 2015.

10.2. Link between the Sovereign Debt Crisis and the Banking Crisis

Sovereigns facing difficulties repaying their international debt obligations are often portrayed as the only culprit who caused the crisis. In the recent crisis episodes, the borrowers who ran into difficulties suffered from macroeconomic and other policy mismanagement as evidenced by higher external indebtedness (measured as external debt per GDP), high inflation, low productivity, fiscal and current account deficits, etc. The resulting inability, but not necessarily unwillingness, to repay the debt put them closer to a potential default. However, the defaulting sovereigns would not have been in a difficult position if the lenders were unwilling to provide the credit in the first place. Those countries that the international banks largely ignored in the run-up to the Latin American debt crisis in the 1980s, such as Colombia, were relatively unaffected by the debt crisis that paralysed their neighbouring countries. More often, the lenders' willingness to make loans irrespective of the underlying risk characteristics of the borrower due to supply side factors (the liquidity glut in the 1970s, excessive expansions in the corporate sectors in the US and other advanced economies in the 1980s, the emergence of 'new economies' industries, i.e., dot-com bubble in the 1990s, and increased lending to the countries in the Eurozone peripheries) also play a vital role in developing sovereign debt crisis episodes.

Furthermore, there is a significant link between the sovereign debt crisis and the banking crisis. A banking crisis can cause sovereign debt concerns, and in turn, a sovereign debt crisis can negatively impact the banking sector in the economy (Correa and Sapriza, 2014, and Reinhart and Rogoff, 2011). *First*, a banking crisis could deteriorate the sovereign's fiscal position enough to cause concern for its ability to service its external debt obligations. This is because the sovereign provides a safety net for the banking sector via a lender-of-last-resort facility, especially for the too big to fail (TBTF) banks in the system. Also, the weakened banking sector will be unable to provide credit to the economy and especially small- to medium-sized firms with no alternative access to credit will suffer. The resulting downturn, if not a total collapse, in economic activities will undermine the sovereign's fiscal position via lower tax revenue when it is needed the most. Also, raising the necessary funds via issuing public debt will be costly as investors are wary of the sovereign's deteriorating fiscal position.

Second, a deteriorating sovereign's fiscal position can impair its banking sector's ability to provide financial intermediation. Banks hold government securities, mostly short-term, for liquidity management purposes, and the value of these securities will fall when the sovereign is in financial distress. In addition, distressed sovereigns are likely to get their credit ratings downgraded. When this occurs, their local banks at the same rating level as their government will also receive a credit rating downgrade since sovereign ratings provide a country ceiling. IMF (2022) reports that emerging market banks' holding of domestic sovereign debt surged during the COVID-19 pandemic period. They held, on average, as much as 20% of assets in domestic sovereign debt and 200% of their regulatory capital. This poses significant challenges as the transmission of risks between the government and the banks can lead to a banking crisis spilling over to a sovereign crisis and vice versa.

Third, financially distressed sovereigns are unlikely to be able to provide the safety net necessary for weaker banks in the economy. As a result, the distressed banking sector is unlikely to receive help from its government, potentially leading to a full-blown banking crisis due to the absence of a government bailout.

10.3. Risks Faced by International Lenders

Cross-border banking is exposed to additional risks that domestic banking is not directly exposed to. In addition to the borrower's credit risk, systemic risk emanating from the country where the borrower is located poses additional challenges for international lenders. Even if the borrower's capacity and willingness to repay are intact, their government could impose limitations or even an outright ban on capital outflows preventing repayment. Also, the deteriorating economic environment of the borrower's country could adversely impact the borrower's profitability, worsening its ability to service the loan. Collectively, *country risk* is the term that refers to these additional risks international lenders face due to systemic risk, which includes transfer, political, and sovereign risks. In addition, currency risk and global systemic risk can also pose challenges.

10.3.1. *Credit risk*

Credit risk refers to the possibility of the inability or unwillingness of the borrower to service the loan. It is an unsystematic risk for the lender. As such, it is possible to reduce the credit risk to individual borrowers by successfully diversifying the loan portfolio, including borrowers with opposite characteristics from as wide geographical areas as possible. The consequences for the lender of loan defaults include the following: the accumulation of bad loans that limits the lending capacity of the bank, especially since the adoption of the successive Basel accords; the need for rescheduling interest and principal repayments that will put pressure on the profitability of the lender; the eventual inability/unwillingness of the borrowers will lead to the bankruptcy and liquidation procedures that will be costly; and the rising NPLs will attract unwanted attention from the regulator and the stock market with negative consequences. Thus, lending banks need to perform an effective credit risk analysis and monitor loan usage to reduce the default probabilities of their loan portfolios as much as possible.

However, individual borrower credit risk may be of less importance in international lending for two reasons. *First*, most international loans are to sovereign entities or are guaranteed by government bodies that do not have default risk in their currencies. *Second*, lenders can select corporate borrowers according to risk characteristics and concentrate on those with lower credit risk. The second point describes well the recent trend of international syndicated lending, whereby the bulk of the international lending goes to developed market borrowers whose credit risk characteristics are considered superior, although less profitable, from the lenders' standpoint. Exhibit 6.2 in Chapter 6 shows that advanced market borrowers dominate the international syndicated loan market. Borrowers from North America, Western Europe, and Japan accounted for as much as 86% (USD 4.6 trillion out of USD 5.4 trillion) of total international syndicated loan volume in 2021.

Credit risk is managed *first* by implementing an appropriate credit risk analysis to screen out the bad risk before granting the loan by the five C approaches: Capital, Capacity, Character, Conditions, and Collateral. The aim is to reduce the information gap as much as possible between the borrower and the lender regarding the borrower's credit quality to arrive at some objective measures (e.g., probability of default) that can aid in the decision-making process. *Second*, the lender must monitor the borrower's loan usage to minimise the moral hazard problem once the loan has been granted. The lender must ensure that the borrower uses the funds only for the approved projects and that the projects perform as planned. Ultimately, the lender charges interest rate spreads for the risk it takes. To the extent that it can reduce the default risk through efficient risk analysis and management, it can stay competitive in the international intermediation business. As most large-volume international loans are syndicated, credit risk assessments and loan usage monitoring are carried out mainly by the lead banks in the syndicate.

10.3.2. *Country risk*

Country risk refers to the possibility of the borrower's inability to service (hard currency-denominated) loans due to the economic or political circumstances of the borrower's country, which may be unrelated to the borrower's credit standing. For example, the government of a borrower may impose a binding capital control that effectively prevents hard currency payments to foreign creditors. Alternatively, political instability in the investment host country may prevent profit and principal repatriation. In addition, when national governments default on their external loans, international lenders face additional uncertainty because the usual legal recourse does not apply to sovereigns. Country risk refers to all of these risks international lenders face, and it is systematic (and systemic) for investments in the country in question in that, regardless of the fortunes of particular borrowers and their industries in that country, all foreign investments in that country are similarly affected. However, international banks that can access multiple countries can diversify individual countries' systematic risk by investing across countries with varying degrees of credit qualities and characteristics, thus turning systematic risk into unsystematic risk. This is one of the advantages of cross-border diversification of investment.

In general, the country risk may be managed *first* by avoiding borrowers from countries with high risk and concentrating on advanced country borrowers with good standing. This is problematic, however, as in most cases, international banks look to emerging market borrowers to increase profitability as the loans to mature market borrowers became increasingly competitive and advanced countries tend to follow similar business cycles. Thus, going back to the saturated market segments meant lower margins for the lenders. *Second*, international banks can continue to lend to emerging market borrowers through syndicated loans that help diversify default risks to some extent. *Third*, they could enforce exposure limits for each country (setting the upward limit on the maximum loan amount). Usually, credit risk rating agencies would be useful in this regard. *Fourth*, lenders can discourage incentives to default by raising the severity of default consequences and making the borrower aware of the possibility of being cut off from future credits if a default occurs.

10.3.2.1. *Political risk*

International investors and lenders face political risk when sudden and unpredictable deterioration in the investment environment occurs in the host country. This could be in the form of higher levels of uncertainty due to regime changes, general strikes, natural disasters, military insurgencies, etc. FDI investors are likely to observe higher volatility in the value of their equity and other investments as a result. International lenders can face a higher incidence of NPLs as local borrowers struggle to generate sufficient cash flows to service their loans. For example, the Russian invasion of Ukraine on 4 February 2022 made the Russian operation of many multinational companies untenable due to strong consumer and investor resistance back home. Many Western companies have curtailed their activities in the Russian market or exited altogether due to the extreme political risk they faced. The notable exits include McDonald's fast food chain, Netflix streaming service, and H&M clothing, to list a few from the long list of companies impacted.[1]

Other deliberate policy changes aimed at foreigners include imposing restrictions on foreign capital investments, lifting the incentives that drew foreign investments into the country (such as tax incentives and subsidies), and introducing a foreign investment ceiling and taxes. The increasing geopolitical tensions from the late 2010s greatly impacted the ability of multinational companies operating in some locations. For example, the trade war between the US and China put Chinese companies' FDI in the US at risk. For example, on 15 May 2019, the US authorities banned Huawei equipment on the country's 5G mobile network and the company's participation in the US telecommunication network. In addition, US companies are banned from supplying software and hardware to the company. Being unable to use US technologies (e.g., Google's Android mobile operating system) in its products forced the company to retreat to its domestic market. There has also been increasing scrutiny of other Chinese companies in the US, raising political risk in their US operations. Political risk in a country can also be due to externally imposed restrictions. For example, the US imposed sanctions on Venezuela in 2019, citing its poor human rights record, links with the illicit drug trade, and government corruption, preventing US corporations from engaging with the country. Other countries on the US sanctions list are North Korea (since 1950), Cuba (since 1958), Iran (1979–1981 and since 1987), and Syria (since 1986). In addition, individuals, organisations, or companies within the banned countries can be targeted for specific bans. Any US companies or foreign companies operating in the US are forbidden to provide any support to the banned entities. Chapter 13 provides some examples of multinational banks penalised by the US government for violating such bans.

An extreme example of political risk faced by multinational companies in a foreign market is the potential nationalisation of their

[1]New York Times (2022) Companies Are Getting Out of Russia, Sometimes at a Cost, 5 July 2022. https://www.nytimes.com/article/russia-invasion-companies.html.

investments. Although this is a hostile measure that is likely to prevent future inward FDIs, and so should be reserved as a last resort despite potential short-term political gains for the political regime. Depending on the level of compensation the host government might offer, the loss to the foreign investor can vary from a total loss of the country's market to minor additional interferences on existing operations. Venezuela, under the Hugo Chavez government from 1998 to 2013, nationalised a string of companies and industries from 2007. Starting with the oil industry in 2007, companies in the cement, steel, rice processing, glass manufacturing, and retail industries were nationalised by 2010, citing national interest. The nationalisation drive adversely impacted the foreign companies that lost the profitable market, but an even bigger impact was felt by the economy of Venezuela, where the national GDP fell from USD 393 billion in 2010 to USD 316 billion in 2021, a mammoth 20% drop (World Development Indicators, World Bank).

10.3.2.2. *Transfer risk*

Transfer risk refers to the likelihood of the borrower being unable to service a hard currency-denominated loan due to an imposition of capital control prohibiting hard currency payments to foreigners. The lender may not face credit risk if the borrower shows the willingness and the capacity to service the loan. However, due to unforeseen events beyond its control, the borrower may not be able to repay the loan in hard currencies due to exchange controls or other capital mobility impediments imposed by the government of the borrower. Capital controls are typically used in countries that have yet to fully liberalise capital accounts to maintain control over capital inflows and outflows. The aim is to regulate capital movements in the absence of an efficient financial market mechanism that can absorb excess liquidity caused by inflows and supply liquidity when capital outflows occur (i.e., effective sterilisation mechanism).

During a financial crisis in a country where rapid capital outflows occur due to foreign investors losing confidence and withdrawing from the host country, the resulting liquidity drain will inevitably destabilise the domestic financial and economic systems. In the absence of an effective sterilisation mechanism to maintain stable domestic money supply levels, imposing capital control measures to introduce an orderly capital movement can be beneficial. For example, during the Asian Financial Crisis period, 1997–1999, Malaysia imposed strict control on capital outflows in

September 1998. Foreign investors were required to hold their proceeds from asset sales in Ringgit for 12 months, thereby preventing capital outflows from foreign investors repatriating their liquidated investments in Malaysia. In addition, they fixed the exchange rate to 3.8 Ringgits per USD to inject stability in the currency. The capital control stayed until September 1999. More recent examples include Iceland, which introduced capital control in 2008 during the GFC, which was later softened to a tax on capital outflows and lasted until 2017. In 2013, Cyprus imposed capital control during its banking crisis episodes, 2012–2013, and lasted until April 2015. Greece implemented capital control from 2015 to 2019 as a delayed measure to control capital flights in the aftermath of its debt crisis that began in 2009.

The borrower who cannot repay in hard currency due to capital controls may offer alternative forms of payments, such as in their domestic currency or in-kind payments with resources that the borrower can secure domestically. For example, in 2010, Indonesia agreed to pay 20% of the development cost of the Korean fighter jet KF-21, in return for one prototype, technical transfer, and local production in Indonesia. It has failed to honour its financial obligations since 2016 and subsequently offered to pay 30% of its commitment in palm oil.

Transfer risk is likely to be prominent in countries with the following characteristics: the insufficient holding of foreign currency reserves; lacking maturity in the financial system to handle abrupt international capital flows; being vulnerable to speculative attacks on their currencies due to economic mismanagement; having non-convertible currencies.

10.3.2.3. *Sovereign risk*

The lender faces sovereign risk when the borrower is a sovereign entity and default occurs, as in Mexico in 1982 and 1994 and Greece in 2012. Sovereigns are free from default risk in their national currencies as they have the constitutional power to raise domestic currency funds to retire domestic currency-denominated debt by monetisation (printing money) or increasing tax revenues. It is only when sovereigns and other government bodies raise funds in foreign currencies that a question of default becomes relevant, as they cannot generate foreign currency by these means. When a sovereign default occurs, the lending bank is unable to declare the sovereign borrower bankrupt and use legal remedies (e.g., seize the defaulting borrower's assets). What is essential for the lender in carrying out a risk analysis is not the borrowers' ability to repay as such but their willingness to repay. This is because political processes can be motivated by short-term gains (loan repudiation and moratorium) at the expense of longer-term costs to the country. However, the borrower may not have the incentive to repudiate the loan (as opposed to requests for rescheduling) since it is likely to be denied credit should attempts be made to access the international capital market again in the future. The Latin American countries that declared loan moratoriums in the early 1980s (e.g., Mexico, Argentina, and Brazil) were essentially denied additional loans throughout the 1980s, robbing them of growth opportunities as their economies were incapable of generating sufficient foreign currency income to finance current account deficits. This led to the 'missing decade' of growth for these defaulting countries, which suffered the longer-term consequence of loan defaults. More recently, some of the economically weaker countries in the Eurozone were exposed to sovereign default risk caused by sustained fiscal and current account imbalances and their inability to address the external imbalance by depreciating their currency.

10.3.2.4. *Currency risk*

Cross-border loans can be denominated in the lender's currency to avoid direct foreign exchange risk or currency risk. US banks lending to foreign borrowers in the USD can avoid the currency risk due to fluctuations in the exchange rate between the USD and the currency of the borrower. In this instance, the currency risk is entirely borne by the borrower, which may appear to benefit the lender. However, if the borrower faces unhedged currency mismatches in its operation, the continued depreciation of the borrower's currency results in a deterioration of its debt servicing and increasing default probabilities. This is because if the borrower invests the borrowed USD funds domestically, it will face difficulty replaying the loan when its currency depreciates against the USD. As the domestic currency income from the investment will be used to repay the USD loans, increasingly higher amounts of domestic currency income are required to service the USD loans if the domestic currency continues to depreciate. The resulting deterioration in profitability could potentially lead to the borrower defaulting on the loan. Thus, despite the lender not facing currency risk, it will face higher default risk if the borrower's currency is expected to depreciate sharply.

For example, during the 1990s, large Indonesian banks borrowed in the USD from the US and Japanese banks due to a lack of sufficient domestic funding sources. The Rupiah fell sharply during the Asian Financial Crisis period from 2,428 IDR/USD in June 1997 to 15,200 in June 1998. Within one year, Indonesian borrowers faced the Rupiah value of their USD borrowing rising by more than six times, forcing most of them into bankruptcy. Another example is the Korean banks that raised USD funds in the short-term money market in Hong Kong and Singapore to satisfy the insatiable expansion drives of their corporate customers, Chaebols. In this case, they faced both currency and maturity mismatches in their balance sheets as short-term USD borrowing funded longer-term Korean Won loans. The Korean Won lost its value rapidly from 986 KRW/USD in November 1997 to 1,665 in February 1998, resulting in a string of bankruptcies of the banks and finance companies exposed to the currency risk. Thus, there has to be an appropriate balance in the trade-off between the management of the currency risk and the default risks for the lender.

On the other hand, cross-border loans can be denominated in the borrower's currency, which is often the case for borrowers in the US and Eurozone countries. In this case, currency risk is entirely borne by the lender who faces a loss if the borrower's currency depreciates against the lender's currency. For example, if the foreign branch of a multinational bank is extending loans in the domestic currency of the host market funded by its headquarters (e.g., a Barclays' US branch makes loans to a local US borrower in the USD), currency risk exists from the foreign branch operation, similar to a cross-border loan denominated in the borrower's currency. Whereas if local USD deposits fund the same loan, no such currency risk exists. In general, only the large multinational corporations from major economies are likely to be able to borrow in their own currencies in the international market, e.g., the US, the UK, and Eurozone country borrowers. The USD and the EUR, in particular, are reserve currencies and held by central banks around the world as foreign currency reserves, so they generally hold their value against other currencies, so the currency risk is unlikely to matter when banks make loans to US and Eurozone borrowers in the borrowers' currencies.

10.4. Country Risk Management

International banks engaging in cross-border lending and other investment activities need to incorporate the country risk of the borrower in assessing overall risk. The first step in this process is to identify the types of country risk (as discussed above) faced as different aspects of the country risk require risk-specific responses. The second step is to quantify the risk faced, which involves the calculation of the probability of the risk becoming a reality (e.g., capital control-induced payment difficulties, sovereigns declaring loan moratorium, and adverse and rapid exchange rate movements). The last step is applying the necessary modifications to the pricing and other loan conditions. For example, banks that face country risk may choose to apply a risk premium to the borrower from high-risk countries, set country limits in loan amounts, or seek guarantees of payment from the government of the borrower. This section discusses two broad types of risk assessment methods: internal and outside models of country risk analysis.

10.4.1. *Internal risk evaluation models*

Bank lenders can rely on their own risk assessment procedures to quantify the country risk of their international borrowers. We consider two types of models: statistical and checklist approaches.

10.4.1.1. *Statistical models of country risk analysis*

The identification phase of the country risk management requires a quantitative assessment of the probability of an adverse event occurring that can compromise the ability of the borrower to service the loan. Banks have their methods of assessing the borrower's credit risk which can also be applied to assess the country risk of the borrower. Both quantitative and qualitative variables are considered as determinants.

Quantitative variables are those that indicate the country's ability to service its foreign currency-denominated external debt. Saunders *et al.* (2020) highlight the importance of the macroeconomic variables of a country in assessing its ability to manage its economies and achieve systemic stability. These include the country's debt service ratio, import ratio, investment ratio, volatility of export income, and domestic money supply stability.

A country's exports are a source of foreign currency income that can be used to repay external debt. Hence, a rising level of export earnings in the country is a positive sign for the debt-repaying capacity of the country and so reduces the probability of transfer risk due to capital control. Specifically, the country's export income is considered in relation to its external debt service obligations. The borrowing country's *debt service ratio (DSR)* is the ratio between the sum of interest and amortisation payments of its external debt divided by export income. The *DSR* measures the share of a debtor country's export income used to service the existing debt. A rise in this ratio indicates a deterioration of its debt-repaying capacity, hence a higher probability of rescheduling or default. Exhibit 10.2 shows the top 40 worst countries in terms of economic risk in 2019. The

Country Rank	(A) External debt Service to Export (%)		(B) Financing Imports from foreign reserves (months)		(C) Net non-Financial Investment to GDP (%)		(D) Share of raw agriculture export (%)		(E) Growth rate of broad money annual (%)	
1	Argentina	38.46	Ireland	0.13	Ukraine	0.14	Benin	57.37	Zimbabwe	249.84
2	Kenya	35.18	Cayman Islands	0.27	Belgium	0.22	Gambia, The	35.49	Turkey	27.24
3	Jamaica	32.83	Slovenia	0.28	Morocco	0.23	Uruguay	15.37	South Sudan	26.82
4	Pakistan	31.13	Luxembourg	0.34	West Bank & Gaza	0.26	Kenya	12.49	Guinea	23.46
5	Ethiopia	28.75	Cyprus	0.36	Canada	0.33	Togo	11.68	Chad	22.71
6	Sri Lanka	25.39	Malta	0.37	Israel	0.34	Latvia	11.68	Burundi	22.69
7	Ecuador	24.21	Netherlands	0.52	China	0.35	New Zealand	11.54	Ghana	21.35
8	Lebanon	24.08	Belgium	0.69	Brazil	0.37	Finland	7.15	Azerbaijan	19.97
9	El Salvador	22.67	Estonia	0.71	Tanzania	0.41	Chile	6.89	Cambodia	18.15
10	Angola	22.24	Slovak Republic	0.83	Guatemala	0.43	Congo, Rep.	5.77	Tajikistan	16.94
11	Montenegro	19.90	West Bank & Gaza	0.85	Argentina	0.54	Brazil	5.66	Georgia	16.66
12	Egypt, Arab Rep.	14.94	Greece	1.12	Germany	0.64	Indonesia	5.45	Uruguay	15.93
13	Brazil	14.69	Ecuador	1.21	Mexico	0.65	Mongolia	5.35	Uganda	15.88
14	Jordan	14.66	Djibouti	1.22	UAE	0.65	Eswatini	5.33	Niger	15.57
15	Tunisia	14.33	Panama	1.29	Moldova	0.68	Suriname	5.24	Myanmar	15.54
16	Colombia	14.26	South Sudan	1.37	Spain	0.76	Ecuador	4.95	Rwanda	15.31
17	Mauritania	13.87	Lithuania	1.43	Belarus	0.83	Bosnia&Herzegovina	4.86	Australia	14.60
18	Mozambique	13.41	Canada	1.46	Barbados	0.88	Colombia	4.53	Sierra Leone	14.39
19	Gambia, The	13.32	Lao PDR	1.54	Switzerland	0.89	Croatia	4.34	Guyana	14.38
20	Armenia	12.69	United States	1.55	Australia	0.98	Thailand	3.85	Uzbekistan	13.85
21	Serbia	12.18	Germany	1.55	Italy	0.98	Canada	3.73	Nepal	13.81
22	Zambia	11.54	Finland	1.58	Mauritius	1.00	Uzbekistan	3.27	Haiti	13.73
23	Sao Tome and Princi	11.45	Guyana	1.66	South Africa	1.11	Belarus	3.27	Seychelles	13.69
24	Maldives	11.02	Austria	1.72	Kazakhstan	1.13	Fiji	3.15	Vietnam	13.62
25	Dominican Republic	10.62	United Kingdom	1.72	Japan	1.15	Lithuania	2.98	Egypt, Arab Rep.	13.28
26	Indonesia	10.19	Spain	1.75	Georgia	1.16	Macao SAR, China	2.94	Kyrgyz Republic	12.83
27	Tanzania	9.78	Australia	1.84	United States	1.23	Netherlands	2.87	Kosovo	12.58
28	Cameroon	9.15	Iraq	1.86	Uruguay	1.23	Guatemala	2.86	Ukraine	12.58
29	Samoa	9.06	Maldives	1.96	Portugal	1.28	Denmark	2.56	Zambia	12.55
30	Ukraine	8.62	Eswatini	2.11	Vanuatu	1.34	Greece	2.49	Bhutan	12.43
31	Congo, Dem. Rep.	8.33	France	2.12	Ireland	1.34	Kyrgyz Republic	2.30	Belarus	12.25
32	Belarus	8.31	Latvia	2.35	Netherlands	1.38	Zimbabwe	2.29	Chile	12.17
33	Malawi	8.30	Belize	2.42	Colombia	1.42	Portugal	2.27	Mozambique	12.11
34	Mexico	8.29	Belarus	2.48	Finland	1.46	Madagascar	2.26	Bangladesh	11.95
35	Belize	8.24	Sweden	2.48	Bosnia&Herzegovina	1.48	United States	2.15	Pakistan	11.67
36	Costa Rica	8.03	Zambia	2.49	France	1.52	Russian Federation	2.15	Dominican Rep.	11.67
37	Tajikistan	7.98	Kosovo	2.53	Cyprus	1.63	Australia	2.13	Honduras	11.66
38	Bolivia	7.55	Hungary	2.54	United Kingdom	1.67	Vietnam	1.90	El Salvador	11.35
39	Albania	7.52	Portugal	2.55	Korea, Rep.	1.67	South Africa	1.88	Armenia	11.18
40	Honduras	7.51	Suriname	2.73	Austria	1.68	Costa Rica	1.87	Mauritania	9.95

Exhibit 10.2. Top 40 countries with economic risk, 2019.

Source: World Bank, World Development Indicators, 2021. https://datatopics.worldbank.org/world-development-indicators/.

country with the highest debt service ratio is Argentina, with 38.46 %, followed by Kenya, with 35.18 % (column A, Exhibit 10.2).

On the flip side, the import of a country is an outflow of foreign currency that potentially contributes to hard currency payment difficulties of the country. *The import ratio (IR)* is measured as the ratio between total imports and total foreign exchange reserves of the country. Alternatively, it can also be measured as the number of months the government's foreign exchange reserves can finance the current level of imports. Imports represent a drain on the foreign currency reserves of the importing country, and so the level of reserves held by the central bank is seen as a safety buffer for the financing of imports. The foreign trade partners of the importers often look to the importer's government should the importer default. Indeed, in the absence of credible financial guarantees by the importer's banks via a letter of credit issued by a reputable bank, the importer's government is often required to take over this role. This can be via a letter of credit provided by the government-owned export/import agencies or a direct standby guarantee. The *IR* thus measures an importing country's ability to finance its imports without external financing. Ireland has the lowest import reserve backing, with only 0.13 months' worth of foreign currency reserve, followed by the Cayman Islands, with 0.27 months (column B, Exhibit 10.2).

Domestic investment is an important component of a country's GDP. A measure of a borrower country's ability to generate sufficient levels of economic activities is the level of business sector investment. The higher the investment, the higher the potential for economic growth in general. *The investment ratio (InvR)* can be measured as the total business investment made in the economy divided by its GDP. This *InvR* shows the country's commitment to invest in its local economy for longer-term economic returns. This might entail a rise in short-term external indebtedness if the domestic saving level is insufficient to finance the investments, which would, in turn, lead to a higher probability of loan rescheduling. On the other hand, the longer-term economic prosperity that might result from investments in infrastructure, capital goods, etc. will lead to competitive import-competing industries and export competitiveness. Thus, a rise in this ratio might also be consistent with a fall in the probability of loan rescheduling or default. The country with the least amount of non-financial investment to GDP in 2019 was Ukraine, with 0.14% of GDP, followed by Belgium, with 0.22% (column C, Exhibit 10.2).

Export concentration and export revenue volatility can materially impact the repaying capacity of a borrowing country. Some of the developing countries have a very narrow focus on commodities (agricultural and raw mineral resources), leading to higher volatility of their export income due to worldwide economic swings. Higher volatility implies more uncertainty regarding short-term liquidity in the borrower country and its deteriorating capacity to repay on schedule. Export income vulnerability can be measured in several ways. For example, *the export concentration of the country (EC)* (e.g., the proportion of commodity exports to the total merchandise export) and *the volatility of export revenue (VER)*. The former measures the extent to which the total export income is concentrated in commodities. Commodities are denominated in the USD, and commodity exporters are generally price takers on the world market. In 2019, Benin, a country in West Africa, had 57% of its aggregate merchandise exports in agricultural raw materials. Cotton was the largest export, and the cotton industry accounted for 40% of its GDP (World Bank, World Development Indicators, 2021). The Gambia, another West African nation, shows the second highest ratio with 35%, and its reliance was on ground nuts (peanuts) which accounted for 7% of GDP in 2018 (column D, Exhibit 10.2). The second method measures the variability of export revenue over time. In general, a country whose export base is less diversified and is concentrated on commodities is vulnerable to worldwide economic swings, leading to higher volatilities in its export earnings. Thus, the higher the export concentration is in commodities, the higher the export income volatility, leading to a higher probability of loan rescheduling.

Economic stability is another key indicator. A range of macroeconomic indicators for a country can be examined to see if its economic system is stable. A common economic mismanagement by the government is monetising its deficits in place of raising tax revenues. This inevitably leads to high levels of inflation (even hyperinflation) and significant loss of currency value. Combined with a potential currency mismatch in its banking system, rapid currency depreciation will strain the repayment capacity of the borrowers in the country. An indicator of this exposure is *the money supply growth (MSG)*. Money growth exceeding the underlying economy will result in a higher inflation rate and a depreciating currency. The higher the money supply growth rate, the higher the probability of a default on hard-currency external debt. In 2019, Zimbabwe recorded a 250% growth rate in its annual broad money growth, and the second highest was 27% in Turkey (column E, Exhibit 10.2).

Unlike economic variables, as discussed above, some factors contributing to country risk are not directly observable. These factors are qualitative variables that reflect a country's political, social, and governmental risks. For example, a borrower country's corruption level is a negative factor in attracting international investments and loans. If the control on corruption is weak, the rule of law and regulation quality are compromised, resulting in an opaque environment for business operations that international lenders and investors find difficult to navigate. In many developing countries, business transactions may require unofficial expenses (i.e., bribes) to be executed, and the nature of legal protection in the case of counterparty default is not well defined, if at all. Moreover, frequent social unrests, labour disputes disrupting industrial production, etc. can add to the difficulty of country risk assessment.

One common approach is to quantify these qualitative variables by subjectively determining the scale of severity of each variable. For example, the level of corruption can be rated on a scale of 0–100, 0 being no corruption and 100 being the maximum level of corruption in the country. Similarly, an index of the strength of the legal and accounting environment can be constructed for each country on a scale of 0–100, using subjective judgement. Once these indexes are calculated, they can be used alongside the quantitative macroeconomic variables discussed above in a statistical model.

Exhibit 10.3 lists the best 20 and worst 20 countries rated by the World Bank's world governance indicators (WGI), which has the most comprehensive country coverage compared to similar indexes. Each country is rated in five categories: the control of corruption, government effectiveness, regulation quality, the rule of law, and voice and accountability. The top 20 countries that score highly in each component are all small-sized advanced countries in Western Europe (Finland, Denmark, and Luxemburg) and Asia Pacific (Australia, New Zealand, and Singapore), with well-defined and transparent legal and political systems. On the other hand, the bottom 20 countries in the table are not integrated with the world, such as North Korea and South Sudan.

Once both quantitative and qualitative variables are obtained and appropriately transformed, they can be used to explain and predict the likelihood of default in a model such as Equation (10.1):

$$P_{Default} = \alpha_c + \sum \beta_i \cdot X_i + \sum \beta_j \cdot Y_j + \varepsilon \tag{10.1}$$

where $P_{Default}$ is the probability of a default event, such as loan moratorium, rescheduling, and restructuring of loan terms, due to country risk, and its values range between zero and one. The X_is are the macroeconomic

Country Rank	Control of Corruption (percentile rank)		Government Effectiveness (percentile rank)		Regulatory Quality (percentile rank)		Rule of Law (percentile rank)		Voice and Accountability (percentile rank)		Composite Index (percentile rank)	
1	Denmark	100.00	Singapore	100.00	Singapore	100.00	Finland	100.00	Norway	100.00	Finland	99.42
2	Finland	99.52	Switzerland	99.52	New Zealand	99.52	Norway	99.52	Finland	99.52	Denmark	98.27
3	Singapore	99.04	Finland	99.04	Finland	99.04	New Zealand	99.04	New Zealand	99.03	Luxembourg	96.92
4	New Zealand	98.56	Norway	98.56	Luxembourg	98.56	Singapore	98.56	Switzerland	98.55	Netherlands	96.63
5	Sweden	98.08	Denmark	98.08	Australia	98.08	Denmark	98.08	Netherlands	98.07	Liechtenstein	94.41
6	Norway	97.60	Netherlands	97.60	Denmark	97.60	Switzerland	97.60	Denmark	97.58	Australia	94.22
7	Switzerland	97.12	Luxembourg	97.12	Hong Kong SAR	97.12	Austria	97.12	Sweden	97.10	Canada	93.84
8	Luxembourg	96.63	Andorra	96.63	Netherlands	96.63	Sweden	96.63	Luxembourg	96.62	Austria	93.84
9	Netherlands	96.15	Liechtenstein	96.15	Macao SAR	96.15	Iceland	96.15	Canada	96.14	Iceland	93.65
10	Liechtenstein	95.67	Sweden	95.67	Norway	95.67	Luxembourg	95.67	Austria	95.65	Germany	92.59
11	Germany	95.19	Hong Kong SAR	95.19	Sweden	95.19	Liechtenstein	95.19	Ireland	95.17	Ireland	91.92
12	Iceland	94.71	Austria	94.71	Liechtenstein	94.71	Netherlands	94.71	Iceland	94.69	Estonia	90.28
13	United Kingdom	94.23	Canada	94.23	Canada	94.23	Greenland	94.23	Germany	94.20	Andorra	90.18
14	Australia	93.75	Australia	93.75	Switzerland	93.75	Jersey	94.23	Uruguay	93.72	Japan	88.73
15	Hong Kong SAR	93.27	Japan	93.27	Germany	93.27	Andorra	93.27	Australia	93.24	Belgium	88.45
16	Bhutan	92.79	New Zealand	92.79	Estonia	92.79	Canada	92.79	Aruba	92.75	Greenland	87.11
17	Estonia	92.31	Taiwan, China	92.31	United Kingdom	92.31	Australia	92.31	French Guiana	92.75	Jersey	87.11
18	Canada	91.83	Bermuda	91.83	Ireland	91.83	Hong Kong SAR	91.83	Greenland	92.75	French Guiana	86.53
19	Ireland	91.35	Iceland	91.35	Iceland	91.35	Germany	91.35	Jersey	92.75	Aruba	85.95
20	Austria	90.87	Ireland	90.87	Austria	90.87	Japan	90.87	Belgium	90.82	France	85.46
190	Iraq	9.13	Marshall Islands	9.13	Algeria	9.13	Nicaragua	9.13	Bahrain	9.18	Haiti	11.66
191	Guinea-Bissau	8.65	Liberia	8.65	Iraq	8.65	Equatorial Guinea	8.65	Belarus	8.70	Zimbabwe	10.69
192	Haiti	8.17	Guinea-Bissau	8.17	Afghanistan	8.17	Guinea	8.17	Iran, Islamic Rep.	8.21	Iraq	10.40
193	Tajikistan	7.69	Congo, Rep.	7.69	Zimbabwe	7.69	Zimbabwe	7.69	Egypt, Arab Rep.	7.73	Congo, Rep.	9.24
194	Eritrea	7.21	Chad	7.21	Congo, Rep.	7.21	Chad	7.21	Venezuela, RB	7.25	Chad	8.38
195	Sudan	6.73	North Korea	6.73	Iran, Islamic Rep.	6.73	Burundi	6.73	Uzbekistan	6.76	Afghanistan	8.10
196	Congo, Rep.	6.25	Equatorial Guinea	6.25	Cuba	6.25	Guinea-Bissau	6.25	Burundi	6.28	Burundi	8.08
197	Chad	5.77	Sudan	5.77	Central African Rep.	5.77	Turkmenistan	5.77	Azerbaijan	5.80	Sudan	7.89
198	Afghanistan	5.29	Afghanistan	5.29	Congo, Dem. Rep.	5.29	Eritrea	5.29	Saudi Arabia	5.31	Central African Rep.	7.71
199	Burundi	4.81	Comoros	4.81	Equatorial Guinea	4.81	North Korea	4.81	China	4.83	Congo, Dem. Rep.	5.88
200	Turkmenistan	4.33	Eritrea	4.33	Sudan	4.33	Central African Rep.	4.33	Yemen, Rep.	4.35	Turkmenistan	5.19
201	Venezuela, RB	3.85	Central African Rep.	3.85	Yemen, Rep.	3.85	Iraq	3.85	Tajikistan	3.86	Equatorial Guinea	4.52
202	Congo, Dem. Rep.	3.37	Congo, Dem. Rep.	3.37	Syrian Arab Rep.	3.37	Yemen, Rep.	3.37	Lao PDR	3.38	Libya	3.76
203	Libya	2.88	Syrian Arab Rep.	2.88	Turkmenistan	2.88	Congo, Dem. Rep.	2.88	Somalia	2.90	Eritrea	3.56
204	Somalia	2.40	Venezuela, RB	2.40	Somalia	2.40	Afghanistan	2.40	South Sudan	2.42	Venezuela, RB	2.99
205	Yemen, Rep.	1.92	Libya	1.92	South Sudan	1.92	South Sudan	1.92	Equatorial Guinea	1.93	Yemen, Rep.	2.79
206	North Korea	1.44	Haiti	1.44	Venezuela, RB	1.44	Libya	1.44	Syrian Arab Rep.	1.45	North Korea	2.60
207	Equatorial Guinea	0.96	Somalia	0.96	Libya	0.96	Syrian Arab Rep.	0.96	Turkmenistan	0.97	Somalia	1.83
208	Syrian Arab Rep.	0.48	Yemen, Rep.	0.48	Eritrea	0.48	Somalia	0.48	Eritrea	0.48	Syrian Arab Rep.	1.83
209	South Sudan	0.00	South Sudan	0.00	North Korea	0.00	Venezuela, RB	0.00	North Korea	0.00	South Sudan	1.25

Exhibit 10.3. Top 20 and bottom 20 countries in World Bank world governance indicators in 2020, in percentile rank.

Source World Bank World Governance Indicators, https://info.worldbank.org/governance/wgi/.

variables that measure the country's economic health and debt service capabilities, as discussed above (DSR, IR, InvR, EC or VER, and MSG). The β_is are the coefficients for the macroeconomic variables and measure the relative contribution of each macroeconomic variable to the default probability. The Y_js are index variables of qualitative risk factors that reflect government, social, and political risks. The β_js are the coefficients for the index variables. The first step is to estimate (Equation (10.1)) using a suitable regression technique (such as a logistic regression model that can restrict the value of the dependent variable between zero and one) using historical data on actual observations of the variables identified above. The estimated coefficients β_is and β_js are then used to make a forecast of the default probability of a country, given the explanatory variables of the country, X_is and Y_is. The estimated default probability of the country is then compared against a threshold value for the lender. For example, if an international bank required at most 30% default event probabilities, it would reject loan requests from any borrower located in a country with an estimated default event probability of more than the threshold value.

Although this approach has been popular with international banks, there are practical and conceptual limitations that need to be weighed against the usefulness of this method. *First*, currently available macroeconomic information reflects economic conditions with lags, whereas future economic variables are needed to judge the probability of future defaults. This reduces the accuracy of the resulting analysis, especially when the economic variables considered are unstable and fluctuate widely over time. If so, the usefulness of using past observations to predict future conditions is reduced. This problem can partially be addressed by employing forecasts of the relevant economic variables, but this introduces the additional problem of bias and forecast errors. *Second*, deciding to put one country into either reschedule or non-reschedule groups can be arbitrary. That is, the choice of a benchmark probability can be subjective. *Third*, the qualitative variables approximated as index variables using subjective judgements are subject to bias.

10.4.1.2. *Internal risk evaluation models: A checklist approach*

An alternative approach to the statistical model of country risk analysis outlined above is a checklist approach that aims to calculate country risk weights rather than default probabilities. The first step is identifying a list of variables contributing to country risk. A similar list of macroeconomic and qualitative variables can be considered. For each variable, a weight is assigned in terms of its perceived importance, and the aggregate weight sums to 1 or 100. The second step is to determine an appropriate score for each of the variables and calculate an aggregate score for the country. For directly observable macroeconomic variables, a suitable transfer equation needs to be worked out. For example, if the weight given to the DSR is 10, then zero can be assigned for the DSR values greater than 100%, whereas ten is given to the values lower than 10%. For qualitative variables, subjective judgement is required to allocate suitable scores. For example, for the control of corruption variable, zero or close to zero is given for countries completely isolated from the world markets, and the government is not accountable to anyone, such as North Korea. Small-sized western countries such as Finland and Denmark could be assigned close to the full score on the other end of the spectrum. Once the aggregate mark of the risks is calculated for each country, the next step is to decide on the minimum acceptable aggregate mark for lending decisions. The last step is using the calculated aggregate score for each country to make decisions on lending to borrowers operating in the country by comparing it with a minimum threshold value of the country's weight. For a country with a higher country score above this threshold, loan requests can be granted to borrowers located in the country, and the appropriate risk premium to be applied will depend on how close the country's aggregate score is to the threshold value. So, a checklist approach can be used by international lenders to analyse existing loan portfolio quality, establish and adjust country loan limits, and price international loans.

Exhibit 10.4 shows a checklist approach using the variables identified in this section. For illustrative purposes, only the two types of variables identified above are used with equal weights. The aggregate country score is out of 100, and a sample of nine countries is included in the calculations: three countries in four different regions, Latin America, East Asia, Eastern/southern Europe, and Africa. The scores for individual variables are linearly transformed from the values listed in Exhibits 10.2 and 10.3. The country score ranges from 36.1 for Brazil to 86.2 for Singapore. If the threshold value is set at 70, then only borrowers in Singapore will be considered. If lowered to 60, Hungary, Poland, and South Africa will also be included in the allowed list but will attract a higher risk premium than the borrowers in Singapore. The country scores will need to be

	Weight	Brazil	Colombia	Mexico	Indonesia	Singapore	Vietnam	Greece	Hungary	Poland	Egypt	Kenya	South Africa
Macroeconomic variables													
External debt Service to Export	10	1.3	1.6	3.5	2.6	9.0	9.0	3.0	4.0	4.0	1.2	0.1	6.6
Financing Imports from foreign	10	3.0	3.0	6.8	3.2	8.9	5.2	1.2	3.9	7.8	10.0	9.1	9.7
Net non-Financial Investment to	10	0.7	3.4	1.3	5.3	5.2	6.0	9.3	9.7	5.7	6.9	4.0	2.3
Share of raw agriculture export	10	1.1	1.8	5.0	1.2	9.8	3.9	3.1	9.4	6.3	4.7	0.3	4.0
Growth rate of broad money	10	7.0	5.5	10.0	8.2	9.8	2.4	6.0	6.9	6.5	2.5	8.6	8.9
World governance indicators													
Control of Corruption	10	4.4	4.8	2.2	3.9	9.9	4.2	5.9	6.1	7.3	2.3	2.1	5.9
Government Effectiveness	10	3.7	5.5	4.6	6.5	10.0	6.2	6.9	7.2	6.6	3.2	3.9	6.3
Regulatory Quality	10	4.6	6.3	5.5	5.5	10.0	4.7	7.2	6.8	7.6	2.5	3.6	6.0
Rule of Law	10	4.8	3.4	2.7	4.2	9.9	4.9	6.3	6.8	6.9	4.0	3.1	5.0
Voice and Accountability	10	5.7	5.3	4.5	5.2	3.8	1.2	7.9	5.9	6.7	0.8	3.6	7.0
Total	**100**	**36.1**	**40.5**	**46.0**	**45.8**	**86.2**	**47.5**	**56.6**	**66.5**	**65.5**	**38.2**	**38.4**	**61.6**

Exhibit 10.4. Checklist approach to country risk analysis, 2019–2020.

Source: Calculated from World Banks' data on World Development Indicators for the year 2019 and World Governance Indicators for the year 2020.

regularly updated so that deteriorations or improvements in some of the variables are reflected in the country scores.

10.4.2. *Outside risk evaluation models*

Accurately assessing country risk requires access to country-specific information that may not be readily available. Smaller lenders lacking an extensive worldwide network of intelligence collection capabilities are unlikely to have access to key variables to assess country risk accurately. In addition, they may be unable to accurately extract the underlying risk characteristics from qualitative variables requiring subjective judgements. In such circumstances, an alternative is utilising the country risk assessments provided by outside parties specialising in the task. There are two broadly different types of country risk assessors. The first is the traditional credit rating agencies that provide ratings for sovereigns as well as individual corporations and their debt obligations. The second is companies that provide aggregate country risk scores using surveys and also their own assessments.

10.4.2.1. *Credit rating agencies*

Credit rating agencies provide a standardised assessment of the risk associated with sovereign lending. They provide market participants with a system of relative creditworthiness by incorporating all the elements of default risk into a single code — the credit rating. Credit ratings are intended to be forward-looking indications of the relative risk that a sovereign will be either unwilling or unable to make full and timely payments over the life of a loan. The three largest global rating agencies are Standard & Poors, Moody's, and Fitch. In addition, there are rating agencies that are specific to regions or countries, specialising in providing ratings to companies and governments in those locations. The US Securities and Exchanges Commission (SEC) recognises ten rating agencies in total as nationally recognised statistical rating organisations (NRSRO), including the big three agencies and other regional agencies.[2] The credit ratings provided for sovereigns are short- and long-term

[2]The other agencies in the list are A.M. Best Rating Services, Inc., DBRS, Inc., Demotech, Inc., Egan-Jones Ratings Co., HR Ratings de México, S.A. de C.V., Japan Credit Rating

obligations of sovereign borrowers in domestic and foreign currency denominations.

Standard & Poor's (https://www.spglobal.com/en/) provides ratings covering both foreign and local currency credit ratings for each country. Its rating scales vary from AAA (highest rating) to D (default grade). It adopts a similar approach to the checklist model outlined in the previous section, and its methodology is detailed in S&P (2017).[3] They consider five key areas of a country's credit risk. These are institutional, economic, external, fiscal and monetary assessments. Each assessment factor is rated on a scale of one to six, one being the strongest and six being the weakest. The next step is to combine the first two factors, institutional and economic, into an institutional and economic profile, and the rest are combined into a flexibility and performance profile. The rating for a country is determined by considering various combinations of these two profiles. For example, for the AAA grade, a county needs to have 2.7 or better (i.e., smaller) score for the first profile when the second is at 1. Alternatively, when the first profile score is 1, the score of the second profile needs to be 2 or better (less than 2). The AA+ and lower ratings are determined in a similar fashion as a combination of the scores of the two profiles.

Moody's (http://www.moodys.com) ratings range from Aaa (highest) to C (default).[4] Its method is very similar to that of S&P's in that it is based on a checklist approach. It considers 'factors' in four broad categories as follows: (1) economic strength, (2) institutions and governance strength, (3) fiscal strength, and (4) susceptibility to event risk. Within the four factors, there are a total of twenty-one subfactors covering quantitative and qualitative (such as World Bank's WGI) variables with varying weights attached to each subfactor. Each subfactor is allocated a score, and an aggregate score for each country is calculated that ranges between 0.5 (highest possible quality) and 20.5 (lowest possible quality). The top rating of Aaa is issued to countries with a score of less than 1.5, Aa2 between 1.5 and 2.5, Aa2 between 2.5 and 3.5 and Aa3 between 3.5 and 4.5, etc., until C with a score equal to 20.5.

Agency, Ltd., and Kroll Bond Rating Agency, Inc. https://www.sec.gov/ocr/ocr-current-nrsros.html.

[3]Standard & Poors (2017) Sovereign Rating Methodology, https://disclosure.spglobal.com/ratings/en/regulatory/article/-/view/sourceId/10221157.

[4]https://www.moodys.com/researchdocumentcontentpage.aspx?docid=PBC_1321715.

Fitch ratings (http://www.fitchratings.com) reports sovereign credit ratings across the same scale as S&P, ranging from AAA to D.[5] A major difference with the S&P methodology, however, is that Fitch uses statistical analyses incorporating both quantitative and qualitative variables. Eighteen variables across four 'analytical pillars' are considered. The four pillars are (1) structural features, (2) macroeconomic performance, policies, and prospects, (3) public finances, and (4) external finances. Its sovereign rating model (SRM) is then estimated via OLS regressions using the collected data for these eighteen variables over a twenty-year period. The estimated coefficients for each variable are then used in the model to estimate a credit score for each country. Finally, a 'notching adjustment' is applied to the score in the aggregate range of +/– 3 notches to account for subjective judgements on the output of the pillars considered inadequate.

Exhibit 10.5 displays the sovereign credit ratings of the three agencies in August 2022. The rating scales are comparable across the three agencies. There are (1) speculative grades: 10 ratings covering AAA to BBB- and Aaa to Baa3, (2) speculative grades: 9 grades ranging from BB+ to CCC– for S&P, 10 grades ranging from Ba1 to Ca for Moody's, and 10 grades from BB+ to CC for Fitch, and (3) default grades: RD, SD, and D for S&P and Fitch, and C for Moody's. The rating assessments largely overlap in each notch across the three agencies. However, there are some inconsistencies within each grade. For example, New Zealand is rated AA+ by S&P, Aaa by Moody's, and AA by Fitch. There are many countries with ratings that differ by one or two notches across the agencies. As long as the ratings stay within the investment grade range, there should be no significant differences in applicable risk premiums. However, Cyprus received the lowest investment grade from S&P (BBB–) and Fitch (BBB–), but the rating from Moody's is in the non-investment grade (Ba1). In this case, lenders would likely be conservative and apply a non-investment grade risk premium to borrowers from Cyprus.

In general, sovereign ratings place upper limits on the borrowers residing in those countries, affecting the ability of both private and sovereign borrowers to raise funds in the international market.[6] That is to say

---

[5] https://www.fitchratings.com/research/sovereigns/sovereign-rating-criteria-11-07-2022.

[6] An example of a sovereign ceiling-induced downgrade occurred when Moody's downgraded Japan's long-term foreign currency rating in November 1998, from Aaa to Aa1. Following this, all other triple-A-rated Japanese borrowers were also downgraded by one notch. Clearly, this creates a problem for companies located in countries with relative political or economic instability, but which otherwise have a strong corporate credit rating.

Standard & Poor's		Moody's		Fitch	
AAA	Australia, Canada, Denmark, Germany, Liechtenstein, Luxembourg, Netherlands, Norway, Singapore, Sweden, Switzerland	Aaa	Australia, Canada, Denmark, European Union, Germany, Luxembourg, Netherlands, New Zealand, Norway, Singapore, Sweden, Switzerland, United States	AAA	Australia, Denmark, European Union, Germany, Luxembourg, Netherlands, Norway, Singapore, Sweden, Switzerland, United States
AA+	Austria, Finland, Hong Kong, New Zealand, Taiwan, United States	Aa1	Austria, Finland	AA+	Austria, Canada, Finland
AA	Belgium, European Union, France, South Korea, United Arab Emirates, United Kingdom	Aa2	France, South Korea, United Arab Emirates	AA	France, Macau, New Zealand, Taiwan
AA-	Czech Republic, Estonia, Ireland, Israel, Qatar, Slovenia	Aa3	Belgium, Cayman Islands, Czech Republic, Hong Kong, Isle of Man, Macau, Qatar, Taiwan, United Kingdom	AA-	Belgium, Czech Republic, Estonia, Hong Kong, Ireland, Kuwait, Qatar, South Korea, United Arab Emirates, United Kingdom
A+	Bermuda, China, Japan, Kuwait, Latvia, Lithuania, Slovakia	A1	Chile, China, Estonia, Ireland, Israel, Japan, Kuwait, Saudi Arabia	A+	China, Israel, Malta
A	Chile, Iceland, Spain	A2	Bermuda, Iceland, Lithuania, Malta, Poland, Slovakia	A	Iceland, Japan, Lithuania, Saudi Arabia, Slovakia, Slovenia
A-	Malaysia, Malta, Poland, Saudi Arabia	A3	Botswana, Latvia, Malaysia, Slovenia	A-	Andorra, Chile, Latvia, Poland, Spain
BBB+	Cyprus, India, Kazakhstan, Montserrat, Romania, Trinidad and Tobago	Baa1	Bulgaria, Peru, Spain, Thailand	BBB+	Croatia, Malaysia, Thailand
BBB	Aruba, Bulgaria, Hungary, Indonesia, Italy, Mexico, Panama, Peru, Portugal, Uruguay	Baa2	Andorra, Colombia, Croatia, Hungary, Indonesia, Kazakhstan, Mexico, Panama, Philippines, Portugal, Uruguay	BBB	Bulgaria, Hungary, Indonesia, Italy, Kazakhstan, Peru, Philippines, Portugal
BBB-	Cyprus, India, Kazakhstan, Montserrat, Romania, Trinidad and Tobago	Baa3	India, Italy, Mauritius, Romania	BBB-	Cyprus, India, Mexico, Panama, Romania, Uruguay
BB+	Azerbaijan, Colombia, Greece, Morocco, Serbia, Vietnam	Ba1	Azerbaijan, Cyprus, Guatemala, Morocco, Paraguay	BB+	Azerbaijan, Colombia, Macedonia, Morocco, Paraguay, San Marino, Serbia
BB	Georgia, Paraguay	Ba2	Brazil, Georgia, Serbia, South Africa, Trinidad and Tobago	BB	Aruba, Georgia, Greece, Oman, Vietnam
BB-	Bangladesh, Brazil, Dominican Republic, Guatemala, Honduras, Ivory Coast, Macedonia, Oman, South Africa, Uzbekistan	Ba3	Armenia, Bahamas, Bangladesh, Dominican Republic, Greece, Ivory Coast, Oman, Senegal, Vietnam	BB-	Bangladesh, Brazil, Dominican Republic, Guatemala, Ivory Coast, Jordan, Namibia, South Africa, Uzbekistan
B+	Albania, Armenia, Bahamas, Bahrain, Benin, Bolivia, Fiji, Jamaica, Jordan, Rwanda, Senegal, Turkey	B1	Albania, Benin, Fiji, Honduras, Jordan, Montenegro, Namibia, Uzbekistan	B+	Armenia, Bahrain, Benin, Egypt, Jamaica, Kenya, Rwanda, Seychelles, Turkmenistan, Uganda
B	Bosnia and Herzegovina, Costa Rica, Egypt, Kenya, Mongolia, Montenegro, Togo, Uganda	B2	Bahrain, Bolivia, Cambodia, Cameroon, Costa Rica, Egypt, Jamaica, Kenya, Nigeria, Papua New Guinea, Rwanda, Tanzania, Uganda	B	Bolivia, Cameroon, Costa Rica, Lesotho, Mongolia, Nigeria, Turkey
B-	Angola, Barbados, Belize, Cameroon, Cape Verde, Congo, Ecuador, Iraq, Nicaragua, Nigeria, Papua New Guinea, Tajikistan	B3	Angola, Bosnia and Herzegovina, Kyrgyzstan, Moldova, Mongolia, Nicaragua, Niger, Pakistan, St Vincent and the Grenadines, Swaziland, Tajikistan, Togo, Turkey	B-	Angola, Cape Verde, Ecuador, Gabon, Iraq, Maldives, Nicaragua, Pakistan
CCC+	Argentina, Burkina Faso, El Salvador, Ghana, Mozambique, Republic of the Congo, Ukraine	Caa1	Barbados, Congo, Gabon, Ghana, Iraq, Maldives, Solomon Islands, Tunisia	CCC+	Mozambique
CCC	Ethiopia	Caa2	Ethiopia, Mali, Mozambique, Republic of the Congo	CCC	Argentina, El Salvador, Ethiopia, Ghana, Republic of the Congo, Tunisia
CCC-		Caa3	Belize, Ecuador, El Salvador, Laos, Suriname, Ukraine	CCC-	Laos
		Ca	Argentina, Belarus, Cuba, Sri Lanka, Zambia	CC	Ukraine
SD	Cambodia, Gabon, Isle of Man, Tunisia, Venezuela	C	Lebanon, Venezuela	C	
				RD	Belarus, Lebanon, Sri Lanka, Suriname, Venezuela, Zambia
D	Lebanon, Poerto Rico			D	
N/A	Cambodia, Gabon, Isle of Man, Tunisia, Venezuela	N/A		N/A	Bermuda
NR	Kyrgyzstan, Russia	NR	Russia	NR	Russia

Exhibit 10.5. Sovereign credit ratings from S&P, Moody's, and Fitch, August 2022.
Source: Websites of the S&P, Moody's, and Fitch.

that borrowers cannot have a risk rating higher than that of their national government's risk rating. This is known as a sovereign ceiling.

Although outside risk rating services are useful for smaller banks that face high costs in carrying out the necessary risk analyses, there are significant shortfalls associated with using these services. *First*, they are based mainly on publicly available information (e.g., macroeconomic variables released with a lag), such as macroeconomic information on rated countries. As such, the changes in ratings are reactive to changes in the economic conditions of the countries involved rather than predictive. *Second*, as a direct result of the first, the rating changes tend to exacerbate business swings. During recessions, the risk ratings of borrowers tend to worsen, which causes the cost of borrowing to rise and further depresses economic activities. However, risk ratings tend to improve during boom periods, leading to increased borrowing.

10.4.2.2. *Other sources of country risk assessments*

International banks may also consider country risk assessments from other country risk providers. Although not as comprehensive as the major credit rating agencies, aggregate country scores provided by alternative risk assessment service providers can be useful to a much-limited extent. Several service providers carry out country risk analyses based on their internal models or by surveying market economists. They make their aggregate or composite country risk scores available to subscribers.

The Euromoney country risk has been provided annually by Euromoney since 1979.[7] Initially, the risk premium attached to a borrower country's debt over LIBOR (adjusted for volume and maturity) was used as an indicator of country risk. This was replaced with an index comprised of economic and political variables that are considered to be of relevance. The Euromoney Country Risk (ECR) score is calculated by the following five categories: political risk (35% weighting), economic risk (35%), structural risk (10%), access to international capital markets (10%), and sovereign debt indicators (10%). The aggregate score out of 100 is assigned to each country. The first four categories are qualitative factors and they are obtained by consulting international experts who are asked to rate subfactors in each category on a scale of 0–10. The score for the quantitative category is calculated using World Bank's WDI data on key macroeconomic factors, such as total debt stock to GNP, debt service to exports, and current account balance to GNP. An aggregate score for each country is then calculated using the scores from qualitative and quantitative categories and sums to 100.

---

[7] https://www.euromoneycountryrisk.com/methodology.

The PRS Group provides country risk assessments in its International Country Risk Guide (ICRG) service. A composite country risk score is calculated for each country covered by the service, and the score ranges from 0 to 100, similar to the ECR scores. The information on the methodology and the formulas used to calculate the composite scores are only made available to subscribers to its service.[8]

The OECD provides Country Risk Classification (CRC) for non-high-income countries. The CRC is based on minimum premium fees required for official export credits provided by Export Credit Agencies (ECA) of various countries (see Chapter 3). The country risk experts from ECAs meet several times a year to produce a risk classification for each country, and it ranges from 0 (no premium required) to 7 (maximum premium required). Both quantitative and qualitative risk assessments are used in its Country Risk Assessment Model (CRAM). The quantitative factors considered include three groups of risk factors: the payment experience by the participating ECAs, and financial and economic situations based on IMF statistics of the country being assessed. It covers only non-high-income countries (OECD and Eurozone countries are not covered).[9]

Other well-known country risk providers include the Economist Group's Economist Intelligence[10] and IHS Markit,[11] among others.

Exhibit 10.6 shows the country risk scores and classifications provided by ECR, ICRG, and OECD. The first two provide composite country risk scores ranging from 0 to 100, and the third classifies each country into each of eight classifications, 0–7. For international lenders, these country risk assessments can be useful in assessing potential country risks faced by lending to borrowers in various countries. *First*, these country risk scores can be used to set country ceilings or risk thresholds. For example, for the ECR and the ICRG scores, 80 can be set as the minimum score that the lender is willing to tolerate. If so, only the best 10 countries in the list (New Zealand being the last) using the ECR and the best 7 countries (Brunei being the last) will make the cut. Using the CRC, if 3 is set as the maximum acceptable risk premium, then the first 22 countries

---

[8] https://www.prsgroup.com/explore-our-products/icrg/.

[9] https://www.oecd.org/trade/topics/export-credits/arrangement-and-sector-understandings/financing-terms-and-conditions/country-risk-classification/.

[10] https://www.eiu.com/n/solutions/country-risk-model/.

[11] https://ihsmarkit.com/industry/economics-country-risk.html#home.

	Euromoney Country Risk Score (Dec 2020) /100		PRS International Country Risk Guide Rating (Jan 2021) /100		OECD Country Risk Classification (Jul 2022) /7	
Rank	Country	Score	Country	Rating	Country	CRC
1	Switzerland	88.16	Switzerland	87.00	Singapore	0
2	Singapore	87.86	Taiwan	84.25	Chinese Taipei	1
3	Norway	87.80	Luxembourg	82.25	China	2
4	Denmark	86.90	Norway	81.50	Hong Kong SAR	2
5	Sweden	84.72	Denmark	81.00	Kuwait	2
6	Luxembourg	84.52	Australia	80.00	Malaysia	2
7	Finland	84.08	Brunei	80.00	Saudi Arabia	2
8	Netherlands	83.85	Singapore	79.50	United Arab Emirates	2
9	Australia	81.21	Sweden	79.00	Botswana	3
10	New Zealand	80.32	Germany	78.25	Bulgaria	3
11	Austria	79.72	Iceland	78.25	India	3
12	Germany	78.90	Korea, Republic	78.25	Indonesia	3
13	Hong Kong SAR	77.31	New Zealand	78.00	Mauritius	3
14	Chile	75.98	Canada	77.75	Mexico	3
15	Canada	74.73	United Arab Emirates	77.25	Morocco	3
16	Ireland	73.93	United Kingdom	77.25	Peru	3
17	United States	72.82	Finland	77.00	Philippines	3
18	Belgium	72.55	Hong Kong	77.00	Qatar	3
19	Slovak Republic	70.90	Netherlands	76.00	Romania	3
20	Taiwan	70.89	Ireland	75.50	Thailand	3
21	Czech Republic	70.63	Japan	75.25	Trinidad and Tobago	3
22	Malta	69.87	Austria	74.50	Uruguay	3
23	France	69.79	Slovakia	73.75	Azerbaijan	4
24	Iceland	69.49	Chile	73.00	Bahamas	4
25	Slovenia	69.12	Czech Republic	73.00	Colombia	4
26	Macau SAR (MSAR)	68.82	Poland	73.00	Costa Rica	4
27	Qatar	66.71	Philippines	72.75	Croatia	4
28	Portugal	66.52	Botswana	72.25	Dominican Republic	4
29	Estonia	66.23	Kazakhstan	72.25	Guatemala	4
30	United Kingdom	65.86	Kuwait	72.00	Panama	4

Exhibit 10.6. Alternative country risk assessments by service providers.

Source: Respective websites of Euromoney country risk, The PRG Group's International Country Risk Guide, and the OECD's Country Risk Classification.
https://www.euromoneycountryrisk.com/methodology.
https://www.prsgroup.com/explore-our-products/icrg/.
https://www.oecd.org/trade/topics/export-credits/arrangement-and-sector-understandings/financing-terms-and-conditions/country-risk-classification/.

in the list (Uruguay being the last) will be included in the group of countries where lending can be considered. *Second*, once the acceptable risk group of countries are selected, the country risk premiums for individual country borrowers will be based on how far the scores deviate from the threshold value in each method. For example, using the ECR and PRS methods, countries with scores ranging between 80 and 85 may receive 50 basis points margin above LIBOR, whereas those between 86 and 90 may receive only 30 basis points. The country risk premiums will rise in the OECD method as their risk classifications rise from 0 to 7.

References

Ariyoshi, A., Habermeier, K., Laurens, B., Otker-Robe, I., Canales-Kriljenko, J. and Kirilenko, A. (2000). Capital Controls: Country Experiences with their Use and Liberalisation. IMF Occasional Paper 190. https://www.imf.org/external/pubs/ft/op/op190/.

Correa, R. and Sapriza, H. (2014). Sovereign debt crises, in The *Oxford Handbook of Banking*, (2nd ed.), Berger, A., Molyneux, P. and Wilson, J. (eds.), The Oxford University Press.

Flores, J. (2016). Capital markets and sovereign defaults: A historical perspective, in *Capital Markets and Sovereign Defaults: A Historical Perspective*, Cassis, Y., Schenk, C. and Grossman, R. (eds.), The Oxford University Press.

IMF (2022). The Sovereign-Bank nexus in Emerging Markets: A Risk Embrace, Chapter 2 in Global Financial Stability Report, April. https://www.imf.org/en/Publications/GFSR/Issues/2022/04/19/global-financial-stability-report-april-2022.

Reinhart, C. and Rogoff, K. S. (2011). From financial crash to debt crisis. *American Economic Review*, 101, 1676–1706.

Saunders, A., Cornett, M. and Erhemhamts, O. (2020). *Financial Institutions Management*, 10th ed., McGraw-Hill, Chapter 14: Sovereign Risk, pp. 423–449.

Chapter 11

International Debt Crisis

11.1. Introduction

There have been numerous international financial crises, as documented in Laeven and Valencia (2018), and also in Beers and Mavalwal (2017). There were 151 banking, 239 currency, and 75 sovereign debt crises identified between 1976 and 2017 (Laeven and Valencia, 2018, Exhibit 11.1). For sovereign debt crises, all incidences of crises occurred in emerging market countries except for two cases, one in 2012 (Greece) and another in 2013 (Cyprus). The most noticeable period of sovereign debt crises is from 1978 to 1986. In particular, between 1981 and 1984, there were 29 sovereign debt crises. The following two sections in this chapter explain the factors behind the sovereign debt crises in emerging economies in the early 1980s and the Eurozone debt crisis events during 2009–2012, respectively.

11.2. Sovereign Debt Crisis in Emerging Economies

As highlighted in Exhibit 11.1, a sovereign debt crisis regularly occur in emerging market countries. The early 1980s saw a concentration of crises across many regions of emerging market countries, including Latin America, Asia, Eastern Europe, and Africa. In most cases, contributing factors include domestic economic mismanagement, financial market underdevelopment, and deteriorating external competitiveness.

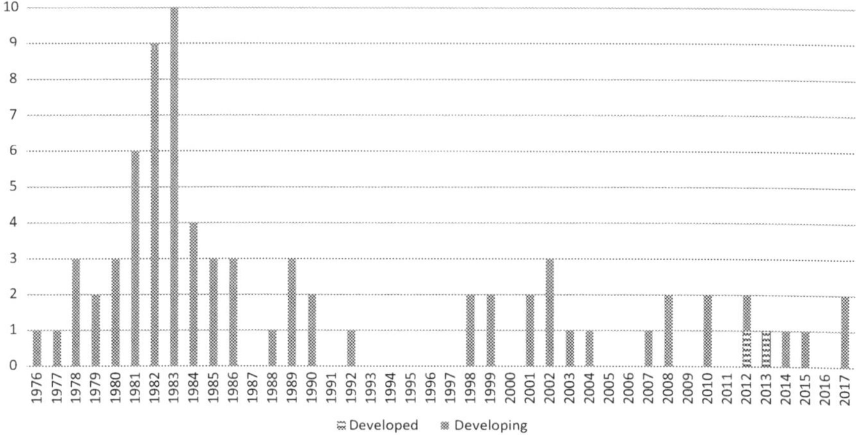

Exhibit 11.1. Incidence of sovereign debt crisis, 1976–2017.

Source: Constructed from Table 11.1 in Laeven and Valencia (2018).

11.2.1. *Emerging economy debt crisis in the 1980s — Latin American crisis*

In Panel A, Exhibit 11.2 shows the external debt stock of all emerging market regions (East Asia & Pacific, Europe and Central Asia, Latin America and Caribbean, Middle East and North Africa, and Sub-Saharan Africa) from 1970 to 1990, in USD billions. External debt grew from USD 52 billion in 1970 to USD 980 billion by 1990, an increase by a factor of 19 and an annual compound growth of 28%. Latin American countries held the bulk of the debt during the period, accounting for 55% of the total emerging market debt in 1970 and 50% in 1982. Panel B shows the debt levels for the four largest debtor countries in Latin America (Argentina, Brazil, Mexico, and Venezuela) for the same period. The aggregate external debt in Latin America grew from USD 28.7 billion in 1970 to USD 281.6 billion in 1990, equivalent to a 21% annual compounded growth. In 1982, the four countries had over USD 257 billion of external debt, accounting for approximately 91% of the total external debt of their region and 46% of the entire emerging market countries' external debt. Out of the four countries, Brazil and Mexico were significantly more

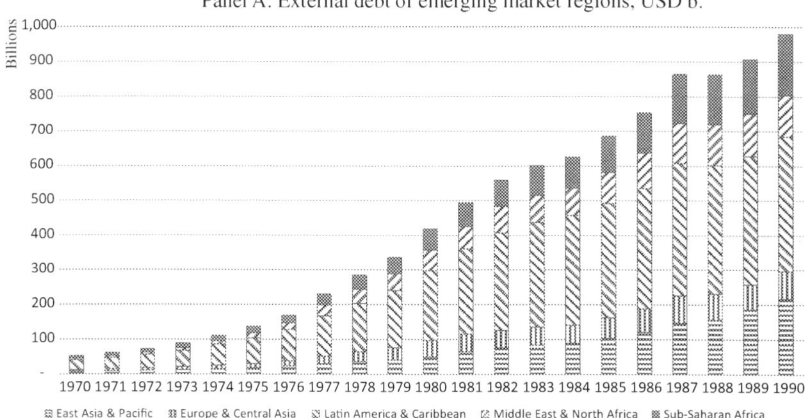

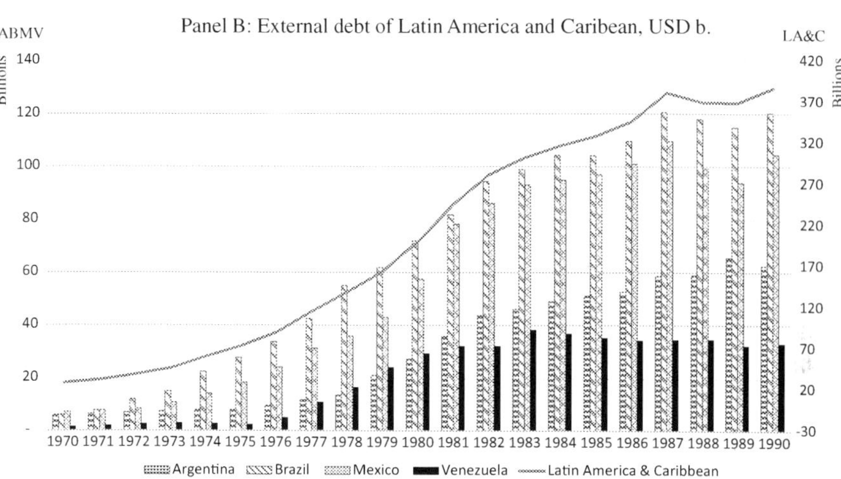

Exhibit 11.2. External debt stock of emerging market countries, in USD b. 1970–1990.

Source: Constructed from World Bank World Development Indicators (2021).

indebted than the other two. By 1982, their external debts were USD 94 billion and 86 billion, respectively.

Exhibit 11.3 summarises the external debt statistics of the four countries in 1982. The additional dimensions of the sizeable gross external debts in all four countries point to their inability to handle the debt load, eventually leading to their defaults in 1982. The common characteristics of the four countries were very high inflation rates, except for Venezuela

	Argentina	Brazil	Mexico	Venezuela
Gross external debt (USD b.)	43.79	94.43	86.27	32.18
Debt to GDP (%)	51.94	34.80	46.73	47.51
Debt service (USD b.)	4.89	19.27	15.71	5.95
Debt service to GDP (%)	63.86	89.91	58.98	35.05
Public debt to total external debt (%)	36.63	56.41	59.98	38.76
Long-term debt to total external debt (%)	62.27	80.90	69.37	54.30
Foreign reserves to external debt (%)	10.29	4.23	2.06	36.71
Current account balance to GDP (%)	−2.79	−6.01	−3.19	−6.27
Annual GDP Deflater (%)	194.54	101.03	61.84	4.28

Exhibit 11.3. External debt statistics for Argentina, Brazil, Mexico, and Venezuela in 1982.

Source: Constructed from World Bank World Development Indicators (2021).

(194% in Argentina, 101% in Brazil and 61% in Mexico); a sizeable current account deficit ranging from 3 to 6% of GDP; and minuscule foreign exchange reserve to external debt ratio (2% in Mexico and 4% in Brazil). The combination of these features in 1982 highlighted the possibility of default in these countries.

Throughout the 1970s, Latin American countries were able to finance their current account deficits by borrowing from international banks, mainly from the US. Large US bank lenders (often referred to as money centre banks) were eager to supply the required funds as they could charge higher interest rates to these government borrowers than domestic US corporate borrowers. They considered lending to sovereign governments and government-guaranteed entities relatively low-risk and high-return investments. Moreover, the oil price shocks in the 1970s created the need to recycle the petrodollars of oil-exporting countries. Oil revenues of petroleum exporting countries grew by USD 70 billion from 1973 to 1976 and by USD 121 billion (1.4% of World GDP) from 1978 to 1981 (Nsouli, 2006). These revenue windfalls were due to the politically motivated oil price hikes in 1973 (USD 2 per barrel in 1973 rose to 12 by 1974) caused by a conflict in the middle east and in 1979 (rising to USD 39.50 per barrel) sparked by an unexpected drop in oil production due to the Iranian revolution in that year. The unplanned windfall was put through to the international banking system, and international banks were pressured to make more loans to recycle the increasing supply of petrodollar, which required lowering lending standards to include borrowers previously deemed high risk. Oil-importing countries were unprepared, especially in the first oil price shock in 1973, and they needed to fund the resulting current account deficits from the international financial market. International banks recycled the accumulating petrodollar from oil-exporting countries to oil-importing countries requiring funding for the growing current account deficits. This contributed to the external debt of emerging market countries rising from USD 52 billion in 1970 to USD 559 billion by 1982. Latin America accounted for 54% (50%) of the entire emerging market debt in 1970 (1982), or USD 29 billion (292 billion). The four largest indebted countries' share of the debt was 71% (91%) of their regional aggregate and 39% (46%) of the total emerging market debt in 1970 (1982). Moreover, long-term debt from international banks dominated Latin American debt, accounting for 81% in Brazil and 70% in Mexico. These were mostly priced at margins above LIBOR, reset every six months, and so susceptible to rising interest rates. In addition, public sector debt (loans to sovereign, sub-sovereign governments, and publicly guaranteed corporate borrowers) amounted to 56% and 60% for the two countries, respectively.[1]

As the size of external debt grew in most of the emerging market countries towards the end of the 1970s, especially in the four Latin American countries, warning bells started to sound from various corners, including the US regulators. However, the belief that sovereign loans were relatively safe despite the growing concerns seemed compelling, so the loan growth continued until 1982, especially in the face of the excess supply of funds in the international banking market after each oil price shock in the 1970s. The growing signs that the Latin American borrowers were facing payment difficulties include domestic economic mismanagement and an increasingly hostile external environment for debtor countries. The failure to control domestic inflation and diversify export income away from commodities resulted in alarmingly high levels of current account deficits in the four countries. The current account deficits ranged from 2.79% of GDP in Argentina to 6.27% of GDP in Venezuela in 1982. The oil price shock induced inflation throughout the 1970s (the average world inflation for the 1970s was 10%, whereas it was 130% for Argentina, 33% for Brazil, 15% for Mexico, and 13% for Venezuela) was part of 'the Great Inflation' of the 1970s. In 1979, newly appointed US Federal Reserve president, Paul Volker, started monetary tightening aimed at reducing inflation that was running at above 10% in the US,

[1] BIS locational banking statistic.

resulting in rising interest rates (three-month LIBOR rose to its peak of 17.68% in January 1980, from 5.7% in October 1977). The USD started to appreciate against all other currencies (by 9.6% and 9.3% in 1981 and 1982, respectively, against major currencies). In addition, the rise in real interest rates in the US due to the unusual mix of tight monetary and easy fiscal policy in the early 1980s created financial hardship for debtor countries that borrowed in the USD. This put the world economy into a severe recession from July 1981 to November 1982. Due to the peg to the USD, its appreciation caused a similar appreciation of the Latin American currencies, which led to the further deterioration of their external competitiveness. In addition, the recession reduced demand for their exports, further deteriorating their balance of payments. Latin American countries that borrowed heavily in USD loans experienced increasing difficulty repaying their debt due to rising interest costs as their debts were mostly on floating rate loans based on LIBOR. These factors contributed to the Latin American countries' rising debt service ratios. Brazil's debt service obligation to its export income was as much as 90%, 64% in Argentina, and 59% in Mexico in 1982 (Exhibit 11.3). Moreover, foreign currency reserves all but evaporated in Mexico and Brazil, where the reserves covered only 2% and 4% of external debt, respectively.

By 1982, all four Latin American countries were in great economic and financial difficulty, and it would not have been unusual to see any of these countries come out and declare a default. However, doing so would cause a long-lasting stigma of starting an international debt crisis and could be blamed for creating an environment where other indebted countries had no choice but to default. Countries that follow suit and default themselves could argue that the toxic environment was the cause of their default and seek more attractive terms for negotiating new debt service terms. Mexico could not hold out any longer and became the first to declare default on their debt service obligations. On 12 August 1982, the Mexican finance minister, Jesús Silva-Herzog, unilaterally declared a 90-day loan moratorium, stating that his country could not meet its debt obligations amounting to USD 86 billion at the time, mostly due to large US banks. By 10 December 1982, US commercial bank lenders rescheduled USD 23 billion, falling due between 23 August 1982 and 31 December 1984. The Mexican default triggered Argentina and Brazil to follow suit, and it quickly spread to other emerging market countries in a similar situation, as well as other Latin American debtor countries. By October 1983, a total of 27 countries rescheduled or were in the process of rescheduling their external debt, and 16 were Latin American countries (FDIC, 1997). Therefore, Latin American countries were the largest contributors to the emerging market debt crisis in the 1980s. Latin American debt during 1973–1984 increased much more than in other regions of the world, and their debt/export and interest/export ratios increased substantially prior to the onset of the crisis. It was mainly a large bank problem, and there was a concentration of loans from large US banks.

11.2.2. *International responses to debt crisis*

The emerging market debt crisis in the 1980s was arguably the most severe international debt crisis since the 1930s, and it took more than a decade before meaningful economic recoveries were seen in the affected countries and the balance sheets of the lending banks were restored (FDIC, 1997). There are several options lenders can consider in the event of a sovereign default. These include rescheduling, restructuring of loan conditions (interest rate base, fee structures, and loan covenants), partial and full loan forgiveness, alternative repayment methods, and loan sales. For lenders, rescheduling payments is the least costly option, and it is viable if the borrower is likely to regain the capacity to service the loan. Payment extensions can be granted in that case, which might involve additional rescheduling fees. Restructuring loan conditions require negotiations with the defaulting sovereign, potentially involving third-party international organisations such as the IMF if a rescue package is being organised. Partial forgiveness of debt, also known as a 'haircut' might be a solution if there is no prospect of the borrowing country being able to repay in full. If there is no indication of the capacity or willingness of the defaulting sovereign to service the debt, full debt forgiveness (or total write-off) might be the only option as there is no practical way to enforce the loan contract (e.g., foreclosure of the country's assets) due to the sovereignty of the borrower. However, if the defaulting sovereign is willing to repay the loan, alternative methods of payment may be negotiated. For example, a repayment in local currency tied to an investment in specific assets in the borrower country can be considered. In a typical debt-for-equity swap arrangement, the creditor can be given an equity stake in a state-owned company of some strategic value. Finally, the lender might be able to sell the defaulted loan to an investor who is willing to see it through to the end, where the borrower recovers sufficiently and profits from the risk-taking. In addition, a secondary market for defaulted sovereign loans would help the lender recoup at least some portion of the loan.

11.2.2.1. *Loan rescheduling*

Borrowers facing problems servicing existing loans ask for loan rescheduling. This may involve deferring both principal and interest payments (i.e., a grace period) and adjustments to the interest rate applicable on the loans (e.g., reduction of the rate, conversion of interest rate denomination from floating to a fixed rate, and change of interest rate base). Loan rescheduling is designed to give temporary relief to problem borrowers in order to induce future repayment in full. Thus, lenders prefer rescheduling, which involves costs to them, to certain defaults in the near future. Lenders might apply additional fees for rescheduling and interest rate base change.

Borrowers benefit from rescheduling because they avert default, temporarily at least. The present values of their liabilities in hard currencies are lower (whether it be payment deferring or a cut in interest rates). However, they may be shut out of future loan markets because of their higher credit risk (higher probability of rescheduling), leading to missed investment opportunities. In addition, this interferes with international trade (credit). Borrower countries who ask for rescheduling may gain short-term benefits in terms of lower present values of loan repayments, but their long-term economic prosperity may be adversely affected if lenders apply penalty rates in future loans or access to future loans is lost due to the current difficulties.

Lenders would prefer rescheduling to default for obvious reasons. Although they might charge renegotiation fees and realise some tax benefits from loan write-downs or -offs, their misfortunes may not be looked upon kindly by their shareholders due to the lower market value and liquidity of their assets. They may also receive more regulatory attention as loan rescheduling is evidence of ineffective credit risk management by lending banks. Since there was invariably more than one lender involved in sovereign default, a coordinated effort was necessary among the lenders. Known as the Paris club, government lenders organised an informal gathering (10 times a year) of member countries[2] to consider debtor countries' requests for debt relief. It provides standardisation in the

[2]There are 20 members in the Paris club. These are Australia, Austria, Belgium, Brazil, Canada, Denmark, Finland, France, Germany, Ireland, Israel, Italy, Japan, the Netherlands, Norway, Russia, South Korea, Spain, Sweden, Switzerland, the UK, and the USA. https://clubdeparis.org/.

loan rescheduling of debtor countries and private sector borrowers guaranteed by their governments on a case-by-case basis. Its inception was following the debt restructuring negotiations between Argentina and government lenders that took place in Paris in 1956. The London club is a private lender counterpart which is an unofficial group of international commercial banks organised to help coordinate debt restructuring of bank loans to debtor countries.

In the Latin American debt defaults, international lenders (mostly US banks) negotiated rescheduling terms from 1983. For example, the US commercial bank lenders rescheduled Mexico's debt obligations of USD 23 billion due between 23 August 1982 and 31 December 1984 by December 1982. However, towards the mid- to late-1980s, it became clear that the rolling rescheduling without improving the debt-repaying capacity of the debtor countries did not prove effective. International lenders started to consider other debt restructuring methods, such as alternative debt repayment methods, debt reduction and the development of a secondary market for sovereign debt. From 1987, creditor banks started to recognise losses and establish loan loss provisions which, by the end of 1989, rose to approximately 50% of their outstanding emerging market loans (FDIC, 1997).

11.2.2.2. *Debt for equity swap*

One of the alternative payment methods potentially available for debtor countries is to offer domestic assets of value to creditors. In-kind payment can be in natural resources of the country (debt for nature swap) or equity stakes in government-owned and controlled enterprises with potential growth prospects (debt for equity swap). Alternatively, any potential assets in the country may be offered in return for a reduction in or replacement for the country's external debt. In this section, we consider the debt-for-equity swap method used to respond to the Latin American debt crisis in the 1980s.

Debt for equity swap refers to a corporate borrower offering debt holders newly issued equity capital in exchange for the retirement of debt. This has been a popular method of retiring debt but has long-term consequences for the borrower as equity stakes represent perpetual ownership claims. The swap applied to international debt is similar to its domestic counterpart. A simplified process is shown in Exhibit 11.4. Assume that a bank has an existing loan to a borrower in a debtor country in the amount

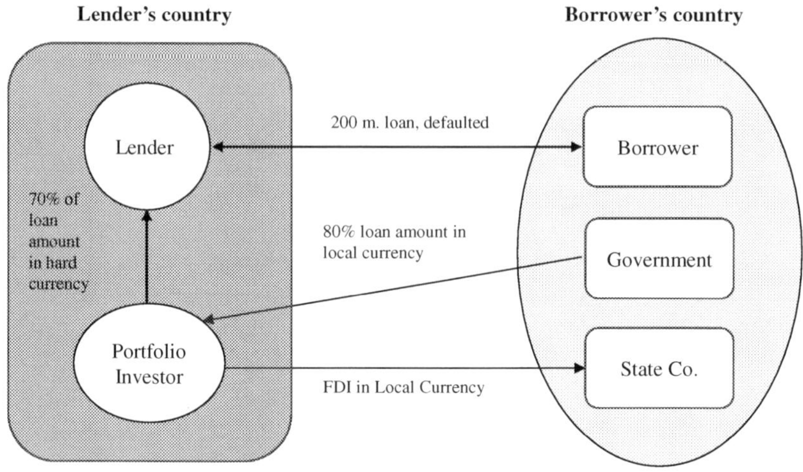

Exhibit 11.4. International debt for equity swap.

of USD 200 million, which is in arrears. Enter the government of the borrower's country and an interested foreign direct investor (FDI) in equities in the debtor country, and we have a potential solution to the problem. The lender will sell the legal rights to the loan at a discount, e.g., 70 cents in the dollar, to a portfolio investor in the lender's country. The investor then surrenders the loan to the government of the borrower's country in return for 80 cents in the dollar of the face value of the loan in equivalent local currency to invest in the equities of nominated companies in the borrower's country.

The benefits of the swap apply to all parties involved. *First*, the lender is able to sell off the non-performing loans that would otherwise be difficult to recoup. Since the borrower is located in a different country, enforcing loan covenants would be difficult or impossible (if the borrower is a sovereign). Moreover, the lender is unlikely to be in a position to continue to allow the rescheduling of payments or involuntary additional emergency loans to the debtor. Thus, the loan sale is an optimal method of exiting the investment position and unloading the non-performing loan from the balance sheet, despite a large discount involved in the loan sale. The swap allows the lender to make more loans to financially sound borrowers by improving its short-term liquidity position. *Second*, the borrower's country is no longer required to make interest or principal payments. This will save valuable hard currency reserves of the country, which can be deployed to more productive uses. Cole (1992) reports that between USD 13 and 18 billion of Latin American debt had been traded in the secondary market for debt-to-equity swap purposes. The most successful case of the swap was for Chile. Between 1985 and 1988, Chile was able to convert at least 5% of its external debt to domestic equities, which resulted in a debt reduction of approximately USD 740 million. Over the same period, its GDP grew by 40%, and the government budget deficit turned from a USD 377 million deficit to an 18 million surplus (Cole, 1992). *Third*, the portfolio investor benefits as the arrangement allows them to access the debtor country's previously inaccessible equity market. Moreover, they can enjoy a competitive and effective exchange rate when converting the debt into local currency funds, leading to cheaper local currency financing.

Despite the benefits outlined, the effects of debt for equity swaps as a debt resolution measure were limited. In Brazil, the swap program period was between 1983 and 1987, and the debt reduction was approximately USD 8 billion (Cole, 1992). This was only 6.6% of the total debt stock in 1987, which was USD 120 billion. In Mexico, the program was much shorter, lasting less than two years, between 1986 and 1987 and only USD 1.1 billion reductions, only 1% of the total debt of USD 109 billion in 1987. Even in the most successful case in Chile, only 10% of debt reduction was achieved by 1989. The limited success of the swap in Latin America was due to its inherent limitations. *First*, for the lender, the loan sale at a discount is not only a financial burden but can also attract more stringent regulatory attention as a result. For example, for lending banks located in jurisdictions that require marking to market accounting rules, other emerging market loans with similar characteristics in their loan portfolios could be required to be marked down. This could pose difficulties for banks already struggling to meet Basel's risk capital ratios. Moreover, the lender's willingness for the swap could set precedence for the lender's other struggling debtor countries. *Second*, for the debtor country, the swap crowds out hard currency investment inflows that would have occurred in its absence. International investors interested in investing in the debtor country would find it attractive to purchase the debtor country's debt in the secondary market and then swap it with the equity investments they desire instead of bringing in hard currency investments into the country. The swap will then replace the hard currency inflow that could have resulted. Moreover, the local currency fund provided to the international investor will be inflationary in the debtor country as it will add to the domestic money supply. The Latin American debtor countries were experiencing high inflation, as shown in Exhibit 11.3. They could not afford the additional inflation the swaps could bring. In Brazil, the swapped debt in 1988 alone was an equivalent of USD 1.8 billion, as much as one-third of the money supply in that year. Moreover, it was speculated that for every USD 100 million swaps there would be a 3–5% rise in inflation (Cole, 1992).

11.2.2.3. *Debt reduction (debt-for-debt swaps, Brady Plan)*

A form of debt-for-debt swap initiated by the US treasury secretary Nicholas Brady was proposed in 1989 as a solution to the 1980s' emerging market debt crisis. In particular, the US was concerned about the health of the large US money centre banks that held the bulk of the Latin American debt. Known as the Brady Plan, this was an initiative to reduce the (sovereign) debt of emerging market countries, especially those in Latin America, by exchanging existing debt for new debt with smaller amounts (discount exchange) or the same amount (par exchange) with lower fixed interest and with generally a longer maturity. The newly created bonds were referred to as Brady bonds, named after the proposer of the plan. The aim of these bonds was to permanently transform the structures of outstanding debt issues and interest arrears into tradable assets. Brady bonds typically were issued at a 30–50% discount on the defaulting bank loans of debtor countries and can be par value or discounted zero coupon bonds with maturities ranging from 10 to 30 years. Brady bonds were denominated in the USD in most cases, but in rare cases, non-USD denominations were used (e.g., the West German Mark, the Japanese Yen, and the Dutch Guilder). The price movements of Brady Bonds provided an accurate indication of the market sentiment toward the sovereign risk of the debtor countries. Debtor countries who observed austerity measures to enhance domestic savings, reduce deficits, etc., received support from the World Bank and the IMF to finance debt buybacks and the collateral used in their Brady bonds.

Exhibit 11.5 presents an example of a Brady bond creation. Step (1): The lender faces a default on a USD 200 million loan to a sovereign, and the two parties agree to enter a Brady plan with a 50% discount on the face value. Step (2): The IMF provides a rescue fund, USD 100 million, on the condition that the debtor country enters into an economic restructuring program. Step (3): The debtor purchases USD 100 million's worth of zero

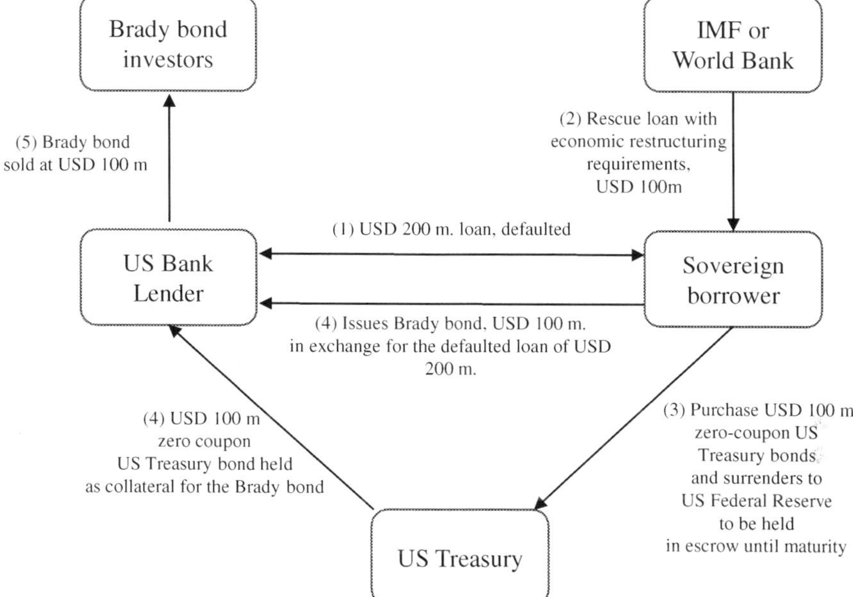

Exhibit 11.5. Brady bond process.

coupon US Treasury bonds with the same maturity as the current bank loan and surrenders the bonds to the US Federal Reserve in escrow. Step (4): The debtor country issues a Brady bond with a USD 100 million face value to the lender in return for the USD 200 million loan. The US Treasury bonds in escrow are used to guarantee the Brady bond. Step (5): The lender sells the Brady bond to an investor in the secondary debt market. At maturity, the Treasury bonds are sold, and the proceed is used to retire the Brady bond. If the debtor defaults on the Brady bonds, the investor receives the principal of the bonds at maturity from the US Treasury bonds.

Mexico was the first debtor country to issue Brady bonds during the Brady plan period of 1989–1990, followed by 18 other emerging market debtor countries,[3] and the aggregate amount of Brady bonds issued was

[3]A total of 19 countries issued Brady bonds. These are Argentina, Brazil, Costa Rica, the Dominican Republic, Ecuador, Panama, Peru, Uruguay, and Venezuela in Latin America; Bulgaria, Poland, and Russia in Eastern Europe; the Philippines and Vietnam in Asia; and Ivory Coast, Jordan and Nigeria in the Middle East and Africa.

over USD 160 billion.[4] By 2005, the trading of Brady bonds accounted for only 2% of total emerging market debt trading, a significant reduction in activity from its peak in 1994 when it accounted for 61% of the market total (USD 1.68 trillion), and by mid-2006, most of the Brady bonds were either retired or exchanged with other debts (EMTA).

11.2.2.4. *Secondary market for emerging market debt*

The secondary market for emerging market debt became an important part of the solution to the emerging market debt crisis of the 1980s. Bank lenders with non-performing loans to debtor countries could sell them to investors who were less risk-averse and had longer-term investment horizons. There are many examples of such perseverance on the part of investors who can sit on non-performing loans until they turn the corner and are handsomely rewarded. Secondary markets catered for such investors who were after defaulted assets at a deep discount to their face values. In particular, many Latin American debtor countries issued Brady bonds to replace bank loans from 1989, and the market for trading Brady bonds became an essential part of the debt reduction initiatives.

Market participants initially were mostly large banks in New York and London, and creditors would reassign rights to future interest and principal to the buyers of debt (a formal transfer of ownership). In the case of syndicated loan sub-participations, reassignment and assignment with novation were used. The secondary markets were supported by the central banks of the debtor countries that sometimes assumed the loans. Also, frequent restructuring of the loans led to them becoming more standardised in terms of risk and duration. This raised the marketability of the restructured loans, increasing the market liquidity. In addition, the collateralisation of bond principals against US Treasuries (in the case of Brady bonds) gave a boost. A conversion into financial instruments with amortisation tied to a debtor's foreign exchange income further increased the attractiveness of the loans to the investors. Overall, due to the role of the secondary debt market, the market value of existing portfolios of emerging market debt can be determined. The trading volume of the emerging market debt grew from only USD 2 billion in 1984 to a peak of USD 6.7 trillion by 2010 before receding to USD 5.1 trillion by 2021 (EMTA).

---

[4]Emerging Market Trade Association (EMTA), https://www.emta.org/.

11.2.3. *Debt crisis in the 1990s*

11.2.3.1. *Mexico 1994*

Mexico was the first country to declare sovereign default in 1982, and it was one of the first to achieve meaningful debt reduction through various debt restructuring activities throughout the rest of the 1980s. The debt reduction program from 1987 resulted in the gross debt falling from its peak of USD 109 billion in 1987 to USD 94 billion in 1989 before rising again to USD 139 billion by 1994. During the same period (1987–1994), external debt to GNI fell from 78% to 27%, and the debt service ratio to export from 44% to 29% (World Development Indicators). It appears that Mexico was making progress on all fronts.

However, the macroeconomic mismanagement and rising political risks in 1994 plunged the country back into the cusp of another sovereign default. In 1994, Mexico was in a presidential election year, and the government was on a spending spree financed by peso-denominated Treasury bills with guaranteed repayment in the USD, called 'tesobonos'. Foreign investors found them attractive because of the USD repayment feature, and the yields were set lower than the traditional Mexican Treasure bills with repayment in the Peso. The rising political instability due to the assassination of the presidential candidate Luis Donaldo Colosio and a violent uprising of the indigenous population in the state of Chiapas raised the risk premium on the Mexican government debt (Boughton, 2001). Moreover, the higher risk premium on Mexican debts and the inflationary pressures from the economic profligacy put immense pressure on the Mexican Peso, which was still pegged to the USD at the time.

The Mexican central bank intervened in the market to maintain the overvalued Peso and keep the peg by selling the USD, funded by issuing USD-denominated government debt. The increasing USD debt service requirement of mounting USD debt (USD 139 billion in 1994) and the rising imports due to the overvalued Peso contributed to the deterioration in the current account balance, which stood at a deficit of 5.6% of GDP. The rising inflation due to the expansionary fiscal policy was as much as 36% in 1993. Eventually, the quickly depleting foreign currency reserves from USD 25 billion in 1993 to USD 6 billion in 1994 forced the government to devalue the Peso from 3.4662 MXN/USD to 3.95 on 20 December 1994, a 13% devaluation (Panel A1, Exhibit 11.6). A further devaluation to 3.997 occurred the following day, and the Peso floated the day after on

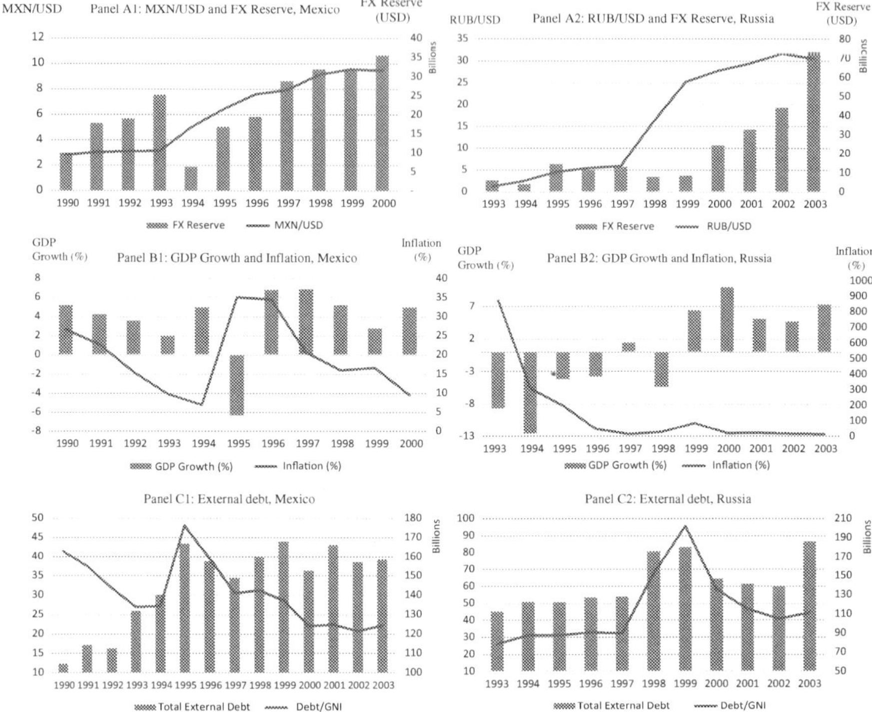

Exhibit 11.6. Economic fundamentals surrounding debt crisis: Mexico 1994 and Russia 1998.

Source: Constructed from World Bank World Development Indicators, 2021.

22 December, and its value fell immediately to 4.85. By 27 December, it depreciated to 5.75, a 50% reduction in the value of the currency in only seven days. By this time, it was clear that the Mexican government could no longer service its USD-denominated government debt, and external assistance was required to prevent another sovereign default. The resulting debt crisis, also known as 'the tequila crisis', had contagion effects in countries in the East Asian region, Australia, and countries with current account deficits.

In January 1995, the US led an international coalition of countries and organisations to arrange a USD 50 billion rescue package for Mexico to allow the restructuring of its USD debts. The USD 50 billion was contributed by the US (20 billion), the IMF (17.8), the BIS (10), and the rest by a group of Latin American countries and Canada. The Mexican government was required to strictly adhere to the monetary and fiscal policies prescribed by the IMF. It suffered a period of recession throughout the rest of the 1990s. The GDP contracted by 6.29% and inflation rose to 35% (Panel B1, Exhibit 11.6), while unemployment rose to 7.1% in 1995. However, from 1996, Mexico showed signs of recovery, including rebuilding the depleted foreign exchange reserve that by 1997 accumulated to USD 29 billion, returning to the pre-crisis level of USD 25 billion in 1993. Moreover, external debt peaked in 1996 at USD 167 billion and at 45% of GNI started to fall. The debt to GNI fell to 22% by 2003 (Panel C1, Exhibit 11.6).

11.2.3.2. *Russia 1998*

The Russian debt crisis of 1998 had the same combination of currency and debt crises as in Mexico's 1994 experience. The sudden devaluation of the Ruble (RUB) followed by its floating in September 1998 (Panel A2, Exhibit 11.6), led to the inability of the Russian government to service its debt to both domestic and international creditors and declaring a loan moratorium for 90 days.

When the Soviet Union was dismantled in 1991, Russia inherited most of its debt which stood at USD 112 billion in 1993. Ninety-two per cent of the external debt in that year was long-term debt, and there was negligible private debt. The aggregate debt remained stable until 1997 (USD 128 billion) before it rose to USD 175 billion in 1998 and then to USD 180 billion the following year before stabilising. The Debt to GNI ratio also reflects a similar peak in 1999 before falling (Panel C2, Exhibit 11.6). The Russian economy was suffering through the breakup of the union as shown by the negative annual GDP growth rate, which averaged –7.4% from 1991 to 1996, and the hyperinflation of 874% per annum in 1993 being reduced to 14.7% by 1997 (Panel B2, Exhibit 11.6). The IMF continuously supported the policies to achieve Ruble stability[5] and provided over USD 18 billion in loans to Russia. It then led to a rescue package of

[5]The Central Bank of the Russian Federation maintained the Ruble to fluctuate within ±15% around the 6.2 Rub/USD central rate from 1 January 1998 before the currency was floated on 2 September 1998. Market interventions to buy and sell Rubles against the USD were required to keep the exchange rate within the target zone.

USD 22.6 billion on 20 July 1998[6] in an attempt to stabilise the Ruble and the Russian economy. Kharas *et al.* (2001) suggest that there were two reasons that both the Russian government and the IMF were keen to maintain the exchange rate arrangement. They wanted to avoid undoing the progress Russia had made in gaining control of inflation since the breakup of the Soviet Union. By 1997, Russia managed to bring its inflation down to 15% from 874% in 1993. Additionally, they wished to avoid the type of financial meltdown following the forced floating of currencies in Mexico in 1994 and during the Asian Financial Crisis of 1997–1998.

Unfortunately, the adverse spillover effects from the Asian Financial Crisis of 1997 showed up in the form of a higher risk premium on Russian debt as the confidence of foreign investors in the progress of the Russian government's fiscal reforms eroded. The relentless attack on the Ruble required the Central Bank of Russia to continue to defend the currency by selling its foreign currency reserves which stood at a mere USD 7.8 billion in 1998 (12.8 billion in 1997). This led to the announcement, on 17 August 1998, of a devaluation of the Ruble from the central rate of 6.3 to 9.5 RUB/USD by the end of the year. The government also declared its intention to restructure all official domestic currency debt and imposed a 90-day moratorium on external debt. Despite the announcement of the devaluation plan, the fast depleting foreign exchange reserves forced them to float the currency on 2 September to avoid total depletion of the foreign exchange reserves (Panel A2, Exhibit 11.6). The Ruble continued to slide in value, and by 9 September, it depreciated to 21 RUB/USD, a mere 30% of its value before the devaluation announcement. With the collapse of the Ruble, the inflation rate started to rise again in 1998, undoing the hard work of getting it down to 15% by 1997. It rose to 28% in 1998 and then to 86% in 1999. The GDP, which grew by 1.4% in 1997 after years of negative growth, contracted by 5.3% in 1998. The external debt grew significantly from USD 128 billion in 1997 to 175 billion in 1998.

The recovery, however, was relatively quick due mostly to the rising oil prices from USD 20.26 per barrel in November 1998 to USD 43.28 by November 1999 (and then to USD 57.53 by November 2000). The current account balance increased from 23 billion in surplus in 1999 to 45 billion in

[6]The 22.6 billion package was provided by the IMF (15.1 b.), the World Bank (1.5 b.), and other countries. However, only 5.5 b., which was earmarked for currency stability, was actually disbursed (Kharas *et al.*, 2001). The Russian Parliament, Duma, did not approve the fiscal conditions associated with the other aspect of the rescue package.

2000. The GDP growth averaged 6.9% from 1999 to 2008. After peaking at USD 180 billion in 1999, the external debt fell to USD 138 billion by 2002.

11.3. Sovereign Debt Crisis in Advanced Economies — Eurozone Debt Crisis

11.3.1. *Overview*

The Eurozone has operated as a single currency monetary union since 1 January 1999 among 11 founding member countries of Austria, Belgium, Finland, France, Germany, Italy, Ireland, Luxembourg, the Netherlands, Portugal, and Spain. By the time Euro notes and coins were introduced on 1 January 2001 and replaced the national currencies of the member countries, Greece became the 12th member. The Maastricht Treaty 1992 specified five criteria for the EU member countries to join the currency union. These were (1) inflation no higher than 1.5% points above the average of the three best-performing member states, (2) government budget deficit to GDP to be less than 3%, (3) government debt to GDP to be less than 60%, (4) stable exchange rate, and finally, (5) long-term interest rate (average 10-year government bond yield in the past year) to be less than 3%. The most apparent and direct benefit of the union was the elimination of foreign exchange risk and currency conversion costs within the zone, stimulating intra-regional trade in goods and services. Equally important was the convergence of the monetary policy conducted by the ECB, which is also entrusted with ensuring the stability of the Euro. Moreover, the opening up of both financial and labour markets in the member countries allowed unrestricted movements of factors of production, including capital (loanable funds) and labour. On the other hand, the monetary union took away an individual country's ability to respond to localised economic instabilities by adjusting monetary policy and exchange rates to stimulate their economies.

The free movement of capital allowed the recycling of the current account surplus from countries such as Germany and the Netherlands to the deficit countries such as Greece, Portugal, and Spain via the unified banking system, without the fear of currency risk or other frictions on cross-border capital flows that existed prior to the union. The movement of capital led to a reduction in long-term interest rates in countries with higher interest rates than in Germany and France. For example, the long-term interest rate in Greece fell from 8.48% in 1998 to 5.3% by 2001.

Also, the ability to easily finance government budget and current account deficits at lower borrowing costs seemed beneficial to both creditor and debtor countries.

However, the adverse impact of the US subprime mortgage crisis from 2007 on major European banks revealed the weakness in the monetary and banking union. The weak points in the union were Greece, Ireland, Italy, Portugal, and Spain (GIIPS). As a consequence, the collapse of the US housing market and the CDO market left some of the large European banks liquidity strapped, and they found it difficult to continue providing funding to the current account deficit countries. Greece and Spain's average current account deficits were 12.6 % and 7.7% to GDP, respectively, from 2015 to 2019. Moreover, by 2009, the budget deficit and government debt positions deteriorated markedly in many countries. The ratios of budget deficit to GDP were 15% in Greece, 14% in Ireland, 11% in Spain, and 7% in Portugal in 2009. Government debt to GDP stood at as high as 136% in Greece and 126% in Italy. These were clear signs of financial difficulties faced by these deficit countries. The trigger that the market needed was the announcement that the Greek government's actual budget deficit for 2009 was significantly higher than what was forecast for the year (15% of GDP compared to the forecast range of 6–8%). Amid the spreading concerns, the three rating agencies downgraded the Greek sovereign credit rating by one notch over the period 8 December to 22 December 2009 (e.g., Fitch downgraded Greece from A– to BBB+). The sovereign ratings of Spain and Portugal were downgraded in April 2010, with more coming later. Considering that the ratings are directly tied to the cost of borrowing, the downgraded sovereigns found it virtually impossible to continue to finance their deficits by issuing more bonds or borrowing from other European banks. Their inability to service their debt, the bulk of which was denominated in the EUR and held within the Eurozone (mostly by German and French banks and investors), required the assistance of the other countries in the currency union.

The deteriorating sovereign credit qualities showed up as the rising sovereign spreads of the five countries affected the most (GIIPS). Exhibit 11.7 shows the USD- and EUR-denominated sovereign debt CDS spreads from 1999 to 2017. All of the spreads rose from early 2010 and reached their peaks in early 2012. Portugal recorded 2,028 basis points on 30 January 2012, and Ireland reached its peak of 1,454 on 19 July 2011. These were very high premiums to pay for the investors of underlying sovereign debt for protection, indicating a severely compromised ability for these sovereigns to raise additional funds, although they were not in

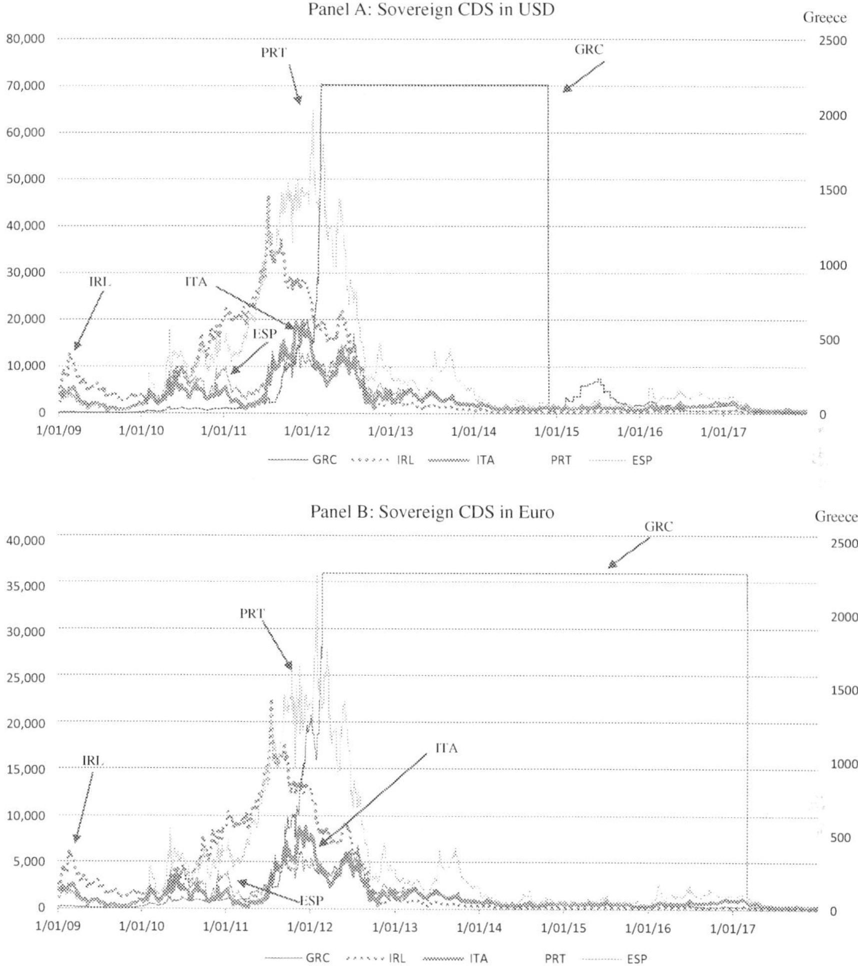

Exhibit 11.7. One-year sovereign CDS spreads of selected Eurozone countries in USD and Euro, 1999–2017.

Source: Refinitiv Eikon.

default. Greece reached a technical default on the USD-denominated one-year CDS on 26 September 2011 when the spread crossed the 10,000 bps threshold to reach 10,123. The peak was reached at 70,194 bps and lasted until 27 November 2014. The start of the default for the EUR-denominated CDS was 17 October 2011, and a peak spread of 35,932 lasted until 3 March 2017. So, the CDS market judged Greece to be in default until October 2017, lasting over five years.

On 9 May 2010, the European Financial Stability Facility (EFSF) was created with up to EUR 750 billion of rescue package. This was topped up to reach 1 trillion in October 2011. At the same time, private creditors (banks) agreed to a 53% write off of their Greek debt. However, EFSF's credit rating was downgraded from AAA to AA+ by the Standard & Poors on 16 January 2012, and it never regained its previous top rating status (as at February 2023, the ratings are AA from S&P and Fitch, and Aaa from Moody's). This was a direct consequence of the sovereign ratings downgrade of 9 European countries on 13 January 2012, where France and Austria lost their AAA ratings. This added to the uncertainty regarding the effectiveness of the EFSF as the funding abilities of some of the contributing countries diminished. In addition, in May 2012, the incumbent governments in France and Greece failed to regain power in their respective national elections, at the time casting doubt over the level of commitment to the continued austerity measures necessary for the resolution of the debt crises.

11.3.2. *Contributing factors*

11.3.2.1. *Current account deficits*

The current account and budget deficits of some countries were identified as one of the factors contributing to the debt crisis. This is despite some observers arguing that for the Eurozone as a whole, the deficits were no worse than those of the US and the UK (Noyer, 2011). However, there are those countries in the Eurozone that have generated unsustainable levels of sovereign debt that they had accumulated throughout the 2000s. It can be argued, however, that had these countries not been a part of the Eurozone, they might not have been able or allowed to continue to finance their deficits in their own currencies. Favaro *et al.* (2010) note that the source of the imbalance for Greece and Portugal was a low domestic saving rate in each country. In contrast, an investment boom was a more important factor for Ireland and Spain.

Exhibit 11.8 shows the current account balances of the 12 early member countries in the Eurozone (11 founding members and Greece that joined one year later). There were distinct surplus countries such as Luxemburg, the Netherlands, Finland, Belgium, France, Germany, and Austria, and distinct deficit countries such as Greece, Ireland, Italy, Portugal and Spain. The monetary and banking union within the Eurozone made it easier for the surplus countries to lend their surplus funds to the deficit countries via intra-Eurozone cross-border bank loans. There were noticeable changes in current account balances across the pre- and post-Eurozone periods. While Luxemburg, the Netherlands and Germany maintained strong surpluses, the positions of all five deficit countries markedly deteriorated until 2009. The deficits were as much as 12.6% of GDP in Greece, 10.3% in Portugal, 7.7% in Spain, 5.2% in Ireland, and 1.7% in Italy for the period 2005–2009. The mostly bank-funded current account deficits resulted in foreign banks holding claims against the deficit countries to explode by 2009 (Exhibit 11.10).

The decade-long accumulation of the current account deficits led to significant levels of government debt in some countries. For Greece, the ratio was over 139% in 2009, and more than half of the debt was held by foreign creditors. Italy and Portugal also accumulated high amounts of external debt by 2009 (126% and 97% of GDP, respectively, Panel B, Exhibit 11.9). However, most of the sovereign debt was held within the Eurozone. As a result, the majority of government debt in the Eurozone was held within the region, which was the basis of the claim that the deficit for the Eurozone was no worse than those of the US and the UK (Noyer, 2011). Indeed, the Euro area current account balance was barely in deficit in the periods of 2000–2004 and 2005–2009, with –0.06% and –0.44% of the Euro area GDP, respectively. However, the rapidly deteriorating deficits and the resulting government debt accumulations in the affected countries

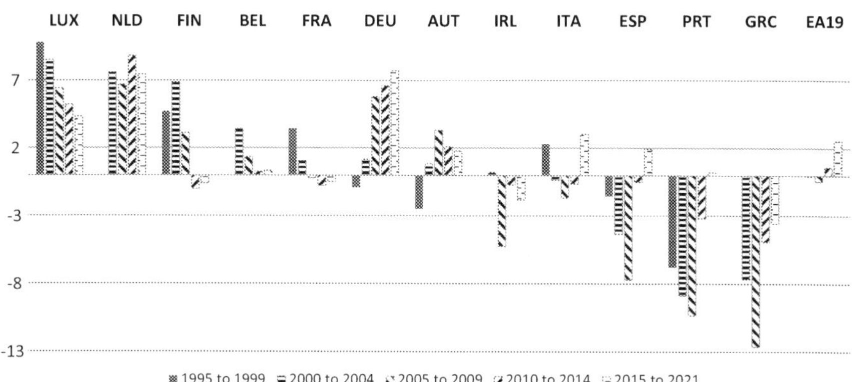

Exhibit 11.8. Current account balance of 12 founding Eurozone countries, % of GDP.
Source: OECD data, https://data.oecd.org/ and ECB.

presented a systemic risk for the union as the potential sovereign defaults posed significant challenges for the banking system within the union.

11.3.2.2. *Government budget deficits*

In concert with current account deficits, government budget deficits also posed a danger in the five countries. Exhibit 11.9 shows the government

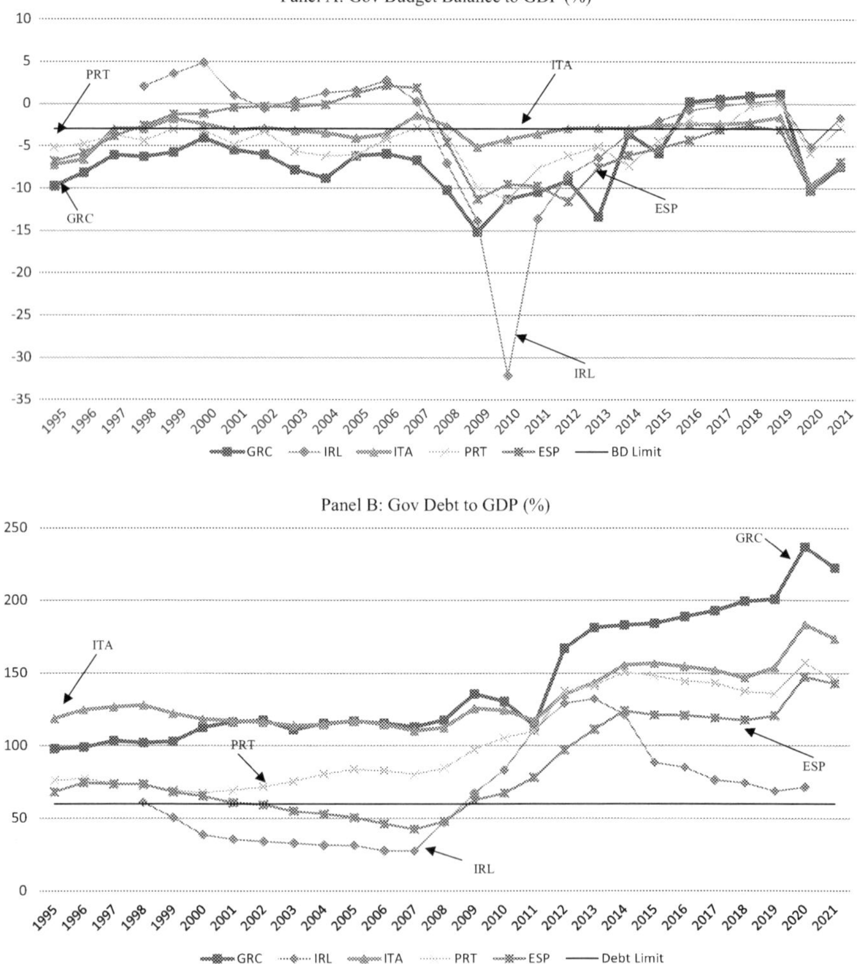

Exhibit 11.9. Government budget deficit and debt, % of GDP.

Source: OECD data, https://data.oecd.org/.

budget balance (Panel A) and debt to GDP (Panel B) for the GIIPS countries since 1995. There was a noticeable deterioration in budget deficits from 2007, when the negative spillover effects from the GFC were beginning to be felt in the most vulnerable economies in the Eurozone. Greece reported a deficit of 15% of GDP in 2009, and Ireland recorded a massive 33% deficit. The 3% of GDP budget deficit requirement as a requirement for a Eurozone membership was clearly not met by any of the countries from 2007 to 2015.

Given that domestic saving rates were generally insufficient to fund government deficits, external sources of funds were needed to secure financing for the deficits. For example, in Greece and Portugal, the national saving rates were negative, –10% of GDP and –5.8% in Portugal in 2009. In the other countries, the saving rates were positive but much less than the budget deficits, 0.25% of GDP to –13% in Ireland, 0.25% to –5.12% in Italy, and 4.56% to –11% in Spain (World Bank, World Development Indicators 2021). Panel B of Exhibit 11.9 shows the impact of the deteriorating government budget deficits on external government debt. For all five countries, government debt started to rise rapidly from 2007 as a direct consequence of the rising government budget deficits. Although Ireland recovered relatively quickly and a significant reduction started in 2013, other countries have yet to achieve meaningful reductions. For the Greek debt, there was a period of recovery between 2010 and 2011, which was due to the 50% debt reduction agreed upon by private lenders in 2011 rather than the Greek economy recovering.

11.3.2.3. *Increased bank flows within the Eurozone*

One of the monetary union's key benefits was the removal of frictions in capital movements within the union, which resulted from the uniform financial sector regulation and the common central bank setting the policy interest rates, in addition to the newly created common currency among the member countries. Banks from current account surplus countries (mostly Germany and France) took full advantage of the banking union, and the resulting availability of funds allowed the current account and budget deficit countries to be funded largely from within the Eurozone. On average, the Eurozone and the UK banks held 80% of cross-border claims against the five countries across the period 1999–2019.

Exhibit 11.10 shows foreign banks' cross-border claims against the five deficit countries at the start of the monetary union (1999–Q1), at the

	Greece			Ireland			Italy			Portugal			Spain		
	1999-Q1	2009-Q4	2019-Q4	1999-Q1	2009-Q4	2019-Q4	1999-Q1	2009-Q4	2019-Q4	1999-Q1	2009-Q4	2019-Q4	1999-Q1	2009-Q4	2019-Q4
Panel A: Total cross-border claims of BIS reporting banks against each country, USD millions and % of GDP for the year															
All reporting countries	**46,215**	**240,817**	**53,373**	**131,881**	**1,170,229**	**728,418**	**404,098**	**1,147,078**	**692,585**	**59,139**	**281,372**	**83,980**	**168,025**	**1,104,452**	**454,730**
	(23%)	(71%)	(16%)	(130%)	(622%)	(169%)	(28%)	(56%)	(26%)	(33%)	(101%)	(23%)	(21%)	(74%)	(23%)
Panel B County of lending banks, USD millions and % share of total															
European Countries	**38,657**	**184,773**	**45,950**	**106,573**	**915,857**	**518,405**	**342,936**	**977,930**	**635,101**	**38,206**	**172,997**	**78,461**	**140,507**	**956,130**	**372,225**
	(84%)	*(77%)*	*(86%)*	*(81%)*	*(78%)*	*(71%)*	*(85%)*	*(85%)*	*(92%)*	*(65%)*	*(61%)*	*(93%)*	*(84%)*	*(87%)*	*(82%)*
Eurozone Countries	**18,905**	**139,526**	**31,895**	**60,863**	**519,449**	**288,090**	**216,737**	**768,486**	**568,706**	**25,502**	**129,105**	**73,278**	**88,585**	**665,228**	**319,957**
	(41%)	*(58%)*	*(60%)*	*(46%)*	*(44%)*	*(40%)*	*(54%)*	*(67%)*	*(82%)*	*(43%)*	*(46%)*	*(87%)*	*(53%)*	*(60%)*	*(70%)*
France	4,700	52,015	2,105	6,799	76,885	73,339	67,226	306,684	290,746	10,398	49,825	22,091	28,982	213,620	117,369
	(10%)	*(22%)*	*(4%)*	*(5%)*	*(7%)*	*(10%)*	*(17%)*	*(27%)*	*(42%)*	*(18%)*	*(18%)*	*(26%)*	*(17%)*	*(19%)*	*(26%)*
Germany	8,825	45,745	24,467	17,433	251,245	41,841	64,995	175,817	80,198	9,226	41,700	8,617	28,821	238,091	77,599
	(19%)	*(19%)*	*(46%)*	*(13%)*	*(21%)*	*(6%)*	*(16%)*	*(15%)*	*(12%)*	*(16%)*	*(15%)*	*(10%)*	*(17%)*	*(22%)*	*(17%)*
United Kingdom	18,780	40,388	12,232	37,892	349,432	209,572	117,821	202,784	58,065	11,575	41,868	3,765	48,253	279,912	43,078
	(41%)	*(17%)*	*(23%)*	*(29%)*	*(30%)*	*(29%)*	*(29%)*	*(18%)*	*(8%)*	*(20%)*	*(15%)*	*(4%)*	*(29%)*	*(25%)*	*(9%)*
Belgium	1,049	6,466	238	10,665	108,131	18,889	16,127	44,886	12,153	1,828	9,096	645	5,632	45,657	12,678
	(2%)	*(3%)*	*(0%)*	*(8%)*	*(9%)*	*(3%)*	*(4%)*	*(4%)*	*(2%)*	*(3%)*	*(3%)*	*(1%)*	*(3%)*	*(4%)*	*(3%)*
Luxembourg	2,377	14,032	1,158	11,479	10,155	11,980	40,489	73,596	31,277	2,165	7,499	4,587	7,731	42,123	11,061
	(5%)	*(6%)*	*(2%)*	*(9%)*	*(1%)*	*(2%)*	*(10%)*	*(6%)*	*(5%)*	*(4%)*	*(3%)*	*(5%)*	*(5%)*	*(4%)*	*(2%)*
Netherlands	1,334	7,941	777	14,144	61,752	68,417	19,077	36,925	14,784	1,294	8,130	2,459	6,224	55,649	16,421
	(3%)	*(3%)*	*(1%)*	*(11%)*	*(5%)*	*(9%)*	*(5%)*	*(3%)*	*(2%)*	*(2%)*	*(3%)*	*(3%)*	*(4%)*	*(5%)*	*(4%)*
United States	742	499	94	3,750	57,777	64,703	9,033	44,398	2,749	1,272	1,975	413	3,499	40,072	5,692

	(2%)	*(0%)*	*(0%)*	*(3%)*	*(5%)*	*(9%)*	*(2%)*	*(4%)*	*(0%)*	*(2%)*	*(1%)*	*(0%)*	*(2%)*	*(4%)*	*(1%)*
Japan	543	5,989	287	4,631	31,346	58,310	10,813	45,980	37,503	405	3,497	1,104	5,973	21,845	36,888
	(1%)	*(2%)*	*(1%)*	*(4%)*	*(3%)*	*(8%)*	*(3%)*	*(4%)*	*(5%)*	*(1%)*	*(1%)*	*(1%)*	*(4%)*	*(2%)*	*(8%)*
Panel C: Claims against banks and non-banks, USD millions and % share of total															
Banks, total	14,984	100,654	15,719	87,852	648,943	212,972	202,554	693,364	326,532	39,297	199,453	39,760	95,362	767,867	213,381
	(32%)	*(42%)*	*(29%)*	*(67%)*	*(55%)*	*(29%)*	*(50%)*	*(60%)*	*(47%)*	*(66%)*	*(71%)*	*(47%)*	*(57%)*	*(70%)*	*(47%)*
Non-banks, total	31,226	140,141	37,626	43,863	521,199	507,403	201,225	453,578	355,414	19,837	81,907	41,171	64,728	336,425	238,774
	(68%)	*(58%)*	*(70%)*	*(33%)*	*(45%)*	*(70%)*	*(50%)*	*(40%)*	*(51%)*	*(34%)*	*(29%)*	*(49%)*	*(39%)*	*(30%)*	*(53%)*
Panel D: Currency denomination of cross-border claims, USD millions and % share of total															
Euro	13,154	207,627	40,977	57,952	714,960	316,298	300,135	1,050,351	642,604	34,656	259,607	78,555	115,849	924,620	397,232
	(28%)	*(86%)*	*(77%)*	*(44%)*	*(61%)*	*(43%)*	*(74%)*	*(92%)*	*(93%)*	*(59%)*	*(92%)*	*(94%)*	*(69%)*	*(84%)*	*(87%)*
US Dollar	11,643	26,786	11,483	47,460	256,155	247,144	62,431	73,045	38,168	14,875	15,526	3,704	38,223	111,785	43,737
	(25%)	*(11%)*	*(22%)*	*(36%)*	*(22%)*	*(34%)*	*(15%)*	*(6%)*	*(6%)*	*(25%)*	*(6%)*	*(4%)*	*(23%)*	*(10%)*	*(10%)*
Pound Sterling	410	1,363	391	15,813	156,608	116,177	14,329	7,813	2,954	2,447	1,154	159	2,822	53,097	4,996
	(1%)	*(1%)*	*(1%)*	*(12%)*	*(13%)*	*(16%)*	*(4%)*	*(1%)*	*(0%)*	*(4%)*	*(0%)*	*(0%)*	*(2%)*	*(5%)*	*(1%)*
Swiss Franc	2,507	1,869	407	3,210	4,867	3,299	6,522	6,046	3,222	423	451	271	1,444	3,419	2,186
	(5%)	*(1%)*	*(1%)*	*(2%)*	*(0%)*	*(0%)*	*(2%)*	*(1%)*	*(0%)*	*(1%)*	*(0%)*	*(0%)*	*(1%)*	*(0%)*	*(0%)*
Japanese Yen	5,832	2,032	24	3,697	12,429	21,110	13,029	4,717	1,262	2,199	958	349	7,206	4,872	1,950
	(13%)	*(1%)*	*(0%)*	*(3%)*	*(1%)*	*(3%)*	*(3%)*	*(0%)*	*(0%)*	*(4%)*	*(0%)*	*(0%)*	*(4%)*	*(0%)*	*(0%)*
Other currencies	12,669	1,140	91	3,749	25,210	24,390	7,652	5,106	4,374	4,539	3,676	942	2,481	6,659	4,628
	(27%)	*(0%)*	*(0%)*	*(3%)*	*(2%)*	*(3%)*	*(2%)*	*(0%)*	*(1%)*	*(8%)*	*(1%)*	*(1%)*	*(1%)*	*(1%)*	*(1%)*

Exhibit 11.10. Foreign banks' cross-border claims on selected Eurozone countries, 1999–2019, in USD millions.

Source: BIS International banking statistics, Locational.

start of the crisis (2009–Q4), and at the point of the aftermath of the crisis (2019–Q4). Between 1999 and 2009, the total foreign bank claims increased by a factor of six to reflect the increasing current account deficits in the five countries (Panel A). The total claims surpassed USD 1 trillion by 2009–Q4 in Ireland, Italy, and Spain. The outstanding foreign banks' claims were a staggering 622% of GDP in Ireland which was partly due to the offshore financial market role it performed. However, relatively high ratios of 101% in Portugal, 71% in Greece, 74% in Spain, and 56% in Italy were of concern. By 2019, foreign banks had largely reduced their exposures by at least 50% of their 2009 claims. The bank funding received by the five countries mostly came from the banks in EU countries (on average, 78% in 2009 across the five countries) and, in particular, the Eurozone countries (55%). The three most important lenders were France, Germany, and the UK, which accounted for 58% of the total (Panel B). The bank claims were relatively larger on non-banking sector borrowers in Greece, accounting for 58% in 2009 and 70% in 2019 (Panel C). The claims against the general government accounted for 54% of the non-banking sector (USD 20 billion out of USD 38 billion in total). In other countries, claims against banks were higher in proportion in general.

In terms of currency denomination, the EUR accounted for 83% of the total, followed by the USD at 11% (Panel D). The two currencies accounted for 94% of foreign bank claims averaged across the five deficit countries. Therefore, the current account deficits of the five countries were mostly funded by the claims of banks within the Eurozone and other EU area countries. Moreover, most of the funding was in the EUR. Although the EUR is the national currency of the deficit countries in question, they lack the ability to either depreciate their currency to gain external competitiveness or expand their money base or change policy interest rates unilaterally to stimulate their domestic economies.

In summary, the patterns of cross-border claims from 1999 to 2019, as shown in Exhibit 11.10, suggest the following. *First*, the creation of the currency and banking union led to a significant increase in the BIS reporting banks' claims against the five countries until 2009. *Second*, the bank flows came mostly from lenders in the Eurozone and the UK, and were denominated in the EUR. *Third*, non-banking sector borrowers received more funds in Greece, whereas banks were the more significant destination in other countries. *Fourth*, all countries show a substantial drop in cross-border claims against them between 2009 and 2019.

11.3.2.4. *Lending boom*

Exhibit 11.10 (Panel C) shows that more than 50% of the cross-border claims held against Ireland, Italy, Portugal, and Spain were directed to the banking sector. Banks in these countries in turn, extended credits to domestic borrowers. The interest rate convergence in the monetary union resulted in the long-term interest rates in the Eurozone rapidly falling until 1999 towards Germany's rate, and the trend continued to reach the Eurozone average of around 3.44% in 2005 (Panel A, Exhibit 11.11). The falling interest rates attracted government and private sector borrowers, resulting in continued government deficits and debt (Exhibit 11.9) and rising private sector investments.

Exhibit 11.11 shows the long-term interest rates, domestic credit extended by banks, housing prices, and bank NPL ratios from 1999 to 2021. The period of falling long-term interest rates from 1999 to 2005 (Panel A) coincides with the rapidly rising domestic bank lending from 2001 to 2008 (Panel B). In particular, the rapid domestic bank credit expansion is noticeable in Ireland, Portugal, and Spain, reaching their peaks of 169%, 159%, and 171% of GDP, respectively, in 2009. The inevitable boom in the housing market following such rapid credit expansions is also visible in all countries except Portugal (Panel C). In all countries except for Portugal, the housing price index rose substantially to its respective peaks in 2007. In Spain, the housing index rose 279% between 1999 and 2007, followed by 187% growth in Italy. The average growth across the four countries was 230% over the eight-year period. From 2005, however, signs started to show in the US of a housing market collapse that eventually led to the GFC in 2007. The housing market collapse in Spain and Ireland started in 2007, and by 2013, the housing price index fell by 35% and 53%, respectively. The falling housing prices were more gradual in Greece and Italy, and Portugal did not experience a similar housing sector boom and subsequent bust cycle.

The banking sector's health deteriorated due to the collapse of the housing market bubble (in all countries except for Portugal) and the difficulties the government faced in their debt repayments following the adverse effect of the GFC. Panel D of Exhibit 11.11 shows the banking

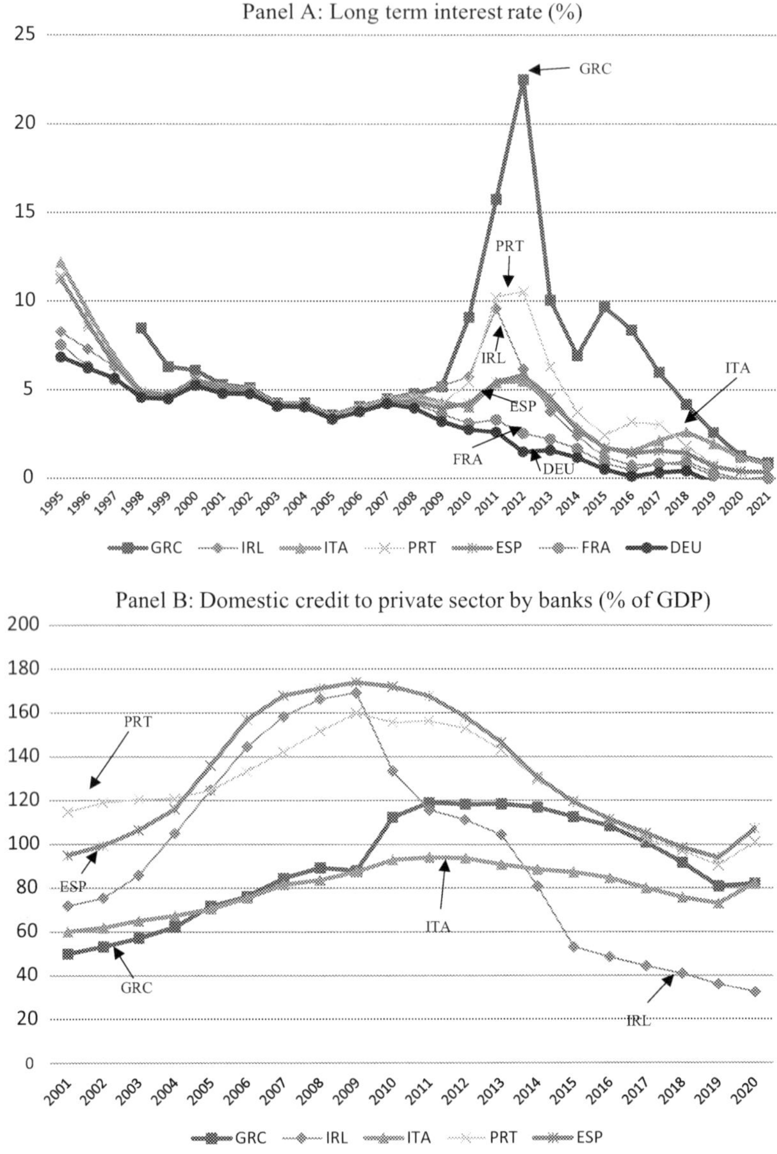

Exhibit 11.11. Bank lending and housing prices in selected Eurozone countries, 1999–2021.

Source: World bank Global Financial Development indicators, https://www.worldbank.org/en/publication/gfdr/data/global-financial-development-database, and OECD data, https://data.oecd.org/.

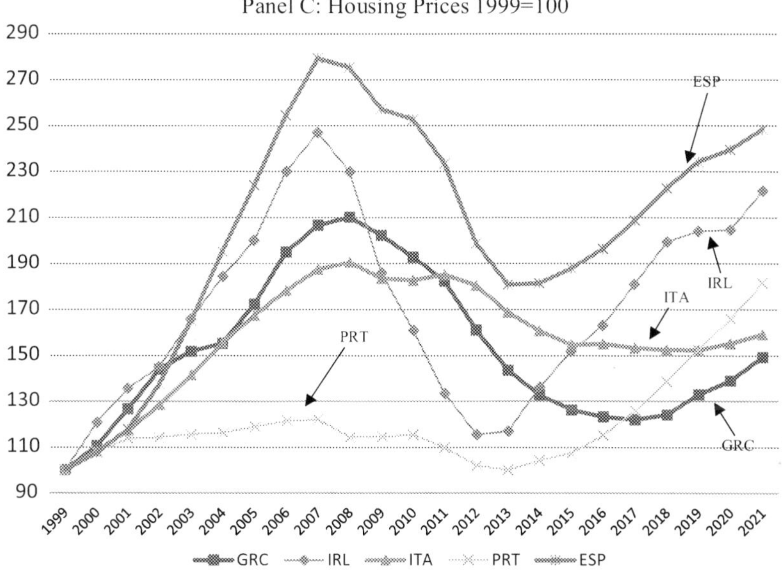

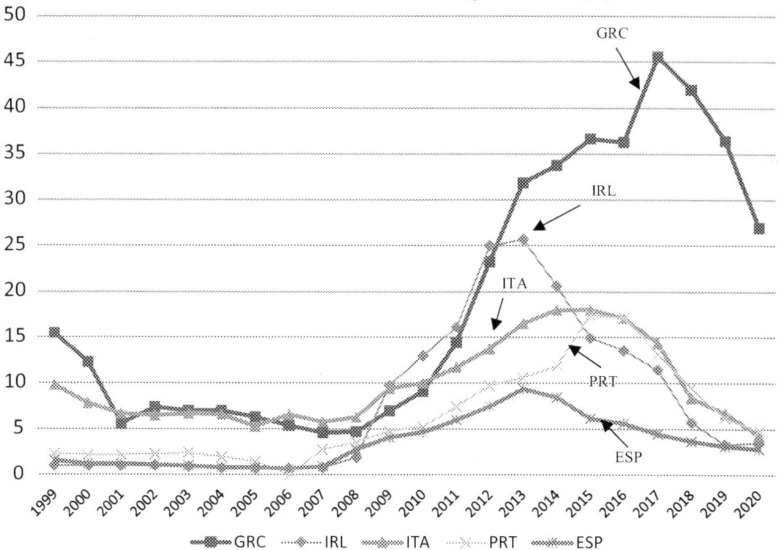

Exhibit 11.11. *(Continued)*

sector NPL ratios to gross loans. In all five countries, the NPL ratio started to deteriorate in 2008, reaching its peak in the early to late-2010s. The NPLs were significantly above the level the individual banking sector could resolve without external assistance. In Ireland, the NPL ratio rose to as high as 26% in 2013 amid the restructuring of two financial institutions, Anglo Irish bank and Irish Industrial Building Society, which were merged in 2011 and later liquidated in 2013. The worst deterioration is in Greece, where the NPL ratio rose to a staggering 46% in 2017, which required the government's help recapitalising troubled banks. The Hellenic Financial Stability Fund, established in 2010, provided recapitalisation support to the troubled banks, including leading the creation of four systemic banks out of 10 banks through M&As.

11.3.2.5. *Weak economic productivity*

Another important contributing factor to the Eurozone sovereign debt crisis was the rapid and significant deterioration of domestic productivity and external competitiveness in the crisis countries. After the union, the liberalisation of movements of factors of production and capital resulted in the conversion of interest rates and labour costs towards those of the two largest economies: France and Germany. Panel A of Exhibit 11.12 shows the unit labour cost of the five countries and the two main economies in the Eurozone. The divergence of the unit labour cost away from France and Germany is clearly visible for all five countries since the start of the union in 1999 to before the crisis erupted in 2009, suggesting that the relative labour costs have been rising in the five crisis countries against France and Germany. In Ireland, the unit labour cost fell from its peak in 2008 equally as rapidly as it rose, eventually becoming more competitive than France and Germany. Panel B shows the GDP generated from one hour of work in the five plus two countries. Apart from Ireland, which has shown significant improvements since 2009, the remaining four crisis countries share a clear and widening gap against France and Germany. Combining the two productivity measures paints a clear picture of rising labour costs and lower labour output compared to the two main economies, suggesting a significant and continuing deterioration of domestic productivity in the crisis countries leading up to the outbreak of the crisis in 2009.

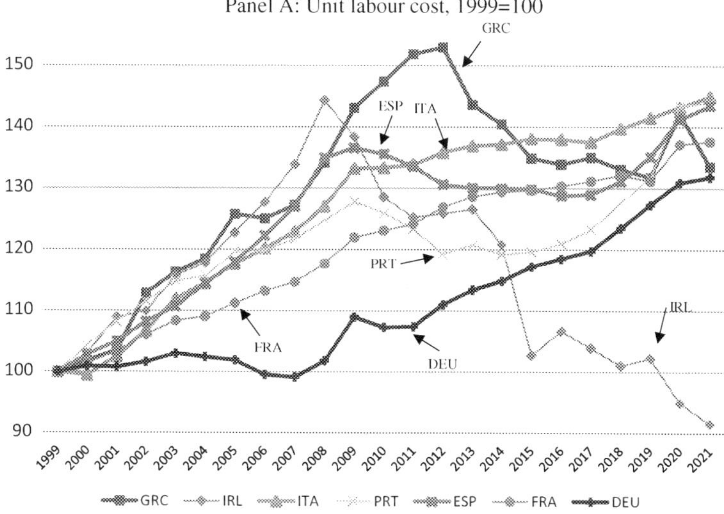

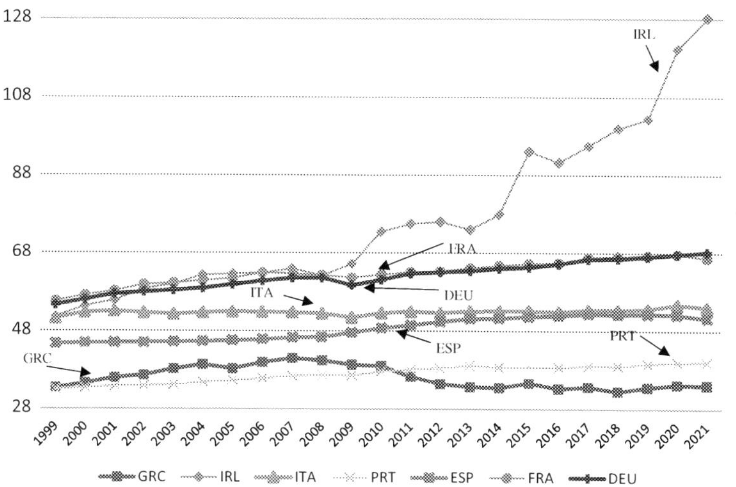

Exhibit 11.12. Economic productivities and performances of selected Eurozone countries, 1999–2021.

Source: OECD data, https://data.oecd.org/.

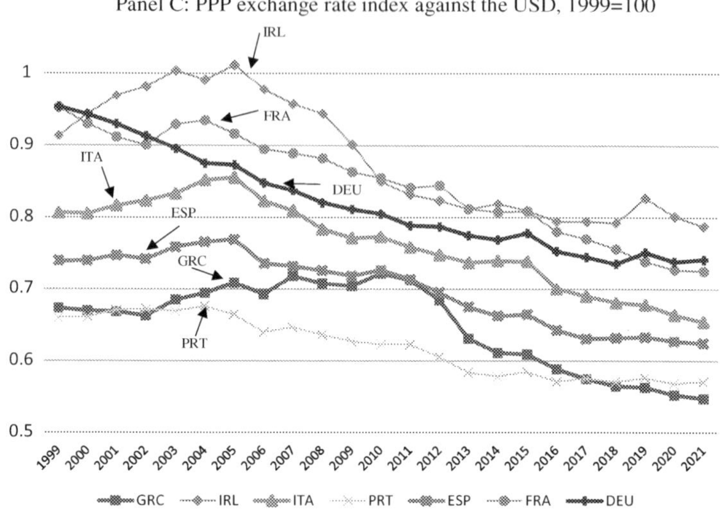

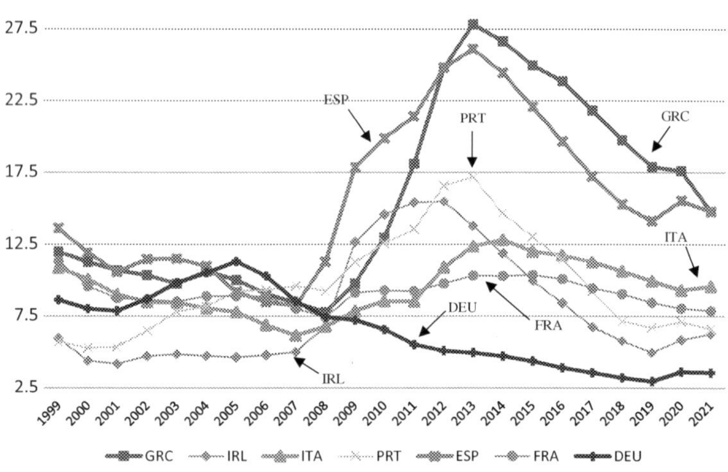

Exhibit 11.12. (*Continued*)

Moreover, the external competitiveness of the crisis countries deteriorated against countries outside the Eurozone, as shown by the falling PPP exchange rate of each of the countries against the USD.[7] In addition, all

[7]A PPP exchange rate is defined as the ratio between the equivalent domestic and the US price indexes and is a measure of the real exchange rate. Although the EUR is the common

crisis countries except Ireland show higher effective exchange rates (shown as lower PPP exchange rates) than Germany, suggesting weaker external competitiveness in these countries.

The deteriorating domestic productivity and uncompetitive external positions, combined with the other factors outlined above, led to economic breakdown in the five countries. The GDP of all five countries contracted in 2009, reaching –1.4% in Greece, –5.3% in Ireland, –2% in Italy, –0.1% in Portugal, and –2.7% in Spain. The Greek economy further shrank in 2010 and 2011 (–8% growth each year). At the same time, unemployment rose significantly in all countries (Panel D), reaching as high as 27.8% in Greece and 26.1% in Spain by 2013.

11.3.3. *Crisis resolution and recovery*

There were efforts made by various parties to resolve the sovereign debt crisis in the five member countries and to prevent them from spilling over to the rest of the union and creating a systemic crisis for the whole Eurozone. In addition to the debtor countries and the private lenders, their respective governments and international organisations became involved. The 'Troika' of the European Commission (EC) government, the ECB, and the IMF provided financial support and policy guidance in the rescue efforts of all the parties involved. Moreover, European Financial Stability Facility (EFSF) was created on 9 May 2010. It was a special purpose vehicle funded by the Eurozone member countries whose purpose was to provide financial assistance to the member countries during the Eurozone debt crisis. It initially had the authority to borrow up to EUR 440 by issuing bonds and bank loans. It was replaced with the European Stability Mechanism (ESM) on 27 September 2012 as a permanent fixture to handle financial instability in the Eurozone, replacing EFSF and the other temporary funding mechanism, European Financial Stability Mechanism (EFSM). ESM serves as a more permanent financial backstop and holds a lending capacity of EUR 500 billion.

The IMF provided rescue packages to Greece (May 2010–August 2018), Ireland (November 2010–December 2013), and Portugal (May 2011–June 2014). In addition, the EC initiatives of EFSF/EFSM and later ESM provided funds to these four countries. Austerity programs were also

---

currency in the Eurozone, each country's price index can differ, resulting in different 'real exchange rates' against non-EUR currencies and also within the Eurozone.

imposed as a condition for the IMF funds. For example, in Greece, measures to reduce current account and budget deficits were required to be implemented. These include freezing public sector wages, cutting public salary bonuses by 30%, increasing consumption tax (VAT) to 21% in March 2010 and then to 23% in July 2010, etc. With a combination of emergency rescue funds and debt reduction (e.g., private sector borrowers eventually agreeing to a 53% Greek debt reduction in March 2012), financial system-wide collapse in the Eurozone was averted and provided a foundation for recovery in the affected countries.

Economic and financial recoveries are evident in all the affected countries, although the nature and the pace of recovery vary. The current account deficits were largely reduced in most countries, even turning to surpluses. Spain's current account balance turned to a surplus of 1.9% of GDP in the 2015–2021 period, and Portugal also recorded a surplus of 0.21% for the sample period. Greece and Ireland still run deficits, but they were much reduced at 3.5% and 1.8% for the period 2015–2021, respectively, down from 12% and 5.2%, respectively, for the period 2005–2009 (Exhibit 11.8).

The government budget deficits have also shown significant improvements in all countries. All five countries once again met the Eurozone budget deficit criterion of 3% of GDP by 2018. In Greece, the budget turned into a surplus between 2016 and 2019 until the COVID-19 induced deficit of 2020. However, except for Ireland, the government's external debt continued to increase. In Greece, although there were periods of improvements in 2010 and 2011 (mostly due to the 'Greek haircut' of 53% of the privately held debt), the continued accumulation of debt is alarming, reaching its peak of 236% of GDP by 2020. The government debt held by external creditors was 154% of GDP, suggesting that foreigners held approximately 64% of its debt in 2020. Other countries also have high government debt, such as Italy (183%), Portugal (157%), and Spain (147%). Ireland is the only country that successfully reduced government debt closer to the required level of 60% of GDP. Its debt fell from its peak of 132% of GDP in 2013 to only 72% by 2020 (Panel B of Exhibit 11.9). Therefore, the silent bomb of high government indebtedness lingers, and unless successfully managed, it could be another trigger for future instability, especially in the interest-rising environment of post-COVID-19 period of 2022 and beyond.

Long-term interest rates started to stabilise after their peaks in 2012. In all five countries, the 10-year government bond rates converged to near zero or even negative by 2020, consistent with those of Germany and France, suggesting that the government's ability to raise funds by issuing bonds has drastically improved since 2012. The banking sector also shows great improvements in the NPLs in all countries, however, it is still a serious concern in Greece. The NPLs peaked at 25.7% in 2013 in Ireland, and then, rapidly dropped to a healthy 3.5% by 2020. In Italy, Spain, and Portugal, improvements were more gradual, but their 2021 NPLs were comparable to that of Ireland. The NPL ratio in Greece was still dangerously high at 27% in 2020, although much smaller than its peak of 45.6% in 2017. The banking sector loans gradually declined to pre-crisis levels in all countries. In particular, in Ireland, there was a substantial drop in bank lending activities to only 32% of GDP in 2020. In combination with the NPL and bank lending reductions, it appears that the banks in the crisis countries partially achieved lower NPLs by reducing their loan portfolios.

The area that the crisis countries have yet to show improvements in is economic productivity. The unit labour cost was still higher than that of Germany, labour productivity still lagged behind France and Germany, and their external competitiveness did not improve by 2021. Ireland is one exception where the combined productivity measures have improved since 2009. Also, the dangerously high unemployment rate reached 26.65% in Greece, and 26.11% in Spain was much less but still unsustainably high at 14.79% in both countries in 2021. In others, much more manageable levels were achieved by 2021.

In short, the emergency liquidity provisions by the Troika managed to avert the system-wide collapse and helped some countries, such as Ireland, to fully recover from the crisis on all accounts. However, there is still lingering danger for other countries, as shown by the rising levels of government debt, weaker labour productivity, and much-reduced banking sector activities in 2021. Given the high-interest-rate environment from 2022, uncomfortably high government debt levels can strain the ability of governments to maintain healthy budgets. In this regard, one of the policy responses is to consider the possibility of a fiscal union in addition to the monetary union among the Eurozone economies. Such a response can potentially have a positive consequence of avoiding a repeat of the crisis but at the cost of losing yet another macroeconomic tool available to address localised economic problems.

References

Beers, D. and Mavalwalla, J. (2017). Database of Sovereign Defaults. Technical Report No. 101, Bank of Canada. https://www.bankofcanada.ca/wp-content/uploads/2016/06/r101-revised-june2017.pdf.

Boughton, J. (2001). Silent Revolution: The International Monetary Fund 1979–1989. https://www.imf.org/external/pubs/ft/history/2001/.

Cole, D. H. (1992). Debt-Equity Conversions, Debt-for-Nature Swaps, and the Continuing World Debt Crisis, Articles by Maurer Faculty. 690. https://www.repository.law.indiana.edu/facpub/690.

Correa, R. and Sapriza, H. (2014). Sovereign Debt Crises, in *The Oxford Handbook of Banking* (2nd ed.), Berger, A., Molyneux, P. and Wilson, J. (eds.), The Oxford University Press, Oxford, UK.

Favaro, E., Li, Y., Pradelli, J. and Van Doorn, R. (2010). Europe's crisis: Origins and policy challenges, Chapter 9 in *Sovereign Debt and the Financial Crisis: Will This Time Be Different?* Carlos A. Primo Braga and Gallina A. Vincelette (eds.), The World Bank. https://documents1.worldbank.org/curated/en/217391468151502378/pdf/Sovereign-debt-and-the-financial-crisis-will-this-time-be-different.pdf.

FDIC (1997). The LDC Debt Crisis, Chapter 5 in History of the 80s Volume I: An Examination of the Banking Crisis of the 1980s and Early 1990s. https://www.fdic.gov/bank/historical/history/vol1.html.

Flores, J. (2016), Capital Markets and Sovereign Defaults: A Historical Perspective, *The Oxford Handbook of Banking and Financial History, Cassis*, Y., Schenk, C. and Grossman, R. (eds.), The Oxford University Press, Oxford, UK.

Kharas, H., Pinto, B. and Ulatov, S. (2001). An Analysis of Russia's 1998 Meltdown: Fundamentals and Market Signals, Brookings Papers on Economic Activity. No. 1. https://www.brookings.edu/wp-content/uploads/2001/01/2001a_bpea_kharas.pdf.

Noyer, C. (2011). Europe — A Financial Crisis, Not a Monetary One, Speech Given to the Paris Europlace Financial Forum, Singapore, 30 November 2011. http://www.bis.org/review/r111202c.pdf.

Nsouli, S. (2006). Petrodollar Recycling and Global Imbalances — Presentation by Saleh M. Nsouli, Director, Offices in Europe, International Monetary Fund at the CESifo's International Spring Conference, March 23–24. https://www.imf.org/en/News/Articles/2015/09/28/04/53/sp032306a.

Chapter 12

Financial Secrecy and Secret Money

12.1. Introduction

One of the functions of international banks that have received much attention in recent years is private banking services. This relationship-driven fee-income service caters mainly to high-net worth individuals and corporations from various countries in their investment and financing requirements. One of the critical aspects of private banking is strict confidentiality in providing financial services within the confines of the law in the countries of operation. However, there can be instances where banks might take this to the level of secrecy, making it difficult even for the national authorities (the financial regulators and the tax authorities) to ascertain the nature of the services provided and the identities of the customers served. Indeed, even some of the largest international banks have been found guilty of providing financial secrecy beyond the legal limits (e.g., Wachovia Bank, Standard Chartered Bank, Danske Bank, and HSBC, see Appendix 13A). In the US, HSBC and PNP Paribas were fined USD 1.9 billion in 2012 and USD 8.9 billion in 2014, respectively, for breaching the US's anti-money laundering regulation. These were cases of bank employees (and management) being more than complicit in facilitating money laundering for their high-net-worth clients. Most advanced countries have enacted laws preventing money laundering activities and strengthened the compliance requirements of their banking systems to prevent even unwitting cases involving banks.[1]

[1] In the US, the Bank Secrecy Act (BSA), enacted in 1970, aims to prevent banks from being used for illegal money laundering activities. Also known as the Currency and

There are, however, legitimate motives for financial confidentiality within the confines of the law. Moreover, some countries provide the legal framework to enable banks domiciled in their jurisdictions to supply anonymity in financial dealings. They are tax havens and offer facilities for anonymous business transactions. Switzerland is one such country offering banking secrecy for foreign customers. In this chapter, we discuss the various reasons for the demand for financial secrecy and what forms the supply of financial secrecy take.

12.2. Demand for Financial Secrecy

Financial secrecy is simply the non-disclosure of financial information of bank customers to third parties, including the tax authorities of the countries where they reside. The demand for secrecy is motivated by personal, business, political, and other legitimate or not-so-legitimate reasons.

Personal reasons include personal safety, financial privacy, business negotiations, etc. Individuals require financial secrecy *firstly* because of the belief that their financial status should be confidential within the confines of the law. Indeed, personal financial privacy is the cornerstone of the modern financial system in developed countries, protected by relevant laws. *Secondly*, they may need their financial information kept from the prying eyes of estranged partners, potential competitors or adversaries. Privacy does not imply secrecy, however. The rights of individuals to financial secrecy are desirable, and they are protected by law except for during the resolution of legal disputes, especially against the government, that require the financial details of the individuals involved. This factor contributes to the demand for personal financial secrecy that can be protected beyond the relevant domestic privacy laws. Individuals then seek to reallocate their wealth to jurisdictions that provide a higher level of confidentiality protection. For example, in the Cypriot banking system in 2013, the vast majority of the foreign deposits, estimated to be around USD 91 billion, were reported to be from Russia due to the attractive conditions offered by the Cypriot banking sector, such as low taxes, lenient financial regulations, and the provision of financial secrecy. In 2016, an investigation by the International Consortium of Investigative

Foreign Transactions Reporting Act, the law requires financial institutions operating in the US to assist in the US government's money laundering investigations.

Journalists (ICIJ) went public with a leak exposing the operations of Panama-headquartered international law firm Mossack Fonseca. The so-called the Panama Papers leak revealed the details of some 40 years of records on more than 214,000 companies in 21 offshore jurisdictions (ICIJ, 2017), with the transfer of funds conducted by more than 500 international banks. While offshore financial activities are not necessarily illegal, the Panama Papers records have become subject to an ongoing investigation by local and international authorities for suspected tax evasion and money laundering activities. As of December 2017, more than USD 500 million had been recovered by tax authorities worldwide following the Panama Papers release, including USD 122 million by authorities in Spain and the authorities in 15 countries have now commented on taxes recovered because of the leak (ICIJ, 2017) (see details in Appendix 13B).

Financial confidentiality in business is a necessary ingredient for a corporation's competitiveness or even its survival, especially when the success or failure of projects depends on the information asymmetry between the corporation and its competitors. Since a corporation's financial information can be regarded as proprietary, it is wise to release such information in a manner that suits its objectives. For instance, merger and acquisition activities require confidentiality of intentions and swift moves are needed to catch competitors unguarded if there are multiple bidders. Effective business negotiations may also require not revealing all of the financial cards that the corporation holds. However, the need for secrecy may lead to situations where the limits of the law may be tested with uncertain outcomes. That is, the need for financial secrecy may conflict with the requirements of fair-trading practices in many industries, and criminal activities might also be hidden under the veil of financial secrecy.

Political, economic, and social uncertainties in a country can lead to outflows of private wealth to foreign jurisdictions (capital flights). Growing uncertainty regarding the safety of ownership of financial assets in a country due to the fear of nationalisation, falling out of favour with the people in power, the introduction of unfavourable taxes, etc. could lead to an increasing need to reallocate assets to a jurisdiction out of reach of the local government. In general, capital flight is not illegal in itself in the absence of legal impediments to international capital movements, e.g., capital control prohibiting hard currency payments to foreigners. Investable funds flow to where the return is higher and the risk is lower globally. So, a deteriorating risk and return relationship for financial investments in a county would lead domestic and foreign investors to reallocate their assets away from that country. However, if such an outflow of capital from domestic residents is politically unwise, even if it is legal, financial confidentially, not necessarily secrecy, is required from the jurisdictions to which the fund is destined. Financial secrecy is also sought for illegal motives which might involve tax evasion, smuggling, money laundering, bribery, corruption activities, etc. As opposed to tax avoidance, which is not illegal, tax evasion refers to activities that falsely declare taxable income or allowable expenses to reduce or avoid tax liabilities illegally.

Tax authorities can be made unaware of foreign assets held by domestic residents if the assets are located in jurisdictions that provide financial secrecy and do not participate in information exchange arrangements with the domestic authorities. Outside assets that are unknown and beyond the grasp of the domestic authorities are thus valued by tax evaders. Tax evasion via moving assets to tax haven jurisdictions has a long history. During the First World War, war taxes imposed on wealthy individuals in France and Germany encouraged them to hide their assets in Switzerland to evade the taxes. Since then, individuals in high-tax jurisdictions have used the financial secrecy services provided by tax haven countries to hide their assets for tax evasion.

Another motive for demanding financial secrecy is related to criminal activities. Due to the illegal nature of certain activities, income generated from them is also illegal and subject to criminal proceedings, including confiscation of ill-gotten gains. Therefore, criminals who generate wealth from illegal activities seek financial secrecy to hide behind. Typical criminal activities include drug trafficking, loan sharking, extortion, organised crimes, and terrorism financing that require anonymity in their financial dealings.

In short, there are legitimate reasons for seeking financial secrecy, and many jurisdictions cater to these demands via private banking services, tax havens, and others. On the other hand, there are criminal activities that generate illegal wealth, leading to the demand for hiding the criminal proceeds away from prying eyes.

12.3. Supply of Financial Secrecy

Financial confidentiality can be provided for financial and physical assets held in onshore and offshore jurisdictions. Privacy and confidentiality of financial information on financial assets held onshore are about non-disclosure of information to unauthorised inquiries from third parties. Bank deposits, certificates of deposits, bonds, equities, and bank checks provide holders with some level of confidentiality. However, government authorities can legally force financial institutions and exchanges to disclose the personal financial information of their clients and their transaction records in the event of civil or criminal proceedings against them. If domestic financial assets were held in proxy by trustworthy individuals such as family members, relatives, and old friends, the legal actions might not be able to reach the custodians unless they themselves are also implicated in the investigation (Walter, 2012). Also, the proxy ownership makes it difficult to prove true ownership in case of a dispute. Therefore, financial confidentiality for onshore assets held by domestic residents depends on the level of confidentiality the law of the land allows. For residents of a jurisdiction with strict bank secrecy, such as Switzerland, the level of protection, even from government authorities, can be substantial.

Financial assets of domestic residents held in foreign jurisdictions as bank deposits, bonds, and other types may enjoy higher levels of protection than domestically held assets, depending on the types of confidentiality offered in the host country and whether there is a binding information exchange program between the host and home countries (e.g., OECD's Common Reporting Requirement). Even if the foreign jurisdictions offer similar levels of financial confidentiality as the home country, additional layers of complexity are added to the pursuit of financial information on assets held in foreign jurisdictions. Further protection can be obtained if shell companies can be created with bearer form ownership and assets are held by the shell companies to achieve anonymity. In this case, such financial secrecy raises confidentiality to the level of non-disclosure of information both to the home and host government authorities.

Physical assets can be hidden away from prying eyes by placing them into vaults, secret locations known only to the owner or bank security deposit boxes. They ideally take the form of high value–low mass assets that can easily be hidden, such as precious metals, collectibles, bearer form securities, or even large denomination cash. Swiss banks have traditionally offered security deposit boxes in vaults in hard-to-access locations, such as in mountain locations that can only be accessed by air and have multiple access controls once the owner of the deposit box arrives at the locations. However, if their locations are discovered, the owner may face unwanted attention or even criminal elements such as fraud, theft, or extortion aimed at securing the asset by third parties.

In this section, we focus on offshore financial assets as a means to secure financial confidentiality. We will discuss how tax havens, offshore financial centres, and Swiss banking system are useful in this regard.

12.3.1. *Tax havens*

Tax havens have attracted much attention in recent years due to the highly publicised data leaks (notably the Panama Papers in 2016 and the Pandora Papers in 2021) that implicated the rich and powerful in many countries, which have led to unwanted attention they had wished to avoid by using the services offered by the tax haven locations in the first place. A common perception of a Tax or financial haven is that it is a jurisdiction that offers financial secrecy to wealthy foreign individuals and businesses to evade taxes and hide assets or, even worse, assist in illegal money laundering via anonymous shell companies. Indeed, traditional tax havens located in Europe, the Caribbean island countries, and developing countries across various regions have perpetuated this perception by offering zero or very close to zero taxes on foreigners' activities, stable legal and political systems with financial secrecy baked in, and an absence of effective financial information exchange arrangements with the countries from which their foreign customers come. They allow foreigners to invest their assets in their financial systems and provide financial secrecy, especially from the authorities of the foreign investors' government authorities. This is done via the financial secrecy provisions and non-cooperation with foreign government authorities on information exchanges.

There are essentially three types of tax havens. *First*, no-tax tax havens are offshore locations that have no direct taxes for foreigners, however, there are various fees associated with foreigners' business activities. These countries tend to have economies that are over-reliant on income from this source. In Exhibit 12.1, the notable no-tax tax haven jurisdictions in 2020 include Anguilla, the Bahamas, Cayman Islands, Turks and Caicos Islands, Bermuda, Guernsey, Isle of Man, Jersey, Bahrein, and Vanuatu. *Second*, low-tax tax havens apply taxes on domestic business activities but at considerably lower rates than no-tax haven countries. The jurisdictions with less than the minimum global corporate

	Country	OECD[1] 2000	Hine[2] 2010	GFTH[3] 2017 SOFC	GFTH[3] 2017 COFC	TJN[4] 2021 CTHI	Corporate[5] Tax Rate 2021 (%)	Individual[5] Tax Rate 2021 (%)
				Africa				
1	Djibouti		✓				25	—
2	Gambia					✓	27	—
3	Ghana					✓	25	30
4	Kenya					✓	30	30
5	Liberia	✓	✓	✓		✓		—
6	Mauritius		✓	✓		✓	15	15
7	Seychelles	✓	✓	✓		✓		—
8	South Africa					✓	28	45
9	Tanzania					✓	30	30
				Americas and the Caribbean				
10	Anguilla	✓	✓	✓		✓	0	0
11	Antigua and Barbuda	✓	✓				25	0
12	Argentina					✓	25	35
13	Aruba	✓	✓			✓	25	52
14	Bahamas	✓	✓	✓		✓	0	0
15	Barbados	✓	✓				5.5	28.5
16	Belize	✓	✓	✓				—
17	Botswana					✓	22	25
18	Brazil					✓	34	27.5
19	British Virgin Islands	✓	✓	✓		✓		—
20	Cayman Islands		✓	✓		✓	0	0
21	Costa Rica		✓			✓	30	25
22	Curaçao			✓		✓		—
23	Dominica	✓	✓				25	35
24	Ecuador					✓	25	35
25	Grenada	✓	✓				28	28
26	Guyana			✓				—
27	Mexico					✓	30	35
28	Montserrat	✓	✓			✓		—
29	Netherlands Antilles	✓	✓					35
30	Panama	✓	✓			✓	25	25
31	Peru					✓	29.5	30
32	St. Kitts and Nevis	✓	✓					—
33	St. Lucia	✓	✓					—
34	St. Martin		✓					—
35	St. Vincent and the Grenadines	✓	✓	✓				—
36	Turks and Caicos Islands	✓	✓			✓	0	—
37	US Virgin Islands	✓						—
38	Bermuda		✓	✓		✓	0	0
39	United States					✓	27	37
				Asia				
40	China					✓	25	45
41	Hong Kong		✓	✓		✓		—
42	Macao		✓			✓		—
43	Maldives	✓	✓					—
44	Singapore		✓		✓	✓	17	22
45	Taiwan			✓		✓	20	40

Exhibit 12.1. List of tax haven countries.

Notes: 1. OECD (2000) Towards Global Tax Co-operation: report to the 2000 Ministerial Council Meeting and Recommendations by the Committee on Fiscal Affairs.

2. Hines, J. R. (2010) Treasure Island, Journal of Economic Perspectives, 24:4, pp. 103–126.
3. Garcia-Bernardo, J. Fichtner, J., Takes, F. and Heemskerk, E. (2017) Uncovering Offshore Financial Centers: Conduits and Sinks in the Global Corporate Ownership Network, Science Reports, 7, pp. 1–7. SOFC is Sink OFC and COFC is Conduit OFC.
4. Tax Justice Network (2021) Corporate Tax haven Index, https://cthi.taxjustice.net/en/, accessed 29 November 2021.
5. Corporate and Personal tax rates as at 2021, KPMG Corporate and Individual Tax Rates Tables, https://kpmg.com/it/it/home/services/tax/tax-tools-and-resources/tax-rates-online/corporate-tax-rates-table.html, accessed 29 November 2021.

	Country	OECD[1] 2000	Hine[2] 2010	GFTH[3] 2017 SOFC	GFTH[3] 2017 COFC	TJN[4] 2021 CTHI	Corporate[5] Tax Rate 2021 (%)	Individual[5] Tax Rate 2021 (%)
				Europe				
46	Andorra	✓	✓			✓	10	—
47	Austria					✓	25	55
48	Belgium					✓	25	50
49	Bulgaria					✓	10	10
50	Czechia					✓		—
51	Croatia					✓	18	30
52	Denmark					✓	22	56.5
53	Estonia					✓	20	20
54	Finland					✓	20	56.95
55	France					✓	26.5	45
56	Gibraltar	✓	✓	✓		✓	10	25
57	Germany					✓	30	45
58	Greece					✓	24	44
59	Guernsey	✓	✓			✓	0	20
60	Hungary					✓	9	15
61	Ireland		✓		✓	✓	12.5	48
62	Isle of Man	✓	✓			✓	0	20
63	Italy					✓	24	43
64	Jersey	✓	✓	✓		✓	0	20
65	Latvia					✓	20	31
66	Liechtenstein	✓	✓	✓		✓	12.5	—
67	Lithuania					✓	15	20
68	Luxembourg		✓	✓		✓	24.94	45.78
69	Malta		✓	✓		✓	35	35
70	Monaco	✓	✓	✓		✓	33	—
71	Poland					✓	19	32
72	Portugal					✓	21	48
73	Romania					✓	16	10
74	San Marino		✓			✓		—
75	Spain					✓	25	47
76	Slovakia					✓	21	25
77	Slovenia					✓	19	50
78	Sweden					✓	20.6	52.85
79	Switzerland		✓		✓	✓	14.93	40
80	The Netherlands				✓	✓		—
81	United Kingdom				✓	✓	19	45
				Middle East				
82	Bahrain	✓	✓				0	0
83	Cyprus		✓	✓		✓	12.5	35
84	Jordan		✓				20	30
85	Lebanon		✓			✓	17	25
86	United Arab Emirates					✓	55	0
				The Pacific Islands				
87	Cook Islands	✓	✓					—
88	Marshall Islands	✓	✓	✓				—
89	Micronesia		✓					—
90	Nauru	✓	✓	✓				—
91	Niue	✓	✓					—
92	Samoa	✓	✓	✓			27	27
93	Tonga	✓	✓					—
94	Vanuatu	✓	✓				0	—
	Total No. of Countries	**35**	**52**	**24**	**5**	**70**		

Exhibit 12.1. (*Continued*)

tax rate of 15% proposed by the G20 in 2020[2] include Barbados (5.5%), Andorra (10%), Bulgaria (10%), Gibraltar (10%), Hungary (9%), Ireland (12.5%), Liechtenstein (12.5%), Switzerland (14.95%), and Cyprus (12.5%). *Third*, special-tax tax havens can exist within a relatively high tax country for purpose-specific business activities. Special legislations exist for exempting tax for some vehicles, such as International Business Corporations[3] and tax breaks for foreign companies to set up manufacturing plants. Also, countries in this category include a newer breed of corporate tax haven countries listed in Exhibit 12.1.

The traditional tax havens, especially the no-tax jurisdictions, are countries that possess characteristics that foreigners find attractive. *First*, they impose little or no direct taxes on (foreign) business activities. Business activities conducted outside the tax haven country are not usually taxed, and there is also very little tax liability on domestically generated income. *Second*, they provide safe environments for establishing tax-free corporations and trusts. The necessary conditions include political stability, a transparent legal system, financial infrastructure, and an absence of binding capital controls.

Third, they provide both protection and invisibility of assets for foreign investors. They provide anonymity of ownership of business corporations through the non-disclosure of company information and with bearer-form equity capital. There usually are no tax treaties with major economies, allowing for tax-effective offshore investment possibilities for residents of high-tax jurisdictions. In general, tax haven countries do not have the incentive to cooperate with the government of the country of residence of their customers because doing so losing their foreign customers, leading to a collapse of their economies. They also provide strict bank secrecy, which can rival the Swiss banking secrecy. Tax haven countries typically have a significant number of financial institutions operating in their jurisdictions. For example, there were 111 banks for a population of 65,720 in the Cayman Islands in 2020. Foreign investors' investment in

---

[2]Dangor, G. (2021) G20 Signs Off On 15% Global Minimum Corporate Tax — Here's How It Will Work, Forbes, 11 July 2011. https://www.forbes.com/sites/graisondangor/2021/07/11/g20-signs-off-on-15-global-minimum-corporate-tax-heres-how-it-will-work/?sh=692b79de1c7e, Accessed 6 December 2021.

[3]An International Business Corporation (or Company), also known as a shell company, is a company incorporated in offshore centres (mostly tax havens) to conduct exclusively offshore business transactions in the country of incorporation, where it enjoys tax-exempt status.

the jurisdiction was worth USD 2.2 trillion that year. However, the foreign financial institutions were present to conduct offshore activities rather than servicing the local economy and customers.

The list of tax haven countries varies according to different definitions and criteria used. Exhibit 12.1 shows four independent lists of tax havens comprising up to 70 countries from five regions of the World. The OECD (2000) list includes 35 countries identified as tax havens that met the OECD tax haven criteria. Interestingly, the list did not include any OECD member country. Hines (2010) shows a more extensive list of 52 countries, including some of the countries that OECD did not consider. Both lists rely more on qualitative information (such as the degrees of cooperation with foreign government authorities, tax structures, and effective tax rates of the host countries), and so the countries in the lists can change over time as the qualitative assessments on them change. On the other hand, Garcia-Bernardo *et al.* (2017) rely purely on quantitative assessments using a big data analysis of ownership chains of 98 million companies connected through 71 million ownership relations. Their approach identified two types of tax havens: Sink Offshore Finance Centre (SOFC) countries and Conduit Offshore Finance Centre (COFC) countries. The former is defined as jurisdictions where foreign capital flows into, and the latter act as an intermediate destination of foreign capital. There are 24 and 5 jurisdictions identified as SOFC and COFC, respectively. The SOFCs are a subset of the Hines (2010) list quantitatively confirming the role these countries play in providing traditional tax haven services to attract international capital. The five COFCs act to channel money between jurisdictions. Singapore, Switzerland, and the UK also function as international financial centres, whereas Ireland and the Netherlands have a narrower focus on servicing corporate customers on tax matters. The fourth list in Exhibit 12.1 contains corporate tax havens where various tools that offer corporate tax minimisation to attract foreign multinational companies. They are mostly jurisdictions with transparent taxation systems and in full compliance with international information exchange programs. Tax Justice Network, in its 2021 list, includes 70 countries that qualify for the definition.

The harmful effects of tax havens on the lost tax revenues are difficult to estimate due to the nature of financial secrecy involved. However, some estimates suggest governments lose somewhere between USD 500 and 600 billion a year globally, and about 200 billion of that is from developing countries that can ill afford such revenue loss (Shaxson, 2019). More modest estimates are provided by Tørsløv *et al.* (2020). They suggest that about 10% (or USD 200 million) of global tax receipts are reduced in a year due to tax shifting to tax havens. There have been international efforts to counter the financial secrecy-induced international capital flows by individual countries such as the US and international country groups, such as the EU and the OECD. These include the efforts to name and shame tax haven jurisdictions, such as the countries listed in the tax haven list shown in Exhibit 12.1, and to list them in the blacklist of countries in terms of their lack of participation in international information exchanges. The increasing and sustained pressures on tax haven jurisdictions resulted in an increasing level of financial information exchange in these countries, and in 2017 the OECD listed only one county, Trinidad and Tobago, as a country that meets all three criteria of being a tax haven, down from 35 in 2000.[4] However, this is somewhat unrealistic as the degree of information exchange can be limited in some cases, and the inherent financial secrecy found in some jurisdictions still allows them to function as havens in the traditional definition.[5] The increasing pressure on tax havens to adopt information exchange agreements resulted in moving the focus of attention from tax havens that offer financial secrecy to those described as corporate tax havens that actively comply with international information exchange agreements but offer vehicles to foreign corporations to achieve low to zero effective tax rates. Corporate tax havens are relatively recent developments where some jurisdictions have relatively higher headline tax rates but offer effective tax rates close to zero via Base Erosion and Profit Shifting (BEPS) tools. These are high transparency jurisdictions but offer very low effective tax rates for foreign businesses that move untaxed income to their jurisdictions. Various BEPS tools allow the erosion of taxable income by inflating the cost base of revenue-generating assets, mostly Intellectual Properties, and shifting remaining untaxed profits to

[4]The three OECD criteria are (1) no or very low (nominal) tax, (2) absence of effective information exchange, such as the OECD's Common Reporting Standard (CRS) and the US's Foreign Account Tax Compliance Act (FACTA), and (3) lack of transparency. The third criterion addresses an issue of a non-transparent legal and financial environment, including financial secrecy, allowing the establishment of anonymous shell companies, for instance.

[5]For example, Switzerland complies with many bilateral and multilateral information exchange arrangements with other countries. However, the financial services provided by their banks are still subject to the Swiss Banking Act.

jurisdictions with very low tax rates. These tax haven countries comply with international information exchanges and have tax treaties so that the reduced tax liabilities achieved through these tools are legally binding in all countries that have entered into these agreements. The two most popular BEPS tools are so-called Double Irish and Dutch sandwiches. In the former, multinationals establish two companies in Ireland, one domestic tax resident company and the other a non-domestic tax resident company. The non-domestic tax resident company is incorporated in another tax haven country. The non-resident company holds intellectual properties against the resident company, and so a flow of income is directed to the second company in a country with very low or zero taxes. Apple Inc. is a very good example of this case whereby they established a second company in Ireland but is a tax resident in Bermuda, which has a zero tax rate.[6] In the second method, a tax loophole in the Netherlands allowed non-EU companies to avoid EU withholding taxes by shifting their royalty payments to non-EU tax havens. Due to the requirement of IP to generate royalty payments, this scheme is useful to those multinationals that possess IPs that generate income flows, such as information technology and pharmaceutical companies. For example, Google Inc. is reported to have shifted EUR 19.9 billion through a Dutch shell company to an Irish company incorporated in Bermuda in 2017 to substantially reduce or eliminate its tax bills.[7]

The OECD suggests that BEPS practices cost between USD 100 and 240 billion per year to the countries from which tax revenue is shifted away.[8] This is especially troublesome for developing countries that rely more heavily on corporate income tax revenues. Exhibit 12.2 shows the extent of profit shifting across tax haven countries based on Tørsløv *et al.*

---

[6]On 1 January 2015, the Irish authority changed the tax residency rule effective from 1 January 2021 that the second company in the Double Irish arrangement would be treated as a tax resident unless it is controlled from a country within the EU or the countries that have tax treaties with Ireland. This significantly reduced the scope of profit-shifting activities of multinationals operating in Ireland.

Doyle, C. (2020), INSIGHT: The Apple Case-Where Are We Now? Bloomberg tax, https://news.bloombergtax.com/daily-tax-report-international/insight-the-apple-case-where-are-we-now, accessed 6 December 202.

[7]Reuters (2019), Google shifted $23 billion to tax haven Bermuda in 2017: Filing, Technology news, 4 January 2019, https://www.reuters.com/article/us-google-taxes-netherlands/google-shifted-23-billion-to-tax-haven-bermuda-in-2017-filing-idUSKCN1OX1G9, accessed 6 December 2021.

[8]https://www.oecd.org/tax/beps/.

Countries	Reported[1] pre-tax profits (USD b)	Of which[1] Local firms (USD b)	Of which[1] Foreign firms (USD b)	Ratio of Foreign and Domestic pre-tax profits	Shifted[1] Profits (USD b)	Corp. tax[1] revenue loss/gain (% collected)	Nominal[2] Corporate tax rate (%)	Effective[1] corporate tax rate (%)	Nominal rate minus effective rate (%)
Belgium	80	48	32	0.67	−13	0.16	33.99	19.00	14.99
Bermuda	25	1	25	25.00	−24		0.00	0.00	0.00
Caribbean Countries	102	4	98	24.50	−97	1.00	0.00	2.00	−2.00
Hong Kong	95	45	50	1.11	−39	0.33	16.50	18.00	−1.50
Ireland	174	58	116	2.00	−106	0.58	12.50	4.00	8.50
Luxembourg	91	40	51	1.28	−47	0.50	29.22	3.00	26.22
Malta	14	1	13	13.00	−12	0.90	35.00	5.00	30.00
Netherlands	195	106	89	0.84	−57	0.32	25.00	10.00	15.00
Puerto Rico	53	10	43	4.30	−42	0.79	37.50	3.00	34.50
Singapore	120	30	90	3.00	−70	0.41	17.00	8.00	9.00
Switzerland	95	35	60	1.71	−58	0.20	17.92	21.00	−3.08
Other Havens					−51				

Exhibit 12.2. Tax shifting and effective tax rate in tax havens.

Notes: 1. Extracts from Table 2 in Tørsløv, T., Wier, L., and Zucman, G. (2020) The missing profits of nations, NBER Working Paper 24701, http://www.nber.org/papers/w24701.

2. KPMG Corporate tax rates table, https://home.kpmg/it/it/home/services/tax/tax-tools-and-resources/tax-rates-online/corporate-tax-rates-table.html, accessed on 29 November 2021.

(2020). Apart from Belgium and the Netherlands, all the haven countries show a ratio of pre-tax profits of foreign companies to domestic companies greater than one. In extreme cases, foreign company profits dominate in Bermuda, the Caribbean Islands, and Malta, which show ratios of 25, 24.5, and 13, respectively. This is typical of traditional small island country tax havens. The shifted profits are all negative, suggesting that they all receive shifted corporate income from the rest of the World. Ireland is the clear standout in this regard with over 100 USD billion inward profit shift. The corporate tax reduction through BEPS tools is noticeably higher in the European tax havens. The effective tax rate for Malta is reduced from the nominal rate by 30 percentage points, followed by Luxemburg (26), Belgium (15), and Ireland (8.5). However, the jurisdiction with the most reduction in their effective tax rate is Puerto Rico, where the nominal tax rate of 37.5% can be reduced to just 3% (a 34.5 percentage point reduction) through BEPS. However, paradoxically some high-tax countries may actually benefit from their multinationals using BEPS tools to avoid foreign taxes. For example, the US government may end up with higher corporate tax revenues as their corporations may pay higher US domestic taxes due to lower foreign tax credits they receive as they pay little or no foreign taxes via BEPS tools (Hines, 2010; Hong and Smart, 2010).

On 8 October 2021, the OECD/G20 BEPS project[9] announced a two-pillar framework tax deal agreed upon by 136 countries covering 90% of the World's GDP. The agreement was formally approved by the G20 leaders at the 2021 G20 meeting in Rome, Italy. The two-pillar policy involves limiting BEPS and setting a global minimum corporate tax rate. The first pillar applies to large multinational companies with a global turnover of more than EUR 20 billion and a pre-tax profitability of 10%. Their pre-tax profits (25% above the 10% threshold) are to be re-distributed to the jurisdictions from which those profits were generated. The OECD estimates that re-distributed profits would be more than USD 125 billion per year among 130 countries, which will have a positive impact disproportionally more on developing countries. The second pillar is a global minimum corporate tax rate of 15% to be applied to companies with revenues of more than EUR 750 million. The estimated additional global tax revenue is USD 150 million per year.[10] They are scheduled to be effective in 2023.

Large multinational technology companies have been using IP-based BEPS tools to avoid taxes by locating in corporate tax haven countries that are highly transparent and have established international information exchange agreements. The OECD measures can be effective in reversing some, if not all, of these tax avoidance practices. Also, the minimum global tax rate will hopefully reduce the ability of those tax havens with effective tax rates close to zero to continue to offer tax avoidance tools. Therefore, the merits of corporate tax havens under the two-pillar global tax agreement are likely to be reduced for larger multinational companies subjected to these rules. However, smaller multinationals under the thresholds would still be able to take advantage of those corporate tax havens. Moreover, those havens that mostly cater to foreigners seeking financial secrecy are unlikely to be affected as much and so would likely continue to offer existing services to foreigners seeking secrecy.

12.3.2. *Offshore financial centres*

Offshore financial centres (OFCs) are countries that provide financial services to foreign financial and non-financial corporations. The Bank for

[9] https://www.oecd.org/tax/beps/.

[10] https://www.oecd.org/tax/international-community-strikes-a-ground-breaking-tax-deal-for-the-digital-age.htm.

	Foreign[1] Banks' Assets (US$ m)	Foreign[1] Banks' Liabilities (US$ m)	Foreign Banks' Assets to GDP	Foreign Banks' Liabilities to GDP	GDP[2] (US$ m)	GDP[2] Per Capita (US$)	% of[3] Primary Sector in GDP (%)	% of[3] Secondary Sector in GDP (%)	% of[3] Tertiary Sector in GDP (%)	Exports[2] (US$ m)	Imports[2] (US$ m)
Offshore Centres (OFC)	5,264,234	4,823,578			—	—	—	—	—	—	—
Aruba	1,653	1,445	0.52	0.45	3,202	30,253	0.4	33.3	66.3	2,363	2,390
Bahamas, The	125,626	123,207	9.65	9.46	13,022	33,768	2.3	7.7	90.0	5,132	4,999
Bahrain	54,162	37,170	1.44	0.99	37,653	23,991	0.3	39.3	60.4	29,959	27,050
Barbados	22,785	31,853	4.48	6.26	5,087	17,745	1.5	9.8	88.7	2,100	2,020
Bermuda	122,902	92,353	17.01	12.78	7,224	113,023	0.9	5.3	93.8	3,704	1,868
Cayman Islands	2,227,112	1,301,302	403.27	235.63	5,523	86,060	0.3	7.4	92.3	3,960	2,520
Curacao	5,919	15,574	1.89	4.98	3,128	19,631	0.7	15.5	83.8	1,930	2,750
Gibraltar	3,823	11,172	1.87	5.47	2,044	61,700	0.0	0.0	100.0	202	—
Guernsey	114,401	113,917			—		3.0	10.0	87.0	—	—
Hong Kong SAR	1,119,223	1,524,985	3.09	4.22	361,692	48,543	0.1	0.6	92.3	681,283	682,056
Isle of Man	17,452	42,821	2.33	5.72	7,492	89,113	1.0	13.0	86.0	—	—
Jersey	203,579	187,748			—		2.0	2.0	96.0	—	—
Lebanon	4,715	31,779	0.09	0.58	54,961	8,013	3.9	13.1	83.0	11,389	26,070
Macao SAR	69,470	104,723	1.26	1.89	55,302	87,555	0.0	6.3	93.7	45,621	18,276
Mauritius	19,746	18,775	1.39	1.32	14,182	11,208	4.0	21.8	74.1	5,809	7,661
Netherlands Antilles		-			—	—	—	—	—	—	—

(*Continued*)

Exhibit 12.3. Cross-border claims and liabilities against offshore financial centres (OFC), 2020.

Notes: 1. BIS reporting banks' total cross-border claims and liabilities against each of the OFC countries as at end of 2020, in USD millions. Three major economies are also shown for comparison. BIS's International Banking Statistics, Consolidated Statistics. www://bis.org.

2. Export and Import in current USD millions for the year 2019. World Bank's World Development Indicators https://databank.worldbank.org/source/world-development-indicators.

3. CIA's world fact book, https://www.cia.gov/the-world-factbook/.

	Foreign[1] Banks' Assets (US$ m)	Foreign[1] Banks' Liabilities (US$ m)	Foreign Banks' Assets to GDP	Foreign Banks' Liabilities to GDP	GDP[2] (US$ m)	GDP[2] Per Capita (US$)	% of[3] Primary Sector in GDP (%)	% of[3] Secondary Sector in GDP (%)	% of[3] Tertiary Sector in GDP (%)	Exports[2] (US$ m)	Imports[2] (US$ m)
Panama	86,527	62,362	1.33	0.96	64,928	15,545	2.4	15.7	82.0	27,719	30,516
Samoa	5,321	727,406	6.48	885.46	821	4,189	10.4	23.6	66.0	281	413
Singapore	727,406		1.93	0.00	375,982	66,679	0.0	24.8	75.2	665,718	557,509
Sint Maarten	465	407	0.39	0.34	1,185	29,160	0.4	18.3	81.3	800	1,236
Switzerland	662,785	698,340	0.90	0.95	735,889	86,430	0.7	25.6	73.7	487,009	394,807
Vanuatu	228	530	0.25	0.58	915	3,125	27.3	11.8	60.8	518	549
West Indies UK	324,697	314,151			—	—	—	—	—	—	—
Major Economies											
Germany	1,859,654	1,896,177	0.47	0.48	3,961,832	47,787	0.7	30.7	68.6	1,876,821	1,633,219
United Kingdom	5,228,073	5,401,139	1.83	1.89	2,857,317	42,993	0.7	20.2	79.2	882,627	916,629
United States	6,129,544	4,410,653	0.30	0.21	20,611,861	63,064	0.9	19.1	80.0	2,528,704	3,138,164

Exhibit 12.3. *(Continued)*

International Settlements has been reporting a broad list of jurisdictions as offshore centres in their international banking statistics (summarised in Exhibit 12.3). In most cases, OFCs are small countries that enjoy domestic political stability, lack regulation on international capital flows, and impose little or no direct taxes on international banking activities they host. Foreign financial institutions established are usually shell branches with all the business decisions made at their headquarters. They are mainly used as booking centres for eurocurrency operations. This is consistent with the IMF's definition of an OFC, as Zorome (2007)'s definition where 'An OFC is a country or jurisdiction that provides financial services to non-residents on a scale that is incommensurate with the size and the financing of its domestic economy (page 7)'. He also states that '..the setting up of an OFC usually results from a conscious effort to specialise the economy in the export of financial services, in order to generate revenues that often constitute a critical proportion of the national income'.

Indeed, many of the jurisdictions listed as OFCs in Exhibit 12.3 show this very characteristic. The first two columns show the BIS reporting banks' cross-border assets and liabilities against the OFCs. The clear standouts are the Cayman Islands, Hong Kong, Singapore, and Switzerland in terms of size. The Cayman Islands is one of the best known tax havens belonging to the traditional definition of a tax haven jurisdiction (Zorome, 2007), a small, independent, politically stable country with an absence of regulation on foreigners' business activities. In 2020, the BIS reporting banks held nominal assets worth USD 2.2 trillion, which is twice as large as the next largest OFC, Hong Kong, and three times as large as the next two, Singapore and Switzerland, which helped achieve the high GDP per capita of USD 86,060. However, the economy of the Cayman Islands is considerably smaller, with its real GDP of USD 5.5 billion, which is approximately 1.5% of that of Hong Kong. The countries in this category share the same characteristics, although not to the extreme extent shown in the case of the Cayman Islands, of disproportionally larger cross-border financial assets and liabilities being held in the jurisdiction compared to the size of their economies, high tertiary sector concentration in their GDPs and enjoy higher GDP per capita compared to the non-tax haven counties of their peers. The smaller jurisdictions offer low tax environments for international financial transactions and host shell banks and corporations for international business corporations. They lack any regulation on international capital flows and have little or no direct taxes on international banking activities. Political stability is also a vital requirement. They are host to shell branches of multinational companies that act as booking centres for profit shifting and other tax avoidance schemes, with all of the business decisions being made at their headquarters.

Hong Kong and Singapore, on the other hand, are considered to be financial centres where multinational financial institutions operate eurocurrency and foreign exchange market operations. They are considered international and regional financial centres by the IMF as well as being an OFC. Switzerland is a traditional safe haven jurisdiction for foreign investments (see the following section). All three also have sizeable economies in addition to their OFC operations, as evidenced by considerably larger GDPs and international trade activities compared to the rest of the countries on the list.

There is a large overlap between offshore financial centres and tax havens. Indeed, GFTH (2017)'s classifications of sink and conduit OFCs cover most of the jurisdictions listed as OFCs in Exhibit 12.3. The notable SOFCs are the Cayman Islands and Hong Kong, where disproportionate amounts of taxable income disappear, routed from the notable COFCs, such as Singapore and Switzerland.

12.3.3. *Swiss banking*

12.3.3.1. *History of bank secrecy*

Switzerland is one of the oldest and better-known tax havens in the World, well known for offering offshore private banking activities catering to many wealthy individuals and corporations from around the World, in addition to watchmaking, the Swiss guards, and the Swiss army knife, among other things. It has been a host of the headquarters of Bank for International Settlement in Basel since 1930. It operates financial centres in three main locations to cater to clients of different language and cultural backgrounds, Geneva for French speakers, Lugano for Italian speakers, and Zürich for German speakers. In 2018, Swiss banks managed around a third of the World's offshore wealth, which amounted to USD 2.3 trillion, which was more than double the second largest, which was Hong Kong's USD 1.1 trillion, followed by Singapore's USD 0.9 trillion.[11] Private banking in Switzerland has always been dependent on its

[11] SWI (2018) Switzerland remains biggest offshore wealth centre, https://www.swissinfo.ch/eng/international-money-_switzerland-remains-biggest-offshore-wealth-centre-/44193170.

banking secrecy used for tax evasion by foreign customers (Walter, 2012). The provision of bank secrecy was the key to this level of success, given the relatively small size of the economy. Indeed, Guex (2000) argues that the maintenance of bank secrecy has consistently been the main objective of the successive Swiss governments' domestic and foreign policy. In 2022, Switzerland was ranked second out of 141 countries in the Financial Secrecy Index, beaten only by the Cayman Islands and the United States.[12]

Switzerland has a long history of bank secrecy dating back to the early 18th century when Swiss banks started to attract deposits from nearby Catholic country monarchs and aristocracy who detested Protestant bankers. The great council of Geneva adopted regulations in 1713 prohibiting bankers from revealing client information to outside parties. This started the tradition of bank secrecy that is characterised as the banker-clients relationship rivalling the priest-penitent privilege. Moreover, being a small country surrounded by major military aggressors of Germany, France, Italy, and Austria throughout the centuries, Switzerland's path to survival was to become a neutral country that posed no threat to its neighbours and to provide indispensable services to the surrounding countries as they needed them without bias. Neutrality was essential as mountainous terrain isolated valley communities or cantons along the lines of three distinct language groups — French, Italian, and German speakers — closely located to their respective origin countries. Taking sides with one country against the other in a conflict was a sure way of dividing the country. In 1815, the Congress of Vienna decreed its neutrality, and so Switzerland, along with its bank secrecy, truly was on its way to becoming a haven country for those who were looking for a safe haven for their assets during times of conflict. Being a safe haven for financial and non-financial assets of the dominant countries at the time as they accumulated plunders from conflicts required unbreakable confidentiality. Switzerland performed this role admirably

[12]The US being ranked first is a surprise. In its report on the US, Tax Justice Network (https://www.taxjustice.net/) suggests that 'While the United States has pioneered powerful ways to defend itself against foreign tax havens, it has not seriously addressed its own role in attracting illicit financial flows and supporting tax evasion'. It highlights the tolerance by some states, such as Delaware and Nevada, of secretive anonymous shell companies. https://fsi.taxjustice.net/.

throughout two world wars and various regional wars, and political upheavals.

The major impetus to the growth of Swiss banking came in the early 1900s when Swiss bankers identified an opportunity to cater for wealthy European individuals wishing to avoid rising domestic taxes. For instance, in October 1901, France greatly increased the inheritance tax and the income tax on the wealthy. Also, during the first World War, the countries on both sides of the War raised war taxes. Increased taxes presented opportunities for Swiss bankers to attract the wealthy to deposit their financial and non-financial wealth with the Swiss banking system under strict confidentiality so that such taxes can be avoided.

12.3.3.2. *Swiss banking Act*

Up until 1934, bank secrecy was a tradition among Swiss bankers who abided by their own code, and although the violation of trust (e.g., breaking the bank-client confidentiality) was a significant civil offence, it was not a criminal matter. Such matters were considered civil violations and resolved by awarding damages. The Federal Act on Banks and Savings Banks in Switzerland, known simply as the Swiss banking Act 1934, was enacted into law, thus codifying the bank secrecy that had been in practice for centuries. As a result, the stringent privacy law regarding financial information disclosure made the Swiss's banking privacy law the tightest in the World.

Article 47 is the key aspect of the law and states that all bank personnel are obliged to maintain the confidentiality of their client information (e.g., identity of bank account holders, the current balance of accounts, confirmation of the existence of accounts, and in general, this covers all the information in relation to the bank's dealing with the customer). Bank employees are required to sign the secrecy portion of the Banking Act as a condition of employment and maintain secrecy not only during the period of employment but also after leaving the current job. They are prohibited from disclosing client information to third parties, including Swiss authorities. The only exceptions are when there is consent from the client and the client account is identified by relevant authorities as directly linked to a crime recognised both in Swiss and the country of the client who is under investigation. However, neither is likely in practice if secrecy is properly maintained. Detected violations of secrecy by current or past bank employees are automatically dealt with in criminal proceedings, irrespective of whether legal action is brought up against the offending employee. The offence attracted a prison term of up to six months and fines of up to CHF 50,000 (30,000 if the information leakage was due to negligence). In a 2008 revision, the penalties have increased to five years of jail time and a CHF 250,000 fine. Both individuals and banks are prosecuted if a breach is discovered, and the violation of financial secrecy remains punishable even after the employee leaves their employment. However, foreign branches of Swiss banks observe the laws of the countries in which they are located. Thus, they may not provide the same level of protection as at home.

In rare cases of accepted criminal complaints, the relevant customer account information can be released to the Swiss authorities for required investigations. If foreign authorities request an investigation into a case, both the Swiss and the requesting foreign authorities must agree that there are criminal elements involved and these activities are punishable in both countries. Appropriate investigations may be conducted in such cases, including the examination of account transactions and the beneficiary of the accounts under investigation. However, the Swiss authorities have a narrower view of what constitutes a financial crime.

In the first few years following the introduction of the 1934 Act, Swiss banks introduced the most well-known account type for ensuring account holder privacy, the *Swiss numbered bank account*. A numbered bank account is identified by a series of numbers, and the identity of the owner is known only to a handful of employees (the account manager and the bank director). A numbered bank account can be opened usually only in person at a local bank in Switzerland. Instead of paying interest, the account requires a minimum deposit of USD 100,000 or its equivalent in the EUR, the CHF, or the GBP, and an approximately USD 300 annual fee. Deposits and withdrawals by the owner are made in the privacy of a closed room assisted by the designated account manager, and third-party deposits to the account are made only with the account owner's consent. Although numbered bank accounts provide an additional layer of protection, the account holder still needs to pass through multiple layers of identity checks and show that the funds to be deposited are from legal sources. Moreover, information about the accounts may be disclosed to the authorities of the account holder's domicile under very limited cases of proven criminality, as explained above.

12.3.3.3. *Attempts to combat bank secrecy and modern amendments to the banking law*

Bank secrecy propelled Switzerland into one of the largest offshore financial centres in the world. However, at the same time, there have been countless attempts by many countries to weaken its secrecy in order to prevent the flight of capital to or even repatriate capital from Switzerland. Guex (2000) presents detailed discussions of the threats faced by Swiss banks in the first half of the 20th century. Immediately after the first World War, France and Belgium put pressure on the Swiss authorities to obtain information on the identities of deposit holders from their countries. The Swiss authorities were, however, able to fend off these pressures by refusing to cooperate. In the 1930s, the Germany and France attempted to prevent or reverse capital flights to Switzerland in order to address their fiscal difficulties during the heights of the great depression. Germany made several decrees to identify all assets of German citizens held in Switzerland with a view to forcing repatriation. In addition, the German authorities attempted to obtain information about the German depositors in Swiss banks from the Swiss bank employees. More serious threats came from France. The French authorities seized documents in the Paris office of some of the Swiss Banks, Basler Handelsbank and the Banque d'Escompte Suisse, and discovered that these Swiss banks aided more than a thousand French citizens in moving their capital to Switzerland to evade French taxes to the tune of 1 billion French Francs (roughly equivalent to 20–40 billion Francs in 2000) (Guex, 2000). The French authorities demanded to search these Swiss banks' offices in Switzerland as well. They also used espionage tactics to obtain information on the French clients and their assets in Switzerland. They even imprisoned Swiss bank employees in Paris for not accommodating their demand for client information. These existential threats to the survival of Swiss banking secrecy contributed to the Swiss Banking Act 1934, which codified bank secrecy into criminal law. Swiss bank employees who divulged their client information to external parties, including the Swiss authorities, were subjected to criminal proceedings leading to imprisonment and a substantial fine.

Another wave of threats came after the Second World War when the US applied pressure. After freezing the Swiss bank assets held in the US (CHF 6 billion, which was equal to approximately half of the GDP of Swiss at the time, Guex, 2000), the US authorities demanded a detailed inventory of all German assets held in Switzerland and the identification of owners of the frozen Swiss bank assets in the US. The investigations were to be supervised by the US authorities so as to identify the exact amount, country of origin, and the identities of the owners of those assets. These demands amounted to the total dismantling of the Swiss bank's secrecy. However, the Swiss authorities and Swiss banks were able to placate the US and survive these attacks with their bank secrecy intact. *First*, they extended much-needed loans to the French and the UK governments to the tune of CHF 300 million and 260 million, respectively, on very favourable terms. The aim was to make Swiss banks indispensable for these allies of the US so that the US would realise that it was in its interest to maintain the credit flows to the French and British governments. *Second*, the Swiss authorities highlighted their humanitarian track record in providing a safe haven for Jewish flight assets from Germany during the Second World War and accepting refugees escaping Nazi persecution, which were all acknowledged by the US. These efforts were largely effective. Although Swiss banks grudgingly agreed to provide information on the German assets they held and eventually repatriated a part of them to the US (only in the 1990s), they escaped the requirement of providing client and account information of the Swiss assets held in the US, which were subsequently unfrozen (Guex, 2000). In short, the Swiss bank secrecy survived the most important threats to its existence up to that point.

From the Second World War to the present day, there have been numerous attempts from many countries to weaken the Swiss banking secrecy by forcing the Swiss authorities and banks to give up client information. Some of these attempts yielded positive outcomes leading to bilateral and multilateral agreements of information exchange between Switzerland and the US and major European countries. Following the US case against UBS and Credit Suisse, and other banks in 2008, the US government successfully obtained information on more than 4,000 UBS clients in 2009 (TJN, 2020). This has led to Switzerland signing the US Foreign Account Tax Compliance Act (FATCA) which requires all non-US financial institutions to supply information to the US Department of the Treasury on the assets and liabilities of the US customers (both residents and citizens) they hold. The pressures coming from major European countries resulted in Switzerland's participation in the European Union Savings Tax Directive (EUSTD) in 2013, which requires automatic information exchange for the EU and affiliated countries. Moreover, Switzerland participates in the OECD's Common Reporting Standard (CRS), which requires the automatic transfer of financial account information.

All of these developments suggest that the Swiss banking secrecy has been significantly weakened, and therefore its status as an international tax haven has been appreciably damaged as a consequence. However, it is premature to predict the demise of the Swiss banking secrecy. *First*, data breaches have so far been limited to US clients, leaving clients from other countries protected. Also, there can also be criticisms that the US itself is not free from the stigma of financial secrecy, as it is ranked higher (first) than Switzerland (second) in the Financial Secrecy Index 2022 (TJN, 2022) due to some of the states' practice of harbouring anonymous shell companies. *Second*, the Swiss government has been successful in using delaying tactics and deliberate obfuscation to extract maximum leverage before signing information exchange agreements so as to water down the negative impact of those agreements. For instance, the reciprocity agreement in the CRS limits partner countries of information exchange to those advanced economies that can provide confidential handling of exchanged information. *Third*, clients from developing countries still enjoy unhindered access to Swiss banking secrecy. Indeed, Switzerland increasingly saw developing countries that lack the power and resolve to combat financial secrecy as the next lucrative markets. For example, UBS started to turn its focus to BRIC countries after its brush with the US law in 2009.[13]

In short, although once mighty Swiss banking secrecy has been dealt a number of blows, none were fatal, and it is likely that Swiss banks will continue to provide services to foreign clients that it has been known for, for quite some time to come. However, they need to adapt to the global norms and regulations in order to maintain their reputation (Poddar *et al.*, 2009).

References

Garcia-Bernardo, J. Fichtner, J., Takes, F. and Heemskerk, E. (2017). Uncovering Offshore Financial Centers: Conduits and Sinks in the Global Corporate Ownership Network. Science Reports, 7, pp. 1–7.

Guex, S. (2000). The origins of the Swiss banking secrecy law and its repercussions for Swiss federal policy. *The Business History Review*, 74(2), 237–266.

[13]https://taxjustice.net/2015/04/22/how-swiss-banks-moved-their-evasion-experts-to-latin-america/.

Hines, J. R. (2010). Treasure Island. *Journal of Economic Perspectives*, 24(4), 103–126.

Hong, Q. and Smart, M. (2010). In praise of tax havens: International tax planning and foreign direct investment. *European Economic Review*, 54, 82–95.

International Consortium of Investigative Journalists (2017). Tax Agencies Draw Up "Target List" of Offshore Enablers. ICIJ. https://www.icij.org/investigations/panama-papers/20170120-oecd-target-list/.

OECD (2000). Towards Global Tax Co-operation: Report to the 2000 Ministerial Council Meeting and Recommendations by the Committee on Fiscal Affairs. https://www.oecd.org/ctp/harmful/2090192.pdf.

OECD/G20 BEPS Project (2021). Statement on a Two-Pillar Solution to Address the Tax Challenges Arising from the Digitalisation of the Economy, 8 October. https://www.oecd.org/tax/beps/statement-on-a-two-pillar-solution-to-address-the-tax-challenges-arising-from-the-digitalisation-of-the-economy-october-2021.pdf.

Poddar, A., Aggarwal, S., and Razdan, P. (2009). The future of bank secrecy and Switzerland. *SSRN Electronic Journal*. doi: 10.2139/ssrn.1460713.

Shaxson, N. (2019, September). Tackling tax havens. *Finance & Development*, 56(3), 6–10.

Tax Justice Network (2022). *Financial Secrecy Index 2022*. Switzerland. https://fsi.taxjustice.net/country-detail/#country=CH&period=22.

Tørsløv, T., Wier, L., and Zucman, G. (2020). The Missing Profits of Nations. NBER Working Paper 24701. http://www.nber.org/papers/w24701.

Walter, I. (2012). Use and Misuse of Financial Secrecy in Global Banking, Chapter 15 in *Socially Responsible Finance and Investing: Financial Institutions, Corporations, Investors, and Activists*, H. Kent Baker and John R. Nofsinger (eds.), John Wiley & Sons, New Jersey, USA.

Zorome, A. (2007). Concept of Offshore Financial Centers: In Search of an Operational Definition. IMF Working Paper, WP/07/87.

Chapter 13

International Banks and Money Laundering

13.1. Introduction

Money laundering refers to the process that aims to disguise or hide the origin of assets currently held to avoid financial or legal scrutiny. Along with tax evasion, it represents a notable application of financial secrecy. However, unlike tax evasion, which is typically provided by traditional tax haven jurisdictions with strong financial secrecy provisions, such as Switzerland and the Cayman Islands, money-laundering activities are not limited to physical locations. Indeed, there are both willing and unwitting providers (financial institutions, legal firms, and legal, accounting and financial professionals) of money-laundering services all across the globe. Also, assets involved in money laundering are likely to have been generated from illegal activities, the discovery of which poses severe consequences (loss of assets involved and criminal prosecution) for the parties involved in the activities. Profitable criminal activities occurring in any jurisdiction can add to the demand for global money laundering. The purpose of money laundering is thus to transform illegally obtained wealth into what appears to be legitimate assets in the eyes of the authorities to utilise the funds to continue to finance those illicit activities that have generated the asset.

It is impossible to accurately measure the size of global money laundering given the illegal nature of the activities where financial transactions are not recorded or reported to the authorities. However, in 1998, the IMF came up with a consensus range of 2–5% of global GDP, amounting to a range of USD 590 million to 1.5 trillion using the 1998 global GDP.[1] The United Nations Office on Drugs and Crime (UNODC, 2011) provides a more updated estimate in its 2011 report. *First*, it suggests that all criminal proceeds (drug trafficking, fraud, loan sharking, extortion, arms trading, etc.) amounted to an average of 3.6% (from a range of 2.3–5.5%) of global GDP in 2009. This is approximately USD 2.1 trillion. The criminal activities that generated the most income were drug trafficking which accounted for 20% of all criminal proceeds or 0.75% of global GDP in 2009. Moreover, approximately 75% of all criminal proceeds (2.7% of global GDP) and 66% of drug trafficking proceeds (0.5% of global GDP) were estimated to be laundered in 2009. *Second*, all criminal proceeds laundered are higher as a proportion of the national GDP in developing countries. This finding indicates that developing countries suffer more in relative terms as measured by GDP loss to money laundering. *Third*, once the criminal proceeds enter the laundering system, it is nearly impossible to detect and intercept it. Once illegal funds enter the money-laundering system, less than one percent of all criminal proceeds are seized and frozen during the laundering process globally.

The availability of highly effective money-laundering services (more than 99% of non-detection, as reported by UNODC, 2011) encourages criminal activities that generate assets to be laundered through the international financial system. Some of the negative consequences of the money-laundering process thus include (1) significant misallocation of economic resources with substantial opportunity costs, which are disproportionally high for developing countries, (2) an increase in the risk of the financial sector, and (3) damage to the credibility of the international monetary system.

In this section, we first provide discussions on the various aspects of the process of money laundering. We then discuss the international efforts to combat money laundering.

13.2. The Process of Money Laundering

Due to the significant amount of illicit funds to be laundered, the laundering process involves financial institutions that can process international fund transfers. Some offshore financial centres attract money-laundering

---

[1] https://www.fatf-gafi.org/en/home.html.

businesses due to their financial secrecy and obstructive laws designed to render financial audit trails difficult. The process of international money laundering typically involves three stages: Placement, Layering, and Integration.

13.2.1. *Placement*

Apart from financial crimes whose proceeds are already in electronic forms, such as financial frauds and other profitable crimes that receive payoffs in bank transfers, proceeds from other criminal activities are likely to be in currency notes. UNODC (2011) reports that drug trafficking-related proceeds laundered through the international financial system accounted for approximately 0.5% of global GDP, or USD 290 billion, in 2009. Given that drug trafficking proceeds are mostly generated in cash from the frontline of retail drug sales, there is a need to transport and transform the drug proceeds in cash away from the location of the crime and into non-cash assets that can be easily transferred to other locations. One method is to physically transport cash proceeds to another location. However, this method may be impractical given the size of the proceeds to be transported. In order to move a large amount of illegally obtained money, it has to be deposited with financial institutions that can transfer funds to different locations. Vast amounts of illegally obtained cash are placed in financial institutions or put through other economic activities to remove the proceeds from the place of acquisition and turn them into other forms of financial assets. Once the money is in the financial system, it can be transferred through the international network of payment systems.

The placement stage is where such a transformation of criminal proceeds takes place. The most obvious place to start the process is banks and other deposit-taking financial institutions, where the cash proceeds can be deposited into accounts controlled either directly or indirectly by the ultimate owner of the cash. Once deposits are accepted without causing unwanted attention, the money can then easily and quickly travel around the World's financial system. If it is practical to transport cash into OFC locations (cash smuggling into Switzerland, for instance), the transferred money can be deposited into local banks in those locations.[2] Other meth-

[2]There is a market for USD deposits outside the US jurisdiction. Feige (2012) suggests that as much as 39% of USD notes in circulation are held outside the US. The money base in

ods of placing the criminal cash proceeds include the following: casinos and other gaming venues where cash can be converted into gaming chips before being converted into cashier's checks; alternative remittance systems where a sender can place the cash with a dealer in one country for a recipient located in another to receive the money in the local currency of that country; an exporter under invoices its exports and an importer pays an over-invoiced contract against shell companies in tax haven countries to transfer funds to an overseas location.[3] The criminal cash proceeds are broken into amounts small enough to avoid suspicion when deposited to banks, and individuals acting for the criminal then deposit them into several bank accounts. This is known as 'smurfing', and the individual depositors are known as 'smurfs'. The criminal proceeds can be blended into legitimate cash income from running a retail cash business, and then the business owners deposit the blended funds into banks.

13.2.2. *Layering*

This stage aims to create complex layers of financial transactions to disguise the true origin of the money and frustrate the audit trail. Various institutions are involved in this process, such as banks and other financial institutions, futures exchanges, and casinos. Alternative remittance systems (such as the Hawala/Hundi system of remittance, the black market

---

the US was USD 5.58 trillion in August 2022, so approximately USD 2.17 trillion would have been held outside the US in 2022. The USD is used as legal tender in some independent countries such as Panama, Ecuador, El Salvador, Zimbabwe, and the US overseas territories in the Pacific and the Caribbean. In addition, many countries hold USD notes as a safe haven currency asset, and banks and other financial institutions in offshore financial centre locations freely accept US dollar deposits.

[3]Other examples include falsely describing goods and services in order to transfer funds to and from overseas locations (FATF, 2006). In general, trade-based money-laundering techniques can be used in the placement stage if the dirty money generated in a country is required to be transferred to another country and in the last leg of the layering stage to bring the funds onshore. In all of these cases, it is necessary for the parties involved to share the benefits resulting from the fraudulent transactions. It is not uncommon for the two parties (business entities) involved to be owned and controlled by a common owner. For example, the offshore partner in these arrangements could be a shell company incorporated in an offshore business centre (or tax haven) country where information on company ownership can remain confidential.

Peso system, and other parallel banking systems) are also involved. These involve the transfer of value from one party to another without alerting the relevant authorities, thus escaping capital control, if applicable, and various forms of audit trails. It is often the case that the laundering process is helped by professionals (lawyers and accountants).

Some examples include the following: the usage of offshore bank accounts of shell companies to electronically transfer funds; a series of loans involving offshore and onshore banks for eventual payment to the originator of the money (low or no income tax from offshore lending and tax-deductibility of the borrowings adds to the effectiveness of the process); a series of stock and other financial asset dealings; cybercash and other Internet-related value transfer systems (crypto-currency) that facilitate immediate and almost anonymous funds transfer.

13.2.3. *Integration*

This is the stage where the laundered money is integrated into the general economy, making it virtually impossible to distinguish it from legitimately sourced funds. For this final leg of the laundering process, the cleaned money can be transferred to the criminal through the financial system. For example, shell companies can be established to loan out laundered money to the originator of the dirty money (interest payments are tax deductible), or the laundered money can be transferred from the shell companies (which can be a shell bank located in a tax haven country) to a legitimate bank in the destination country. Once the criminals have possession of the cleaned money, they can invest in real estate and financial markets,[4] purchase luxury goods and precious metals, etc., hoping that the cleaned money cannot be linked to the original criminal activities that generated the dirty money.

---

[4]Real estate sector investment vehicles can be used in the final stage of the money-laundering process. For example, loans from a domestic bank secured by an offshore bank deposit can be used to finance an acquisition or an expansion of real estate assets with rental income streams. Criminals who have access to funds being cleaned in the international financial system can deposit them in an offshore bank. This is used as collateral for a domestic loan that the borrower intends to default at some future date. After a default, the domestic bank will collect the offshore bank deposit, and the criminal will keep the loan amount. No money has actually moved onshore in this arrangement, but the criminal has successfully transferred offshore funds into a legitimate domestic asset, FATF (2007).

Exhibit 13.1 illustrates examples of the money-laundering process in various cases. Cash criminal proceeds are converted into bank deposits via a number of different methods depending on the location of the criminal activities and the availability of professional assistance to evade attention. Depositing directly to banks in the location of the cash proceeds usually requires a large number of 'smurfs' who will deposit to designated bank accounts amounts small enough to avoid unnecessary attention. Alternatively, complicit bank employees will either look the other way or actively engage in assisting in the placement stage. If depositing cash proceeds in the domestic financial system is impractical, cash proceeds might be physically transported to a foreign location where banks are not as stringent in checking the origin of deposits. If criminal proceeds are large in amount, physical transportation of cash is very difficult, if not impossible.[5] If so, the criminal cash proceeds can be used to purchase expensive but small-volume goods such as jewellery, artwork, gold bars, etc., then smuggled to other countries, converted back into cash (might be in another currency) before the funds are deposited into the financial system of that country. Another option for moving cash to another location is to use Alternative Remittance Systems (ARS), which do not require physically moving the cash across borders. Once the converted cash is received in the destination country, it can be deposited to the local banking system. Criminal activities can generate financial proceeds such as a direct deposit into a numbered Swiss bank account or accounts in a shell bank in OFC locations. In these cases, the placement stage has already been completed.

Once the criminal proceeds are in the financial system, a multitude of techniques are used to obscure the audit trails of the movements of funds. Innovations in payment technologies, including crypto assets, the improved speed in the movements of electronic funds, and the provision of financial

[5]For example, USD notes weigh one gram irrespective of denomination. So, one million dollars weigh a ton in one dollar notes, 100 kilograms in 10 dollar notes, and 10 kilograms in 100 dollar notes. As typical proceeds from illegal drug sales are on street corners, most common dollar denominations are likely to be in the tens and twenties. So, storing and transporting large amounts of USD notes poses non-trivial problems for the criminals who wish to be undetected in this process. Therefore, a crucial process in money laundering is to transform cash into financial assets that can easily be transferred to entities located away from the location source of the cash.

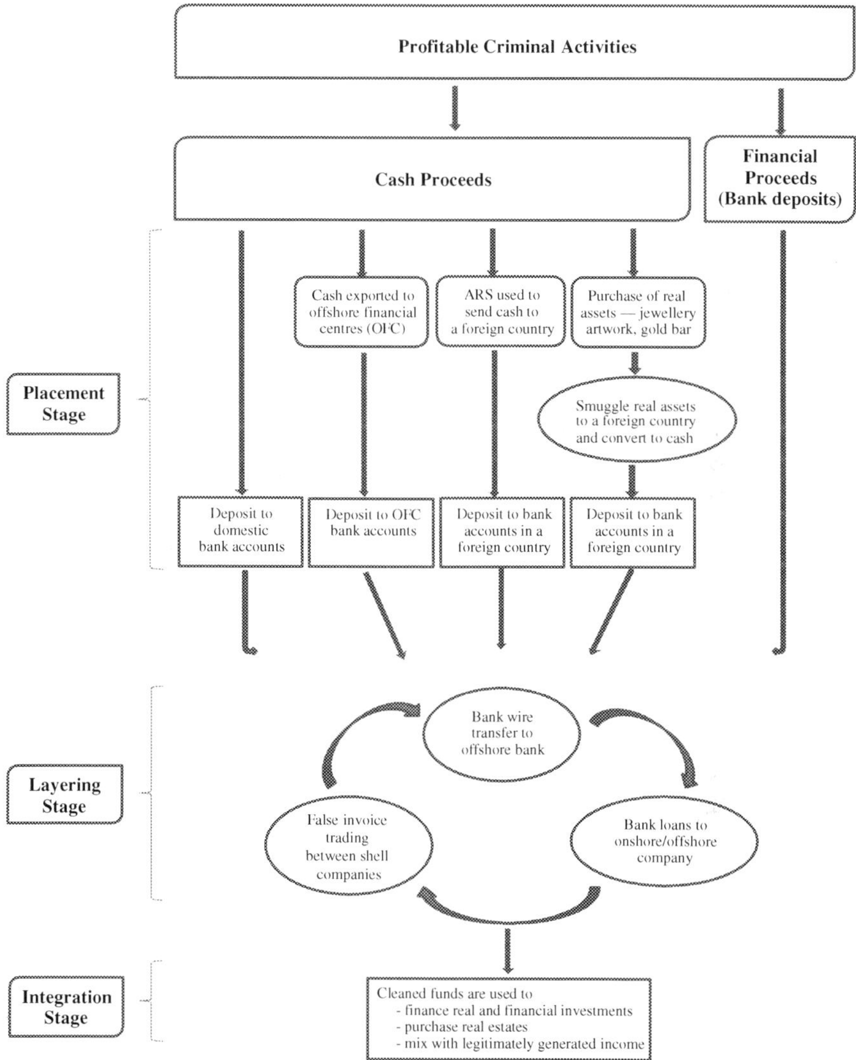

Exhibit 13.1. Examples of money laundering process.

secrecy in OFCs greatly assist the money-laundering process in the layering stage.

In the final integration stage, 'cleaned' funds are moved onshore and finance legitimate investments in real estate, financial and real assets, and business operations with legitimate income flows. Once funds are 'cleaned' and integrated into the economic system of the destination county, it would be virtually impossible to successfully prosecute the criminals for holding 'cleaned' assets. Indeed, UNODC (2011, p. 7) reports that only one percent of laundered amounts are seized and frozen.

13.3. Alternative Remittance System

International transfer of funds typically goes through the global financial system, specifically Society for Worldwide Interbank Financial Telecommunications (SWIFT), where banks take centre stage. Such official transfers leave a record of each transaction fulfilled, such as the parties involved, the amount and the currency denomination of the transaction, which is what the money-laundering process aims to avoid. Other forms of international remittance that escape official record-keeping are thus required. An Alternative Remittance System (ARS) refers to a system of monetary/value transfer from one country to another in such a way as to bypass the official channel of transfer via the financial system. ARSs rely on a network of brokers who are bound by an honour system. Hawala is the best-known example of an ARS and is often used by migrant workers to send money to their families and relatives in their home countries. The reason for their use might not be related to the money-laundering motives but rather due to the underdevelopment of the financial system of their home countries that make official transfers too costly or even unavailable.

ARS providers share similar characteristics as listed in FATF (2013, p. 13). They run cash-based businesses that can easily facilitate personal remittance service, operating in areas with a sufficient number of expatriate workers wishing to send money to their home countries. They already have some level of personal or business relationship with their customers (e.g., as a shop owner, a clergy, or a school teacher in the same community) and belong to a network of ARS brokers located in other countries. When communicating with the ARS broker in the country where the payment is going to, they provide only the bare essential information (usually coded) to facilitate the transaction.

Exhibit 13.2 illustrates a typical process of an international transfer of funds via an ARS. This process starts with a person located in country A who wishes to transfer funds to their associate, a family member, or a

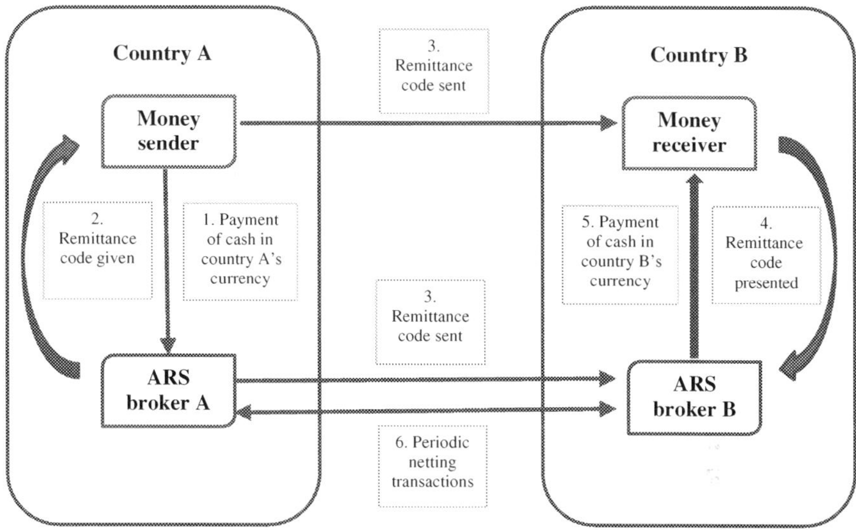

Exhibit 13.2. Alternative remittance system.

friend in their home country, country B. The money sender approaches an ARS broker, who is typically a well-known member of the community that the sender belongs to. Once a rate of exchange is agreed upon, the sender pays broker A the required amount in the currency of country A (Step 1). Upon receipt of the payment, Broker A gives a remittance code to the money sender, which can be a secret keyword or series of numbers that can easily be transmitted by phone, email, or messaging apps to the money receiver located in country B. In the pre-Internet era, remittance codes were sent by telex, by international mail, and in the case of a physical object, by couriers to the money receiver in the destination country. For example, one half of a currency note torn in two halves is given to the money sender as a remittance token (Step 2). ARS broker A then sends the remittance code (or the second half of the torn currency note) and the payment instructions to its counterpart in country B, ARS broker B (Step 3). The money receiver presents the remittance code to the ARS broker B (Step 4) for a cash payment in the currency of country B (Step 5). ARS brokers rarely achieve perfectly balanced positions across incoming and outgoing transfers. Brokers in one location may accumulate incoming transfers, while its counterpart in another location may accumulate outgoing payments. So, it is necessary for the brokers in a given network to regularly settle their net positions (e.g., weekly or monthly) at exchange rates that ensure profits for all parties in the network (Step 6). The settlements can be between the two brokers or involve a third party in a triangular settlement arrangement. In addition to cash settlements which include physical transportation of cash across borders, value settlement can also be used, such as over and under-invoicing other existing transactions between the brokers.

There are many reasons why an ARS is used throughout the World instead of the formal banking system. *First*, an ARS replaces or complements an underdeveloped financial system. In countries where the financial system is not well developed or not reaching some parts of the country, a shadow banking system develops instead to service the unbanked. In this case, ARS brokers provide a range of financial services, including loans and currency exchanges in addition to remittance services. So, when migrant workers from financially underdeveloped countries want to send money back to their countries, an ARS might be the only option available to them. *Second*, there is a significant cost advantage. Even if transfers via the banking system are possible, ARS transfers are usually much cheaper than official bank transfers. FATF (2013) reports that ARS brokers charge less than half of the equivalence bank charges and offer much more attractive exchange rates. *Third*, ARS transfers are usually very quick, taking only a few hours at most, given the time zone difference, compared to the days that bank transfers would take. This is because of the unofficial nature of the transaction, which is rarely regulated or taxed. More importantly, no money is transported physically or electronically between the two locations for individual transactions. *Fourth*, they are reliable due to their simplicity and, in most cases, due to the existing professional or personal relationship the ARS brokers have with their customers. The brokers operate in their respective communities as established businessmen, religious figures, etc. and so enjoy respect and trust. On the other hand, the official financial system might be either unavailable or impractical due to restrictive conditions required for international remittances, such as identification checks, the requirement to supply the purpose of fund transfer, unfavourable official exchange rates applicable, and restrictions on the amount that can be transferred. *Fifth*, ARSs have existed in some parts of the World (e.g., known as Hawala in south Asia and the Middle Eastern countries)[6] for

[6]Hawala is Arabic, meaning 'change' or 'transform'. A Hawala operator/dealer is known as 'Hawalada'. In Hindi (Indian), 'Hundi' and 'Hundiwalar' are equivalents.

centuries and provided not only remittance services but also a range of other financial services, including trade financing in place of formal banking systems. As such, businesses and individuals from countries where ARSs are common and well accepted prefer to use the ARS they are familiar with.

FATF (2013) categorise ARS into three categories: pure traditional, hybrid traditional, and criminal. In the pure traditional ARS, international remittances are likely from migrant workers sending money back to their home countries, and the recipients reside in a location where banking services are scarce. Remittances are in relatively small amounts, and the sender and the receiver share common cultural, religious, and other socio-economic characteristics. Due to the small size of individual transactions and the important financial services provided, pure traditional ARSs are often tolerated by authorities and are unregulated. Hybrid traditional ARSs are similar to pure traditional ARSs in that remittances are in small denominations, and there are shared characteristics between the sender and the receiver, etc. But one key difference is that the same service can also be used for illicit money transfers for tax evaders and those who wish to avoid capital controls and other governmental restrictions on international remittance. They are not usually a part of a criminal network, however. *Finally*, criminal ARSs are those that are set up by criminal networks for the purpose of laundering illicit money from criminal activities or to finance terrorism. Also, they can evolve from pure traditional and hybrid traditional ARSs as they grow in remittance size and international network coverage. Criminal ARSs differ in key characteristics from the other two forms of ARS. As the name suggests, they are used mostly for criminal motives by criminal and terrorist networks to send large amounts of money to locations that have developed and regulated financial systems. Moreover, there are no apparent shared characteristics between the sender and the receiver regarding cultural, socio-economic, or geographical background.

In general, ARSs can be an effective tool in circumventing capital controls, and it represents a cost-effective method of transferring money for personal and business reasons. Apart from the criminal ARSs purposefully set up to launder criminal proceeds and terrorism funds, the other forms of ARSs have been in existence for centuries in some countries and have been providing remittance and trade finance services. However, due to the characteristics identified above, ARSs can be used for money-laundering purposes. Since they are a remittance system, they can be used in all three phases of the laundering process.

In the placement stage, the usual checks aimed at detecting the placing of illicit money into financial institutions can be bypassed. The ARS brokers who run cash-intensive businesses can usually justify the money they receive as proceeds from their normal business activities, and they would deposit the money received for remittance along with their regular cash deposits to the bank. The layering and integration stages can also involve the system as there will mostly be no paper trail, and so the transformation of illegally generated funds to legitimate assets will be easily accomplished.

A typical hawala or other ARS transaction is virtually without paper trails or has confusing record-keeping and difficult-to-understand invoicing system in the eyes of the authorities. Legitimate and illegitimate remittances are mixed, and remittances can be spread across multiple transactions over time. So, the Hawala system can be a very effective tool in the layering stage as well.

In the final stage of integration, the money received by an ARS broker (a Hawalada in the Hawala system) can easily be integrated into their legitimate business by paying expenses or making new investments using the transferred (or cleaned money). Due to the effectiveness of hiding the audit trails and the ARS broker running a legitimate business, the cleaned money can be integrated into the economy.

All throughout this process, ARS brokers will not keep any record of the transactions that can be used by outsiders or the authorities to identify the details of the transfers and will be bound by the code of confidentiality so that it would be virtually impossible for the authorities to identify and confiscate the remittances from the receivers. The money senders and receivers can remain anonymous as far as the authorities are concerned. Siddiqui (2018) reports that the Hawala system has been used in a variety of illegal activities, such as illicit drug trafficking, terrorism financing, people smuggling, welfare fraud, insider trading, gambling, and tax evasion, virtually all types of criminal activities that require money-laundering services. As a result, ARSs are mostly unregulated and can be illegal in some countries. For example, Hawala is illegal in India and Pakistan due to their imposition of capital controls aimed at maintaining official exchange rates, and the penalty in India is up to three times the size of the amount transferred but is capped at 200,000 rupees (equivalent to USD 2,600). However, Hawala is legal and regulated in other countries, e.g., Dubai. FATF (2013) reports that a handful of countries permit Hawala and other ARSs. Eleven developed countries and four developing countries regulated ARSs via licensing, registration, or both on ARS brokers.

13.4. Fighting Money Laundering

The availability of effective financial secrecy and money-laundering services in various forms facilitates criminal activities that take advantage of those facilities. UNODC (2011) report that approximately 2.7% of global GDP or USD 1.6 trillion in 2009 was available for laundering. The opportunity cost of economic resources consumed by criminal activities and the subsequent money-laundering transactions is disproportionately high for developing countries that can ill afford such harmful activities as they can rob them of economic growth opportunities. Moreover, increasing attention has been paid to terrorist financing via traditional money-laundering channels, especially after the 9/11 attack on US soil in 2001. This represents reverse money laundering in that the objective is not to hide the origin of money; rather, the focus is more on using the money to fund terrorist activities. Siddiqui (2018) states that the amount transferred from bin Laden to finance the 9/11 attack was approximately USD 500,000, which caused the estimated monetary damage well in excess of USD 135 billion, not counting the human cost. The preferred method of channelling funds to the various locations of terror cells and targets has been Hawala and other ARSs.

13.4.1. *Role of banks and ARSs*

Combatting money laundering and terrorism financing requires both domestic and international efforts due to their cross-border nature. Efforts need to be directed in the first two stages of money laundering as it would be virtually impossible to identify cleaned money from other legitimately sourced income once the integration stage has successfully been completed. In the placement stage, money launders are greatly assisted by willing or unwitting bank employees. The most critical barrier in this stage is banks that are vigilant in identifying the beneficiaries of deposits and reporting suspicious transactions. In the US, the Bank Secrecy Act of 1970 requires financial institutions in the US to provide assistance to the government in detecting and preventing money laundering. However, there are several cases of the major US and other international banks or their employees systemically being involved in facilitating money laundering. Appendix 13.A details some of the largest and the most well-known cases of multinational banks being used in the first two stages of money laundering. For example, the Bank of Credit, Commerce International (BCCI) was set up to service international criminals and assist them in all three stages of money laundering. Wachovia Bank in the US and HSBC USA were used by drug cartels in Mexico and Colombia to launder their drug money by exploiting their weak or non-existent Anti-Money-Laundering (AML) procedures. The drug cartels had little trouble depositing large sums of cash into their branches in the US and Mexico. The common issues across the cases against the large multinational banks discussed in Appendix 13.A are that money laundering happens when inadequate and ineffective AML measures are exploited, global headquarters do not have effective information collection and processing across their global operations, and bank management is slow to respond to warning signs. Moreover, corporations and government entities on the US sanctions list have used multinational banks, such as Standard Chartered and BNP Paribas, to channel their US dollar funds through the US financial system. Banks have played a vital role in facilitating international money laundering for criminal organisations and US-sanctioned entities by accepting deposits from them and putting them through payment systems. Therefore, banks must play an equally vital role in preventing money laundering.

In addition to banks, ARSs have been used to launder money, and Hawala systems have been popular among terrorists in channelling funds to various terror cell locations. In most countries, ARSs are too small in terms of the amount transacted, integrated into local communities, and are a part of everyday lives. In these cases, regulating these traditional ARSs may be of only marginal benefit in itself. However, preventing them from becoming hybrid traditional and criminal ARSs used for terrorism financing and money laundering is of paramount importance. Thus, identifying and regulating ARSs go a long way to preserving the desirable role that ARSs play in unbanked societies and preventing them from being used for illegal fund transfers.

Combatting money laundering requires strong AML procedures set in place in the first two stages of money laundering. For deposit-taking and cash-handling businesses that can be used in the placement stage, it is vital that they correctly identify depositors, the source of deposits, and the beneficiary of the deposit if they are deposited into the accounts of someone other than the person making the deposits. This is the 'Know Your Customer (KYC)' principle. Moreover, the beneficiary of the funds being transferred through the financial system needs to receive similar attention in the layering stage. In addition, various mechanisms are set in place to monitor relatively large denomination wire transfers (e.g., amounts greater than USD 10,000 (US), AUD 10,000 and its equivalent (Australia), and EUR 15,000 (the Eurozone) are reported to the relevant authorities for record-keeping). However, monitoring each and every payment transaction is impossible in the layering stage, given the breakneck speed of the electronic transfer of funds and the involvement of tax haven jurisdictions that may not fully cooperate in international information exchange arrangements. For this reason, pattern recognition has emerged as a method of identifying suspicious transactions. Recent technical developments, in particular big data and artificial intelligence technologies, can be useful in identifying suspicious transactions by the nature of fund movements that fit certain profiles (e.g., repeated wire transfers to accounts in tax haven jurisdictions and relatively large number of transfers from one account in a short space of time).

13.4.2. *International organisations*

International efforts directed at setting AML standards for financial institutions and national authorities have resulted in two complementary initiatives. The first is the establishment of the Financial Action Task Force on Money Laundering (FATF, https://www.fatf-gafi.org/) in 1989 within the OECD, which is an intergovernmental body that sets international standards for governments to prevent global money laundering and terrorist financing. FATF released forty recommendations in 1990, which were updated multiple times, and the latest recommendations are contained in its 2021 publication. The 40 recommendations are in six groups to achieve the following aims.

'(1) identify the risks, and develop policies and domestic coordination; (2) pursue money laundering, terrorist financing and the financing of proliferation; (3) apply preventive measures for the financial sector and other designated sectors; (4) establish powers and responsibilities for the competent authorities (e.g., investigative, law enforcement and supervisory authorities) and other institutional measures; (5) enhance the transparency and availability of beneficial ownership information of legal persons and arrangements; and (6) facilitate international cooperation'. (FATF, 2021, p. 7)

The second international organisation is a coalition of global banks (started with 11 in 2000 and 13 currently) that created a non-governmental organisation with the aim of developing financial industry standards for AML, Know your customer (KYC) and combatting terrorist financing. It is known as the Wolfsberg group (https://www.wolfsberg-principles.com/). Wolfsberg's proposed standards may be regarded as an extension to the KYC principle relating to business transactions involving wealthy clients in private banking.

13.4.3. *US government sanctions against criminal cartels and terrorist organisations*

The Office of Foreign Asset Control (OFAC) within the US Department of the Treasury administers and enforces economic and trade sanctions against foreign countries, organisations and individuals, such as terrorists and criminal organisations, on the ground of US national security and foreign and economic policies. Entities on the sanctions list[7] can have their assets in the US ceased and frozen, fines levied and be barred from operating in the US, including processing financial payments through the US financial system. The list includes broad sanctions at the country level, such as Iran, Cuba, North Korea, Sudan, and Zimbabwe, and targeted against specific companies and individuals and their associates, such as Al Qaeda organisation, Arellano Felix organisation (also known as Tijuana Cartel), and Sinaloa drug cartel associates. Banks and other financial institutions, foreign ones included, are prevented from acting on behalf of the sanctioned countries and entities to process funds through the US financial system.

There are hefty penalties involved in violating sanctions, as BNP Paribas and Standard Chartered Bank found out. They agreed to pay USD 8.9 billion in 2014 and USD 947 million in 2012, respectively, in return for a deferred prosecution agreement with the US department of justice. Although the size of these fines is very large and can serve as a warning

[7]A specially designated nationals list is available at the OFAC website. https://home.treasury.gov/policy-issues/financial-sanctions/specially-designated-nationals-and-blocked-persons-list-sdn-human-readable-lists.

to other global banks that either knowingly or unwittingly process funds for sanctioned entities, they are not crippling enough for the banks involved, given the size of their global incomes and so future violations, deliberate or otherwise, may not be completely prevented with these penalties unless they are expelled from the USD clearing network.[8]

13.4.4. *Tax havens — information exchange*

Tax havens that provided strict financial secrecy, such as the traditional tax haven countries in the Caribbean locations and Switzerland, have been used in both the placement and the layering stages of the money-laundering process. US dollar notes are often smuggled and deposited into the banking system of the tax haven countries to start the placement stage. Given the traditionally lenient standards of KYC and financial secrecy, the placement stage is usually uneventful, and the layering stage can then be started via the tax haven country banks' participation in the global financial system. As a result, money-laundering activities that involve tax haven countries, at least in one of the transactions during the layering stage, can be almost impossible to trace. Therefore, the key challenge for the government authorities is to break down the financial secrecy and force the tax haven countries' cooperation in sharing information on the financial transactions their banking system processes for their non-resident customers, especially those that involve individuals or organisations that are of interest to the authorities.

There have been a number of effective international schemes at various country groups designed to increase the transparency of financial information for the national tax and legal authorities. These include the US's Foreign Account Tax Compliance Act (FACTA), EU's European Savings Tax Directive (EUSTD), and OECD's Common Reporting Standard (CRS). The US FACTA, introduced in 2010, requires US citizens to report their assets held outside the US to the Internal Revenue Service (IRS) annually. Similarly, non-US financial institutions are

---

[8]The average annual net income of BNP Paribas over the period 2010–2020 was EUR 7 billion. It even had a positive net income of EUR 157 in 2014, even after paying the USD 8.9 billion penalties. Standard Chartered Bank's net income over the same period was USD 2 billion, so USD 947 million was not close to crippling its operations.

required to report the assets of US citizens they hold to the US Department of Justice. Given the tendency of the US government to prosecute both US and non-US banks for sanctions violations (see above), the imposition of FACTA makes it more difficult for tax haven countries to provide financial secrecy to US citizens and organisations. The EU equivalent of anti-tax evasion information exchange measure was EU's EUSTD (known as Directive 2003/48/EC) which required the EU member states to report interest paid to non-resident investors from other EU member states to the authorities of those countries. This was replaced by the Directive 2014/107/EU in 2015, which requires the automatic and mandatory exchange of information within the EU member states.[9] The OECD's CRS, initially agreed on by 47 countries in 2014 and 97 by 2020, is much broader in scope, covers a wider range of countries, and is also known as a global version of the US's FACTA.[10] The CRS requires countries to automatically exchange financial information from their institutions with other countries annually. Tax haven countries have been under pressure to participate in these information exchange agreements to prevent tax evasion and money laundering.

OECD's FATF maintains a record of countries that are not cooperating with international efforts in investigating financial crimes, tax evasion and money laundering so as to put pressure on them to comply. Initially, this was met with considerable resistance from those tax haven countries that depend heavily on income generated from providing financial secrecy to non-residents. In 2000, OECD published its list of non-cooperating jurisdictions, which included the following tax haven countries: the Bahamas, Cayman Islands, Cook Islands, Dominica, Israel, Lebanon, Liechtenstein, Marshall Islands, Nauru, Niue, Panama, Philippines, Russia, St. Kitts and Nevis, St. Vincent, and the Grenadines. Since 2000, the continued pressures on tax haven countries to participate in international information exchange agreements resulted in only one country remaining on the list by 2017: Trinidad and Tobago.

OECD's FATF also reports countries considered to be high-risk, requiring monitoring for money-laundering weaknesses. As of March 2023, the following 23 countries were identified as Jurisdictions with strategic deficiencies (grey list): Albania, Barbados, Burkina Faso, Cayman Islands, Democratic Republic of Congo, Gibraltar, Haiti,

---

[9] https://eur-lex.europa.eu/legal-content/EN/TXT/?uri=celex%3A32014L0107.

[10] https://www.oecd.org/tax/automatic-exchange/.

Jamaica, Jordan, Mali, Mozambique, Nigeria, Panama, Philippines, Senegal, South Africa, South Sudan, Syria, Tanzania, Türkiye, Uganda, United Arab Emirates, Yemen. In addition, there are black listed countries subject to a call for action: North Korea, Iran and Myanmar.[11]

In addition to the voluntary (or forced) information disclosures, there have been information leaks that exposed vast amounts of financial information protected by financial secrecy (see Appendix 13B). In 2016, the Panama Papers (11.5 million documents in 2.6 terabyes of data) exposed the 40 years' worth of client records of an international law firm in Panama, Mossack Fonseca. The leak exposed the details of offshore financial transactions of its clients, wealthy individuals from around the World. The subsequent investigations by national authorities of these clients resulted in more than USD 500 million collected by their tax authorities. In a similar information leak in 2021, the International Consortium of Investigative Journalists (ICIJ) released another data leak named the Pandora Papers. This time, the leaks are larger, covering 11.9 million documents in 2.9 terabytes of data. The leaks cover 35 current and former world leaders and 330 high-net-worth individuals from around the World. These data leaks brought to light the extent of the offshore activities of wealthy individuals in an effort to hide their activities. Although offshore transactions themselves are not illegal, there can still be reputational damage for the individuals exposed, and possible audits and investigations by the relevant tax and legal authorities could follow. As data leaks such as these are more likely to occur as there are continuing efforts to expose offshore financial activities, both the demand for and supply of financial secrecy could be adversely affected.

13.4.5. *Cryptocurrency and money laundering — Regulation*

New payment systems in the forms of online banking, Internet commerce, smart cards, e-cash, etc. that enhance the speed of value transfer over many jurisdictions with the anonymity of the source of funds represent a new breed of problems. Blockchain-based cryptocurrencies such as bitcoin pose a significant challenge to national authorities. Cryptocurrencies have been used to facilitate illicit activities, both domestically and internationally. However, due to the decentralised nature of blockchain

---

[11] https://www.fatf-gafi.org/en/countries/black-and-grey-lists.html.

technology, it would be very difficult to audit the change of ownership from one party to another in business transactions, making it a perfect vehicle for money laundering (especially in the layering stage). Chainalysis (2022) reports that in 2021 approximately USD 8.6 billion were laundered through cryptocurrencies (USD 33 billion between 2017 and 2021). Although the amount is significant and has been growing, this represents only 0.25% of the total laundered amount in that year.[12]

Nevertheless, coordinated efforts are required to combat money laundering through this channel as the volume of flows to illicit wallets is rising (Chainalysis, 2022). FATF (2018) reports that G20 finance ministers and central bank governors provided a commitment to implement the FATF standards for virtual/crypto-currencies in March 2018. One example of such an effort is to regulate the trading of cryptocurrencies on private exchanges, which some jurisdictions have already implemented. Another example is to require a license to conduct a virtual currency transaction. In the US, the state of New York enacted the BitLicense regulation in 2015 to require companies engaging in virtual currency transactions to obtain a license (BitLicense) from New York state's department of financial services and implement AML procedures.

Appendix 13A. Bank and Money Laundering

13.A.1. *Bank of Credit, Commerce International* (*BCCI*)

The most notable example of bank involvement in money laundering is Bank of Credit, Commerce International (BCCI). BCCI was established in the UK in 1972 as an Islamic bank to cater to the needs of the Islamic World. It quickly established itself as the World's fastest growing bank, on the back of the enormous flow of petrodollars, with 146 branches in 34 countries and a total asset of 1.6 USD billion in 1976. It was later revealed that, until its collapse in 1991, most (approximately 70%) of its business customers were involved in criminal activities, and the structure of BCCI was deliberately complex to confuse authorities' audit trails. The United States Senate Committee reported that BCCI was involved in a long list of criminal activities such as 'including fraud by BCCI and BCCI

[12]UNODC (2011)'s estimate of the annual average money laundering is 3.6% World's GDP. Using 2021's world GDP of USD 96.1 trillion, the total amount laundered in 2021 would have been USD 3.5 trillion.

customers involving billions of dollars; money laundering in Europe, Africa, Asia, and the America; BCCI's bribery of officials in most of those locations; its support of terrorism, arms trafficking, and the sale of nuclear technologies; its management of prostitution; its commission and facilitation of income tax evasion, smuggling, and illegal immigration; its illicit purchases of banks and real estate' (Kerry and Brown, 1992).

13.A.2. *Wachovia Bank*

Wachovia bank in the US agreed to pay USD 160 million penalties to the US government in 2010 to avoid prosecution for facilitating laundering of drug money from Colombian and Mexican drug cartels. At the time, the amount was the largest fine ever imposed on a bank for violating the Bank Secrecy Act, 1970 (Fletcher, 2010).

Before being acquired by Wells Fargo bank in 2008, Wachovia was a financial services company headquartered in Charlotte, North Carolina, US. As one of the largest bank holding companies in the US (the fourth largest in 2008 before it was forced to be sold to Wells Fargo to avoid the GFC induced collapse), Wachovia operated a nationwide network of financial centres to provide a range of commercial and retail banking services across 21 states in the US and 41 foreign offices. Wachovia was accused of allowing Mexican drug cartels to launder as much as USD 378.4 billion (approximately equal to one-third of Mexico's GDP at the time) through its branches via corresponding accounts belonging to Mexican currency exchange services ('casas de cambio' or 'CDCs') (Vulliamy, 2011). The Mexican drug cartels smuggled the cash proceeds from drug sales in the US across the Mexican border. They deposited the US notes to Mexican banks where the legal requirements for identifying the source of the deposits and the beneficiaries were not as stringent as in the US, or the cartels bypassed them through a captured bank or bank employees who would look the other way. The deposited funds were then wire transferred to the accounts of the Mexican CDC with Wachovia bank branches. In addition, Wachovia allowed the cartels to use its cash transport service to move the US notes back to the US. So, the drug proceeds in cash from the US were smuggled into Mexico, and then some of them were returned to the US by the Mexican CDCs via bank wire transfers and cash transport services offered by Wachovia. It was shown that some of the money moved back to the US was used to purchase aeroplanes (USD 13 million over the period 2004–2007) that were used to smuggle drugs into the US (UNODC, 2010). The investigation was triggered when narcotics were found aboard an aeroplane by a sniffer dog at Florida Opa Locka airport in 2005 (Fletcher, 2010). The money trails eventually revealed the connections among the owner of the aeroplane, Wachovia bank accounts, CDCs, and the Mexican cartels.

Wachovia management ignored all the red flags raised by both employees and government authorities (Vulliamy, 2011). The eventual whistleblower Martin Woods, who joined the London office of the bank as a money-laundering reporting officer in 2005, raised concerns about irregular and suspicious deposits of checks originating from the Mexican exchange offices (Vulliamy, 2011). Some of these include multiple wire transfers on a single day for the same account, deposits of traveller's checks with sequential numbers and unusual markings, and large cash transfers from Mexican CDCs that were much larger than (up to 50% more) Wachovia was informed to expect. However, his concerns were fell on deaf ears. In 2005, the US Drug Enforcement Agency (DEA) warned the US financial sector that the Mexican CDCs were used by Mexican drug cartels to launder their criminal proceeds. Wachovia chose to continue to allow Mexican CDCs to transfer money from Mexico. Eventually, the US Attorney's office, the DEA and other agencies started to investigate Wachovia's role in the Mexican drug cartel's money laundering via CDCs. They found that at least USD 110 million worth of drug money was laundered through the CDCs' accounts held at Wachovia (UNODC, 2010). The USD 160 million fine was composed of the confiscation of 110 million and a penalty of 50 million. The case was settled in 2010, and Wells Fargo accepted the judgement against Wachovia, which it had acquired two years prior.

13.A.3. *Standard Chartered Bank* (*SCB*)

Standard Chartered bank is a London headquartered global bank with a focus on commercial and retail banking in developing countries in Africa, Asia and the Middle East, where it draws most of its profits. It does not have a retail banking presence in its headquarters in the UK or the US but maintains business banking operations in these two major markets. In 2019, it agreed to pay a combined USD 1.1 billion to UK and US authorities (GBP 102 million and USD 947 million, respectively) for money laundering and repeatedly breaching US sanctions (The Guardian, 2019).

The UK's Financial Conduct Authority (FCA) imposed a penalty of GBP 102 million for the bank's failure to follow anti-money-laundering practices. These violations occurred in the correspondent banking business in the UK between 2010 to 2013 and in its branches in the United Arab Emirates between 2009 and 2014. In its news release (FCA, 2019), some examples were given on the nature of these violations.

> '1. Opening an account with 3 million UAE Dirham in cash in a suitcase (just over GBP 500,000) with little evidence that the origin of the funds had been investigated; 2. failing to collect sufficient information on a customer exporting a commercial product which could, potentially, have a military application. This product was exported to over 75 countries, including two jurisdictions where armed conflict was taking place or was likely to be taking place; 3. and not reviewing due diligence on a customer despite repeated red flags such as a blocked transaction from another bank indicating a link to a sanctioned entity'.

SCB's brush with the US authorities was due to its violation of the US sanctions against various countries of interest, such as Cuba, Iran, Myanmar, Sudan, Syria, and Zimbabwe (The Guardian, 2019). The US Department of Justice states in its 2019 justice news that 'during the period 2007 and 2011, SCB processed approximately 9,500 financial transactions worth approximately USD 240 million through US financial institutions for the benefit of Iranian entities' (USDJ, 2019). The total penalty imposed amounted to USD 947 million for the violations. This follows the USD 667 million penalty it paid in 2012 to settle the case against the US government on sanction breaches between 2001 and 2007. Apparently, the threat of the financial penalty had little effect on improving its compliance with the US sanctions. For the 2018 financial year, SCB reported a statutory profit of USD 2.5 billion (Coppola, 2019) which was more than enough to cover the penalty. However, SCB claims that such violations did not occur after 2014. The year 2014 is significant in that BNP Paribas paid a record breaking penalty of USD 8.8 billion (composed of a forfeiture of 8.8 billion and a 140 million fine) for breaking US sanctions, and their access to global USD clearing was temporarily denied. It appears that it took the case of BNP Paribas for SBC to take the US sanctions seriously when financial penalties were an insufficient motivation given the overall level of profits from its global operations. Being shut out of the USD clearing network would put its core business of lending to developing countries, which are mostly denominated in the USD, in jeopardy.

13.A.4. *BNP Paribas*

BNP Paribas is an international banking group headquartered in Paris, France. It was formed as a result of the merger between BNP and Paribas in 2000 and became the second largest banking group in Europe, after HSBC, and ninth overall in the World in terms of total assets in 2020 (see Exhibit 1.2). In June 2014, it was hit with a penalty of USD 8.9736 billion (composed of forfeiture of 8.8336 billion illegally processed funds and a fine of 140 million), the largest ever amount against a foreign bank by the US Justice Department, for knowingly violating the International Emergency Economic Powers Act and the Trading with the Enemy Act of the US for the period 2004–2012. The US Department of Justice report states that BNP Paribas channelled more than USD 8.8 billion through the US financial system for its clients in Susan, Iran and Cuba, violating the US sanctions against these countries (USDJ, 2014). This amount includes transactions in excess of USD 4.3 billion involving entities specifically banned from the US financial system. USDJ (2014) report that BNP Paribas made significant efforts to disguise the identities of the transactions via various sophisticated schemes and by hiding the names of the parties involved. Moreover, it asked its partner banks not to mention the names of the sanctioned clients in processing payments and to remove references to them from payment messages so that the US authorities cannot detect the funds going through the US financial system (USDJ, 2014). It even set up satellite banks to disguise its involvement in processing sanctioned entities' funds through the US financial system. It chose to ignore warnings by its own lawyers and the US authorities and continued to engage in transactions that benefited sanctioned entities. It actively participated in putting through the funds from the sanctioned entities in the US financial system, thereby assisting them in the layering stage of the money-laundering cycle. In addition to the hefty penalty, it was barred from the USD clearing network for 12 months from the start of 2015 and was required to terminate 13 employees who were involved in the illegal activities, including the group's chief operating officer and other senior executives. However, despite the unprecedented severity of the penalties, BNP Paribas maintained that its operations would remain solid (BBC, 2014).

The troubles of BNP Paribas did not end with the US fines and the suspension of the USD clearing network access in 2014-2015. In 2017, the French financial watchdog ACPR (Autorité de contrôle prudential et de resolution) issued a fine of EUR 10 million to the bank for lacking adequate controls of Anti-Money Laundering (Reuters, 2017). More recently, in 2021, it was charged with assisting the family of the deceased president of Gabon to acquire real estate assets worth EUR 32 million in Paris and Nice by being involved in the money laundering process (Sebang, 2021). It appears that the unprecedented penalties issued in 2014 by the US authorities and by the French authorities in 2017 failed to change the business mindset of the bank, which appears to continuously seek alternative sources of profit even at the risk of severe penalties.

13.A.5. *Danske Bank*

Danske Bank is headquartered in Copenhagen, Denmark, with a long history of banking presence in the country since 1871. It is the largest bank in Denmark and operates a number of branches across the Nordic region and Ireland. In 2007 it acquired the banking operation of Sampo bank in Estonia, which became a branch of Danske bank. The money-laundering problem was concentrated in this one branch of the bank. It is reported that around EUR 200 billion (equivalent to USD 222 at the 2015 exchange rate) worth of funds, mainly in the EUR and the USD with a questionable origin, flowed through the Estonian branch during the period 2007 to 2015 (with an annual average of USD 24.6 billion) (Bruun and Hjejle, 2018). Estonia is a small country with a nominal GDP of USD 23 billion in 2015, so an equivalent of the country's annual GDP was processed by one bank branch every year during the nine-year period. This itself should have caused an alarm bell for the bank and the Estonian and Danish regulators. Large deposits to the Estonian branch came mostly from Russia and other CIS states.

The root cause of the problem was that Sampo bank had a substantial non-resident customer portfolio (NRP) the Estonian branch of Danske bank inherited. Bruun and Hjejle (2018) report that the number of non-resident customers was estimated to be approximately 4,000 at any given time and over 10,000 in total from 2007 to 2015. Most of the customers in the NRP were from CIS states, and most (at least the 6,000 customers investigated) of their origins and activities were considered to be suspicious (Bruun and Hjejle (2018). The NRP accounted for more than 44% of the total deposits the branch processed in 2013. Serious breaches of anti-money-laundering procedures concerning customers in the CIS states were found in the bank's 2014 internal investigations. An investigation by a law firm Bruun and Hjejle (2018) also found the same breaches. The Estonian branch failed to properly identify and record the identities of depositors, the source of the funds and the beneficiaries of the fund transfers. Moreover, screening for customers and their payments was done manually, which was inadequate considering the size and scope of the deposits they processed. Finally, they failed to act in response to suspicious customers and their transactions.

To complicate matters further, the Estonian branch had its own IT platform inherited from the Sampo bank era and records were kept in either Estonian or Russian. This made overseeing the branch operation from the headquarters difficult, especially in ensuring anti-money-laundering (AML) measures. However, Danske bank failed to integrate the system into its main IT system due to cost, thus allowing the suspicious activities to continue.

Danske bank had multiple opportunities to detect and address the money-laundering activities at its Estonian branch. *First*, shortly after it acquired Sampo bank in 2007, the Russian central bank informed the bank via the Danish regulator (Financial Supervisory Authority) that potential tax evasion and money-laundering activities estimated at billions of Rubles per month were suspected at Sampo bank. Danske bank failed to act on this information. *Second*, in 2013 a correspondent bank clearing USD transactions out of the Estonian branch terminated the correspondent banking relationship citing issues with the AML measures at the branch. This led to an incomplete and ineffective review of the NRP business at the branch. *Third*, a whistle blowing in the branch in late 2013 led to another review in 2014 and changes were made to some of the procedures. However, the allegations by the whistleblower were not properly investigated, and NRP activities were allowed to continue (Bruun and Hjejle, 2018).

The NRP was eventually closed in 2015 following repeated warning signs that the Estonian branch was facilitating deposits and fund transfers related to money laundering and other illegal activities, such as tax evasion through the NRP. The last of the accounts was closed in early 2016. In the end, 42 Estonian branch employees and agents were reported to the Estonian Finance Intelligence Unit, and six were reported to the police.

The end result is that Danske bank allowed its Estonian branch to process approximately 7.5 million payment transactions in the placement and the layering stages of money laundering to the tune of EUR 200 billion during the nine-year period from 2007 to 2015. The contributing factors were ineffective AML procedures at the Estonian branch that allowed active collusion between branch employees and its non-resident customers in the NRP, ineffective IT integration of the branch with the main office in Denmark that was not able to detect suspicious transactions, and inaction by the Danske bank headquarters despite mounting evidence of foul play at the branch until 2015.

In December 2022, the investigations by the US Department of Justice were concluded on the matter of US banks being defrauded by Danske bank by allowing access to the US financial system for its high-risk customers in the Estonian branch. Danske bank agreed to forfeit USD 2 billion as a penalty (USDJ, 2022). This appears to be the final resolution to conclude the investigations by the US depart of Justice, US SEC and the Danish serious crime unit (Danske Bank, 2023).

13.A.6. *HSBC*

Hong Kong and Shanghai Banking Corporation (HSBC) is a global financial group founded in 1866 and is headquartered in the UK. It was the largest European bank in terms of total assets and the 6th largest globally in 2020 (see Exhibit 1.2). It maintains offices in 64 countries across the globe and provides services in commercial, investment and personal banking, and wealth management.

In 2012, it agreed to pay the US justice department a penalty of USD 1.9 billion for being used in the process of laundering drug money and for violating US sanctions. The penalty was made up of USD 1.256 billion forfeiture of laundered money and a civil penalty of 665 million (USDJ, 2012). HSBC was accused of allowing at least USD 881 million of drug money to be laundered through its branches and breaking US sanctions by conducting transactions through the US financial system for their clients Cuba, Iran, Libya, Myanmar and Sudan. It was in breach of the US Bank Secrecy Act (BSA), the International Emergency Economic Powers Act (IEEPA) and the Trading with the Enemy Act (TWEA). HSBC admitted it they failed in its Anti-Money Laundering procedures and lacked due diligence on some customers (Viswanatha and Wolf, 2012).

USDJ (2012) states that during the period 2006–2010, HSBC USA classified Mexico as a low-risk country for money laundering and significantly understaffed its AML compliance department in Mexico. Its compliance department of just 1 or 2 employees handled the transactions of up to five to six thousand customers. As a result, drug cartels in Mexico (the Sinaloa Cartel) and Colombia (the Norte del Valle Cartel) were able to deposit and move their drug money through the US financial system via HSBC's Mexican branches. In their Mexican branches, deposits were made by carrying cash into boxes specifically made to fit the tellers' windows. Purchases of billions of USD bank notes failed to raise alarm bells. It is also reported in the Justice news of the US Department of Justice (2012) that the Colombian Black Market Peso Exchange method was extensively used to move drug money from the US to the drug cartels outside the US.[13] As a result, HSBC USA failed to properly monitor wire transfers of USD 670 million and in excess of USD 9.4 billion cash purchases of the USD. This allowed the drug cartels to launder an estimated USD 881 million through HSBC USA.

In addition, HSBC was found to have allowed transactions involving sanctioned entities from mid-1990 to 2006. HSBC affiliates were accused of consciously hiding the identities of their clients in international USD transactions when payment messages were sent. They deliberately used opaque payment messages in the transactions and inserted instructions in their messages to not mention the sanctioned entity or the participating bank affiliates (USDJ, 2012). This shows that HSBC affiliates knowingly transacted with the US-sanctioned entities in direct violation of the IEEPA and TWEA. The HSBC group became aware of these violations in 2000, but allowed these practices to continue until 2003.

In addition to the fines, HSBC was required to substantially upgrade its AML procedures as a condition for the deferred persecution deal

[13]Colombian black market Peso exchange is a scheme whereby drug cartels employ money-laundering brokers to transfer the USD drug proceeds in the US into local currency funds in Colombia. It involves the brokers employing 'smurfs' in the US to collect and deposit the drug money into shell US bank accounts and then using the checks drawn on the accounts to facilitate legitimate international business transactions. The drug cartel will be paid in local currency by the brokers from the payment they receive from the sale of the US dollar checks. This process is detailed in the FATF's 1998 annual report. https://www.fatf-gafi.org/media/fatf/documents/reports/1997%201998%20ENG.pdf.

entered with the US department of justice. This involved launching a global review of 'know your customer' files, estimated to cost the bank USD 700 million over five years.

Appendix 13.B. Leaked Offshore Financial Activity Documents

13.B.1. *The Panama Papers 2016*

In 2016, an investigation by the International Consortium of Investigative Journalists (ICIJ) went public with a leak exposing the operations of Panama-headquartered international law firm Mossack Fonseca. The leak exposed details of 40 years of records on more than 214,000 companies in 21 offshore jurisdictions (ICIJ, 2017a), with the transfer of funds conducted by more than 500 banks. The 2.6 terabytes of data leaks cover 11.5 million confidential documents detailing the offshore financial activities of clients, including 140 politicians and public officials and their families, business executives, sports and media stars from countries around the World, including Russia, China, the UK, the US, and Australia. While offshore financial activities are not necessarily illegal, the 'Panama Papers' records are subject to an ongoing investigation by local and international authorities for tax evasion and money laundering.

As of December 2017, more than USD 500 million had been recovered by tax authorities worldwide following the Panama Papers release, including USD 122 million by the authorities in Spain. Moreover, the audits of individuals in a total of 15 countries (including Canada, South Korea, Germany, and Denmark) resulted in taxes being recovered because of the papers (ICIJ, 2017b). Over 1000 people in Australia were reportedly under investigation by the Australian Taxation Office. Banks involved have also been investigated by authorities in many countries, including Denmark and the US. The public impact of the Panama Papers has been substantial. Tax agencies from 30 jurisdictions met in Paris in January 2016 to share information in their Panama Papers related investigations (ICIJ, 2017b). O'Donovan *et al.* (2016) found the fallout from the Panama Papers wiped 'USD 135 billion in market capitalisation among 397 public firms that the authors traced to "users of offshore vehicles exposed in the leak."'

13.B.2. *The Pandora Papers 2021*

On 3 October 2021, ICIJ released its latest findings from their investigations on offshore financial transactions of individuals from around the World (ICIJ, 2021a). Its finding, referred to as 'the Pandora papers', reveals the financial dealings of 35 current and former leaders of various countries and more than 330 public officials, politicians, billionaires, sports stars, entertainers and other high net worth individuals from around the World. The documents were from 14 offshore services firms that helped set up offshore shell companies and other financial vehicles for clients who wished to hide their offshore financial activities from relevant authorities. ICIJ (2021a, 2021b) details some of the cases of how and where some of the world leaders hid their wealth, even those who championed anti-corruption causes for their political platform.

The instances of the Panama and the Pandora Papers made it clear that despite the promised financial secrecy, there are no foolproof methods to safeguard sensitive and confidential (and compromising) information, especially if kept in electronic forms. Information leaks such as these should reduce moral hazard on the part of current and potential customers of financial security providers, and this would discourage illicit activities with financial secrecy protection until new and better-protected methods become available.

References

BBC (2014). BNP Paribas to pay $9bn to settle sanctions violations, BBC news, 1 July 2014. https://www.bbc.com/news/business-28099694.

Bruun and Hjejle (2018). Report on the Non-Resident Portfolio at Danske Bank's Estonian Branch. https://danskebank.com/-/media/danske-bank-com/file-cloud/2018/9/report-on-the-non-resident-portfolio-at-danske-banks-estonian-branch.pdf.

Chainalysis (2022). The 2022 Crypto Crime Report: Original Data and Research into Cryptocurrency-Based Crime, February 2022. https://www.chainalysis.com/.

Coppola, F. (2019). Standard Chartered Bank's Long History Of Financial Crime, Forbes, 10 April 2019. https://www.forbes.com/sites/francescoppola/2019/04/10/standard-chartered-banks-long-history-of-financial-crime/?sh=5e37dc5d3909.

Danske Bank (2023). Resolution in terms of the Estonian matter. https://danskebank.com/about-us/corporate-governance/resolution-in-terms-of-the-estonia-matter, accessed, March 2023.

FATF (2005). Money Laundering and Terrorist Financing Typologies 2004–2005 (Chapter 1). https://www.fatf-gafi.org/en/publications/Methodsandtrends/Moneylaunderingandterroristfinancingtypologies2004-2005.html.

FATF (2012 and 2021). International Standards on Combating Money Laundering and the Financing of Terrorism & Proliferation. The FATF Recommendations. https://www.fatf-gafi.org/en/publications/Fatfrecommendations/Fatf-recommendations.html.

FATF (2013). The Role of Hawala and Other Similar Service Providers in Money Laundering and Terrorist Financing, October 2013. https://www.fatf-gafi.org/media/fatf/documents/reports/Role-of-hawala-and-similar-in-ml-tf.pdf.

FATF (2018). FATF Report to the G20 Finance Ministers and Central Banks Governors, July. https://www.fatf-gafi.org/media/fatf/documents/reports/FATF-Report-G20-FM-CBG-July-2018.pdf.

Feige, E. L. (2012). The myth of the "cashless society": How much of America's currency is overseas?, Working paper. https://www.bundesbank.de/resource/blob/634976/06c32c73f4488278407d159075571593/mL/2012-02-27-eltville-03-feige-paper-data.pdf.

Fletcher, P. (2010). Wachovia pays $160 million to settle drug money probe, Reuters U.S. News, March 18, 2010. https://www.reuters.com/article/us-wachovia-settlement/wachovia-pays-160-million-to-settle-drug-money-probe-idUSTRE62G35720100317?feedType=RSS&feedName=domesticNews.

International Consortium of Investigative Journalists (2017a). Explore the Panama Papers Key Figures ICIJ. https://www.icij.org/investigations/panama-papers/explore-panama-papers-key-figures/.

International Consortium of Investigative Journalists (2017b). Tax Agencies Draw Up "Target List" of Offshore Enablers, ICIJ. https://www.icij.org/investigations/panama-papers/20170120-oecd-target-list/.

International Consortium of Investigative Journalists (2021). Offshore havens and hidden riches of world leaders and billionaires exposed in unprecedented leak. https://www.icij.org/investigations/pandora-papers/global-investigation-tax-havens-offshore/.

International Consortium of Investigative Journalists (2021). Pandora papers. https://www.icij.org/investigations/pandora-papers.

Kerry, J. and Brown, H. (1992). The BCCI Affair, Report to the Committee on Foreign Relations, United States Senate, by Senator John Kerry and Senator Hank Brown, 102d Congress 2d Session Senate Print 102–140.

O'Donovan, J., Wagner, H. F. and Zeume, S. (2016). The Value of Offshore Secrets — Evidence from the Panama Papers. https://doi.org/10.2139/ssrn.2771095.

OECD (2000). Towards Global Tax Cooperation: Report to the 2000 Ministerial Council Meeting and Recommendations by the Committee on Fiscal Affairs. https://www.oecd.org/ctp/harmful/2090192.pdf.

OECD/G20 BEPS Project (2021). Statement on a Two-Pillar Solution to Address the Tax Challenges Arising from the Digitalisation of the Economy, 8 October. https://www.oecd.org/tax/beps/statement-on-a-two-pillar-solution-to-address-the-tax-challenges-arising-from-the-digitalisation-of-the-economy-october-2021.pdf.

Sebang, G. (2021). BNP charged for laundering ill-gotten assets linked to Gabon, Bloomberg, 21 May 2021. https://www.bloomberg.com/news/articles/2021-05-20/bnp-charged-for-laundering-ill-gotten-assets-linked-to-gabon.

Shaxson, N. (2019, September). Tackling tax havens. *Finance & Development*, 56(3), 6–10.

Siddiqui, D. A. (2018). Alternative Remittance Systems and Its Impact on Money Laundering (2018), SSRN Working Paper 3271778. Alternative Remittance Systems and Its Impact on Money Laundering by Danish Ahmed Siddiqui :: SSRN.

The BCCI Affair (1992). 102d Congress 2d Session Senate Print 102–140. http://www.fas.org/irp/congress/1992_rpt/bcci/.

The Financial Conduct Authority (2019). FCA fines Standard Chartered Bank £102.2 million for poor AML controls, *FCA Press Release*, 9 April. https://www.fca.org.uk/news/press-releases/fca-fines-standard-chartered-bank-102-2-million-poor-aml-controls.

The Guardian (2011). How a big US bank laundered billions from Mexico's murderous drug gangs, 3 April. https://www.theguardian.com/world/2011/apr/03/us-bank-mexico-drug-gangs.

The US Department of Justice (2012). HSBC Holdings Plc. and HSBC Bank USA N.A. Admit to Anti-Money Laundering and Sanctions Violations, Forfeit $1.256 Billion in Deferred Prosecution Agreement, *Justice News*, 11 December. https://www.justice.gov/opa/pr/hsbc-holdings-plc-and-hsbc-bank-usa-na-admit-anti-money-laundering-and-sanctions-violations.

The US Department of Justice (2014). BNP Paribas Agrees to Plead Guilty and to Pay $8.9 Billion for Illegally Processing Financial Transactions for Countries Subject to U.S. Economic Sanctions, *Justice News*, 30 June. https://www.justice.gov/opa/pr/bnp-paribas-agrees-plead-guilty-and-pay-89-billion-illegally-processing-financial.

The US Department of Justice (USDJ, 2019). Standard Chartered Bank Admits to Illegally Processing Transactions in Violation of Iranian Sanctions and Agrees to Pay More Than $1 Billion, *Justice News*, 9 April. https://www.justice.gov/opa/pr/standard-chartered-bank-admits-illegally-processing-transactions-violation-iranian-sanctions.

The US Department of Justice (USDJ, 2022). Danske Bank pleads guilty to fraud on U.S. banks in multi-billion dollar scheme to access the U.S. financial system, *Justice News*, 13 December 2022. https://www.justice.gov/opa/pr/

danske-bank-pleads-guilty-fraud-us-banks-multi-billion-dollar-scheme-access-us-financial.

United Nations Office on Drugs and Crime (UNODC, 2011). Estimating Illicit Financial Flows Resulting from Drug Trafficking and Other Transnational Organised Crimes, *Research Report*. https://www.unodc.org/documents/data-and-analysis/Studies/Illicit_financial_flows_2011_web.pdf.

UNODC (2010). United States of America v. Wachovia bank, Case law database. https://sherloc.unodc.org/cld/case-law-doc/moneylaunderingcrimetype/usa/2010/united_states_of_america_v._wachovia_bank.html?lng=en&tmpl=sherloc.

Viswanatha, A. and Wolf, B. (2012). HSBC to Pay $1.9 Billion U.S. Fine in Money-Laundering Case, *Reuters Breaking News*, 11 December. https://www.reuters.com/article/us-hsbc-probe-idUSBRE8BA05M20121211.

Vulliamy, E. (2011). How a big US bank laundered billions from Mexico's murderous drug gangs, *The Guardian*, 3 April 2011. https://www.theguardian.com/world/2011/apr/03/us-bank-mexico-drug-gangs.

Walter, I. (2012). Use and Misuse of Financial Secrecy in Global Banking, Chapter 15 in *Socially Responsible Finance and Investing: Financial Institutions, Corporations, Investors, and Activists*, H. Kent Baker and John R. Nofsinger (eds.), John Wiley & Sons.

Index

G

H

I

O

P

Q

Printed in the United States
by Baker & Taylor Publisher Services